THE BIG RED MACHINE

STEPHEN CLARKSON

THE BIG RED MACHINE

How the Liberal Party Dominates Canadian Politics

UBCPress · Vancouver · Toronto

15 14 13 12 11 10 09 08 07 06 05   5 4 3 2 1

This book is printed on ancient-forest-free (100% post-consumer recycled) paper that is processed chlorine- and acid-free, with vegetable-based inks.

Library and Archives Canada Cataloguing in Publication

Clarkson, Stephen, 1937-
    The big red machine : how the Liberal Party dominates Canadian politics / Stephen Clarkson.

Includes bibliographical references and index.
ISBN-13: 978-0-7748-1195-8 (bound); 978-0-7748-1196-5 (pbk)
ISBN-10: 0-7748-1195-1 (bound); 0-7748-1196-x (pbk)

    1. Liberal Party of Canada – History. 2. Canada – Politics and government. I. Title.

JL197.L5C52 2005   324.27106   C2005-904559-0

Canada

UBC Press gratefully acknowledges the financial support for our publishing program of the Government of Canada through the Book Publishing Industry Development Program (BPIDP), and of the Canada Council for the Arts, and the British Columbia Arts Council.

UBC Press
The University of British Columbia
2029 West Mall
Vancouver, BC V6T 1Z2
604-822-5959 / Fax: 604-822-6083
www.ubcpress.ca

Pierre Elliott Trudeau once recounted how his first experience
with politics came through his ardently Conservative francophone father.
What he remembered best from the election nights of his childhood was
Charlie Trudeau's friends damning the Liberals and their all-too-often
successful "machine rouge" with round and righteous fury.
Impressed by these outbursts, Pierre had visualized this red machine well
into his teens as some huge Rube Goldbergian device that whirred, clicked,
and threw off sparks with diabolical effects on the electorate.

– CHRISTINA McCALL, *GLOBE AND MAIL*, 1975

Contents

Preface
The Joy of Winning

Our fascination is chronic. Nothing captures Canadians' political attention more predictably and compellingly than an election campaign. During these frantic weeks every few years, when the entire federal stage is handed over to electioneering, the governing process goes into temporary hibernation, and Canada's political culture enters a special mode. The electorate is courted by the nation's political leaders as they attempt to gain its support and mobilize their own rank and file. From Newfoundland to British Columbia, from the American border to the Arctic Ocean, the citizenry is bombarded with competing messages broadcast over radio and television, printed in the newspapers, sent through the mail, voiced at the doorstep and, more recently, transmitted via e-mail, listed on various sites on the World Wide Web, and harangued about on individual blogs. The media corps changes its criteria for reporting, giving credence to upstart challengers and hardened critics who are generally ignored in times of political peace. Signs and billboards clutter the roadsides. Pledges are solemnly declared and bitterly contested. Accusations are made and refuted. Policies are proposed and opposed. Hopes are raised and dashed.

Orchestrating this bedlam, partisan politics comes briefly into the light of day. An unusual institution, the political party is the vehicle for translating hundreds of thousands of hours of intensive campaigning and millions of separately cast votes into a final decision – the joy of winning and the heady reins of power, or defeat and either political oblivion or the ungrateful task of toiling in opposition.

This book focuses tightly on a single federal party's electoral behaviour during the last thirty years, providing the story of the Liberal Party of Canada's (LPC's) nine election campaigns from 1974 through 2004. In their original form, each of these studies appeared shortly after the actual election as a chapter for the scholarly work that has been published on every Canadian federal campaign starting in 1974. These books gave a complete overview of each election, with scholars describing each of the contending parties' campaign performances, as well as the behaviour of the media and, of course, the voters.[1]

It would be an understatement to say that these election volumes had a limited circulation. None enjoyed commercial distribution or widespread media attention of the kind enjoyed by Graham Fraser's *Playing for Keeps* or Rick

Salutin's *Waiting for Democracy* following the dramatic 1988 free trade election. None won prizes as did John Duffy's recent *Fights of Our Lives: Elections, Leadership, and the Making of Canada,* which reviews his selection of important battles in Canadian history. Apart from professional politicians and their advisers, academic specialists in election studies, and students taking courses on Canadian political parties, few would have known of these tomes' existence, and fewer still read their contents.

The reason for revising my own contributions to these studies and putting them together between one set of covers does not lie in their individual merit. After all, each party's campaign in each election is *sui generis,* a unique event that is important in the context of that historical moment, but of little general interest. When put end to end, however, the stories of one party's campaigns may tell us a good deal about that particular organization. And when this party happens to have held power in Ottawa for 78 of the past 110 years, then its campaign practices, communications techniques, and leadership styles should be of greater interest. The LPC's electoral savvy may help us better understand not just how it has come out on top of the heap in nineteen out of twenty-eight elections in the twentieth century, but also what its prospects are for keeping up this winning record into the twenty-first.

These nine elections span two periods in Canada's evolving political economy. The mid-1970s saw the Keynesian welfare state at its apogee as it began its inexorable decline in the face of neoconservatives' demands for a leaner and meaner state. By 2004 Canada had entered a turbulent phase, having experienced almost two decades of liberalized trade on the North American continent and the corresponding cutbacks of the social, cultural, and environmental programs built up under Keynesian governments. Observing the Liberal Party's electoral practices during a broad process of social, economic, political, and ideological change should shed some light on how the Canadian party system itself evolved in the transition from one policy paradigm to another.

The Big Red Machine has two distinct publics in mind. For citizens who are passionate fans of Canada's most popular spectator sport after hockey, it provides a wealth of detail, helping them to understand the inner workings of the Liberal Party in its electoral mode and the general dynamics of election campaigns at the federal level. For specialists, these studies touch on an issue that is the subject of much scholarly debate – the character of Canada's party system, which some consider is undergoing a historic transformation.

These chapters do not appear here as originally published. Because much more research has subsequently been done, they incorporate material that was not available at the original time of writing – most notably, the financial data reported by the parties to the chief electoral officer of Canada and the extensive survey research executed by my political-science colleagues. Besides these works,

I have profited from various papers presented at the annual meetings of the Canadian Political Science Association, articles published in learned journals, memoirs of political figures, journalistic treatments of campaigns, and that work-horse of Canadian political history, the *Canadian Annual Review of Politics and Public Affairs*. Following critiques received by two anonymous peers who read the manuscript's first draft for the University of British Columbia Press, every chapter has been restructured to sharpen its argument and provide more con-sistency in the treatment of each campaign.

The body of the book now consists of the nine contests themselves, begin-ning with the campaign of 1974 and ending with the election of 2004. Given the central importance of political leaders in setting the tone and defining the char-acter of Canadian parties, these narratives fall into four sections – Pierre Trudeau's mixed record of success (1974), defeat (1979), and re-conquest (1980) in his last three campaigns; John Turner's two failed efforts of 1984 and 1988; Jean Chrétien's three subsequent victories in 1993, 1997, and 2000; and, finally, Paul Martin's skin-of-his-teeth win of 2004.

These nine essays are preceded by an introduction that, by sketching in the historical background on Canadian party politics to 1974, provides a context for understanding how the federal party system passed through various transfor-mations from Confederation on; how national policies evolved to suit the chang-ing requirements of Canadian society; what kind of organizational and financial base the Liberal Party had developed; why Pierre Trudeau attempted unsuccess-fully to introduce democratic practices to the internal workings of the party: in short, how the Liberal Party had come to be what it was at the time of the 1974 election.

The conclusion relates the record of six electoral wins and three losses by Canada's hegemonic party from 1974 to 2004 to the contradictory nature of the evolving party system, with both its internal fragmentation and its integration into a global marketplace.

Before passing to the analysis, the reader should know that I was myself a Liberal Party member for seven years. Having become excited – along with mil-lions of other Canadians in 1968 – by Pierre Trudeau's charismatic sweep to power, I joined the LPC in order to contest the nomination for the Toronto riding of Davenport that had become open on the Hon. Walter L. Gordon's re-tirement from politics.

Bloodied by this experience, but intrigued by the many social issues facing Toronto at a time when the urban question was becoming extremely conten-tious, I became active in the effort to create a municipal Liberal Party and found myself elected its candidate for the mayoralty in the 1969 municipal election.[2] Following this dramatic, albeit unsuccessful, initiation into the practical reali-ties of electoral politics, I remained active in the extra-parliamentary, citizen side of the Liberal Party, serving on its policy committees at both the federal and provincial levels, and working in its election campaigns.

During these years, I shifted part of my teaching and my research toward parties and elections. By the time I left the Liberal Party in 1975, I was already researching the study in Howard Penniman's first *Canada at the Polls* that appears here as the entry for 1974.

Finally, a word about the title of this preface. Some are attracted to politics to change the world. Others are drawn to the battle itself. For Jean Chrétien, the previous leader of the Liberal Party of Canada who lived and breathed political combat, politics was less about the ends than the means, less about policy than politics, more about the hunt than the quarry. Visiting a classroom of Canadian children in China toward the end of his prime ministership, the "iron man" was asked by a schoolboy what he liked best about his job. "The most enjoyable thing is to win an election. The day after, we have a lot of work to do, but *the joy of winning* an election is something," the veteran politician responded – straight from the heart.[3]

This spontaneous comment reveals a side of electoral politics that neither scholars nor journalists ever seem to catch. While elections are historical events pregnant with serious implications for the country, they can also be hugely exciting experiences for the combatants. When teams of volunteers, many of whom have worked in campaign after campaign, get back together to do political battle, they manage the tremendous tensions by developing an esprit de corps and enjoying the intense experience. Liberals, in particular, pride themselves on having a good time while they smite their enemies.

The men and women who collectively make up the Big Red Machine don't fight elections to proselytize for liberalism, whatever they may mean by their party's label. Most especially, they don't fight them to lose. As a party activist from Cape Breton once put it, "You can't turn off the Big Red Machine; you just shut it down for maintenance." After decades of experience, the essence of the Liberals' approach to political campaigning can be summed up in Chrétien's telling phrase. It's about the joy of winning.

Reader, read on.

Acknowledgments

Three groups made possible the studies that became this book.

First come the politicians, primarily active Liberals, who helped me in my research, particularly on the 1974 and 1979 elections, whether in informal conversations or formal interviews. Many of these people are identified in these chapters' references.

Second are the many colleagues with whom I have discussed and from whom I have learned over the decades, most notably the dean of party analysts in Canada, John Meisel at Queen's University, and his former student, Jon Pammett, who combines speed with quality in editing each federal election's scholarly volume.

Third, I need to recognize the students I recruited in the 1980s and 1990s to help me carry out the research during each subsequent campaign. In a class of their own are three of these recruits, whom I engaged once I had decided to turn these studies into a book. Tracey Rynark reworked the financial data provided by the chief electoral officer of Canada to provide comparable statistics for every election for which they were available. Priya Suagh started the process of turning the independent election studies into chapters for a stand-alone monograph. Vivek Krishnamurthy took on the final phase of standardizing the chapters' approaches, chasing missing data in the tables, tracking down errant bibliographical references, and helping me incorporate suggestions made by the UBC Press readers.

Over the years, grants from the Social Sciences and Humanities Research Council of Canada helped make possible some of my research.

This book would not exist without these substantial contributions, but my late partner, Christina McCall (with whom I fell in love as we discussed the Liberals' 1974 election campaign) is the one with whom I most enjoyed discussing Canadian politics and from whom I gleaned the greatest insights about the Liberal Party in all its big-red-machine guises for the past three decades.

THE BIG RED MACHINE

Introduction:
Party Systems and Liberal Leaders

In the age of the Internet, some say that there is no use for history. Why should there be, when change has been so rapid in the last two decades that even the meaning of some common words has evolved beyond recognition? "Reform," for instance, once described efforts to redress economic injustice and foster well-being by expanding the state's capacity for enacting the requisite social measures. Spelled with a capital letter in the 1990s, "Reform" became identified with the political movement dedicated to roll back government, curbing its capacity to address social ills.[1] The connotation of "liberal" has mutated just as radically over the decades. Quite apart from the peculiarity in Canadian usage that distinguishes between "big L" Liberal, Liberals, and Liberalism designating the party, its members, and its ideology and "small l" liberal, liberals, and liberalism referring to a more general attitude, those who share it, and the philosophical basis of their beliefs, the concept has morphed from a description of the anti-government, pro-market, *sauve-qui-peut* thinking at the turn of the twentieth century to its market-regulating, generous, big-government opposite a hundred years later.

Those for whom history has become irrelevant would do well to fast forward to the campaign narratives that begin with the next chapter, on the federal election of 1974. Those readers who still think chronologically and are interested in the more general implications of electoral behaviour may wish to have their memories refreshed in the following sections, which trace the roots from which the Liberal Party of Canada (LPC) springs and provide the electoral context on the eve of the 1974 campaign.

Specifically, this introduction introduces the *party system approach* as the context for analyzing the evolution of partisan politics in Canada. First, it reviews the LPC's tumultuous evolution from radical movement to governing party by establishing how the imprints left on the country by its various leaders have reflected not just its party system but also the evolving character of Canada's political economy. It then shows how these leaders would not so often have occupied the prime minister's office had they not profited from the peculiar bias of the country's electoral system, which favours the winning party. Next, it describes both the attitudinal make-up of the LPC's supporters and the organizational foundation of its apparatus by the time Pierre Trudeau came to power. Finally, it summarizes the impact on both party practices and member morale of Trudeau's flirtation with and betrayal of the notion of participatory democracy.

This saga of dashed expectations will prepare us to consider a disturbing paradox when we reach the conclusion, where we will review the reasons for the Big Red Machine's persisting dominance over Canadian party politics. The LPC's continuing hegemony has much to do with its remaining the most autocratic in the field, even while demonstrating such democratic qualities as higher participation rates, a better gender balance, and younger, better-educated activists than its rivals.

Canada's Successive Party Systems

If history is to be something more than an accumulation of seemingly unrelated events, we require some organizing principle to group disparate phenomena into meaningful categories that can be compared with one another, for it is through the comparative method that much of what we know in the social sciences has been learned. The dominant analytical framework for understanding the evolution of Canadian partisan politics is the *party system approach*, which was developed independently in the 1970s by David Smith[2] at the University of Saskatchewan and R. Kenneth Carty[3] at the University of British Columbia. Their central notion divides the history of Canadian party politics into three functionally distinct periods – or systems – each of which possesses certain unique characteristics that distinguish it from the others. The first, the *clientelistic* system, spanned the period from Confederation in 1867 to the end of the First World War. The second, the *brokerage* system, lasted from the 1920s to the 1950s. The third, the *pan-Canadian* system, was born in the political and social tumult of the early 1960s.

Over the past decade, political scientists have discussed at length whether a fourth party system has emerged to supplant the pan-Canadian one. The leading proponents of this thesis, the scholarly trio R.K. Carty, Lisa Young, and William Cross, assert in their *Rebuilding Canadian Party Politics* that the 1993 federal election was a watershed marking the transition from the pan-Canadian system to a fourth, regionally balkanized party system.[4] James Bickerton, Alain Gagnon, and Patrick J. Smith make a similar argument in *Ties That Bind*, although they contend that the shift to the fourth party system began with the election of Brian Mulroney in 1984, not with Jean Chrétien's electoral triumph nine years later.[5]

This book plots a middle course between the Bickerton and Carty positions. The Trudeau section, which covers the elections of 1974, 1979, and 1980, looks at the Liberal Party at the height of the third party system. The Turner section, on the elections of 1984 and 1988, covers a period of transition. Finally, the Chrétien and Martin sections, which deal with the elections of 1993, 1997, 2000, and 2004, assess the Liberals in the putative fourth system.

From Radical Movement to Governing Party

Dominant though it became in each of these four party systems, the Liberal Party's origins predate those of Canada itself. Surprisingly for a party that ultimately helped build and manage the capitalist state, it emerged to express the grievances and demands for social justice and economic freedom of those oppressed by the oligarchic power structure that prevailed in the British North American colonies during the first half of the nineteenth century. Following the military suppression of armed rebellions led by the firebrand William Lyon Mackenzie in Upper Canada (later Ontario) and Louis-Joseph Papineau in Lower Canada (later Quebec) during 1837, the anti-establishment, Protestant, and anglophone Clear Grits[6] and the anticlerical, Catholic, and francophone Rouges developed a reform movement focused on achieving their goal of destroying the power of the incumbent colonial aristocracies – the Family Compact and the Château Clique. To be liberal in their tumultuous times was to profess with John Stuart Mill the equality and dignity of the individual and to believe with Adam Smith in a free-trading marketplace unconstrained by such mercantilist regulations as tariffs. Committed to peaceable, electoral means, Canadian Liberalism's nineteenth-century history records long decades in parliamentary opposition spent espousing these reform principles under leaders who were generally unsuccessful at the polls.

Wilfrid Laurier and the Clientelistic Party System

Although they were effective in expressing the dissatisfaction among Queen Victoria's North American subjects, neither George Brown, Alexander Mackenzie, nor Edward Blake – the first three parliamentary leaders of the Liberal faction in Canada – achieved the balance between principle and pragmatism needed to gain, wield, and hold on to political power.

George Brown personified the paradox of what was more commonly called "reform politics" in the nineteenth century. He was unrepentantly partisan, to a degree that few twentieth-century politicians would dare emulate. A natural fighter who nursed grudges, Brown used his Toronto newspaper, *The Globe*, to trumpet the interests of his reform-minded confederates in the Province of Canada, which grouped Upper and Lower Canada into a single colony in 1841. Perceived by many as being anti-Catholic and anti-French, Brown was nevertheless able to hold together like-minded "Reformers" from both linguistic communities in opposition to the Conservatives (Tories) led by John A. Macdonald:

It is true that Mr. Brown knew the value of party organization, and, if we do not mistake, could connive at arguments in a campaign that were not presented from the housetops, and found lodgement in the voter's pocket rather than in his intellect ... No man ever knew Ontario better than George Brown. He searched every corner of the province for candidates. He knew the tendencies, sympathies and prejudices of every constituency. He knew who might win here and who must fail there.[7]

Thanks to these skills, Brown even succeeded in forming a short-lived government with A.A. Dorion, the leader of the Rouges, in 1858.

The paradox in Brown surfaced when, as chair of a committee of the province's legislature, he helped develop a constitution for the proposed federation of the British North American colonies. Despite the strength of his partisanship, Brown's desire to ensure that the new federal parliament would be organized according to the principle of "representation by population" led him to treat with partisan enemies such as Macdonald and the conservative Quebec Bleus to attain his goal.[8] In 1864 Brown went so far as to join Macdonald in a coalition government to provide the Confederation project with enough political support to pass in the Canadian legislature, even though this meant abandoning his ideological confreres among Dorion's Rouges. Ultimately, it could be said that Brown "had no reverence for party except as an instrument of reform, and that he ranked progressive measures far above stagnant office-holding."[9]

Alexander Mackenzie became Canada's first Liberal prime minister not because of his credentials as a Grit reformer, but because of what he was not. Specifically, Mackenzie was not John A. Macdonald, and as such was blameless in the Pacific Scandal that swept from office the new Dominion of Canada's first government in 1873.[10] Like Brown, Mackenzie came from Clear Grit politics in Ontario to the stage of the newborn nation. He expounded the principles of nineteenth-century liberalism concerning taxes and free trade, once declaring in the House of Commons that "there is no policy more consistent with what we call the Dark Ages of the world than that of protection as principle. There is no principle more consonant with the advance of human freedom, no principle more in accordance with the great prosperity that prevails in our time than the absolute freedom of commerce."[11] Unfortunately for Mackenzie, many electors felt that protection was the cure for, rather than the cause of, their economic woes. Since his advocacy of free trade principles coincided with a severe economic downturn in the late 1870s, the Dominion's first Grit premier was easily defeated in 1878 by a rehabilitated John A. Macdonald, who promised to introduce a bundle of protectionist measures that came to be known as the National Policy.

Edward Blake, who led his party from 1880 to 1887, was the only federal Liberal leader never to become prime minister. A brilliant but nakedly ambitious man who had served as the first Liberal premier of Ontario in 1871-2, Blake switched to Dominion politics in 1872 and soon made it known that he would only continue to serve in the national party if he could be its leader. When Blake did attain that position in 1880, the opportunity for success was ripe. Macdonald's National Policy was seen to be failing, and cost overruns on the Canadian Pacific Railway were pushing the national treasury toward bankruptcy. Thus, much of the blame for the Liberals' failure to displace the Tories was placed on Blake's shoulders, as he did little to attract new recruits from outside Ontario and could not match Macdonald in the cut and thrust of parliamentary debate.

In these first decades of Canadian nationhood, the party system operated on the "clientelistic" principle by which party leaders, as patrons, delivered material benefits to their supporters, the voting clients who kept them in power. Although clientelism persists to some extent even in our contemporary party system, in the era before universal literacy and mass communications, electoral candidates had difficulty appealing to the imagination of the electorate and were forced to solicit votes by making a more direct appeal to their material interests. Only briefly having held power, however, Liberal politicians did not have access to the material means with which to build a solid political apparatus that could rival the patronage-dispensing machine that Macdonald had constructed over his long years as prime minister. Following his death in 1891, and thanks to the incompetence of Sir John A's several successors – four within the five years of the 1891-6 ministry – an opportunity opened up for the Liberals to switch places in the House of Commons with their long-time rivals.

This fascinating reversal took place in the 1896 election, when the Liberal Party broadened its formerly restricted appeal to become the national political formation that would govern Canada for most of the next century. As Hugh Thorburn observed, it was "only when the Liberals abandoned their reformist posture as defender of the agrarian underdog and spokesperson for reform did they succeed; but once they patterned themselves on Macdonald's Conservatives they beat the Tories at their own game – and they have, with notable gaps, continued to do so."[12] The credit for this transformation goes to Wilfrid Laurier, who took over the Liberal Party's leadership in 1887. Turning his back on the Rouges, republican, and anticlerical principles he had championed in his youth, Laurier now declared himself a Liberal in the more pragmatic style of Sir William Gladstone – the greatest of nineteenth-century British crusading politicians.

The party's political fortunes started to change in 1893, when Laurier convened his party's first national convention. Previously, Grits had met with local notables in regional or provincial conclaves, proclaiming policy resolutions that were often in conflict with those passed by other Liberals congregating else-where across the Dominion. At his groundbreaking convention, Laurier ma-noeuvred his supporters into passing resolutions that created a single set of planks to be used in his next electoral platform.

Beyond ideological coherence, he developed partisan muscle. Opening the Reform Club that year in Ottawa, Laurier declaimed, "It is not enough to have good principles; we must have organization also. Principles without organiza-tion may lose, but organization without principles may often win."[13] In two sen-tences, Laurier defined the Liberal Party's ethos for the twentieth century, a stance subordinating principle to pragmatism. Under him, the party ceased to be a hard-line group of radicals representing the regional grievances of their con-stituencies. He saw policy flexibility as the keystone of electoral success and ac-cordingly set his party on its new course. His election in 1896 was to prove the watershed in Canadian Liberalism's long history.

Wilfrid Laurier's primary achievement in the 1896 election was to win Quebec's support, and so wrest power there from the Conservative Party, despite the hos-tility of the Catholic Church hierarchy to a liberal political philosophy that it considered radical and dangerously atheistic. Laurier went on to win the next three elections by unapologetically adopting Macdonald's fourfold formula for success – a nationwide coalition of supporters, an expansionary role for govern-ment, an intimate connection with business, and an accommodation between the French and the English. Tempering his silver-tongued orations about Lib-eral principles with plentiful doses of steely-eyed opportunism, he built his elec-toral coalition in English Canada on the organizational backs of Liberal provincial premiers whom he brought into his cabinet as patronage-dispensing power brokers for their regions. He endorsed the aggressive immigration policy of his Manitoba minister, Clifford Sifton, who was bent on settling what he saw as the empty Canadian West. He entered into the same kind of transcontinental railway-building collaboration with the Grand Trunk and Canadian Northern that his caucus had denounced in the 1880s when sponsored by Macdonald with the Canadian Pacific Railway. And he kept his hand on every aspect of party activ-ity, particularly appointments to government jobs and the allocation of govern-ment contracts – patronage that he used in order to maintain his party in power by securing the support of the ambitious and rewarding the fealty of the faithful.

In this calculated pursuit of clientelism, Laurier reinforced the nation-building that characterized Canada's first party system. Politicians did not just get elected to an office in those days. They created the offices and staffed them with their own partisan supporters as the Canadian government's embryonic structure took shape. One telling example: Laurier invited a reliable industrial-relations spe-cialist – trustworthy because he was the son of a loyal Liberal partisan in Toronto and the grandson of the great firebrand William Lyon Mackenzie – to be his deputy minister of labour, instructing him to create a federal department to manage the problem of growing working-class unrest. The young man's name was William Lyon Mackenzie King.

Mackenzie King and the Brokerage Party System

By the interwar period, the rise of meritocratic norms had led to the professionalization of the Dominion bureaucracy, a development that deprived the parties of their direct role in recruiting government personnel. This left politicians with the more public role of "brokering" between the various, and very often conflicting, provincial interests within a federation that, by 1905, had grown from four to nine provinces. By the Great Depression, the two-party system that had existed since Confederation had become a two-plus-two system, with two "old" parties that could credibly aspire to form a government (the Liberals and the Conservatives) and two "new" parties that brought to Ottawa the angers of their class (the left-wing Co-operative Commonwealth Federation – CCF) or their region (the right-wing Social Credit from the Prairies).

After being elected leader at the Liberal Party's second national convention following Laurier's death in 1919, Mackenzie King went on to prove the most enduring prime minister in Canadian history. His long tenures as party leader (1919-48) and prime minister (1921-30 and 1935-48) coincided with this second party system, which encompassed years of rapid urbanization and industrialization, emerging class conflict, disastrous depression, and mobilization for total war. Where Laurier had done battle with only one rival party, King saw new, more radical formations emerge on his left and his right, both regionally and nationally. In the mould of his mentor, however, King's style of politics was at once conservative and reformist. Reluctant to make new departures or take bold steps in policy matters, he was nonetheless ready to head off electoral threats from the left by adopting the forward-looking, social-justice planks of the CCF's social democrats.

King's success has been ascribed by his critics to his uncanny talent for blurring political issues so as to maintain support among such ideologically opposed groups as farmers in the West, who demanded free trade, and manufacturers in central Canada, who demanded tariff protection. His genius for obfuscation was epitomized by his vacuous but successful 1935 campaign slogan, "King or Chaos." Historians have paid less-grudging tribute to his shrewd recognition of the importance of sustaining his party's support in Quebec, especially during the Second World War. With his Delphic position, "conscription if necessary but not necessarily conscription," he successfully walked the tightrope between English-Canadian militarists and French-Canadian isolationists during the hostilities, forestalling the armed suppression of rioting that had almost destroyed the party's Quebec wing in the previous global war.

King also had Laurier's talent for attracting strong politicians with regional power bases to his cabinet, where he made savvy use of their abilities and connections. He straddled the political middle ground by impressing the business communities in Montreal and Toronto with the government's managerial competence and its responsiveness to their concerns, while leaning slightly to the left on social issues in order to appeal to the broader electorate. In wartime, he craftily used the CCF's surging popularity and a parallel increase in labour militancy to push his pro-business caucus members into accepting the welfare programs – unemployment insurance, family allowances, and pensions within the framework of a moderately interventionist state – that his supporters in the extra-parliamentary National Liberal Federation endorsed as party policy, at his behest, in 1943.[14] In short, he fashioned "a party drawing support from all regions, all classes and all cultural groups."[15]

It was during Mackenzie King's second decade as party leader that the membership wing of the Liberal Party began to assume its present form. Formerly a loose association of citizens who identified with the vision of the party's leadership, the National Liberal Federation (NLF) was reformed in 1932 by King when he was the opposition leader striving to make an electoral comeback. He felt the party organization should be more directly connected to the party's grassroots. While the party faithful had previously been members of the NLF by virtue of belonging to a provincial Liberal organization, individuals wishing to belong to the reformed NLF now had to pay membership dues of $1 per year for this privilege.[16] In return, members could look forward to receiving a copy of a new party magazine, the *Liberal Monthly* (which despite its name was published only bimonthly from 1933 to 1936). One dollar per year bought the rank and file little real influence over the party's internal operations, policy outlook, or leadership selection process – all of which remained under the collective thumb of the prime minister and his ministers. As Reg Whitaker observed, Mackenzie King "never gave the slightest indication that he harboured any belief in intra-party democracy, especially when the definition of party extended beyond the cabinet and parliamentary caucus."[17]

While his democratic credentials may have been lacking, there is no question that King was a highly skilled political recruiter who was able to attract progressive intellectuals to the federal civil service and draw on their nation-building ideas for his partisan needs. Between 1939 and 1945, these civil servants ran what was essentially a centrally planned economy in close co-operation with the cabinet and a handful of capitalists from Montreal and Toronto who had come to Ottawa to help steer the country through the Second World War. Proximity, patriotism, and the sense of mission that came out of this wartime environment produced the tightly knit Anglo-Canadian elite that dominated early postwar Canada. Though some of its members leaned to the left (the civil servants), some steered to the right (the businessmen), and some zigzagged around the middle (the elected politicians), their networks had developed – in the crucible of their intense wartime collaboration – a consensus about what became the framework for postwar Canada's mixed economy and welfare system. By the late 1940s, the "mandarins" in Ottawa had become so influential with Liberal politicians – and by extension with their allies in business who returned to more entrepreneurial pursuits after the war – that their Keynesian economic ideas and pro-American orientation became the main pillars of Liberal government policy for the next quarter-century.

King's hand-picked successor, Louis St. Laurent, was much admired in bureaucratic and business circles when he became party leader – and ipso facto prime minister – at the Liberals' 1948 leadership convention, because he espoused the continentalist economic views most powerfully advocated by C.D. Howe, his American-born "minister of everything." Howe felt Canada needed American capital in order to exploit its vast natural resource endowment. Canada also needed the American market, which, as a rapidly expanding and rearming economy, was sufficiently secure to guarantee its northern neighbour's continuing prosperity, given Great Britain's failure to regain its pre-war capacity to buy Canada's staple exports. But St. Laurent was not Laurier in modern dress. Burdened by office and prone to depression, he became a sad old man, captive to his cabinet and the astute bureaucrats who served it backstage. His regime saw the erosion of King's governing formula and the beginning of the Liberal Party's persistent estrangement from western Canada.[18] St. Laurent had always been bored by the petty brokerage of provincial demands that fuelled the second party system, and, on his watch, the Liberal Party hierarchy grew increasingly insensitive to the electorate. The party's regional fiefdoms continued to be controlled by cabinet ministers who supervised with great diligence the dispensation of patronage and the selection of candidates at the local level. But, disposed as they were to leave the running of their departments to their trusty deputy ministers,[19] they were mostly indifferent to broader issues of ideology and policies for national development.

During the second party system's four decades, the Liberal Party's fusion with the Canadian state and the business community was almost taken for granted. Hardly anyone at the time bothered to object when Cockfield, Brown, and Co., the government's advertising agency, paid the salary of the party's national director. It was taken for granted that the Liberals' fundraising efforts consisted primarily of systematically dunning those companies that secured government contracts to supply weapons or build infrastructure projects such as the St. Lawrence Seaway, a process that was supplemented by corporate cash raised on St James Street in Montreal and Bay Street in Toronto.[20]

While fundraising practices that today would be considered unethical, and even illegal, were not enough to convince the public to oust the Liberals after twenty-two consecutive years in power, the desire for a change in national direction ultimately led to St. Laurent's defeat in the 1957 election at the hands of John Diefenbaker, whose Progressive Conservatives managed to eke out a minority government. The next year, the Liberals would suffer humiliating electoral defeat under their inexperienced new leader, the former diplomat Lester Pearson. Diefenbaker won 208 of the House of Commons' 265 seats, reducing the politically green Nobel Peace Prize winner to leading a rump of just forty-nine MPs.

The Election System's Bias

Although public opinion had begun to turn against St. Laurent and the Liberals as early as 1956, one important factor contributing to the magnitude of Diefenbaker's 1958 victory was Canada's plurality or "first-past-the-post" electoral system.[21] Despite capturing 33 percent of the popular vote in the 1958 contest, the Liberals won a mere 19 percent of the seats in the House of Commons, whereas the Diefenbaker Conservatives captured over 78 percent of the seats in Parliament with just over 53 percent the popular vote, making this the largest electoral landslide in Canadian history.[22]

As much as the Liberals suffered in 1958, there is no question that they have been the chief beneficiary over the last century of an electoral system so favouring

Figure 1

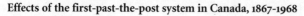

Effects of the first-past-the-post system in Canada, 1867-1968

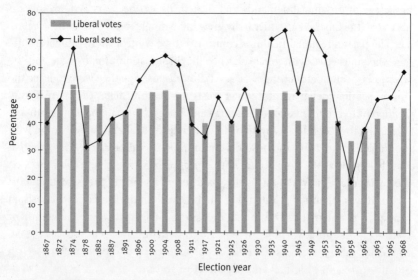

Source: Aggregated from J.M. Beck, *Pendulum of Power: Canada's Federal Elections* (Scarborough, ON: Prentice-Hall, 1968).

the party in power that the system has been christened "one-party dominance."[23] As can be seen from Figure 1, prior to the 1974 election the Liberal Party had received a higher proportion of seats than votes in eighteen out of twenty-three elections since 1896, getting over ten percentage points more seats than votes in eight of those contests. This discrepancy between votes cast and seats won is considerably larger under the plurality system than it would be under some variety of proportional representation.

The most powerful illustration of the winner's premium is in the province of Quebec, where, as Figure 2 shows, the Liberal Party had historically received 50 to 60 percent of the vote, yet had generally made off with some 70 percent of the seats. Only once in the course of twenty-three elections had the Liberals received a smaller proportion of the seats than of the votes cast in the province. This was in 1958 – the great Diefenbaker landslide. That year, voting support for the Liberal Party was 46 percent, which, in an adverse national swing, only yielded the Liberals twenty-five of the province's seventy-five seats. During the

Figure 2

Effects of the first-past-the-post system in Quebec, 1867-1968

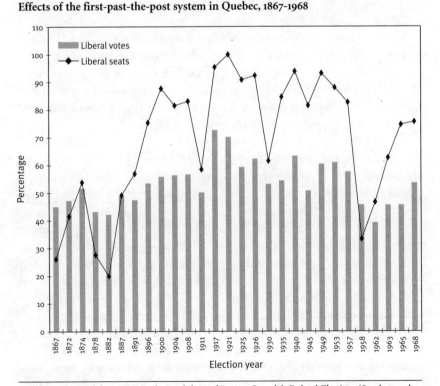

Source: Aggregated from J.M. Beck, *Pendulum of Power: Canada's Federal Elections* (Scarborough, ON: Prentice-Hall, 1968).

1963 and 1965 elections, however, the same 46 percent of the provincial vote yielded forty-seven and fifty-six seats – 63 percent and 75 percent of the total seats from the province. This simple illustration points out how unpredictable are the returns in seats from a given level of votes, and how the fortunes of a party often depend more on a few hundred ballots cast in key marginal ridings than on large swings in the whole electorate. It is the parties' awareness of how a small shift in the vote may determine their fates that accounts for much of their election campaigns' intensity. A two-percentage-point shift of the popular vote can lead to a thirteen-percentage-point gain in seats, as it did in Ontario in 1968, when these extra seats made the difference between a minority and majority government for Pierre Trudeau.

The effect of exaggerated wins or losses resulting from the electoral system, combined with the fragmentation of the Canadian political system along geographical, historical, religious, and even ethnic lines, has been to increase the unevenness of political party representation in the federal Parliament. For example, whereas the Liberals have been historically overrepresented in Quebec, they had managed to win an average of only 9 percent of the seats available in the Prairies over the last ten elections before 1974, despite having drawn nearly a quarter of the votes in these three provinces.

Many academics and politicians have attempted to develop alternatives that reduce the distortions created by the present plurality system in the partisan composition of our parliamentary representatives. Nothing has ever come of any of these proposals, however, for no party in power has ever been willing to do away with an electoral system that allows it to win large parliamentary majorities with the support of only a minority of Canadians.

Pierre Trudeau and the Pan-Canadian Party System

Once the provinces began to rival the federal government in their technocratic capacity and interventionist zeal at the end of the 1950s, the federal parties lost their brokerage role to what became known as "federal-provincial diplomacy," whose periodic first ministers' conferences captured an inordinate amount of the national media's attention. Instead of brokering inter-regional conflicts, the parties developed a "pan-Canadian" mission, by which they performed an integrating function from coast to coast through policies aimed at constructing a national identity (multiculturalism, bilingualism, and the adoption of the maple-leaf flag) and societal cohesion (medicare, pensions, and other social security measures).

This shift in partisan politics away from the regional concerns of the second party system to a national agenda focusing on issues that mattered to Canadians as individuals was facilitated by new communications technologies, most especially television. Unlike "cool" print and radio, which were the media of choice for electioneering during the first and second party systems, respectively, the "hot" medium of television allowed the parties to make the same emotive appeals to the voters' nascent sense of a Canadian identity from coast to coast to coast.[24] By the end of the 1950s, Canadian elections were no longer fought on the region-by-region basis on which campaigns had been waged since Confederation. Instead, they became country-wide contests in which three national political leaders – their personality-enhancing images transmitted by television's hot images – appealed to a single pan-Canadian electorate sharing the same basic concerns, irrespective of their regional, provincial, or ethnic loyalties. This tectonic shift in the way elections were contested would result in the most dramatic shake-up in the internal workings of Canadian political parties since the birth of radical parties in the 1930s.

Lester Pearson, who had made his mark internationally as minister for external affairs under St. Laurent, was the leader who saw the Liberals through the transition from the second to the third party system. Serving as prime minister from 1963 to 1968, "Mike" kept Canada on the path of collective security in foreign policy, which, in practice, meant close collaboration with the United States, primarily in the North Atlantic alliance (NATO) but also in such disastrous adventures as the Vietnam War.[25] At home, Pearson's attainments were similarly ambivalent. The broad system of social welfare first dreamed of by Mackenzie King was completed, but at the cost of further concessions to the increasingly demanding provincial governments who, more and more, were calling the tune for Ottawa. Meanwhile the economy, increasingly dominated by American multinational corporations, continued on its path of satellitic integration with the United States. Its vast resource endowment supplied American industry with cheap raw materials, while its manufacturing sector was little more than a tariff-protected network of inefficient, US-owned "branch-plants" assembling US-made components into finished products for sale only in Canada. That this most unpolitical of Liberal leaders managed to establish his control over a rebuilt party organization was largely thanks to the organizational skills and reformist convictions of his close friend, adviser, and eventual cabinet colleague, Walter Lockhart Gordon.

Gordon applied his dual talents as an experienced management consultant and a self-assured policy reformer to restructure, reorient, and reanimate the Liberal party after its 1958 debacle. He cleared out the deadwood in the party's national organization, reduced the influence of the party's old regional chieftains, created centralized advisory groups for the leader, and supported the efforts of an energetic group of young Toronto Liberals, known as Cell 13, who talked idealistically about bringing democracy to the party's internal operations. Gordon's efforts in English Canada were mirrored in Quebec by an energetic reformer named Maurice Lamontagne, who brought a measure of internal democracy to the party's organization in that province and who cleaned out the corrupt party machine that was widely known as "la poubelle – the garbage can – de Montréal."[26]

On the policy front, Gordon also helped to ensure that progressive ideas on foreign-policy independence, social welfare, state-supplied medical care, and economic intervention were ratified by resolutions passed in January 1961 at a policy convention in Ottawa – the first the party had seen fit to hold since 1919, and only the second since 1893. He then based the party's manifesto for the 1962 election on these resolutions.

With a view to modernizing the Liberals' campaign techniques, Gordon named as national organizer the Toronto advertising salesman Keith Davey and hired the American pollster Lou Harris – who had been central to the recent presidential victory of John F. Kennedy – in order to adopt American electoral techniques, which combined opinion polling with advertising and image-making. As if these efforts were not enough, Gordon recruited a new fundraising team and acted as the Liberals' campaign strategist. In what was still a two-plus-two party system, Gordon received the credit for reducing Diefenbaker from an overwhelming majority to a bare minority in the 1962 federal election and then for winning the Liberals a minority of their own in 1963. As Pearson's first minister of finance, Gordon also led a fight to limit the growth of foreign control in the economy, but his proposal in the 1963 federal budget speech to introduce new tax measures to obstruct foreign takeovers of Canadian companies earned him so much hostility from an already continentalist business community that he lost his pre-eminence in the government and left the cabinet in 1965.

Though it is always difficult to encapsulate the ideology of a party at any particular time, assessments by political scientists Gad Horowitz and John Meisel succeed in capturing the position of the Liberal Party before its 1968 change of leadership:

> The Liberal Party has continued to speak the language of King: ambiguous and ambivalent, presenting first its radical face and then its conservative face, urging reform and warning against hasty, ill-considered change, calling for increased state responsibility but stopping short of socialism openly, speaking for the common people but preaching the solidarity of classes.[27]

> The Liberal Party is notable for its sympathies with the United States and for its willingness to accept the increasing integration of Canada in the English-speaking part of the North American community ... At the same time the Liberals have shown an unmistakable enthusiasm for collective security in international politics, based on vigorous participation in the United Nations and in regional pacts like NATO.[28]

Attitudinal and Organizational Foundations of the Party

Its long record of dominance, its broad geographic distribution of electoral support, and its parliamentary representation helped make the Liberals the most broadly supported political party throughout the various ethnic, religious, occupational, and class groupings in Canadian society. Opinion surveys confirmed that, by the late 1960s, they appealed more effectively than any other party to members of all occupations, apart from farmers. John Meisel summed up his analysis of the 1965 and 1968 federal election data with this observation:

> In Canada, as a whole, the Liberals continued to receive above-average support from Catholics, people with high-ranking occupations, a higher class self-image and more years of formal schooling. They also drew a somewhat disproportionately large number of new Canadians, particularly those who arrived since the end of the Second World War, and they continue to be strongly favoured by French-speaking Canadians, by younger rather than older voters, by the most urbanized segments of the population and, ever so slightly, by men.[29]

Meisel's attitudinal analysis of the electorate indicated that Liberal voters – despite the fact "that a sizeable portion of them live in Quebec – showed themselves to be the most progressive, liberal, secular and politically interested, and to feel politically effective":

> The support for Mr. Trudeau's party varied directly with religiosity, moral liberalism, interest in foreign affairs, greater importance being attached to the central government, interest in the election, a sense of efficacy, general optimism about the future and economic expectations; it varied inversely with authoritarianism, respect for law and order ... and cynicism.[30]

In short, when Pierre Trudeau burst onto the political scene, Liberal voters, more than those of the other parties, included the most industrialized, urbanized, technocratic and managerial Canadians. In terms of its supporters, therefore, the Liberal party could be thought of as being the most progressive or modern, in the sense of appealing to those elements in society who felt at home in the so-called "advanced," urbanized and highly technological world usually associated with urban North America.[31]

Learning of the advantage that the Liberal Party enjoyed in the distribution of its geographical and social support, its history of electoral success, and the clear dominance it had exerted over the government of the Canadian federation, a newcomer to the country in the 1960s might well have expected that its organization would be highly developed, enjoying a broadly based, active membership, a sophisticated structural framework, and a deeply entrenched political culture. In reality the opposite was true. The size of the party's membership varied considerably not only from region to region, but even from year to year. In more traditional political cultures, such as that of the Atlantic provinces, where society was not as highly urbanized as in central Canada, the actual paid-up membership of the party organization was low, while the extent of party identification by citizens was extremely high – to the point where a taxi driver in Charlottetown, Prince Edward Island, could indicate to the tourist the political affiliation of virtually every household on any street. In urbanized areas like Toronto or Vancouver, riding-association membership fluctuated enormously. When a nomination race was hotly contested, hundreds, and in some cases even thousands, of new members could be recruited by candidates signing up citizens to support them at the nomination meeting.[32] Once the nomination effort ended, however, the active membership would drop to its core of just a few hundred, supplemented by the winning candidate's immediate supporters.

Since national parties in Canada were federal organizations made up of provincially organized components, and since the different regions of the country were often in very basic opposition to each other (industrial areas historically wanted high tariffs and other forms of government protection while rural provinces pressed for free trade; poor provinces favoured a strong federal government able to redistribute national income in their direction but rich areas demanded local autonomy and lower taxes), the internal workings of national parties were often notable more for dissension than solidarity. Prime Minister Pearson, for instance, was barely on speaking terms with Ross Thatcher, the Liberal premier of Saskatchewan, who opposed the welfare-state direction in which the federal party was moving. At the same time, Pearson was being urged by Joey Smallwood, Liberal premier of poverty-stricken Newfoundland, to increase federal spending on social services. From a third side, he was under extreme pressure from Jean Lesage, the Liberal premier of Quebec, to hand over operational responsibility for whole areas of federal jurisdiction. At the 1973 national meeting of the party, rank-and-file western delegates attacked their federal government for keeping down oil prices to favour the Maritimes, whose own deputations inveighed against the excessive nationalism of their central Canadian confreres, who for their part wished to slow down the influx of foreign capital into the country's industrial heartland.

More astonishing to the outside observer than the ideological and geographical divisions within what John Meisel famously called this "omnibus party" was its organizational underdevelopment. Having originally been spontaneous operations set up just at election time to coordinate campaigning, Canadian parties were long characterized by their structural impermanence. It was only in 1932 that the Liberal Party first established a permanent central office. Since it was closed down from 1940 to 1943 due to the war, the Liberal Party's "permanent" central office was just over thirty years old by the time of the 1974 election.[33] None of the Canadian parties approached any of their British or American counterparts in the size and sophistication of their head offices and professional staff. That the Liberal Party under Lester Pearson was thought to be the best organized, most rationalized, efficient party organization in its use of public opinion polls and fulltime staff – "Canada's most American party" – should be taken as a measure of the more underdeveloped state of the other parties than as a comment on its institutional maturity.[34]

Even by 1974, when the Liberal Party headquarters occupied a whole floor of a small Ottawa office building, where it employed a full-time staff and had developed a considerable communications capacity, the party organization was anything but coherent. Confusion over their lines of authority characterized the party's operatives, not simple chains of command. Far from following a rational, bureaucratic model, the party bore some similarity to what Samuel Eldersveld called a "stratarchy":[35] a collection of power centres, often overlapping, sometimes even conflicting with each other. The party's national headquarters in Ottawa could not reign supreme over other branches of the party when it had to rely on cash transfers from the autonomous provincial Liberal associations in order to finance its operations.[36] Moreover, it had to compete for influence with the authoritative Prime Minister's Office, the cabinet ministers' departments, and the caucus – the Liberal members of Parliament who were not in cabinet but who commanded a staff of researchers with a government-funded budget. Outside Ottawa, the centres of power multiplied in geometric progression: each province had its own party organization, with regional and district sub-organizations enjoying varying degrees of autonomy. Lowest in the hierarchy came the individual riding associations, which numbered 264 in 1974. Small though their capacity may have been to influence and control the actions of the federal party, they were jealous of their autonomy when it came to exercising their major function: nominating candidates at election time. Since the overwhelming bulk of the personnel staffing the party's power centres in the provinces, regions, districts, and ridings were unpaid volunteers, their turnover was frequent, thus further decreasing the continuity, cohesion, and influence of the grassroots. This weakness of the rank and file increased in areas where the party was not electorally successful and so offered little prospect of patronage or advancement to attract ambitious recruits.

The kaleidoscopic nature of the Liberal Party's internal organization was a manifestation of its failure to evolve from its simple beginnings as an electoral alliance into a "modern" mass structure. This is not to deny that efforts had been made to democratize the party and expand its mass base. In 1957 Diefenbaker had ousted a party whose finances depended on kick-backs from corporations with government contracts, whose election platforms were elaborations on the government's record and were designed largely by civil servants, and whose organizational tasks were undertaken regionally by individual cabinet ministers. Defeat left the party with neither funding to fuel its machine, nor policy direction to attract new recruits, nor a structure that could marshal its forces for a counteroffensive. Accordingly, during the Pearson period, Liberal activists worked with some success to have considerable power removed from the hands of the leader and placed under the control of the party executive, elected at its biennial convention.

Cell 13, the group of reformers from Toronto who took control of the Liberal Party under Walter Gordon's aegis in the late 1950s, intended to remedy the party's failings with a more democratic strategy. As one of the group's intellectuals put it,

> their new concept of the role of a political party – the Liberal Party of Canada –
> is the recognition that the Party's main function is not restricted in fact to the
> election of Liberal Party members until a government is formed and thereafter
> to merely maintain the government in power ... [but includes] the recognition
> that the organization Party ... should be interested in not merely obtaining power
> but the use and exercise of this power. It is not enough to talk of democratizing
> the Party without ensuring that its role for policy making can be effective.[37]

This statement expressed the desire to create a party organization that was built on a broad base of members who had a constitutionally defined role in deciding its policies. However, the party would still remain dependent on corporate largesse rather than rely on its individual members in order to finance its electoral machine.

Although the loss of power in 1957 had motivated activists to press for reforms, such as writing a new party constitution and holding a policy convention in 1961 to produce a member-made platform for the next election campaign, electoral victory in 1963 blunted the cutting edge of reform within the party.[38] The Liberals' recapture of power in 1963 had far more to do with the organizational talents of Walter Gordon working quietly behind the scenes than with the speeches of party delegates debating their policies in a convention under the public's eye.[39] Nevertheless, the rejuvenation of the federal Liberals was not simply a matter of this distinguished business consultant bringing sound management principles to bear on the political planning of a rusty machine that did little more than drag voters to the polls on election day and dispense patronage thereafter. As a result of Walter Gordon's fall from grace after his 1963 budget debacle, continued internecine bickering within the caucus, and the cliff-hanging uncertainties of running a minority government, the party's reformers could still complain by 1967 that "the party wing has not solved the problem of continuing policy development within the Party structure. There are still no signs of new initiatives or structural innovations for policy making in the Party."[40] The only real sign of significant change was an amendment to the party's constitution that made the leader answerable to the regular party convention and "accountable" to the delegates' secret ballot vote on whether a new leadership convention should be called.[41]

Seduction and Betrayal: Participatory Democracy from Above

The leadership convention necessitated by the retirement of Lester Pearson in 1968 caught the imagination of the Canadian public more than anything that the Liberal Party had done for decades. It appeared to be a moment of decision that would shape the party's direction for many years to come. As is normal for parties that have enjoyed long years in office, there was no lack of serious candidates for the leadership. Most prominent was Paul Martin Sr., a long-time cabinet workhorse who was holding down the same external affairs portfolio that both Lester Pearson and Louis St. Laurent had used as their springboard to the political summit. Most powerful in his corporate backing was Robert Winters, who had been minister of trade and commerce and was then a major figure among the country's captains of industry. Not to be discounted as serious contenders for the leadership were Paul Hellyer, who had made his national mark as defence minister by integrating the three branches of the armed forces under a single uniform, and Mitchell Sharp, the articulate minister of finance who had succeeded two years earlier in rallying the party's continentalist wing to defeat the "economic nationalists" supporting Walter Gordon. Then there was the handsome, ambitious, but younger John Turner, who would certainly try for the leadership a second time if he failed to win on his first effort. The economist, businessman, and nationalist intellectual Eric Keirans alone injected some pointed discussion of policy issues into the leadership campaign.[42]

That all of these substantial Liberal figures were outdistanced by a political neophyte who had been first elected in 1965 and had but a year's experience in the cabinet indicates how successfully Pierre Elliott Trudeau managed to appeal to the desire for renewal that was again beating in the breasts of the party's rank and file. Excited by the press attention Trudeau was getting for his tough-love approach to Quebec separatists as minister of justice, Liberal delegates ignored the stories they had heard about his past disdain for their kind and rallied to his campaign by the hundreds.[43] A virtual unknown to the party's grassroots in November, Trudeau went to the April 1968 leadership convention in Ottawa as the candidate to beat.

The choice of Pierre Elliott Trudeau as Pearson's successor at that convention first appeared to be a dangerous departure from the governing party's prudent tradition of leadership selection, but the change of style masked continuity of substance. That he was a Quebecker confirmed the Liberal Party's alternation between anglophone and francophone leaders, recommitting it to that electorate whose support was so crucial to its national dominance. The choice of this former radical, albeit millionaire and intellectual, reaffirmed the Janus-like stance of a centrist party with a record of co-opting personalities and policies from the left while maintaining a more conservative approach when in office.

Trudeau proceeded to stage a brilliant, if ambivalent, election campaign two months later, exciting radical aspirations with his themes of "participatory democracy" and a "just society," while remaining fiscally conservative by rejecting the notion that the state could play Santa Claus.[44] The campaign was cleverly stage-managed by professional political handlers who saw the vote-getting value of Trudeau's daredevil persona. In between his philosophical speeches with their titillating bilingual touch, he was encouraged to do jackknife dives into hotel swimming pools and backflips on trampolines, to kiss every pretty girl in sight, and to be as provocative in his rhetoric as need demanded. The decisive victory that came to the party on June 25 was almost anticlimatic. Years later, Keith Davey described the campaign as "not an election at all, it was a coronation. It didn't teach Pierre Trudeau anything about politics or about the Liberal Party. All he had to do was to show his face and make his speech about the Just Society and participatory democracy and all that jazz. He didn't need the Liberal Party to win and he didn't know what the Liberal Party was about."[45]

Although his rousing electoral success in 1968 has rightly been attributed more to his charisma than to any burning desire among the electorate to get more involved in the processes of governance, Pierre Trudeau's prior selection as party leader was largely the result of his more specific allure to the many Liberals who still felt isolated from the decision-making mechanisms of their own party. Thus, after June 25, 1968, when activists could contemplate four years of secure power, the party leadership returned to its unfinished agenda of the previous decade: increasing the power of the rank-and-file members of the extra-parliamentary party vis-à-vis the cabinet and caucus.

To be sure, "participatory democracy" was an unusual slogan for any Canadian prime minister to use when addressing his followers, and particularly unusual to be heard in the Liberal Party, whose prolonged tenure in federal office through the twentieth century had owed next to nothing to the involvement of party members – let alone ordinary Canadians – in policy making. As a veteran of the campaign waged in the 1950s to make provincial politics in Quebec more open and democratic, however, Pierre Trudeau was clearly committed to bringing participatory democracy to the Liberal Party.[46] In order to provide substance to this commitment, he gave Senator Richard Stanbury, the party's new president, a mandate to design an ambitious new policy-making process.

Because they understood that the party's attempts at policy making earlier in the 1960s had suffered from an elitist reliance on experts, inadequate input from the ridings, undemocratic procedures at the policy convention, and a leadership that was arbitrary in its acceptance or rejection of grassroots views, Senator Stanbury and his federal policy committee created an elaborate battle plan designed to address the democratic deficits of the old process. The whole policy operation was to be stretched over two years to allow enough time for party members to respond to the proposals received from an array of experts at the first stage of the three-phase process – a "thinkers' conference" held in November 1969 at Harrison Hot Springs, British Columbia. At this salt-spring spa, the party leader told his participating activists,

> Our concept of a political party, which is attuned to the needs of our society, is ... one which reaches out to absorb the ideas and to reflect the aspirations of all Canadians ... [to] encourage the widest possible participation by those interested in questions of public policy.[47]

> We are like the pilots of a supersonic aeroplane. By the time an airport comes into the pilot's field of vision, it is too late to begin the landing procedure. Such planes must be navigated by radar. A political party, in formulating policy, can act as a society's radar.[48]

The second phase of the process would allow the best part of a year for discussions at the grassroots level, giving the ridings, the districts, and finally the provincial party associations plenty of time to act as society's radar by submitting resolutions on issues that concerned them. Third, a redesigned policy convention would give delegates the chance to make policy without being deterred by caucus discipline or cabinet control. Finally, the resolutions that were passed in convention would be drafted into a platform for the next federal election campaign.

Unfortunately for the cause of extra-parliamentary party democratization, each part of this plan to correct the deficiencies of the old policy-making process fell victim to new difficulties of its own. Stretching the process to two years assumed, to start with, that those party members who attended the thinkers' conference would communicate the experts' views back to their ridings, which would respond to these challenges during phase two. This hope was unrealistic. Of the fifty-four delegates from the Toronto & District (T&D) Liberal Association who attended the thinkers' conference in British Columbia, only six attended the phase-two regional and provincial conferences before going to the final policy convention. Of the 154 T&D delegates to this final convention in October 1970, 25 percent had been to no previous conference in this process, and 40 percent had attended only one such conclave.[49]

The concept of a second phase that would articulate the ridings' views also assumed that the grassroots of the party were anxious to contribute to party policy. In actual practice, the party's grassroots turned out to be disconcertingly shallow, with only a minority of its federal riding associations actually submitting resolutions for the final policy convention. The several thousand pages of analysis presented at Harrison Hot Springs enjoyed little circulation in the ridings, and a paperback selection of these fifty-nine papers was not available for the delegates' use until after the final policy convention had adjourned.[50] When riding presidents in the Toronto district were interviewed, more turned out to be hostile than favourable toward policy activities in their constituencies. "Policy is for nuts," said one contemptuously, revealing a distinctly authoritarian political culture in the ranks. The decision-making process within the party had little credibility among riding executives, who continued to suspect that the policy conventions were controlled by the party's elite. In any case, they had no expectation that their government would listen to the party's opinions.[51]

The third major assumption underlying the Liberals' policy process was that a final convention would be able to aggregate the various conflicting views and proposals advanced during the first two phases so as to provide the parliamentary wing of the party with a coherent policy charter for use in the next general election. In many respects, the Liberals' policy convention in 1970 did mark a milestone in the history of party policy-making. Resolutions received from the ridings and the regions were collated and edited by task forces of the federal policy committee and mailed as draft resolutions to the delegates some weeks in advance of the convention to allow them time to discuss the resolutions with fellow party members and their communities in their home ridings. The procedures at the convention in Ottawa further encouraged delegates to amend these drafts or suggest new resolutions for consideration, and the convention's format gave the delegates substantial capacity to resist any attempted manipulation by the party's hierarchy. When Edmonton publisher and bookseller Mel Hurtig, the task force chair for international relations, complained that the nationalist thrust of his foreign-policy resolutions had been emasculated by party hacks in Ottawa before being circulated to the delegates, the convention proceeded to restore the original meaning of his resolutions despite the disapproving presence at the debate of the ministers of external affairs and national defence and of Pierre Trudeau himself. Since delegates voted in secret and at their own convenience on printed ballots (rather than by show of hand in crowded plenary sessions), there was little chance for them to be swayed by eloquent or influential party leaders in their private decisions on the four hundred resolutions that they had before them.

The separation of the convention into distinct operations – considering the draft resolutions in concurrent forums, debating the amended material in plenary sessions, and voting on written ballots after the debates – increased the productivity of the convention and reduced the time lost over procedural wrangling. Yet for all its procedural advantages, the Liberals' convention technique developed a number of flaws that created ambiguities and thus undermined its impact. For example, delegates had to vote on resolutions that had different meanings in their English and French versions. Contradictory resolutions were passed that allowed both economic nationalists and their continentalist opponents to claim victory.

The Liberal Party's Trudeau-inspired exercise in participatory democracy ultimately came to grief not on a question of semantics but on the issue of power. Even before grassroots-authored resolutions favouring a guaranteed annual income were debated and passed, the prime minister made clear in his "accountability session" with the delegates that he was not prepared to implement such a major change in his government's approach to welfare. On November 23, 1970, the day following the phase-three policy convention, Trudeau took pains publicly to repudiate a convention resolution directing his government to establish a review board that would monitor civil rights during the application of the War Measures Act to deal with the terrorist Front de libération du Québec. The leader thereby himself invalidated the fourth crucial assumption on which his participatory process had been based: that the party leadership would listen and act if the membership expressed itself on policy matters in a responsible, representative, and therefore legitimate way.

Once the convention was over, the party lost most of its influence over the leadership in Ottawa. Party president Richard Stanbury continued to meet with the ministers in a periodical "political cabinet." A consultative council continued to mail out resolutions for the delegates to vote on. Staff in the Prime Minister's Office (PMO) continued to monitor activities in the party across the country. Nevertheless, the extra-parliamentary party's policy output could not compete with the weight of other political inputs: the continuing influence of the ministers' own policy departments; the constant pressures from corporate and other interest groups; the daily advice from editorials in the media; the insistent demands coming from alert members of the caucus; the regular public-opinion polling by professional researchers; and above all, the hourly advice coming to Trudeau from his clique of confidants in the PMO. When the cabinet told the party policy chair to forget his proposed electoral charter that had been drafted as planned from the convention's resolutions, there was nothing for him to do but pick up his text and make as dignified a retreat as the aborting of three years' hard effort made possible.

Pierre Trudeau's promise of participation and Senator Stanbury's implementation of an elaborate policy process had generated unprecedented activity within the Liberal Party's ranks. Despite the imperfections in the process, many hundreds of Liberals had devoted substantial energies to developing what they considered a relevant and progressive policy platform for their party. When it became clear that none of their policy positions would be adopted for the 1972 election campaign platform, the morale of the party core fell noticeably. By December 1972, the most active members of the Liberal Party in Ontario showed a striking level of unhappiness with their political involvement. When asked the simple question, "Are you satisfied with your activity in the Liberal party?" 46 percent responded, "Dissatisfied." Far from constituting the base for a vibrant, participatory political culture, card-carrying Liberals felt as alienated as ever from the internal workings of their party.[52]

This widespread discontent among the party's rank and file was an important factor in the near-disaster suffered by Trudeau in the 1972 election campaign. In Ontario, for example, 55 percent of Liberal activists surveyed reported that campaign workers' morale was worse than it had been in the 1968 election campaign, and 67 percent recounted that it was harder to recruit volunteers in 1972 than in 1968.[53] What little manpower the Liberals did manage to attract was not used as effectively as it could have been, due to a lack of coherent leadership to direct the campaign at the national level. The two campaign co-chairs, Robert Andras and Jean Marchand – the ministers of manpower and regional expansion, respectively, were too busy fighting re-election battles of their own to devote sufficient attention to the larger task of organizing and supervising the campaign in all twelve provinces and territories. In the end, Andras and Marchand's failure to provide the campaign with leadership was not the decisive factor in the Liberals' poor showing in 1972. Whatever decisions they did manage to make were "consistently overruled by members of Trudeau's own staff [in the PMO], mainly Ivan Head and Jim Davey, who had no experience with electoral politics other than the coronation election of 1968."[54]

Planning badly at the national level, Liberal headquarters in Ottawa failed to produce a strategy paper for the provincial campaign chairs, while the ridings were understaffed by volunteers because so many Liberals had been alienated by Trudeau's attitudes and policies. Although the Liberals' campaign slogan, "The Land Is Strong," was trying to meet Trudeau's staff's insistence that he was running not an ordinary election campaign but a "dialogue with the people," they failed to address economic problems that were troubling the electorate. As Christina McCall wrote, "Trudeau and his closest staff members felt that he didn't need to worry about the party. 'The people' would understand. They didn't seem to realize that 'the people,' like the party, were puzzled by his seeming indifference to the feelings of large blocs of Canadians."[55]

Widespread grumbling about the prime minister's evident lack of interest in ordinary citizens' concern about unemployment and inflation further eroded his public support, though this problem, too, was ignored by Trudeau's supporters as a media-induced chimera. They seemed to believe that all he would have to do to win a new mandate when the time came was to present himself on the hustings, hold a dialogue with Canadians, and wait for the Liberal votes to come pouring in. Their surprise was palpable on October 22, 1972, when they found themselves clinging to power by a scant two-seat edge over the Progressive Conservatives, whose own unglamorous leader, Robert Stanfield, had conducted a dogged campaign devoted to economic issues.

Unfortunately for Stanfield, his miss was to prove as good as the proverbial mile. Pierre Trudeau proceeded to shed his philosopher-king pretensions, to abandon his dreams of turning Canadian politics into an Athenian agora, to recruit the partisan hacks he had previously spurned, and, with their tutoring, to learn the trade of partisan politics so well that he could run and win decisively less than two years later.

Pierre Trudeau
Victory, Fall, and Recovery

1974

The Liberal Party and Pierre Trudeau: The Jockey and the Horse

The 1974 federal election in Canada was both a mind-boggling puzzle and the most straightforward event a political analyst could ever hope to study. At a time of world upheaval, international monetary disasters, global energy crises, national bankruptcies, coalition governments, and, on the domestic front, worsening economic conditions, the Canadian electorate returned to power the very party that had presided over the country's fortunes and misfortunes for the previous decade – that is, the organization generally identified with the alarming inflation over which the election campaign was fought. Or, to reframe the issue in terms of Canada's federal political culture, the voters renewed the mandate of a compelling leader who commanded an efficient and experienced political machine with a long history of governmental dominance.

If the 1972 election results were a warning that Trudeau did not know his own party, the 1974 campaign was to show that this unpolitical politician had mastered new skills. That Trudeau became a "seasoned professional" in the 1974 election was due, paradoxically enough, to the amateur and anarchic nature of his party. For this conversion was largely the work of a small group of prominent Liberal activists in Toronto who set themselves up in the wake of the 1972 reversal to advise their leader, just as their predecessors in Cell 13 had acted in the late 1950s as Lester Pearson's brain trust. Meeting without any formal mandate in lawyer Jerry Grafstein's office, they were held together by a sense of loyalty to the party. They were concerned about its policy drift, its lack of leadership, and its shaken will to govern. They were worried about Trudeau's remoteness from the heart of the party and quickly came to the conclusion that there was no chance of reversing the party's fortunes in the next election unless a capable campaign chair was appointed soon enough to be able to mobilize the party's energies and orchestrate its efforts. In a meeting at the prime minister's residence, the Grafstein group put the issue to their leader. "You cannot be both horse and jockey," one Toronto lawyer told Trudeau.[1] The message was strong and clear: Trudeau was the horse, and a satisfactory chair was needed to play jockey.

Who that person should be was quite another matter. The Toronto group had canvassed the possibilities and made up its mind: Cell 13 alumnus Keith Davey was their man. Already awarded by Pearson with a seat in the Senate, for his work as the party's national director in the mid-1960s, he had the time for what might be a year's intense preparatory work for the next campaign. As a perennial optimist, he had the enthusiasm and energy needed to guide the party through this trying period in its fortunes.

The party as a whole did not share the Toronto Liberals' confidence in the controversial and flamboyant party hack. As campaign director for the elections of 1962, 1963, and 1965, he was associated with the Liberals' failure to achieve a clear majority during Lester B. Pearson's tenure. Dubbed "the rainmaker" for his apparent capacity to fumble great opportunities, Davey provoked as much alarm as enthusiasm among caucus members when they heard his name bruited about as the next campaign chair. Reluctant to appear too anxious for another election, Trudeau asked party president Richard Stanbury to canvas the party's influentials. Weeks dragged into months before a consensus emerged: Davey was the only Liberal available who had the seniority, the connections, and the authority to establish a game plan and make it stick.

As a result of the prime minister's willingness to put this jockey in the saddle and run flat out under his direction, the 1974 Liberal campaign became a study in contrast with the previous election. Rather than re-establishing the bicephalous campaign committee of 1972 that had been doomed to frustration because the two cabinet ministers that co-chaired it, Robert Andras and Jean Marchand, were themselves seeking re-election, the Quebec Liberals were left alone to run their own unique political show while the campaign organization for the rest of Canada was managed by a single full-time, politically experienced organizer.

Those who expected the 1974 campaign to be a rerun of 1972 did not appreciate the changes that had taken place in Trudeau and his government between the euphoric years of their majority government (1968-72) and the less comfortable times of minority rule (1972-4). In his first term, Trudeau had flown high at the beginning only to crash at the end. The political wunderkind and apostle of rationalism in politics, who had come to power declaring the need to reassess and review all areas of policy before launching out in new directions, had actually accomplished remarkably little during his first four years in power. Foreign policy, fiscal policy, social policy – each area of government was examined and re-examined, but in the end, little change was made from previous patterns.

Insignificant results did not necessarily induce electoral consequences, since only the intellectual community was truly disappointed by the lack of significant change. Far more politically damaging was Trudeau's personal feat of offending almost every major group in the population. Whether it was Quebec nationalists and civil libertarians he had dismayed with his heavy-handed response to the October Crisis of 1970, or Western Canadians he had alienated with the introduction of official bilingualism in 1969; whether it was church people and social activists whose efforts on behalf of the Ibo people's struggle for self-determination in Nigeria he had dismissed with his contemptuous question, "Where's Biafra?" or the large Slavic communities in Canada he had outraged by equating Ukrainian nationalism with Quebec separatism: it seemed that he could not have done worse by a deliberate program to alienate almost every important group in the country.

But having come within a hair's breadth of losing office in 1972, the Trudeau cabinet performed in a decisively different way during their year-and-a-half experience with minority government. Crisis management was the order of the day: at any moment they could have been defeated by the New Democratic Party switching its voting power from the governing Grits to the opposition Tories. Despite the many difficulties of running a government in these circumstances, the Trudeau government's output was more impressive in this period than it had been in the preceding four years of majority rule. Important legislation was brought in and passed in a number of areas, including innovative measures on foreign investment control and a radically progressive reform of election financing. More important in electoral terms, the successful recovery of the 1972 fumble had a positive impact on the morale of the party leader, his cabinet, the parliamentary caucus, and even the rank and file. Having weathered the first hours, days, and then weeks of their precarious position, the Liberals soon regained their usual self-confidence, while keeping their infamous arrogance under apparent control.

Liberal planning for the election went on quietly behind the scenes, as the government continued to keep the initiative in its own hands and away from the frustrated Progressive Conservatives. Even though the Liberals succeeded in holding off the Tory assault during this minority period, their political situation on the eve of the election campaign looked bleak. Despite the favourable trends in Gallup poll results (see Table 1), Trudeau was the underdog in the estimation of the English-Canadian media, who had tasted blood and were generally supporting Robert Stanfield and the PCs on their editorial pages.[2]

Not surprisingly, the Conservatives were spoiling for the fight. Their eagerness was understandable, given the calibre of candidates they were attracting. The fact that Duff Roblin, former premier of Manitoba, Ron Collister, senior news reporter for the Canadian Broadcasting Corporation, and Ronald Ritchie, former vice president of Imperial Oil, were anxious to run for them was an indication of the confidence and eagerness in the Conservatives' camp, which could also legitimately be gratified by opinion polls confirming that inflation

Table 1

Gallup poll measures of party popularity, 1974

Party	Before campaign (%)		During campaign (%)		Votes received (%)	
	6 February	10 April	5 June	22 June	6 July	8 July
Liberal	42	39	40	42	43.0	43.2
PC	31	34	33	34	35.0	35.5
NDP	21	18	21	19	16.5	15.5
Other	6	9	6	6	5.5	6.0

Source: Canadian Institute of Public Opinion, *Gallup Report,* 1974; Stephen Clarkson, "Pierre Trudeau and the Liberal Party: The Jockey and the Horse," in *Canada at the Polls: The Federal Election of 1974,* ed. Howard Penniman (Washington, DC: American Enterprise Institute, 1976), 79.

was the number-one issue in the public mind and that wage and price controls (the official Conservative policy on the matter since the 1972 election campaign) was the most popular solution.[3] Given this context, the tale of the 1974 federal election can either be told as the Conservative story of defeat snatched from the jaws of victory or – the gist of this chapter – the Liberal story of victory snatched from the jaws of defeat.

Victory from the Jaws of Defeat: The Expert Amateurs
Seen in retrospect, the 1974 Liberal campaign was a model operation, run by a group of experienced but non-professional men and women who rallied, as usual following the election call, to a political leader who had been able to learn from his past mistakes.

Strategy
Rather than revive the vague and unsuccessful approach of the 1972 campaign, which Prime Minister Trudeau had billed as an intellectual "conversation with Canadians," the Liberals chose to articulate a clear strategy on the basis of a careful analysis of survey research aimed at identifying the opposition's weaknesses and their own strengths. An opinion survey they carried out in the spring of 1974 had again shown the public's intense concern about inflation. This was a serious problem for Davey, since there was clear public support for the Conservatives' proposed solution – wage and price controls.

As bad as the situation appeared, the Liberal command group had long known that the Conservatives' major liability was Robert Stanfield. Even before the campaign started, the polls were indicating greater public confidence in the Liberal than in the Conservative leader (see Table 2). Trudeau outpolled Stanfield by 41

Table 2

Attitudes toward the three major party leaders before the 1974 federal election

Opinion	Pierre Trudeau (Liberal) (%)	Robert Stanfield (PC) (%)	David Lewis (NDP) (%)
Liked least	19.4	39.7	27.0
Most intelligent	63.8	11.0	7.2
Best leader	55.9	14.7	16.4
Most believable	33.2	25.7	17.6
Most capable of running Canada	54.6	15.7	11.7
Speaks best	67.6	3.7	21.3
Most concerned with Canada's future	37.3	17.8	15.4
Most capable of creating jobs	34.6	12.9	19.9
Best for the under-25 voters	49.3	6.4	24.8
Best to handle energy crisis	45.3	12.6	14.2
Best for Canadian unity	54.1	18.0	12.7
Best representative in foreign affairs	67.7	13.8	5.7

Source: Boyd Upper, speech to Ontario Liberal Candidates' College, May 18, 1974, York University.

percentage points as best leader, by 8 percent as most believable, by 39 percent as most capable of running Canada, by 64 percent as best speaker, by 20 percent as most concerned with Canada's future, by 22 percent as most capable of creating jobs, by 43 percent as best for the under twenty-five-year-old voters, by 33 percent as best able to handle another energy crisis, by 36 percent as best for Canadian unity, and by 54 percent as best representative in foreign affairs.

Given this enormous margin in favour of their leader, the Liberals' strategy focused on turning the issue on which the campaign was waged from inflation to leadership. This was to be done by exploiting Trudeau's dynamism, taking the offensive in attacking the Conservatives, seizing the initiative in presenting new policy issues to the public, and, very simply, running flat out while trying hard not to make any mistakes. The objective was to force the Conservatives to fight on the Liberal issue of leadership and back down from their issue of inflation.

Once the strategy had been worked out, Keith Davey's role as campaign chair was to captain the team, refusing to allow his players to budge from the game plan, monitoring the work of his regional campaign committees, and, in particular, telling the party leader – who was now ready to listen – what to do during every hour of every day.

The Leader's Campaign

The basic message that the prime minister gave his candidates at party meetings across the country in the early days of the campaign was to take the offensive: "Last time," Pierre Trudeau told the Ontario candidates assembled for a campaign college at York University on May 18, "the campaign was a conversation with Canadians. Well, we are still going to talk to the Canadian people ... but there is not going to be any backing up and apologizing and bowing our head. We are going to be on the attack and we are going to show the Canadian people that Liberalism is the way for Canada now."[4]

This time there were no plodding texts read by Trudeau and no aimless intellectual arguments with anonymous callers on radio shows, as in 1972. The party leader that Liberal workers saw on their television screens or heard at public meetings was a fighting politician giving an ad lib speech that repeated over and over again a powerful attack on the Conservatives and a strong case for the Liberals. Trudeau defended his record, including the proposed budget whose defeat had provoked the election call, and defended it aggressively:

> This budget ... was cutting taxes, income taxes ... was ensuring lower prices for your clothing and your shoes because we were cutting the 12 percent federal sales tax on those items. This is the budget that the Tories and the NDP preferred to defeat. (Toronto, June 17, 1974)[5]

> If [the opposition] talk to you about great profits of great corporations ask them why they voted against a budget which was increasing corporate taxes by 25 percent over last year's, which was increasing corporate taxes by $800,000,000 in order that the government would have $800,000,000 to redistribute to those in our society who need it most. (Montague, PEI, May 20, 1974)[6]

As for the Tories' policy of wage and price controls, Trudeau attacked it with his rhetoric in high gear:

> How is price control going to keep down the price of petroleum? Is it going to stop the war in the Middle East? Is it going to make Arabs bring their petroleum down threefold? Have they got a better solution than ours, which is giving Canadians 40 percent cheaper petroleum than the world? They don't. Wage and price controls is not an answer. Is wage and price controls an answer to the high cost of food which you are paying here? What is price control going to do about food that we import from other countries? Either from the U.S. or from less developed nations, like our coffee or our sugar or our cocoa or our tea? You can't put wage and price controls on what's being produced elsewhere. (Winnipeg, June 14, 1974)[7]

The message was repeated tirelessly:

> You'll be stuck with a policy you have seen in operation in the United States, if
> you've seen on your television or heard on your radio, about farmers gassing
> their chickens and slaughtering their cattle. Even if we freeze prices and wages,
> we can't freeze the price of the farm machinery coming in from the United
> States – they won't accept our freeze. And ... we can't freeze the pesticides, which
> come from out of Canada. So the cost to the farmer goes up. He can increase the
> price of his product but nobody will buy it because they can't resell it at higher
> prices. (North Battleford, Saskatchewan, May 23, 1974)[8]

The leader's campaign was a cunning, neo-traditional mixture of old-fashioned
optics with modern media management. For four days Trudeau was seques-
tered on a train, doing a whistle stop tour of the Maritime provinces. But it was
Jim Coutts, Keith Davey's immediate lieutenant on the prime minister's tour,
who was in control of the media on the tour. When his regular press officer,
Pierre O'Neill, wanted to allow the journalists covering the tour to have interviews with Trudeau, Coutts overruled him; they were to be kept at a distance.
This way, readers of the *Globe and Mail* of May 27 found on the front page a
nostalgic photograph of crowds gathered around the rear platform of a small
passenger train and read a long article describing Trudeau's campaigning and
warm crowd response, with no follow-up critique of his policy thinking.

Media Management
Whistle stopping and campaign promises restored an air of traditional political
reality to Trudeau the campaigner, but the men in charge of the 1974 campaign
made very modern decisions about how to relate to the media. Aware of press
hostility toward him, Trudeau was kept off the open-line shows on which he
had spent so much time in 1972. By one stroke of campaign policy, the quick-
tempered intellectual capable of annoying countless voters by a sharp reply to a
provocative question disappeared for the duration of the campaign. Whether it
was Finance Minister John Turner whom the private television network (CTV)
wished to have debate with the chief opposition finance critic, or the national
campaign chair who was asked for interviews by the press, the same rule applied: no public appearances were to be made by high-profile candidates or campaign staff except under controlled and favourable circumstances. The prime
minister gave one interview to the media magnate John Bassett on his Toronto
station, CFTO-TV, and another on the CBC to an old friend, the smooth Robert
Mackenzie of the London School of Economics, and a former supporter, the
broadcaster Patrick Watson. But except for these occasions, Trudeau campaigned

directly before the public, forcing the press to follow on his heels. The goal was to receive maximum coverage with minimal confrontation.[9]

Trudeau's speeches announcing new government programs or promising new measures were timed so as to force the media to report these initiatives while forestalling intensive grilling of either the party leader or his staff. When the paths of the prime minister and the leader of the opposition crossed one day in Winnipeg, Trudeau upstaged his challenger by issuing a government announcement that Air Canada would move its repair facilities to that prairie city and thereby create 800 new jobs. The next day it was the prime minister, not Stanfield, who dominated the headlines on the front page of the press, national as well as local.[10] This media approach was the most controversial of the three parties': journalists were frustrated by the lack of opportunities for critical reporting during the campaign.[11]

In the end, the tactic was eminently successful. Of the ten major policy announcements made by Trudeau himself, seven were reported on the front page of the *Globe and Mail*.[12] During the campaign, the *Globe* carried nineteen news items bearing on the Liberal campaign on its front page, only four of which were negative, as well as eleven policy statements and four government announcements. In all, from May 4 to July 8 the prime minister was on the front page of the *Globe* twenty-one times, compared to nine times for Stanfield. Coverage of the Liberals' campaign was even more favourable in the French-language media, with *La Presse* carrying fourteen front-page stories on the Grits, of which only two were negative.[13] By contrast, Robert Stanfield's Conservatives garnered just four mentions on the front-page of North America's largest French-language daily.[14]

Less successful at sweeping the front pages, but probably far more important to the campaign, was the Liberals' most powerful secret weapon: the prime minister's wife. Strategists running the Liberal campaign were convinced that her image as a beautiful and devoted young wife and mother could be used to the party's advantage. Introducing the prime minister to a political meeting in West Vancouver on June 4, she said, "I want to speak of him as a person, as a loving human being who has taught me in the three years we have been married and in the few years before that, a lot about loving." By talking about her husband in this romantic vein, Margaret Trudeau opened the hearts of many a politically indifferent voter. Analysts and reporters now began to describe the "Margaret factor" as important in the election calculations.[15] She was the rookie star of the campaign, a fresh face to be photographed, a new theme on which to play journalistic variations in an otherwise dull reporting scene. Having been kept out of bounds to the press by her husband since their marriage, she was a novelty – a godsend to a business that thrives on the new.

Publicity

Although the Liberals had made English-language television advertising a prerogative of the national office as early as 1962, Liberal public relations in the 1972 campaign had been run without any coordination or coherence. The disastrous slogan "The Land Is Strong" had been worked out by an ad agency representative without clear input from the campaign committee headed by Marchand and Andras. It had provoked general dismay among party workers, especially in rural areas where farmers retorted with such blunt jibes as, "It's horse shit, not Liberal shit, that makes the land strong." By contrast, the advertising effort in 1974 was run in close coordination with the campaign strategy. Rather than employ just one ad agency to produce its English-language advertisements, as the party continued to do in Quebec, the Liberals followed the example of the Conservatives from the 1972 campaign and set up their own. A fixture in every subsequent Liberal campaign, Red Leaf Communications, Ltd., was a consortium of advertising specialists drawn from various ad agencies and headed by a high-ranking Liberal who ensured that the party's messaging was consistent with its overall campaign strategy. In 1974 this responsibility for oversight went to Jerry Grafstein, still a close associate of Keith Davey.[16] Assembled just prior to the election call, and dismantled soon after the votes were counted, the members of the Red Leaf consortium were not paid for their services during the campaign, although it was understood that their agencies would be first in line to receive lucrative government advertising contracts should the Liberals win.[17]

Following this rationalization of the Liberals' public relations machinery, the advertising message in the 1974 campaign successfully reiterated and reinforced the basic strategy and message of the campaign. Instead of creating a campaign themselves, the ad men simply highlighted the effort being made by the leader on his tour. In a full-page print ad that ran in the Saturday newspapers across the country on June 29, the headline read, "Issues Change from Year to Year. The Ability to Lead Does Not." Leaning on the same survey research and strategic judgment that underlay the prime minister's campaign, the ad went on, "The leadership of Canada is the ultimate issue in this campaign. Who can do the best job for Canada in the years ahead? For every thinking Canadian there can be only one answer: Pierre Trudeau and the Liberal Party." Tying in with the Ontario candidates' proposed stump speech it went on,

> Remember 1971? The issue that year was unemployment. You don't hear much from Mr. Stanfield about a job crisis today. Could that possibly be because from 1971 through 1973 880,000 new jobs have been created in Canada? Could it possibly be because that rate of job formation was the highest in the history of this country? Could it possibly be because the number of jobs created in Canada was greater than the number created in all the Common Market countries combined? That's the record the Liberal Party is building on.[18]

The impact of all these efforts could be measured on July 6, just two days before the election, when the political scientist Peter Regenstrief reported the results of his poll in the *Toronto Star*.[19] The Liberals had increased their level of popular support from 40 percent in May to 43 percent. For the first time in twenty years and eight federal elections, they had maintained their support right through to the last week of the campaign. The momentum had been kept up, almost no mistakes had been made, and the Liberals had succeeded in replacing leadership for inflation as the main issue of the campaign.[20] The sweetest news of all, however, came from a poll conducted for CTV in mid-June that reported that 49 percent considered the Liberals had the best policy to control inflation compared to 24 percent for the Conservatives.[21] The Conservatives' major attack weapon of the campaign had been turned to the Liberals' advantage.

Policies for the Left
In 1972, the party faithful and the public had waited in vain for the prime minister to present the policies that he intended to implement if re-elected – despite the 1970 policy convention that had created more party policy than could comfortably be effected in ten years. In 1974 Pierre Trudeau had no recent party resolutions to worry about, but nonetheless the prime minister did announce a large number of policies designed to grab the front pages of the newspapers across the country, to dominate radio and television news reporting, and so to appeal to the uncommitted "transient" vote that campaign strategists guessed was hovering to the left of the Liberals. Formulated by an ad hoc committee created by Keith Davey, policy statements for the campaign had been approved by the cabinet for periodic releases timed to garner maximum media impact during the sixty-five-day campaign.

Trudeau used ten of these major statements between June 5 and 28, the priorities having been determined by the party's survey research.[22] First came three sets of announcements on housing that made it less financially burdensome for middle-class Canadians to purchase a home (low down-payment mortgages for moderately priced homes, doubling interest rate reduction grants and allowing these over a wider income range, and $500 cash grants for first-home buyers).[23] Transportation policies were also spun over three detailed proposals. The first, announced in Edmonton, promised fair freight rates for farmers; the second, released in Toronto, promised federal aid for urban transit; and the third, issued in Cornwall, Ontario, focused on improving intercity bus and train travel. A large agricultural policy designed to stabilize and guarantee farm incomes was unveiled in Humboldt, Saskatchewan, and a social security platform broadening the guaranteed annual income for pensioners and the disabled was announced in Trois-Rivières, Quebec. In Ottawa, a consumer affairs platform was announced, and, finally, on June 28 a nationalist industrial development strategy was unveiled.

More than a Leader

A government may have one commander-in-chief, but it must have more than one general. Just like the prime minister's schedule, individual ministers' itineraries were organized to get the maximum media mileage out of the better-known personalities from the cabinet. Rough-spoken Agriculture Minister Eugene Whelan, for example, was in demand as a speaker across the country. Finance Minister Turner and Secretary of State for External Affairs Mitchell Sharp travelled widely in addition to running campaigns in their ridings, where each was under heavy fire from a strong Conservative candidate. Whatever the temptations, internecine bickering was absent among the Liberals – in striking contrast to the Conservative camp. Again, there was a payoff in terms of media coverage. The *Globe and Mail* had twelve front-page stories dealing with Liberal cabinet ministers. Of these, only two were negative, reporting Labour Minister John Munro's involvement in a patronage scandal. By contrast, Conservative personalities other than Stanfield only made the front page of the *Globe and Mail* five times, twice in connection with a politically embarrassing Conservative candidate, the former mayor of Moncton, New Brunswick, who had defied Stanfield's accommodating stance on the issue of bilingualism.

Below the leadership and ministerial level, the Liberal campaign was managed nationally, regionally, and at the constituency level. From the national office, material was sent out in the form of telexed "candidates' updates" aimed at maintaining consistency in the message delivered by Liberal candidates at the grassroots level and at supplying information on the prime minister's announcements. The updates also supplied such "ad lib" ammunition for candidates' speeches as this striking remark made by John Turner: "Don't compare him [Trudeau] to the Almighty; compare him to the alternative."[24]

Far more important than the national office, however, were the provincial campaign operations. In a class by itself was Quebec, whose campaign had been run independently of English Canada since the days of Laurier.[25] As in the last two elections, the Quebec campaign was run by Trudeau's lieutenant in the province, the recently appointed Transportation Minister Jean Marchand. The organizational separateness of the Quebec campaign was originally born of its linguistic distinctiveness, which made communicating to the electorate there a separate matter. As Quebec politics took on a distinctly nationalist flavour following the Quiet Revolution of the early 1960s, the initial rationale for maintaining a separate electoral machine in Quebec was supplemented by a need to appeal to French-speaking voters' desire for *survivance* (survival) and *épanouissement* (opening out) within a renewed Canadian federation – themes that played poorly in English-speaking Canada.[26]

In Ontario, which was the most crucial province for the Liberal Party, a woman with long campaign experience was made the regional chair. Tempering her own knowledge of experienced party members with the advice of her colleagues, Dorothy Petrie put together a campaign committee that was, in the words of Gordon Dryden (the party's historical memory and financial controller), "the best campaign committee that Ontario had ever seen."[27] Of the sixteen members of this committee, only two required some financial reimbursement. The others, as is usual at election time, put in some forty hours of volunteer time per week in addition to their own jobs, with two people doing policy research, two running the prime minister's tour in Ontario, two organizing the other ministers' movements, two more organizing special events, such as a mass rally that took place at the University of Toronto's Varsity Stadium, one raising funds, and another administering surveys in critical ridings. The national chair, Keith Davey, attended the Ontario committee's weekly meetings, as did Jerry Grafstein, coordinator of the federal publicity campaign. It was a group of experienced campaigners, most of whom had already worked together several times for the Liberals in provincial and federal elections. Decentralization was the organizing principle of this instant campaign operation, with two dozen campaign coordinators being responsible for finding candidates and supervising the campaigns in the four or five ridings under their charge. The cumulative experience of these middle-level leaders was impressive. While their job was performed almost without a serious error, it retained the non-professional quality that characterized the Liberals' extra-parliamentary wing.

Although amateur in its staffing, the Ontario campaign, like the others, was modern in its techniques. A telex linked the provincial with the federal office for instant communication; a monitor team recorded news broadcasts so that when, for example, CBC television news made an apparently exaggerated estimate of the costs of the Liberal campaign promises, the policy research staff was able to respond vigorously and demand a correction from the news service. The two-person policy research staff took pride in trying to outdo the federal party office in research documentation produced for Liberal candidates. Bulletins were prepared and circulated to candidates on issues such as wage and price controls, inflation, budgetary deficits, energy, and growth in the federal civil service. A fighting speech was adapted from Trudeau's performances by the Ontario party policy chair, Boyd Upper, to provide any Ontario candidates who were inexperienced speakers with a basic line in best platform style:

Remember 1970? The issue was national unity. What leadership did Mr. Stanfield offer? His leadership was Two Nations. When Diefenbaker got done with him the Tories almost had two parties.

What did Prime Minister Trudeau offer? One Canada and no appeasement of separatists.

Remember 1971 and 1972? The issue was unemployment. In the past 3 years new job formation in Canada has exceeded 880,000. That is more new jobs than have been created in the whole of Western Europe in the same period. I'm not saying that unemployment has disappeared. What I'm saying is that unemployment today is not the number one issue in Ontario. It is not number two (energy) or number three (housing) or number four (welfare abuse). It is fifth.

What is number one issue now? It is inflation and the cost of living.

What does Mr. Stanfield offer? His answer to inflation is "wage and price control;" a 90-day freeze followed by some thing he hasn't defined and that no one else can guess.

Wage and price controls aren't new. They aren't innovative. They aren't magic. They have been tried and tried and always found wanting. Wage and price controls do not work. The distortions they create, the shortages they develop and the pent up pressure for wages unleash more serious problems than those the controls set out to solve.

What Mr. Stanfield's position amounts to is this. Prices aren't right. Wages aren't right. But, by gosh, the freeze is right.

In a world of dramatic and dynamic change Mr. Stanfield's response is: "Stop the world, I want to get off – for a 90-day freeze."

It is a dumb position that even Tories can't defend with much enthusiasm. Stanfield's 90-day wage and price freezes is not just simplistic – it is simple minded. It is a snow job and Mr. Stanfield is the Abominable Snowman.[28]

Finances

The Liberal Party had long relied overwhelmingly on corporate support to finance its election campaigns, with large donations from a small number of corporations making up the bulk of its election revenue.[29] Under pressure from the NDP, which held the balance of power in his minority government, Lester Pearson had struck a three-party task force in 1964 to correct a system stacked against fair election conditions. After extensive research and consultation, the Barbeau Commission reached a consensus by 1966. The Liberals then managed to delay implementing its sweeping recommendations year after year, since their governing position gave them the strongest call on corporate generosity. Enjoying the balance of power once again in 1972, the NDP pressed to put the Barbeau Commission report into legislation, but the Trudeauites successfully delayed implementation of the proposed reforms so that the 1974 election was run according to the old lax rules.

Most of the Liberals' funds were raised in Toronto and Montreal but were distributed through the national headquarters amongst the provincial and territorial associations. Although candidates were expected to disclose both revenues and expenditures, the resulting numbers were not audited, and public disclosure was not legally mandatory. Many candidates did not bother to disclose at all.[30] The Liberals had the best record of candidates reporting expenditures: 92 percent versus the Conservatives' 82 percent and the NDP's 80 percent. The total amount disclosed by Liberal candidates for 1974 was $4,961,127 ($18.98 million in 2002 dollars).[31] The Treasury Committee was responsible for fundraising, and it reported revenues of $6.2 million ($23.7 million) for the election, of which $5.5 million was spent, including $2.6 million ($9.9 million) in disbursements to candidates.[32]

Defeat from the Jaws of Victory: Old Generals for New Wars

While the Liberals were fighting hard to win, their two major opponents managed to help them along. The New Democratic Party, which had precipitated the election by voting against the government's budget, failed to generate an attention-grabbing issue as powerful as its 1972 attack on "corporate welfare bums." Their leader, David Lewis, had lost his impact. Appreciated by some for his influential role during the last year and a half of minority government ("the best policy chairman the Liberals ever had" was one joke at the time) and reviled by others for collaborating with the Liberals in return for marginal improvements in their legislation, he was generally castigated for having precipitated an expensive and unnecessary election. The voters' resentment was dramatically demonstrated on election night when Lewis lost his own seat to a neophyte Liberal. While his policy speeches were reported, they seemed to make little impression. Only two news stories and one policy story on the NDP appeared on the front page of the *Globe and Mail* during the whole election, while four stories on the NDP appeared on the front page of *La Presse*.

The greatest impact of the left-wing party was in adding weight to the Liberal attack on the Conservatives' wage-and-price-freeze policy. Early in the campaign, David Lewis used his keynote speech to the annual convention of the Canadian Labour Congress to attack wage and price controls, and labour leaders followed suit throughout the campaign by speaking out against the Conservative position. Such regional factors as the mid-term unpopularity of David Barrett's NDP government in British Columbia helped to undermine the party's appeal. But it was the campaign policy designed and implemented by the NDP leadership that deprived the social democrats of their toehold in the centre, failed to win them new support from the inaudible left, and at the same time helped to neutralize the political right.

The Progressive Conservatives were caught even more hopelessly in skeins of their own spinning. Like generals who had prepared to fight the battles of the last war, they had mapped out plans and built their organization months in advance. Knowing that the public's major concern was inflation and that wage and price control was considered the right solution, they went into battle rigidly over-prepared. The highly reputed, professionally staffed Big Blue Machine (the BBM, as the political brain trust of Ontario Premier William Davis was known), wrote Robert Stanfield's speeches in Toronto – a procedure that prevented the Conservative leader from responding quickly to issues as they developed. A series of policy announcements to focus on the wage-and-price-control solution to the inflation issue was also prepared by the BBM with a view to attracting media attention. But inflation is an abstract problem, and wage and price controls conveyed a direct message to everyone, especially to the majority of voters whose wages would be frozen and who may have had legitimate doubts about how frozen prices would remain.

As the campaign progressed, the credibility of the simple, tough control policy was undermined by the Conservatives themselves. First, the leader kept adding qualifications to his initially strong policy: union contracts with built-in escalation clauses would still be valid; the prices of farm produce would not be frozen; stock prices and interest rates would be exempted, and so on. Candidates' reservations were voiced with increasing volume as the concern about wage freezes rose. And vendettas against Robert Stanfield left over from the party's previous leadership convention led to further questioning of the wage-and-price-control idea by the old guard of the party. Urged to go on tour for the Conservatives, former Prime Minister John Diefenbaker managed in one sentence in a speech in Prince Edward Island to add to the policy debacle: wages should not be frozen, he told his audience, until they had caught up with price increases. Subsequent explanation by aides could not undo the damage that the Conservatives were inflicting on their own policy, nor could it take back the opportunities these gaffes were offering the Liberals, and which Trudeau was quick to seize. How, he asked an audience of 13,000 in the University of Toronto's Varsity Stadium, could Stanfield control inflation if he could not even impose discipline on his own party? "This is the art of politics. It's to put forth a team which is united, and if the other team can't even control its own members in an election, how do you believe it's going to control the whole economy ... [and] put price and wage controls on the Canadian people, when it can't even control its own supporters?"[33]

The Trudeau attack, on platform after platform across the country and again on videotape before millions of television news watchers at night, was hammered home at candidates' meetings in ridings throughout Canada and on doorsteps when canvassers knocked on behalf of the Liberal Party.

Though the wage-and-price-freeze policy never worked to the advantage of the party, the Tory campaigners clung to it, doggedly pursuing their pre-election plan. Furthermore, just as the NDP was to lose votes because of feelings against the provincial NDP in British Columbia, so the Progressive Conservatives would suffer from anger at Ontario's government. Its premier, William Davis, who did some campaigning with the federal opposition leader in his province, was sometimes booed when introducing Stanfield – not the most welcoming of fanfares for a candidate whose lack of forcefulness was already a serious liability.

The Results: Predictably Surprising

The almost universal surprise that greeted the Liberals' decisive victory on election night appeared less astonishing in retrospect. Even though they had fought an incomparably better campaign, the 1974 election was still generally perceived by reporters in terms of 1972. Not only did the Conservatives replay their 1972 strategy, but the media also reported the news as if the events of 1972 were repeating themselves. Although public opinion polls taken by newspapers, television stations, and the parties themselves showed the Liberals and Pierre Trudeau consistently ahead of the Conservatives and Robert Stanfield, the press kept discounting the figures by remarking that in 1972 the Liberals had also had a lead, which had narrowed considerably in the last weeks of the campaign.

What was not given credence by the polls' interpreters was the public's clear desire for greater political stability: 72 percent of the respondents to CTV's last poll of the campaign expressed a strong preference for majority over minority governments.[34] News pundits also failed to assess how badly the Conservatives were faring in the newsmaking of the campaign, not so much in terms of quantity as of quality. Of fourteen news items relating to the Conservatives on the front page of the Globe and Mail during the campaign, five were negative: Stanfield's discipline problems when a New Brunswick riding association nominated an unacceptably anti-French candidate, the objections in the local press to the "parachuting" of Duff Roblin into the Ontario riding of Peterborough, plus three photographs showing Stanfield fumbling a football, wearing his trousers incorrectly inside cowboy boots, and bearing a Liberal sticker on his back.[35] The Conservatives were never on top of their newsmaking. Thus, while editorialists and columnists were generally hostile to Trudeau (all three Toronto daily newspapers supported the Conservatives), the opinion columns appear to have had less effect than the news copy, which consistently showed the Liberals in a better light than the Conservatives: more united, more positive, more decisive, more authoritative, more aggressive.

The payoff for the Liberals' superiority in leadership and campaign management was 43 percent of the popular vote (compared to 35 percent for the Conservatives, 16 percent for the NDP, and 5 percent for Social Credit). Their victory was not a landslide – only marginal gains were made in the Atlantic provinces and in Quebec, and the West remained nearly as Tory as before, except in British Columbia, where the Liberals doubled their seats (but only from four to eight). It was, nevertheless, a major victory, since Ontario fell to the Liberal attack, with nineteen new seats being added to the thirty-six they had held there before. Ontario constituted a feather in the Liberals' cap for another reason: they had attracted an overwhelming 70 percent of the new voters in the eighteen-to-twenty age bracket. (In the country as a whole, the Liberals had received 45 percent of the newly eligible votes, compared to 17 and 10 percent going to the Conservatives and New Democrats.)[36]

A Gallup poll taken in May 1974, just prior to the defeat of the Liberals' budget, showed them with 40 percent of the decided respondents, compared to the Conservatives' 33 percent and the NDP's 21 percent. With more than a third of all voters surveyed being "undecided," it might have been predicted that the campaign itself would prove to be more important than is normally the case.[37] Indeed the success of the Liberal effort can be gauged by the fact that two weeks prior to the election, the Grits' issue of leadership, which was non-existent before the writs were issued, was cited by 43 percent of those surveyed as most important, while the Conservative issue of inflation had fallen since October 1973,[38] when 43 percent of Canadians believed inflation was "the most important problem facing Canada today."[39] Even so, the voters' concern with economic issues such as inflation had not turned to any single party's advantage, for, in spite of the media's saturation coverage of these issues, the electorate had not linked inflation or any other economic issue with any one party.[40] Although the Conservatives enjoyed a slight advantage among those who in 1974 switched their partisan allegiances based on the parties' stance on these issues, new and transient voters who defined economic issues as most important preferred the Liberals."[41] Although wage and price controls had been associated with the Progressive Conservative Party since the 1972 election, less than half of the 7 percent of the electorate who considered this policy the most important issue supported the Liberals in the 1974 contest (see Table 3).[42] While the short-term issues of inflation and economic uncertainty were an asset to the Conservatives, they were overshadowed by concern over another minority government and Trudeau's personal popularity.[43]

In terms of their leader, the Liberal Party had a clear advantage. Not only did Pierre Trudeau have a substantial lead over Robert Stanfield in terms of personal appeal, but his personal popularity had risen significantly since 1972.[44]

Table 3

Effects of issues in the 1974 federal election

Most important issue mentioned (voting pattern)		1974 vote		
		Liberal (%)	PC (%)	NDP (%)
All economic issues	Switch to	3.4	5.1	1.8
	Remain	16.3	11.5	4.7
	Enter/reenter	3.2	1.5	1.8
	Total	22.9	18.1	8.3
Wage and price controls	Switch to	0.4	0.6	0.2
	Remain	1.7	2.2	0.9
	Enter/reenter	0.5	0.3	–
	Total	2.6	3.1	1.1

Note: Percentage of total electorate.
Source: Harold D. Clarke, Lawrence LeDuc, Jane Jenson, and Jon H. Pammett, *Absent Mandate: Interpreting Change in Canadian Elections*, 2nd ed. (Toronto: Gage, 1991), 136, table 7.4.

Public discontent over Trudeau's "aloofness" and "arrogance" had declined – Liberal strategists had made use of his successful management of a minority government situation to reshape his badly damaged public image.[45] Campaigning "differently" with his wife and young children, Trudeau's public image recovered as polls "recorded the public's conviction that Trudeau had changed, in ways that were generally seen as positive."[46] Although leader effects resulted in relatively little vote-switching, the cumulative effect of attracting enough of the permanent, transient, and newly eligible components of the electorate through a series of small steps, while maintaining their electoral base, was the key to the Liberals' victory in 1974.

One such step was the Grits' success in attracting a large share of the female vote with their stance on women's issues. Under pressure from women within and outside the party to act on the recommendations of the 1970 Royal Commission on the Status of Women (RCSW), which had identified the absence of women in public life as a significant obstacle to the achievement of equality for Canadian women, Trudeau had urged senior organizers to recruit women as candidates for the 1972 election. This effort was successful in Quebec, where the party recruited eight moderate feminists, the most prominent being Monique Bégin, a founding member of the Fédération des femmes du Québec, and Executive Secretary of the RCSW. In the rest of Canada, party organizers were more hesitant, and only two women were nominated, neither of whom was elected.[47] Embarrassed by these results, the Liberal Party made a clear effort in

1974 to find women and place them in winnable ridings in English Canada.[48] Of the nine women elected to the House of Commons in 1974, five were elected under the Liberal banner.[49]

In one sense, the meaning of the election was clear. First and foremost, it was a personal triumph and vindication for Pierre Trudeau. He had shown himself to be a seasoned leader, lasting through the honeymoon with the media in 1968, but also weathering its hostility in 1972. As Keith Davey would later say, "it was his victory. He campaigned as hard as anyone and the fact that he wanted to win came across."[50] Trudeau had proved that his appeal was solid in Ontario and the Maritimes, and significant in the West. By the end of this third term in office, he would have been prime minister for ten years, the longest Liberal tenure after Mackenzie King's.

For the Liberal Party, though, the meaning of the victory was unclear. When a cabinet is firmly installed in government, it generally ignores its own party. There was no indication that the traditionally quiescent role of the party between elections would be altered. Nor was there any reason to think that the party organization would develop any new inter-election role, although the "Daveymobile," as the party machine had been dubbed, received far more attention from the prime minister in the twelve months following the 1974 victory than it did during his first period of majority government.[51]

The loss of the NDP's balancing role in Parliament only facilitated a return to a more conservative style of governing, especially in a situation where inflation had to be dealt with, even if this meant postponing or tabling the Liberals' more expensive election promises. Given the complete control that the cabinet exerts over the civil service in a parliamentary system, the Grits' return to the governing benches indicated that no change in policy was likely to come from the federal bureaucracy, although a generational change shifting senior personnel in the Ottawa ministries should have produced some new thinking at the top.

The election results were sufficiently favourable to make the Liberal Party optimistic about its future. At the same time as the Liberals managed to expand their position in Quebec, their complete sweep of all Montreal seats confirmed the party's appeal to the non-French elements in that province. Their success in Ontario, where the Liberals won fifty-five of eighty-eight federal seats, appeared to be the key to the party's future fortunes. All eleven cabinet ministers from Ontario were re-elected – even Labour Minister John Munro, despite the adverse publicity he had received from media reports implicating him in a patronage scandal.

As for party morale, there seemed little doubt that, at the top at least, it was excellent. As one strong Liberal put it, the party's mission in Canada was to reconfederate the nation at each generation. Trudeau re-established the Quebec-central Canada confederation in his first term. He regained Ontario in his second term. Now he faced the challenge of bringing the Prairie provinces back into the federation through his party.[52] Whether the flexible Liberal Party that, even under an anti-nationalist leader, managed to take on nationalist hues in the 1974 election campaign, would ever be able to bring the western provinces back into the Liberal fold was uncertain. Whether Trudeau could pull off a third political coup remained to be seen. But as one observer put it in answering an open-line caller after the election, "Lady, when a man like Trudeau has both his sons born on Christmas Day, he has something special going for him up There."

The Government's Defeat, the Party's Decline, and the Leader's (Temporary) Fall

A decade and a half of Liberal ascendancy in federal politics had obscured how vulnerable Canadian governments can be to dramatic election reverses. The electorate is not mainly composed of loyal partisans who vote for their party through thick and thin, but of "transient" and new voters who make up their minds in response to shorter-term considerations of issue or image.[1] The manner in which the Liberal Party lost the 1979 election illustrated this vulnerability to voter displeasure in three dimensions:

- The Liberal government that was elected with a clear majority in 1974 proceeded to defeat itself by its indecisiveness, its incompetence, and its improprieties.
- The extra-parliamentary party, whose power had waxed during the brief period of minority government from 1972 to 1974, saw its authority wane and its members' morale consequently fall as the Prime Minister's Office (PMO) appropriated its main functions.
- Finally, in the long-delayed election campaign, the efficiency of the Liberals' organization could not compensate for their strategy's lack of coherence, their policies' lack of content, and their leader's lack of conviction.

This chapter shows that the Liberal Party began to lose the 1979 election from the day it resumed office in July 1974. By the time the formal campaign was finally launched in March 1979, the party could do little more than struggle to stem a remorseless tide in the hope that it would turn in their favour before it was too late.

How the Government Beat Itself
Having made its comeback to majority rule in 1974 with a campaign based on the claim of strong leadership and the promise of a dozen major policy ventures, the Liberal government relapsed into inaction. Its leader, Pierre Trudeau,

appeared devoid of the initiative and ability to launch long-range strategies. His cabinet showed signs of disintegration in its ranks, ineptitude in its managerial functions, and malfeasance in many ministers' handling of their political responsibilities. Perhaps most damaging, as far as Grit loyalists were concerned, was the government's drift away from those moderately reformist principles the party had traditionally claimed as its raison d'être.

Perhaps Trudeau was rewarding himself with a long period of relaxation after the rigours of his successful election campaign, as his biographer, George Radwanski, hypothesized. Maybe his still undisclosed marital difficulties were depressing him, as his wife's autobiography suggests. Possibly he lost interest in the problems of governing for other reasons. In any case, his failure to provide leadership to the government produced an atmosphere of indecision in Ottawa.[2] A vague throne speech in September 1974 gave the lie to the dramatic campaign promises he had made that summer. The insubstantial achievements of the Thirtieth Parliament, which did little more than deal with the backlog left over from the Twenty-ninth, perpetuated "a sense of drift not only in the expected political leadership of a triumphant majority but also in the management of the ordinary business of the House of Commons."[3]

John Turner's resignation from the government in September 1975 left Trudeau looking not just adrift, but weak. Serving as finance minister during a period of increasing stagflation – simultaneous inflation and unemployment, which was hitting the public in its pocketbook – was injurious to both Turner's self-esteem and his long-term ambitions. After a difficult exchange with the prime minister, during which Turner tried in vain to extract reassurances about his future, he resigned from the cabinet. When he was offered a partnership in the Toronto corporate law firm of McMillan, Binch, he accepted with alacrity, thereby becoming a valuable mole operating in the heart of the anti-Trudeau Bay Street business community."[4] Although inside opinion generally contradicted the popular view that Turner had been a strong finance minister, the self-exile from Ottawa of this perpetual dauphin reduced the Liberals' credibility in English Canada and their prestige within the business world just as the government was about to introduce a dramatic, if belated, anti-inflation program of wage and price controls.

Even in the atmosphere of crisis surrounding Quebec nationalism, Pierre Trudeau could not sustain his appeal as unchallenged champion of national unity. During the bitter dispute over whether air-traffic control services should be provided in both French and English during the summer of 1976, Trudeau was seen as the villain both by francophone Canadians, who felt that the cabinet had capitulated to the English-speaking majority, and by anglophone Canadians, who saw bilingualism in the air as more evidence of creeping "French power."[5] Significantly, Trudeau lost two ministers within as many months over these issues – Jean Marchand (environment), who resigned over the compromise with the unilingual air-traffic controllers, and James Richardson (national defence), who departed in protest against Trudeau's determination to see French protected in an eventual new constitution.

By the fall of 1976, according to a Gallup poll, 36 percent of those with opinions on the nation's leadership felt that the newly chosen and still largely unknown Conservative leader, Joe Clark ("Joe Who?" had been the headline announcing his victory in the Tory leadership race), would make a better prime minister. Only 28 percent felt Trudeau was still the best-qualified man. It took the momentary shock of René Lévesque's election as premier of a separatist Quebec government in November to bring Pierre Trudeau back into the political spotlight with fire in his belly. In early 1977, he was able to win standing ovations before such crucial audiences as the Chamber of Commerce in Quebec City and the US Congress in Washington, and respected Canadian commentators began to say again that only Trudeau could save Canada from Balkanization.

This rise in the prime minister's fortunes could not be sustained against the difficulties he encountered in managing his cabinet. Every time another minister departed from exhaustion or old age, attention was drawn to the government's continuing hemorrhage. In September 1976 alone, two more veterans left – Bryce Mackasey, minister of consumer and corporate affairs, and Mitchell Sharp, president of the privy council. They were followed the next spring by John Turner's successor in the finance portfolio, Donald S. Macdonald, who had been a Trudeau stalwart since 1968. Even before Macdonald's resignation in 1977, commentators began speaking of "the weakest cabinet since the sorry days of R.B. Bennett or Mackenzie Bowell."[6]

Disintegration in cabinet ranks bred mismanagement, the way stagnant pools breed algae. Despite its numerically secure position in the House, the government continually ran into difficulties when trying to push its legislative proposals through Parliament. The bill to rescind tax concessions on advertising sold in the Canadian editions of *Time* and *Reader's Digest* (1975), the peace and security package on gun control and electronic eavesdropping plus the long overdue competition bill (1976), and the revision of the Immigration Act (1977): time after time the government found itself forced to withdraw or amend its own legislation, often in response to revolts from its own backbenchers. While the government could point to some achievements, such as its measures to help farmers, its establishment of Petro-Canada, and its popular decision to appoint former NDP Premier of Manitoba Ed Schreyer governor general, much of the goodwill generated by these measures was offset by the government's obvious failures.[7]

As political mishap followed political accident, a poisonous aura of recrimination gathered over the government benches. Personal hostilities came to the surface when the minister of national defence and the minister of supply and services bickered publicly about who was to blame for negotiating a major military equipment contract with the scandal-struck Lockheed company. When the auditor general tabled his annual report in November 1976, he administered the funeral oration for the earthly remains of the Liberals' reputation for administrative competence: "Parliament – and indeed the Government – has lost, or is close to losing, effective control of the public purse."[8] Such a strong warning was no surprise to editorial writers, who had generally come to the conclusion that the cabinet knew neither where it was going nor how it proposed to get there.

With this air of incompetence came the stink of malfeasance. Whether because the Watergate scandal in the United States in 1973 had over-sensitized the media to every hint of wrongdoing (as Liberals complained), or whether because the cabinet had become arrogant, careless, or corrupt with majority power (as their opponents maintained), allegations of improprieties plagued the government over these years, while inquiries and investigations kept the issues before political spectators across the country. There was Harbourgate, a price-fixing scheme by companies contracted to dredge Hamilton's harbour that implicated Labour Minister John Munro; then there was Sky Shops, an influence-peddling scandal that allegedly had Quebec Liberal bagman Senator Louis Giguère and Jean Marchand (when he was minister of transport) receiving $95,000 for securing a lease renewal for a duty-free shop at Montreal's Dorval Airport; Nannygate focused on the improper use of government aircraft for personal purposes by another minister of transport, Otto Lang; Dial-a-Judge implicated Marc Lalonde, Bud Drury, and André Ouellet, the ministers of health and welfare, science and technology, and consumer and corporate affairs, respectively, for trying to influence a judge. These scandals, celebrated enough to boast their own labels, did not exhaust the list. There were also wrongdoings in the crown corporations that were flagships for government enterprise: at Air Canada, over senior management cockups, and at Polysar and Atomic Energy of Canada, over bribes and kickbacks to secure foreign contracts and over the uranium cartel that the government had established along with a "gag law" to prevent its disclosure to the public. The increasing tendency of the government to hide under a veil of secrecy was best exemplified by its refusal to introduce the much-promised Freedom of Information Act.[9]

Most damaging in its extent, and most corrosive of the Liberal Party's core support, was the seemingly endless string of revelations about wrongdoing, illegality, and dishonesty, both among the ministers charged with national security and in the federal police force placed under their responsibility. Whether it was a blacklist of bureaucrats compiled for the solicitor general by the Royal Canadian Mounted Police (RCMP) from files stolen during the arson of the Praxis building (a centre in Toronto that housed such "subversive" groups as a tenants' union and an anti-expressway coalition) or a break-in at a Montreal office to steal the list of financial contributors to the perfectly legitimate Parti Québécois; whether it was the surveillance of members of the NDP or the practice of mail interception, which had lasted for over a decade: the cabinet's response developed a monotonous pattern. Initial outraged denials of the allegations would be followed by the publication of further revelations. Ultimately, investigation into the issue was turned over to the Royal Commission of Inquiry into Certain Activities of the RCMP (the McDonald Commission), which was established in October 1977 to take the political heat off the government. The Canadian Civil Liberties Association, that keeper of the nation's civil rights conscience, had turned against the government in protest, not so much against the evidence of RCMP wrongdoing as against the cabinet's condoning of these illegalities. As John Meisel commented, "No member of the Liberal administration, under which the law was repeatedly broken by the RCMP, acknowledged any negligence or wrongdoing, no one resigned, nor has a single officer involved in any of the RCMP's illegal acts and acting on the instructions of his superiors been brought to trial."[10]

Civil libertarians were not alone in their alarm at ministerial statements affirming that it was sometimes proper for the police to break the law. When Francis Fox, the solicitor general and minister responsible for the RCMP, stated on television that there was a need to change the law to permit "the commission of certain activities which normally would constitute a criminal code offense if brought to light,"[11] he chopped off one of the Liberal Party's most vital assets – its small-l liberal supporters. Their first shock had come in October 1975 when wage and price controls were announced, just over a year after Trudeau had won his second majority mandate with a campaign that attacked the very idea of a freeze. The establishment of the Anti-Inflation Board was worse than a mere dramatic flip-flop: it signalled the Liberals' abandonment of the prevailing social-democratic belief that an ever-expanding economic pie could continue to be divided among an ever-more-prospering public.[12] Once these controls were lifted in 1978, the cabinet had to grasp another economic nettle, the federal deficit.

Perhaps one of the most obvious indicators of Ottawa's loss of control was the quintupling of the budget deficit from $2 billion to $10.5 billion between 1973 and 1978. Returning in August 1978 from a G7 economic summit in West Germany, where his friend and ideological ally, Chancellor Helmut Schmidt, had persuaded him that social democrats had to be fiscally responsible, Prime Minister Trudeau abruptly announced what amounted to a mini-budget: "a $2 billion shake-up in expenditures, including large budget cuts, a major tax reduction, and a freeze in public service [expansion]."[13] Not only did the "Guns of August," as the incident would soon be dubbed, undermine Trudeau's public support, it surprised even his cabinet and especially his finance minister, who was not consulted about the cuts before their public announcement. It was a humiliating affront to Jean Chrétien, who felt that "in relations between a prime minister and his minister of finance, it was a snub the likes of which the country had never seen."[14] While it is doubtful whether this born-again conversion to fiscal prudence was convincing to the right; it is certain that the budget cuts confused those supporters on the left who were still committed to the Liberal Party as a vehicle of social reform.

They were soon to have all the more reason to be baffled. Back in 1976, their leader had enjoyed what Richard Gwyn called his "finest parliamentary hour" with an eloquent appeal for the House of Commons to abolish the death penalty: "If penalties applied by the state against lawbreakers cannot be justified for their rehabilitative, punitive or deterrent value, they cannot be justified at all – not in a civilized society. Capital punishment fails on all three counts. To retain it in the Criminal Code of Canada would be to abandon reason in favour of vengeance; to abandon hope and confidence in favour of a despairing acceptance of our inability to cope with violent crime except with violence."[15] Although this had been a free vote in which the MPs officially could vote as their conscience dictated, the prime minister had put considerable pressure on his caucus to support abolition. In September 1978, on the other hand (with Proposition 13 in California generating waves of conservatism in Canadian political waters), Trudeau let his principles capsize.[16] He stated that the referendum on hanging proposed by Otto Lang in the justice portfolio would not be against his conscience. After championing abolition in a rare display of leadership in 1976, the prime minister appeared ready to abandon it in 1978.

Having shaken the faith of its lower-income and working-class supporters, having offended the principles of the left-leaning and the values of the right-leaning, the government had only to finish by alienating its supporters among the professional classes. This it proceeded to do in 1978 with its budget, which wiped out the tax shelters previously available to such upwardly mobile professionals as dentists, lawyers, and realtors – self-employed high earners who tended to work for or at least support the government party.

It is impossible to know with certainty what damage these reversals of position on economic policy or social principle did to the loyalty of the Liberal Party's core of active workers. It stands to reason that the economic and social conservatives who were originally offended by the imposition of controls and the abolition of the death penalty would not have been entirely mollified by the budget cuts and the talk of a referendum on hanging, whereas those leaning toward economic and social reform, who had been pleased by the government's more activist policy stance in 1975 and 1976, would have been alienated by the reversals of 1978. Rather than winning the support of one wing of the party or the other, Trudeau and his entourage seem to have lost support from both sides by appearing so opportunistic as to be callously unprincipled. What unquestionably shocked party militants across the entire ideological spectrum, however, was the seduction of Jack Horner.

How the Party Defeated Itself

Jack Horner, the member of Parliament from Crowfoot, Alberta, had long led the redneck faction within the Progressive Conservative caucus that virulently opposed not just the abolition of hanging but the institution of bilingualism. When tensions that had been simmering between Horner and his party leader, Joe Clark, came to the surface over newly merged ridings, and who would run where in the next election, a meeting was secretly arranged between the disaffected Tory and the prime minister. As a result of Trudeau's blandishments, Jack Horner crossed the floor of the House on April 20, 1977, and the next day entered the Liberal cabinet after nineteen years as a Tory backbencher. This apparently desperate attempt to buy a toehold for the Liberal Party in its political wasteland proved self-defeating in the long term, an act that would hang like a millstone round the Liberals' collective neck. The problem was not just that Horner's dubious conversion blurred the party's image, further confusing the general public and eventually losing votes for the Liberal Party at the next election. More serious was the immediate impact that the Tory cat had among the Liberal pigeons. "When I read the news of Horner in the *Globe*," said Roy MacLaren, a rising Toronto Liberal who was planning to contest a nomination in 1979, "I wondered why I was a Liberal."[17] He was not alone in his bewilderment. Kathy Robinson, a ten-year veteran of the party elite in Ontario who was an active organizer throughout the long period of pre-electoral preparation, felt that the Horner episode had "hurt our own people."[18] By inviting into the bosom of his own shaky government, one of the most vituperative of his old-time enemies who had voted against that cornerstone of his own national unity program, the Official Languages Act of 1969, Trudeau had indicated that his politics were now guided by sheer opportunism. As his pollster Martin Goldfarb confirmed, the destructive result of putting pragmatism so frequently ahead of principle was to turn off the thinking, ideologically motivated Liberals who traditionally rallied as the front ranks of the party's workers at election time.[19]

If courting Jack Horner was an immediate cause of low morale in the party's core, a more basic explanation for the decline in its battle-worthiness was to be found in a subtle but substantial shift of power away from the LPC's elected executive into the PMO. The real stuff of party politics when an election is not looming is fundraising and patronage. An attempt had been made by former party president Richard Stanbury to bring fundraising under the aegis of the extra-parliamentary party executive, but the chief bagman for English Canada,

John Godfrey, had successfully insisted that a direct, personal connection with the prime minister was necessary if the fundraisers were to be motivated to meet their annual targets. Presumably included in that rationale was the prospect of having successful performance in the job rewarded by appointment to the Senate – a delicious eventuality that the prime minister had already delivered to Mr. Godfrey in 1973. Thus, fundraising remained beyond the control of the elected party organization or its membership.

The handling of patronage appointments represented a different kind of ministerial power. On paper, decisions about the several hundred annual appointments to government boards and commissions that lay within the prime minister's purview were made collectively by the cabinet. In practice, routine appointments were handled by the ten cabinet ministers designated to oversee the dispensation of patronage in their respective provinces, and only the most important appointments were discussed at full cabinet meetings.[20] The patronage function thus remained a prerogative of the government, not the party.

One sign of the growing power of the PMO was the consolidation of the revamped system of geographical ministerial reporting that had been developed during its minority government years. Although the purported aim of this system was to make cabinet ministers responsible for the political well-being of a certain number of ridings in areas assigned to them by the prime minister, in reality the system represented a considerable shift from ministerial politics toward control of the party by the prime minister's personal bureaucracy.[21] In the name of election preparedness, ministers' attention to their partisan responsibilities in their assigned ridings was monitored by the PMO staff, and delinquents were chided by the prime minister in personal audiences if they did not visit "their" ridings and submit their reports as often as his office required.

However understandable may have been the rationale for maintaining the Liberal constituency associations in good repair, the transfer of this monitoring function to the PMO reinforced the shift that was quietly taking place in the Liberal Party. From its origins as a cadre organization – that is, an organization dominated by a small number of influential members working in co-operation with the party leader and the cabinet in the first and second party systems – the Liberal Party had become a personal clique in which the leader and his personal staff dominated both the cabinet and the parliamentary party on the one hand, and the extra-parliamentary party on the other.[22] In stark contrast with the efforts during his first majority government to mobilize ideas and proposals from the country's grassroots and so counterbalance the continuous flow of policy advice from the bureaucracy, business, and the media, the prime minister was now remaking the party in the image of his own technocratic style, apparently believing that regular visits from ministerial assistants, occasional gatherings with a minister, and intermittent form letters from himself to riding presidents would keep the party core in fighting trim.[23] It was as if a large but inchoate body of partisan supporters spread across the country's 282 ridings could have their loyalties and motivations primed by a PMO monitoring system run by Colin Kenny, whose relentless managerial skills had been honed at Dartmouth College's prestigious business school.[24]

A further indication of the power shift within the party's command structure came in 1975 with the appointment of Jim Coutts as principal secretary in the PMO. For a year after the 1974 election, the concept of grassroots participation had been kept alive by the monthly meeting of a tripartite group made up of the two chief figures from each of the party's three major power groupings: the national executive (Gill Molgat, the elected president, and Blair Williams, the appointed national director); the party cadre (Keith Davey and Jim Coutts); and the PMO (Pierre O'Neill, the press secretary, and Jack Austin, the principal secretary). When alleged irregularities in Austin's previous business undertakings made him an embarrassment in the PMO – though not, apparently, in the Senate, to which he was duly elevated – Davey successfully urged Trudeau to take on Coutts, a long-time Liberal who had proved his loyalty gallantly by running for election in a staunchly Tory Alberta riding in 1962, and by serving as provincial campaign chair for that province in 1963. He had also gained political experience as appointments secretary for Prime Minister Pearson from 1963 to 1966, and, before coming back to the aid of the party in the 1974 campaign, he was said to have amassed considerable wealth as a partner in a management consultancy firm on the strength of business acumen honed at Harvard.

The principal secretary's master was neither the party president, whom he would see occasionally, nor the campaign co-chair, whom he would see weekly, but the prime minister, whom he saw almost hourly. Teamed with Michael Pitfield, whose job as clerk of the privy council was to advise the prime minister concerning government matters, Jim Coutts was charged with providing Pierre Trudeau political advice. To the extent that he advised on partisan affairs – and his range of political responsibilities spread far wider than mere party concerns, which party activists were to grumble about and journalists were to allege – his function was to bend the party to the needs of the prime minister, rather than the prime minister to the needs of the party.

It did not take the media long to decide that the Coutts-Davey combo was doing with the PMO what it had done with the 1974 campaign – insulating Trudeau from the public in general and the press in particular. Calling Coutts "an honest Bob Haldeman," *Maclean's* irreverent columnist Allan Fotheringham opined that the "remarkable plunge in popularity of Trudeau and the Liberals since their smashing majority win in 1974 is due in large part to [this] new firm of merchandisers and packagers who now wall off the PM from the world."[25] Leading members of the extra-parliamentary party came to share the view that, far from giving grassroots members access to their leader, the PMO under Coutts was spinning a cocoon to shield the prime minister from his party. Among many instances reported by rank-and-file Liberals of party opinion being filtered out before reaching Trudeau, a "perfect recent example was the 'buying' of Jack Horner in the face of the prime minister's initial distaste. It was only after the event that we discovered that the strong opposition of several key Alberta Liberals had apparently been kept from him although these views had been expressed strongly."[26] In vain did party officers write earnest briefs urging a "true democratization of the power structure within the party so that political power is vested in elected, rather than appointed officials."[27] The Liberal Party's concern for democracy in its internal affairs had diminished to the point where it would cut off its nose to spite its face.

The leader-dominated party of the late 1970s left a considerable, though secondary, role to the parliamentary party. The normal power that the prime minister exercised over Parliament kept the caucus generally acquiescent, although on several occasions in 1977, when the backbenchers developed their own consensus in revolt against the cabinet, they managed to secure substantial changes to proposed legislation on unemployment insurance, immigration, and electronic eavesdropping.[28] Such successes were exceptional. In the main, MPs kept relearning the old lesson of parliamentary politics: black sheep don't get ahead. Those independently minded backbenchers who dared to express their own thoughts and cross swords with their leader demonstrated by their exclusion from cabinet how the ministers of the Trudeau government had been politically castrated. Exhausted from being rotated too frequently to head different departments, cabinet ministers were reduced to what one former national director of the party tartly called mere "salesmen of programs devised elsewhere."[29]

With its supporters' enthusiasm low, the caucus quiescent, and the cabinet drained of any surviving strength, the government stumbled on toward the end of its mandate, deciding its actions less by long-term strategy than by tactics devoted to catching the media's short-term attention. The national party executive had long since abandoned any pretence that it was interested in ideas or policy, while the parallel structure of the campaign committee appointed by Trudeau, again chaired for English Canada by Keith Davey and for Quebec by Marc Lalonde, held the real reins of party power outside Parliament. Any doubt that the Liberals had become a clique dominated by their leader and his entourage was finally removed in the months leading up to the 1979 election, when the campaign committee failed to impose itself on Trudeau either in the planning or in the execution of the campaign.

How the Campaign Organization Failed to Save the Situation
A surprising, and temporary, improvement in Liberal fortunes recorded by the

polls in 1977 brought the party's clique to a significant watershed in its relationship with the leader. Conscious that Trudeau's popularity was as volatile as the
Canadian dollar, and knowing that his resurrection from plunging lows in 1976
had come less from long-term policies than from a chance event (the previous
November's election of a separatist government in Quebec under René Lévesque,
whose vision of independence had revalidated Trudeau's claim to stand for national unity), the reconstituted national campaign committee pressed for a fall
election. Keith Davey was bullish by the summer of 1977, all the more since the
party's pollster, Martin Goldfarb, warned that the Liberals' lead would be unlikely to last for more than six months.[30]

Although policy materials were prepared for an election in the autumn of
1977, few in the Liberal caucus were eager to throw themselves into two months
of campaigning after just three years in office. In the end, it was Trudeau himself
who vetoed the plan for a fall campaign. That he had valid personal reasons is
not the point here (he had not recovered his equilibrium following his wife's
banner-headline escapades as Canada's most famous runaway wife). Nor is it
germane that hindsight shows how this procrastination pronounced the (admittedly temporary) death sentence on his government, a sentence that neither
brilliant tactics by the principal secretary nor repeated gaffes by the leader of the
opposition could reverse. Trudeau's rejection of his party experts' advice to call
an election while his popularity was at a peak meant that even the clique's power
had waned in campaign-strategy making. Where it should have remained decisive and where it had enjoyed supremacy during the previous minority government, it was as if Trudeau, the champion thoroughbred, had thrown off his rider
once again, determined to leave his jockey at the starting gate along with his
other stable attendants. The seasoned team of experts – professionals like Senator Keith Davey and market researcher Martin Goldfarb, volunteers like advertising coordinator Jerry Grafstein and party financial agent Torrance Wylie –
saw their influence diminish from this point. Their former campaign colleague
Jim Coutts changed, in their words, "from one of Us to one of Them," demanding loyalty and complete faith from the campaign clique, dismissing dissent,
reducing the give-and-take of campaign committee meetings, and blocking access to the prime minister so that even this inner elite felt cut off from participation in formulating strategy for the eventual campaign.

Despite the superficial evidence suggesting that a slightly broader cadre party
was still in operation – regular meetings of the campaign committee throughout 1977 and 1978 (to debate the pros and cons of various suggested election
dates) and weekly meetings of the political cabinet composed of ministers and
the party president every Tuesday morning – the top members of the inner
elite themselves felt that communications, in the words of one of them, were
"absolutely nil ... the oxygen to the party leader had been cut off." Just as the

centralization of policy-making authority in the PMO had led to the constipation of the Liberal government's policy output, so the assumption by the leader's office of executive authority over campaign planning had led to a paralysis of political strategizing. The leader's staff people may have been admirably skilled in their preparation of schedules and policy material for a campaign expected first in the spring, then the fall of 1978, but they had taken over from the party cadre the command functions for which its talents had been best suited.

When the writs were eventually issued for the dissolution of Parliament, the Liberal campaign showed time after time how the party's bleeding by its own leader had changed its major asset, Pierre Trudeau, into its chief liability. Trudeau was the first among unequals, the captain of a team with neither a seasoned first string to support him in defence nor an enthusiastic line of rookies to give power to his offence. If few cabinet ministers shared the leader's speaking chores during the election campaign, it was because the best and the brightest of them had left in some manner, honourable or dishonourable, over the previous five years. Herb Gray (consumer and corporate affairs) and Robert Stanbury (national revenue) had been dropped from the cabinet shortly after the 1974 election. Tony Abbott had been demoted from consumer and corporate affairs in 1977, and Joseph Guay (national revenue) had been elevated to the Senate in 1978. Francis Fox (solicitor general), John Munro (labour), and André Ouellet (consumer and corporate affairs) had tendered their resignations under clouds of their own making. Bryce Mackasey (consumer and corporate affairs), John Turner (finance), James Richardson (defence), and Jean Marchand (environment) had resigned in protest or anger. Bud Drury (public works), Donald Macdonald (finance), Ron Basford (justice), Mitchell Sharp (privy council), Jean-Pierre Goyer (supply and services), and Joe Greene (energy, mines, and resources) had retired from politics during the life of the Parliament. Of the seventeen, Ouellet was rehabilitated to cabinet rank after what many felt an unduly short stay in backbench purgatory, while only Gray, Abbott, and Fox remained in the caucus to fight the next election.

Unfortunately for the new candidates who were coaxed into the limelight by the party's talent scouts, the flow of public anger at Trudeau and the Liberal Party was so great by 1978 that, when fifteen by-elections were called for October 16 (in lieu of a general election, which the Liberals knew they would lose decisively at that time), the would-be stars, who had been billed as the party's great hope for cabinet and even as leadership material, went down to ignominious defeat. In Toronto, where anti-Liberal hatred burned strongest, the rout was complete: the Liberals lost all four of the ridings they had held. Of great psychological importance was the defeat of their two "big name" novice candidates: Doris Anderson, former editor of the biggest women's magazine, *Chatelaine*, and John Evans, former president of the prestigious University of Toronto. Across

English Canada, the Liberals lost six by-elections to the Progressive Conservatives, who retained possession of four other seats. Only in Quebec did the Liberals do well, winning Claude Wagner's vacated seat from the PCs, keeping Bud Drury's Westmount, and reducing the Créditiste lead in Lotbinière.

Such gains in French Canada were no help to the morale of the other Grit candidates who had been lined up to contest ridings held by opposition parties. The mini-election of October 16 was a crushing blow, making it evident to many an aspirant that the Liberals were engaged in a hopeless fight. As the tacticians in the PMO scanned the political horizon, consulting the polls and watching for the perfect wave on which they could surf to one more victory, many would-be politicians abandoned the quest. Candidate after candidate stepped down, stoutly claiming they believed the Liberals would win but, alas, they had to forego their expected victory for reasons of professional advancement or business exigency (taking over a McDonald's franchise in the case of the candidate in Northumberland; taking over a large American corporation in the case of Maurice Strong, candidate in Scarborough Centre). By the spring of 1979, the Liberals' Ontario farm team had been decimated by the premature resignation of fourteen of its rookie nominees.[31] As late as March 1, just three weeks before the election call, eighteen ridings in Ontario remained without a candidate.

Crisarchy

A federal party's campaign structure is an impressive but peculiar institution. It is informal, not enjoying the constitutional legitimacy of the party's official structure, to which it is a less visible but more powerful parallel organism. Short-lived though a campaign organization may be, it operates on an impressively large scale, spending some $10 million in 2002 dollars in the space of two months' campaigning – the equivalent of a corporation with an annual turnover of $60 million.[32] The structure of a party campaign organization is partially determined by the federal nature of the political system, partially imposed by law (such as the 1974 Election Expenses Act, which defined the period for advertising and set limits on each party's expenditures), partially established by precedents and the experience of previous campaigns, and partially improvised by the response of those in charge to the problems and crises that arise. A campaign organization is idiosyncratic: its active mandate lasts for just eight weeks, during which it is largely autonomous, controlling the politicians who normally control the party, and deciding the fate of hundreds of politicians front-stage and back. The decision-making structure is essentially authoritarian, with power deriving from the party leader, who appoints the campaign co-chairs who in turn appoint their staff. In the battle-like tension of the campaign atmosphere, in the secrecy of its strategic planning, and in the war-game nature of its tactical execution, the campaign organization is like a military operation whose purpose is to implement a battle plan and respond to the crises generated by its troops' daily skirmishes and its enemies' manoeuvres.

In 1979, the national campaign committee was the visible supreme body of the Liberals' electoral apparatus. It was chaired not by the party leader but by Keith Davey and Marc Lalonde. Its membership consisted of the eleven chairs of the provincial and territorial campaign committees together with the party's national director, president, and financial agent, plus Jim Coutts, the leader's principal secretary. Although it met some sixteen times over the two years leading up to the campaign and twice during the campaign itself, it was not the effective strategy-making body for the campaign, since this responsibility had been appropriated by the PMO. This left the national campaign committee with little more than a reporting and endorsing function. During the campaign, the clique, generally consisting of Coutts, Davey, and Lalonde, would meet on Sunday afternoons at the prime minister's residence to review strategy and decide tactics for the week ahead. For the remaining chief players of the campaign – those in charge of planning the leader's tour, writing the speeches, making the commercials, polling the public, answering the needs of candidates, and executing the campaign in each province – a sense of their alienation from the campaign's strategy making became a major irritant. "There was no exchange, no debate, no input to be made," one complained.

Below this command level, the campaign structure operated on three levels: national campaign operations, binational campaign functions, and provincial campaign coordination.

National Campaign Operations
There were four principal centres of activity in the national campaign structure: the leader's tour, the leader's office, the national party office, and the coordination of fundraising.

The Leader's Tour
What turns an election campaign into an organizational nightmare is the fact that the party leader (who is de jure commander-in-chief) and his principal adviser (who is generally de facto commander-in-chief) are isolated from the party's operational centres for the bulk of the campaign, travelling by airplane, train, or bus on a demanding itinerary. They require a continuous flow of intelligence from headquarters, as well as a continual supply of fresh speeches. At the same time, they have to make decisions and issue commands to the key players in the campaign, who are located in the national and provincial capitals across the country. The pressures and tensions are understandably enormous.

The tour is organized primarily to generate favourable news for the national television, radio, and print media. Because reporters routinely comment on the quality of the leader's events (whether they are well or poorly attended, by sympathetic or hostile crowds, in symbolically interesting or telegenically boring locations) a crucial component of the leader's tour is the "advancing" – the planning and organization of the events in each town visited by the leader. In 1979, three advance men (in what was still a male preserve) prepared events in the western provinces, a team of eight to ten worked in Ontario, and two to three people "advanced" in the Atlantic provinces, with Quebec events being organized as independently as ever by that province's campaign committee.

Because the nature of campaign news reporting can be determined by the capricious humour of the reporters who accompany the leader on his tour, catering to the needs of the "boys on the bus" is a further priority, requiring in 1979 half a dozen people to handle baggage, look after hotel accommodations, provide entertainment, and generally coddle the press pack. An executive assistant ministered to the leader's personal needs and maintained contact several times a day with the PMO in Ottawa, where the advance work was coordinated and the speeches were drafted. Apart from Pierre Trudeau himself, the key personage on the tour was his principal secretary, Jim Coutts, who acted as master strategist, planner, and tactician, constantly reassessing the political situation, checking with Ottawa and Keith Davey as often as phone communication permitted, rewriting draft speeches that arrived a few hours before their scheduled delivery, advising the prime minister about the next audience's expected characteristics, reviewing the situation with him at the end of the day, acting as his buffer with the press in the back of the plane, reporting to the weekly strategy meeting in Ottawa on Sundays, and taking a hand in all the other major decisions that had to be made day by day and hour by hour. Having been the aide-de-camp of the 1974 campaign and having become principal secretary in 1975, Coutts was, by 1979, the most powerful figure after Trudeau in the party, with more weight than both national campaign co-chairs combined.

The Leader's Office

The organizational base of Coutts's power was the PMO, which, having planned the major aspects of the campaign, now acted as its central command. It was here that the policies for the campaign had been prepared for cabinet approval and were drafted into speeches by a team of four anglophone and two francophone writers under the command of Tom Axworthy, chief policy adviser in the PMO. It was here too that the leader's tour had been planned, almost to the hour, by Colin Kenny. The leader was to spend six days in British Columbia, five in the Prairies, ten and a half in Ontario, seven in Quebec, and five and a half in the Atlantic provinces, with five and a half more allowed for travel time and fifteen days "off" scheduled so he could attend to government business and be with his children on weekends and at Easter.

The National Party Office

Dwarfed by an eighty-strong PMO, the two dozen staffers in the Liberal Party's national office handled the less glamorous job of providing campaign materials for the party's other 281 candidates. In conjunction with the caucus research bureau, they produced a "Briefing Book on Issues and Policies" – a loose-leaf binder that gave the candidates a defence of the government's record in 139 pages, an apologia that did not once mention "Liberalism," "principle," or even, apart from the cover page, the "Liberal Party." The national party office circulated answers for all imaginable questions, hostile or not, prepared in the caucus research bureau by the former journalist and future senator Philip Deane Gigantes. As the campaign proceeded, the communications staff sent copies of the leader's main speeches to the candidates, along with a dozen "Campaign '79 Bulletins" with selected data designed to keep up candidates' morale and furnish them ammunition for their own speeches and debates. A brochure proclaiming the government's record, *Our Economy Second to None,* was produced and printed for candidates' use in the ridings. Press releases were drafted and issued to the House of Commons press gallery to keep journalists in the capital informed of the leader's movements and any ministerial engagements.

Apart from producing information for candidates, the national party office received urgent demands for information from candidates through their provincial campaign headquarters, with which the national office was linked by telex. These queries would be relayed to government departments or the caucus research bureau for answers, which would then be telexed back to the provincial office.

Fundraising

The large amounts of money required for election campaigns had long generated a suspicion of backroom control of governments, due to the ruling parties' dependence on corporate donors. After decades of debate and years of study, sections of the Canada Elections Act (CEA), the Income Tax Act, and the Broadcasting Act that dealt with election financing were finally amended in 1974 by the CEA, which included several important features pertinent to the Liberals' finances:

- Every registered political party was to appoint a chief financial agent who had to submit to the chief electoral officer (CEO) a professionally audited financial return, detailing its election receipts and expenses.
- All candidates also had to appoint official agents who had to submit an audited return to the CEO detailing their own election receipts and expenses.

- Expenditure limits were established for each riding by a formula that took into account the number of its electors.
- Limits to the national parties' campaign expenditures were set.
- Registered political parties were entitled to a reimbursement by the state for 22.5 percent of declared election expenses, provided the party obtained 2 percent of the national votes, or in individual ridings more than 5 percent of the votes cast.
- Candidates were entitled to reimbursement by the state for 50 percent of their declared election expenses provided they received at least 15 percent of the votes.
- Advertising was limited to the time period between twenty-nine days and two days before the vote.[33]

Although the CEA did not limit the amount that could be contributed to a party or candidate, the Income Tax Act provided a graduated tax credit to a maximum of $500, with donations under $100 receiving the maximum tax credit of 75 percent. The source of all donations over $99 had to be disclosed by the party.

To comply with these long-delayed reforms, the Liberal Party had to change many of its ways of doing business, but internal disorganization following the PMO's appropriation of many responsibilities delayed the party in making the necessary adjustments. Arrogance also played a role, for, as Donald Johnston stated, "The party suffers from years in government when popular fundraising was not necessary. We never learned how to do it."[34] As a result, the Grits were the slowest of the three parties to respond to their own new rules, still relying on their tried-and-true methods of raising funds from a small number of large corporations.

By comparison, the Progressive Conservatives moved quickly to focus on soliciting individual contributions. Getting technical assistance from the Republican Party's fundraisers south of the border, they developed a direct-mail program targeted at raising a large number of small contributions from individuals. By 1979 the difference was apparent. Although the average size of an individual's donation to both the Liberals and Conservatives was $91, the Conservatives received 34,952 such contributions, while the Liberals garnered only 13,025 (see Table A.3, p. 288). Individuals contributed 38 percent of the Conservatives' revenue in 1979 but only 23 percent of the Liberals', who still relied on corporate contributions for 74 percent of their revenue, a figure that compared to 60 percent for the PCs.[35]

The Liberal Party's federated structure was an organizational problem in terms of finances. LPC members belonged to one of twelve provincial or territorial associations (PTAs). In accordance with the legislation, PTAs had to appoint registered agents to submit audited returns detailing campaign expenses to Elections Canada. Although responsibility for disclosure was placed on the Federal Liberal Agency of Canada, which did not take on any fundraising duties, responsibility for the majority of fundraising remained at the constituency level.[36] The PTA received a quarter of this money, and the riding received another quarter; the remaining half was held in trust for constituency election expenses. No money was sent to national headquarters.[37] Meanwhile, the party's national treasury committee remained responsible for soliciting funds from large corporations.

The problems generated by this confusing system soon became apparent, since the effect on the party's national election budget was drastic. In 1979 the transfers to candidates from national headquarters only amounted to $300,000 ($750,000 in 2002 dollars), compared to the $2.6 million ($9.9 million) that were transferred in 1974.[38] Under the new dispensation, the party's constituencies were least in need of funds, since they were to be reimbursed for half of their election expenses as long as they received 15 percent of the vote, while the federal party would be reimbursed for only 22.5 percent of election expenses (see Table A.2, p. 287). The riding organizations' relative affluence ultimately caused the national office to try to claim a portion of the candidates' reimbursements. The response came too late for 1979, by which time the Liberals' federal campaign was already facing financial difficulties (see Table A.1, p. 285).

Torrance Wylie, former national director of the party, was appointed chair of the Federal Liberal Agency of Canada. In conjunction with the party's treasury committee and the national campaign committee, he had to decide how much money was to be spent in each province. Wylie established a campaign budget of $3.9 million ($9.8 million in 2002 dollars) – somewhat below the $4.5 million ($11.3 million) limit for the Liberals set by the legislation's formula. Each of the four western provinces had its budget approved by Wylie and was responsible for raising its own money from business and assigning levies on the refunds with which the candidates would be reimbursed by the chief electoral officer. The Maritime provinces were also self-financed, but they did not impose a levy on the candidates. For Newfoundland and the territories, the national campaign contributed small amounts. The Ontario, Quebec, and national campaigns were treated as one package for budgeting purposes, thus reducing the previous financial autonomy of the Quebec campaign. The treasury committee met in Ottawa twice during the campaign to report on progress made with corporate donations and to assess the problems of meeting the financial targets. Wylie himself was formally connected with the campaign structure as a member of the national campaign committee, and informally by regular communication with the PMO.

Binational Campaign Functions

Some $2.4 million ($6.0 million in 2002 dollars), or 62 percent of the campaign budget, was spent on advertising, an activity again divided between BCP Publicité, a francophone agency in Montreal, and Red Leaf Communications in Toronto (see Table A.5, p. 290). Provincial campaign chairs and local candidates were free to do their own advertising if they could afford it from their own budgets, and those who were unhappy with the national English-language advertising campaign did just that. In Alberta, for instance, where the popular connotation of the word "Liberal" was almost obscene, the provincial campaign committee placed a series of full-page ads headed, "And now a good word from the 'bad guys' in this election." The Manitoba committee also developed a separate provincial advertising campaign to exploit the growing hostility toward Sterling Lyon's Conservative provincial government.

Unlike the English-language advertising, which was centrally prepared in Toronto for the whole of English Canada, the French-language advertising was created as an integral part of the Quebec campaign committee's operations. In further contrast to their confreres' uphill struggle in English Canada, Quebec Liberals knew they were winning. From having taken 51 percent of the votes and 84 percent of the seats in 1974, they were actually gaining ground. According to the polls, by May 22 they had 60 percent of the vote and 89 percent of the seats. Their slogan, "Parle fort Québec avec Trudeau et tout le Canada," expressed their self-confidence. Rouge advertising emphasized the theme of national unity and the positive accomplishments on Trudeau's balance sheet after eleven years in power – themes that could be used as well for the French-speaking ridings of New Brunswick and the English-speaking ridings of Montreal, where Trudeau's somewhat faded charisma was still an unqualified electoral asset.

Provincial Campaign Coordination

The organizational framework for the Quebec campaign was bicephalous. Marc Lalonde, the national co-chair, also chaired the Quebec campaign committee and was responsible for overall strategy, while André Ouellet acted as chief organizer in charge of the daily operations of this carefully oiled electoral machine. In the Liberal Party of Canada's Quebec office, eight to ten people looked after public relations, while others coordinated ministerial visits to marginal ridings. A policy committee of six to eight volunteers met every evening and drafted material that a full-time staff person sent out daily to the candidates. For the prime minister's few visits to Quebec, the Montreal office performed the advance work.

With ten provincial and territorial campaigns to coordinate, the function of the English national co-chair, Keith Davey, was both more complex and more demanding than Lalonde's. From his office in the Senate, he maintained daily phone contact with each provincial campaign. The Newfoundland Liberals were struggling to hold on to their four of the province's seven seats against a resurgent NDP. In Nova Scotia, where the Liberals held but two of the eleven seats, the NDP was also threatening. The Grits' position in New Brunswick was stronger: they held six out of ten seats and had a fourteen-percentage-point lead over the Conservatives. In Prince Edward Island, on the other hand, their only MP was in danger of losing his seat.

In the West, the Liberals had run second in each province in the 1974 election, but by 1979 prospects for holding the few ridings they had won five years before were looking so grim that they decided to concentrate their scarce electoral resources further east in Ontario.

In Canada's most populous province, where fifty-five of the eighty-eight Liberals candidates had won in 1974 thanks to a ten-percentage-point lead in the vote, they were now in danger of losing twenty-five to thirty seats, since they were ten percentage points behind in the polls. Given the strategic importance of Ontario to the fortunes of the Liberal Party, Keith Davey devoted a disproportionate amount of his time to liaise with the Ontario campaign committee, since his choice for Ontario campaign chair had been controversial. Not only had Royce Frith not been actively involved in politics for many years. He had been rewarded in advance for his services by being appointed to the Senate – a fact that raised as many party eyebrows as did his old-fashioned managerial style. More controversial still was the relationship between the PMO and the Ontario committee. The leader had ten and a half days of campaigning scheduled for this pivotal province, and Colin Kenny, the officer in the PMO responsible for Ontario, was determined that the prime minister's Ontario events should work flawlessly. Back in 1977, a year and a half before the election call, Kenny had decided that the campaign should open in Earlton, Ontario. He knew, in the words of a colleague, that they could "close down the whole town" for Trudeau. Though it was a small and relatively unknown place, Kenny could be sure of a "big event."

Kenny prided himself on guaranteeing that the prime minister always had big events with the appropriate school bands, enthusiastic handmade signs waved by normal-looking youngsters, and hecklers muted by well-drilled, soft-arm ushers. The "advance man's advance man," as insiders admiringly called him, Kenny had been recruiting his eleven blitz team captains and his 300 volunteers for two years. He had selected sites and chosen ridings that could perform according to his criteria; that is, provide good television coverage for the prime minister and give him three, four, or five stages every day to use as platforms for his policy message. Once selected, the ridings had been conditioned: campaign colleges were held and candidates impressed with the poll data showing that the prime minister was more popular than the party and the party more popular than the candidates. For most candidates, Trudeau's visit to their ridings offered the sole chance during the campaign to get their pictures and names on the front page of their local papers. Ridings were played off against each other, being encouraged to bid for a prime ministerial visit. If one constituency could promise two bands and a turnout of 400 bodies while another could marshal three bands and an audience of 600, there was no question that Kenny would send Trudeau to the latter. The ever-present crowds in the background on the nightly television news were a tribute to the organizational power of Kenny and his advance men.

As successful as many of these events were, when it came to their scheduling, the PMO ran roughshod over the local campaign committees, often changing at the last minute plans that had been devotedly and laboriously made. At least one provincial campaign chair complained that the PMO was more interested in sticking to its schedule than in winning votes. The response from the PMO to such criticisms was always the same: the party people were lucky to have the prime minister grace their city or riding with his presence. When the PMO arbitrarily cancelled the leader's appearance on a popular Winnipeg radio talk show, an event that Lloyd Axworthy had spent many days setting up, Axworthy was furious. As the star candidate in Manitoba, and chair of the provincial campaign committee, he did not hesitate to use his weight, threatening to resign if Trudeau did not appear. In this case, the PMO backed down, and the talk show went on the air with the prime minister.

Tension between the Prime Minister's Office and the Ontario ridings was but one of the problems resulting from this complex organization with its enormous communications problems. Overlapping authority was bound to create conflicts. When Jerry Grafstein, the head of Red Leaf Communications, requested another hour of the leader's time to film commercials after one shooting had failed, he was refused: Kenny's schedule took precedence over the production of national ads. Grafstein might be a member of the national campaign committee, but the PMO controlled his master's voice.

There was also tension between the Quebec campaign and the PMO. Quebec's strategy called for Trudeau to spend his time working in marginal seats, so the poor crowds that turned out at his Quebec meetings contrasted with the hundreds or even thousands who were organized for similar events in English Canada. Worse still, Trudeau's apparently poor reception in Quebec contradicted the Liberals' image of superiority in that province. The PMO was not amused.

Considering the communications difficulties, the decision bottlenecks, and the personality conflicts that are endemic to such an ungainly, crisis-centred organization, most Liberal insiders felt the campaign organization had been technically excellent. Three, four, or five stages surrounded by applauding partisans were made available to the leader every day. But when the leader's message was delivered, it turned out day after day to be intellectually barren.

Policy

For those who had observed the shift of power from the party's cadre to the prime ministerial clique, it came as no surprise that the decisions about policy for the campaign had not come under the aegis of Keith Davey, as it had in 1974, but had become part of the speechmaking functions of the PMO. While it was not startling that the policy function should also have been absorbed by the leader's office, opponents, observers, and supporters alike were dumbfounded when Trudeau's campaign turned out to be devoid of substance. At the press conference with which he launched his campaign, Trudeau intoned the phrase, a "decade of development" for Canada, as if this slogan heralded a series of initiatives to be announced as the campaign progressed. These words were not to be heard again. Energy formed the major issue of Trudeau's first two weeks on the hustings, but even with news reports of queues forming at California gas stations and with Petro-Canada's successes in the energy field confounding the Progressive Conservatives' commitment to its abolition, Trudeau had difficulty establishing in his speeches why only his re-election would spare the country another fuel crisis. The Liberals' defence of a strong central government as a crucial component of federalism was different from the Conservatives' position, but the theme of national unity was not presented to the public in a meaningful way.

Although the Grits had adroitly exploited their policy announcements in 1974, Mr. Trudeau's use of policy was ineffective in 1979. In Nova Scotia, Trudeau proposed an employee stock-ownership incentive plan, but this hesitant gesture toward democracy in the workplace was never again mentioned during the campaign. An Agriculture Export Corporation was announced hurriedly in Vancouver on April 23, by the prime minister and the minister of agriculture, who had been rushed out to British Columbia to give the notion some weight and to divert press attention from Trudeau's indiscretion the previous week about clinging to power even if defeated.

Like the other two leaders, Trudeau refused to participate in a "women's issues" debate sponsored by the National Action Committee on the Status of Women (NAC). However, while his New Democratic and Conservative counterparts addressed women's issues during the campaign, Trudeau neither met with NAC representatives separately nor addressed women's concerns explicitly.[39] The Liberals chose not to release any policy statements on women's issues in the campaign, falling back on a previously released government report entitled "Towards Equality," of which NAC was critical "largely because it promised further studies in areas in which NAC believed action could be taken without further study."[40] In fact, as Janine Brodie and Jill Vickers reported, the governing party's only offering to women "was a commitment to act at last on its long-standing promise to permit homemakers to participate on a voluntary basis in the Canadian Pension Plan."[41]

As for actual promises that the voter could associate with a new Liberal government, there was little beyond a pledge to reform the pension system. The promised changes won the approval of pension fund experts but went over the heads of most observers. In her form letter sent to citizens who requested copies of the Liberal Party's platform, Audrey Gill, the communications coordinator in the party's federal office, wrote,

> As you may have noticed by now, Mr. Trudeau is not conducting a campaign of "promises" in the traditional sense of promising to spend the taxpayers' money on big government programs. He is, on the contrary, talking about the larger issues that face the country at this time, and how the Liberal government would deal with them. Enclosed are copies of the "announcements" he has made. They are, in some cases, expansions or further details on existing programs; in other cases they are new programs or proposals for action where the provinces are involved (e.g., pensions). They could not, taken together, be called a "platform."[42]

It is true that the Liberals had failed to keep the promises made in the 1974 campaign and that they knew the press corps was wary of again being manipulated into uncritical reporting of the government party's announcements. It is also true that Trudeau felt his options limited by his impulsive pruning, in August 1978, of $2 billion from the federal expenditures to reduce the alarming growth of the government's deficit. Nevertheless, it is remarkable that this seasoned campaigner could not manage to establish a consistent tone for his appeal to the public – if only a mood of restraint as the one responsible position to take at a time when the growth of government spending had to be contained in order to grapple with inflation.

During the previous five years, the prime minister and the associates he had chosen had confused their public image (attacking, then imposing, wage and price controls; fighting for, then questioning, the abolition of capital punishment; expanding, then constraining, government expenditures). Now the same team, whose modus operandi in government had approached a state of policy paralysis, was caught in the contradictions of its own making. These confusions jumped from the page of the campaign co-chair's strategy document. On the one hand, the prime minister was to talk growth: "He will describe new economic policies which will strengthen the country by strengthening the regional economies; projects which will stimulate the economy." On the other hand, he was to talk retrenchment: "Canadians want responsible government which will end the free rides and give Canadians their money's worth for their tax dollars – more bang for their tax buck."[43]

Even in trying to establish the campaign's mood, Trudeau was caught in the skeins of his own subliminal ambivalence. His primary appeal was pitched to the need for strong leadership to preserve national unity. This meant "Prime Minister Trudeau will reassure Canadians about our future together, and about our potential for economic growth." Boosting the country's confidence was to be the mood message: "If at the end of sixty days Canadians are more optimistic than pessimistic about the country's prospects ... the government will be returned. Ours must be a campaign that builds confidence." At the same time, Trudeau had to reinforce Canadians' fear of separatism, since his issue of national unity was primarily the fight against Quebec declaring its independence: "Because Canadians worry more about the economy than about unity it is important that we consistently point out that growth in the Canadian economy is inextricably linked with the uncertainty about separation. The threat of Quebec separating is harmful both spiritually and economically to all Canadians."[44] If Trudeau aimed simultaneously to build confidence and to increase insecurity, it is not surprising that he failed to generate a coherent theme that could correct the mixed messages his government had conveyed.

The apparent exception to this record of ambiguity was the Liberal Party's refusal to adopt as its own the Progressive Conservatives' promise to allow property taxes and mortgage interest to be deducted from taxable income. Again, there were sound reasons for this Liberal stand. Officials in the finance department feared its impact on the government deficit and on the value of the Canadian dollar, while many among the rank and file in the Liberal Party opposed the plan because it would help the well-to-do, who already owned homes and had relatively comfortable incomes, at the expense of the poor. Meanwhile, the caucus and the cadre pressed for an alternative scheme that was less regressive and included relief for tenants to counter the strong appeal that the Conservatives' policy had for middle-class voters. The campaign co-chair and his intimates felt that a Liberal shelter plan was crucial to their meagre chances for success, but once again the cadre lost out to the clique. The Liberal response was to be a "non response."[45] The party would have to sink with its leader being just as firmly – and just as temporarily – opposed to the Progressive Conservatives' major policy as he had been in 1974. It is small wonder that, when Trudeau shouted at his huge audience in Maple Leaf Gardens in Toronto, "We are the party with the policies," he did not manage to bring even these sympathetic listeners to their feet.

Internal Campaign Communications

"It will be imperative for all of us – the Prime Minister, Ministers, candidates, and every last worker to say the same thing, in the same way, at the same time. This is how we maximize impact. Timing will be an essential ingredient of our campaign. Please follow the Prime Minister's lead." Thus spoke the Davey strategy document to the candidates. But although they were instructed to follow their leader, the candidates received few cues to guide their own campaigns. Since election legislation prohibited advertising until the final four weeks of the campaign, candidates had to rely at first on the news media to bring their party's national campaign message to their ridings. As Trudeau's campaign was based on the premise that his feistiness rather than a concrete platform would create the news, the message received by Liberal candidates in the ridings was more likely to be the news of an insult that Trudeau had hurled at a heckler than the report of an attractive program that he was offering. "What campaign?" responded Bill Rompkey, an ultimately successful Liberal candidate in Newfoundland, when asked about the impact in his riding of the national campaign. "I felt stark naked," quipped Roy MacLaren, another successful new candidate from metropolitan Toronto who, not knowing what to say when asked at all-candidates meetings about Liberal policies, learned to improvise his own version on the spot.

The federal party office mailed out documents to candidates every week to give them the basic outline of Trudeau's major announcements, but Ontario candidates' requests for information indicated, according to the Ontario policy chair, that "the public asks questions about our policy announcements well before our candidates get any information. Although Audrey Gill is doing a good job of getting information out, still many of the calls indicate that our candidates are being left behind in the information flow. (What happened to the Great Plans for Telex?)"[46] Telex messages were indeed sent to candidates from the national party office, but the speed of their transmission was not an index of their contents' importance:

May 12 from Keith Davey: "I spent the morning with the Prime Minister. He is in great shape. We are going to win."
May 16 from Keith Davey: "Our campaign is cresting at exactly the right moment."
May 20 mini bulletin: "Heard this one? Question: What do you do if Clark throws a pin at you? Answer: Run, because he's got a grenade in his mouth."

Pathetic Joe Clark jokes, selected quotations from the press, laundered poll data, anti-Tory items: such vapid material was hardly the kind of communication to help the party's 281 candidates follow the prime minister's lead and "say the same thing, in the same way, at the same time." An exception to this treatment of the candidates as future "nobodies" fifty yards from Parliament Hill[47] was the Ontario policy committee, which sent out thirteen policy bulletins of its own with substantial analysis and data on such subjects as labour force statistics, youth unemployment, abortion law, the dollar, energy, and small business policy. Many of these were solidly written by Fred Lazar, a professor of economics at York University, but even the best mailings to the candidates could do little to close the large gap that separated the leader from his candidates in the field. The lucky ones received a personal boost from a prime ministerial visit, an anointing, as it were, with the momentary presence of the leader. Apart from such fleeting contact, for which the candidate was expected to provide that "best event" platform so that there would be a prime ministerial clip on the national news, the candidates had no effective contact with their leader.

Even on such an important question as how to respond to the Tory promise to move the Canadian embassy in Israel from Tel Aviv to Jerusalem, candidates who were directly affected by this dilemma in predominantly Jewish areas of Toronto found Trudeau indifferent to their concerns and inaccessible to their pleas. They approached Coutts, who reported back that Trudeau would neither budge nor listen to their case any more.

The leader kept himself shielded from his party to the end. The advertising teams had nothing to use but Trudeau playing the strong leader, ads that may have reinforced his image as the better leader but may equally have reinforced the public's anti-Trudeau feelings. The lack of inspiring and unequivocal appeal from their leader left party activists bewildered. Party workers did not go door to door in their ridings believing strongly in their leader, their party, and their policies. Old stalwarts were apparently no longer sure just why they were Liberals. The party's traditional supporters had been given no appeal to Liberal values that might have brought them back to the fold. The independent-minded, who thought before they voted, had been given no clear diagnosis of Canada's problems or blueprint that the Liberals undertook to implement if elected. Nor had they gained a sense that a team of candidates was there ready to take office and govern competently. Only in one major respect had the Liberal campaign been successful. It had managed to make and keep Pierre Elliott Trudeau as the burning issue of the campaign – for better but also for worse.

Strategy

"This election is about Canada, Prime Minister Trudeau and leadership – specifically which leader, the Prime Minister or Joe Clark, has the experience and ability necessary to make the tough decisions the times require – tough decisions to keep Canada together, strong and free."[48] Thus spoke the opening sentence of the Grit strategy paper. Candidates reading Davey's campaign document learned that Trudeau was going to "reassure Canadians about our future together" and "describe new economic policies which will strengthen the country." In short, the Liberal Party would be relying on Pierre Trudeau, the brilliant campaigner of 1974, to save the bacon that he himself had already burned. Although the 1979 command group comprised many of the same people who had kept Trudeau in line in 1974, it was not at all the same body it had been in the heady days of the previous campaign – and not just because sideburns were greyer and scalps were balder. ·

The relationships of personality and power had shifted subtly, but crucially. Jim Coutts, who had travelled with the leader in 1974 as second-in-command to Keith Davey, the campaign strategist, was now the more powerful of the two. As "political tactician," Coutts now had far more direct control over the campaign than Davey, the nominal campaign co-chair.[49] Because of his less frequent access to the leader, the chief strategist of 1974 was restricted in 1979 to a secondary position as coordinator with the provinces. Since there was nobody in the command structure who had both the perspective and the authority to impose a battle plan geared to political realities outside Ottawa, Trudeau could repeat the error of his second campaign in 1972 and impose his personal style as the strategy itself. His approach was subject to modification in detail, but not to alteration in principle, by his entourage of political technicians, who had learned under his thrall over previous years in office to put tactics before strategy and intelligent obedience before independent judgment. Because the PMO staff knew they could catch the opposition leader off guard by calling the election a bit earlier than expected, the decision was made "to go early" – even though Trudeau had promised his candidates they would not have to campaign in the slush of late winter and even though Keith Davey and his Toronto experts wanted to wait for a summer election, when the mood of the country could be expected to improve.

The truth was that there was no coherent strategy for the leader's campaign. The strategy document was the product of an uneasy compromise between the apparent needs of the campaign and the actual dictates of Pierre Trudeau.

The Leader's Campaign

"Canadians associate leadership with toughness and intelligence – qualities which even the Prime Minister's critics acknowledge are his principal characteristics," read the Davey strategy memo on one page, while on the next it forecast that "this campaign will demonstrate the Prime Minister's compassion and concern for ordinary Canadians."[50] The campaign did confirm that Pierre Trudeau was a brilliant political performer but also that he was erratic. He managed to alienate some audiences with harsh responses to hecklers (charging in Quebec that farmers were chronic grumblers, lashing out at a postal worker in Victoria for being "greedy," and shouting in British Columbia that those protesting unemployment should "get off their ass"). As L. Ian

MacDonald of the *Montreal Gazette* noted, Trudeau "seemed to make his way across the country insulting one group of Canadians after another."[51] On another occasion, he could just as easily entrance an audience (in Vancouver) with his vision of Canada or impress a high school (in Toronto) with his masterly command of the most subtle questions of public policy.

Realizing that a repeat of their carefully manipulated 1974 campaign would generate too much media hostility, and hoping to overcome the press corps' long-standing suspicion and resentment of their leader, the Liberals chose an open media policy.[52] "The Liberal strategy was to compare Trudeau with Clark as a leader and to stress national unity and energy policy issues."[53] Making the prime minister available to journalists was intended to contrast the closely controlled and carefully scripted aspirant with the seasoned incumbent who could address a crowd without a note, face down hecklers with his own wit, and respond to unscreened questions without counsel. Although this bold approach did point out the difference between the two leaders, it left Pierre Trudeau as the player prone to errors, while Joe Clark managed not to make a serious political blunder.

Election campaigns have always focused on the words and deeds of party leaders, but the preoccupation of television news with the personal and the colourful had magnified the newsworthiness of chance comments made with rapier wit by Trudeau when prodded by his irritation and tension.[54] In the first week of the campaign, he fired a salvo at the provincial premiers as he made his pitch for a strong federal government. But he did not restrict his attack to the scapegoat of Canada's fuel-price problem, Alberta Premier Peter Lougheed, whose province held no prospective seats for the Liberals. In Ontario's capital he included Premier William Davis among the threats to national unity, thereby turning a previously neutral Conservative into one of the most effective campaigners at Joe Clark's side.

During the fourth week of the campaign, in an informal conversation with CBC television reporter Mark Phillips, Trudeau allowed himself to speculate that he might hold on to power as head of a minority government enjoying NDP support even if he lost by a few seats to the Progressive Conservatives, thereby handing Clark the chance to tell his listeners that, while Trudeau had ignored their views in the past now he was going to ignore their votes. Despite the fact that this could be hypothetically appropriate parliamentary behaviour should the Liberals win more votes than the Conservatives but lose by a only few seats, Clark castigated Trudeau's remark as "part of a pattern of contempt for democracy that he's indicated throughout his time in public life."[55]

As the campaign wore on, the Liberals chose to attack the Conservative leader as being incompetent, and his polices as ill-considered, rather than defend their own record.[56] Repeating Finance Minister Jean Chrétien's statement that the

Conservative promises would cost more than $7 billion, Mr. Trudeau told a Winnipeg audience on April 5 that Joe Clark had gone from being a "red Tory" to being a "red ink Tory" and dubbed the opposition leader the "seven billion dollar man."[57] In response to Clark's statement that Trudeau had pitted "Canadian against Canadian" and that he "sometimes seems almost proud that he can't get agreement from the provinces,"[58] Trudeau retorted that Clark's notion of political consensus threatened the country with disintegration. The opposition leader was a "yes-man," the "headwaiter" for the predominantly Conservative provincial premiers.[59] Liberal ads attempted to project the same message. They contrasted a strong, experienced Trudeau with an inexperienced, "wimpy" Clark. Many television spots showed Mr. Trudeau in his famous "gunslinger" pose – standing alone in front of a Canadian flag with his thumbs hooked in his belt loops, speaking ad lib, and attacking Joe Clark's "fuzziness" on key issues.[60]

For months and months Davey and Coutts had been keeping up morale among Liberal candidates by insisting that, however low the polls might show the party, Trudeau could save them because he was an unrivalled campaigner.

Although no other politician possessed his charisma, Davey and Coutts had not considered in their calculations the impact of personal stress on their leader. The "Margaret factor" that had worked so brilliantly in Trudeau's favour in 1974 was now working against him. An intensely private politician, who could not tolerate published reports about the details of his family life, Trudeau was now subjected almost every day to reading press excerpts from his estranged wife's tastelessly revealing autobiography, *Beyond Reason,* and juicy fragments from the still more outrageous elaborations that Margaret Trudeau was making for interviewers as she promoted her newly released, tell-all book in the United States.[61]

The Campaign in the Media

Because Trudeau was the only focus of the Liberal campaign, no attempt was made to build up the image of his team of experienced ministers or incoming new candidates, many of whom were of considerable stature. In English Canada he appeared to be running a one-man show, an impression the Tories were only too happy to reinforce in one of their ads, which featured pictures of prominent Liberal ministers who had retired from politics since the previous election and implied that only the prime minister was left on the Liberal team.[62]

No efforts were made by the LPC to use its free broadcast time or its television advertising to appeal to that strong plurality of Canadian voters who habitually supported the Grits but whose loyalty had been shaken by Trudeau's personal performance. Instead, the free-time programs replayed for half an hour at a time videotapes of Trudeau's public addresses in front of huge crowds, speeches that showed him shouting at the thousands in Maple Leaf Gardens, doing nothing to convey the impression that he was a politician with "compassion and concern for ordinary Canadians." The commercials showed Trudeau with Israeli Prime Minister Menachem Begin or on campaign platforms, and they never failed to close with the slogan to end all tautologies, "A Leader Must Be a Leader." Reviving John Turner's by then tired line from 1974, the strategy paper urged candidates to ask Canadians "to compare the Prime Minister not to the Almighty, but rather to the alternative." Such arrogance helped Clark become the alternative of choice, notwithstanding his uncertain debating skills.

The 1979 leaders' debate – "Encounter '79" – was the topic of much subsequent journalistic analysis.[63] This two-hour media event, the second of its kind in Canadian history, was held one week before the election and drew an audience of almost 7.5 million (nearly half the English-speaking population).[64] Although there was a risk that Trudeau's erratic behaviour during the campaign would resurface as arrogant disdain,[65] the Liberals prayed that the debate would show Trudeau as the superior leader. Designed as three thirty-minute dialogues, the first (Broadbent/Clark) centred on tax policy, the federal deficit, and economic incentives; the second (Broadbent/Trudeau) focused on the Quebec question; and the third (Trudeau/Clark) was taken up by Trudeau's accusations that the Conservative leader had vacillated on important issues from foreign affairs to federal-provincial relations, and on Joe Clark's counter-charge that the prime minister was merely diverting attention from his government's failures. Although the leaders merely recited familiar themes from their platforms, Trudeau was quicker and more confident, allowing viewers to contrast his dramatic intellectual presence with Clark's verbal stiffness.[66] For every two viewers who thought Clark had lost the debate, one thought he had won. For Trudeau, the opposite was true – for every one who thought he lost, two thought he won. It was a hollow victory.[67]

The overall hostility of the media to the Liberals could be measured by a continuing stream of editorials against the Trudeau party.[68] Traditionally Liberal papers rebelled: the *Toronto Star* supported the NDP, while the *Ottawa Citizen* and *Montreal Star* opted for the Progressive Conservatives. With the Atlantic papers remaining Conservative, only *La Presse* and the *Winnipeg Free Press* endorsed the Liberals, but even these few editorial endorsements were grudging.[69] As Frederick Fletcher wrote, "Editorial writers across Canada seemed to agree that the Trudeau government was worn out, that it suffered from hardening of the arteries, and, more specifically, that its economic polices were bankrupt."[70]

The fact that Maple Leaf Gardens was filled to the rafters two hours before Trudeau appeared for his rally there did not mean that the Liberals were winning Toronto. "Only one man could draw 10,000 people to the Toronto-Dominion Centre plaza," reported Michael Valpy on CBC Radio's *Sunday Morning* about a later mass event. Trudeau was spontaneous, exciting, alive. Only he could "switch on Disco Toronto."[71] He was Canada's great political star, and voters turned out by the thousands to see him, even if their silent message was the same as the one an airplane trailed through the sky above the same rally: "GOOD-BYE PIERRE."

Through most of the campaign, Trudeau behaved almost as though he believed this aerial message and was making his farewell to the public. He knew that the Progressive Conservatives had entered the campaign with such a lead in English Canada that only a disastrous performance by Clark or a flawlessly electrifying campaign of his own could save him. He knew he was his party's chief asset, the one who could get candidates onto the front page of the regional newspapers. But he knew that he was also its chief liability, the personification of the problems the public associated with the federal government, "French power," the symbol and lightning-rod attraction for the anger and frustrations of the average Canadian. Alone, on stage after stage, he talked to his audiences as if he were a tragic figure scripting the lines for his approaching downfall.

Never one to enjoy being managed by lesser minds, he set aside the texts that had been prepared for his introductory and concluding remarks in the three-leader debate, discarded the speech that his office had produced for his climactic appearance at Maple Leaf Gardens, and insisted that the last two weeks of the campaign be spent talking about the patriation of the constitution. Party polls might show that "national unity" was far down the list of issues thought crucial by the public outside his Quebec stronghold, but Pierre Elliott Trudeau wanted to be defeated – if defeat was unavoidable – on his issue, not those of his advisers.[72]

In the last eight days of the campaign, spurred perhaps by his triumph in the direct encounter with Clark during the leaders' debate, he seemed at last to want to win. He delivered passionate lectures on the national shame of Canada's not being able to amend its own constitution without approval from Westminster. He warned the public that "this is not the time to bring on the second string." While the PCs coasted for the last week, secure in their lead, Trudeau, ever the political athlete, turned on a final spurt in the home stretch, straining to the last minute. On the evening of May 21, just hours before campaigning legally had to end, Pierre Trudeau appeared in the stands to watch the Montreal Canadiens win the Stanley Cup. Millions of viewers of Hockey Night in Canada saw the crowd at the Forum come to its feet in applause, but to no avail for the electoral fortunes of Pierre Trudeau.

"When politicians," Christopher Lasch has written, "have no other aim than to sell their leadership to the public, they deprive themselves of intelligible standards by which to define the goals of specific policies or to evaluate success or failure."[73] Whether he was talking about the tired issue of the constitution or returning again and again to the need for strong central government, Trudeau appeared to have no idea to sell other than leadership as a blank cheque that he would fill in as he wished upon re-election. The leader no longer knew how to galvanize his troops' energies or command his public's loyalty. He had failed to convince the nation that this was indeed a historic campaign that would decide the future of the country.

The Results: Time for a Change

On May 22, 1979, the Liberal Party of Canada received 62 percent of the vote in Quebec and took sixty-seven of the province's seventy-five seats, while the Conservatives fell from second to third place there with 14 percent of the vote and two seats. Simultaneously, in the rest of Canada, Trudeau's support fell from 40 percent of the vote and 43 percent of the seats (eighty-one members) to 32 percent of the vote and 23 percent of the seats (forty-seven members). Not only did the party lose twenty-three seats in Ontario, seven in British Columbia, and a crucial three in Saskatchewan, but it also saw more than a dozen cabinet ministers go down to defeat. Among those who lost their seats were Daniel MacDonald in PEI, Otto Lang, who ran third in Saskatoon East, Norman Cafik, Alastair Gillespie, Anthony Abbott, John Roberts, Barney Danson, Hugh Faulkner, Bud Cullen, and Martin O'Connell, all in southern Ontario, Leonard Marchand and Iona Campagnolo in British Columbia, and the albatross Jack Horner in Alberta. Five other Liberal incumbents also ran third in their ridings. So great were their cabinet losses that one Liberal aide remarked that it was "almost as if the voters were blaming them for their association with Trudeau."[74]

The five-point Liberal lead of April had disappeared by May, as a large part of the public expressed its hostility to, or disappointment with, the government.[75] Surveys during the campaign indicated that the Liberal vote had softened: a mid-campaign poll conducted by Carleton University and the CBC showed that of those who had voted Liberal in 1974, only 57 percent remained faithful, while 14 percent switched to the Conservatives and 6 percent to the NDP (21 percent being undecided).[76] Surveyed by Gallup after the election, 37 percent of the citizenry felt the May 22 vote had meant that it was time for a change, that the voters desired something new and wanted to get rid of the Liberals. Sixteen percent felt it had been an anti-Trudeau vote, more personal than partisan.[77] Evidently, the public had not felt that Canada was in such precarious shape that it could not afford to give the alternative a chance at last.

While the Liberals had, in the words of one insider, run a Tory-like campaign with Tory results, the Progressive Conservatives had run a Liberal-like campaign, making substantial, newsworthy promises for every region. Their advertising had been strong, vitriolic, and effective. The mistakes they had made had not hurt them. In riding after riding, they benefited from a flood of volunteers fervently working to throw out the Liberals. Difficult though it was to differentiate the impact of the Progressive Conservatives' campaign in general, from the effect of their individual promises, it was nevertheless striking that in those Ontario ridings where the proportion of homeowners who had mortgages was 50 percent or more of the total households, the Liberal Party lost 100 percent of its seats to the PCs; where the proportion of mortgage holders was 40 to 49 percent, they lost 69 percent of their seats to the PCs; in ridings with 30 to 39 percent of homeowners having mortgages, they lost 42 percent of their seats; and in ridings with under 30 percent of homeowners having mortgages, they lost 26 percent of their seats to the PCs. Not only had the Progressive Conservatives' policy of allowing a proportion of interest paid on mortgages to be deductible from income tax been a highly salient issue, it had been clearly identified with them. Although the NDP had finally advanced a scheme of its own to ease the impact of high mortgage payments, the Liberals had not managed to blunt this Tory proposal's appeal to the broad middle class of English Canada. While Trudeau's technical knockout of Clark in the debate and his strong last week of campaigning may have denied the Conservatives a majority victory, the powerful impact of the mortgage plan may well have been the decisive factor in preventing the Liberals from salvaging a minority government position. The Tories' triumph with mortgage interest deductibility illustrated the textbook argument that in order to be electorally effective, an issue had to be salient – that is, important to the public – and the specific policy had to be clearly identified with one party.[78] Whatever the might-have-beens of the campaign, the Liberal Party emerged on May 23 as the third party throughout the western provinces and the second party in Ontario and half of Atlantic Canada.

The limited nature of the 1979 Conservative victory reflected the "complex mix of issue effects on voter choice but also the manner in which various segments related to the leaders."[79] Even at a time when Trudeau's popularity had slipped to record lows, leadership remained an issue in 1979 that favoured the Liberals. A Gallup poll published in May showed 43 percent of Canadians perceived Trudeau as best for prime minister, a sentiment that held constant across all regions.[80] At the same time, there is little evidence that leadership had an increased effect in 1979. The overall pattern amongst those voters that identified leadership as most important was very similar to that of 1974, except that the Liberal advantage was smaller, due in part to Clark's marginal increase in popularity and Trudeau's overall decline (see Table 4). While leadership itself did not motivate vote-switching to any particular party (on both sides they were almost equal), Trudeau's image had a reinforcing effect motivating Liberal supporters to remain with the party. Trudeau also managed to enhance his party's attractiveness to new voters and transients.[81] Although it is difficult to isolate the debate's

Table 4

Effects of party leaders in the 1974 and 1979 federal elections

Voting pattern		Liberal (%)	PC (%)	NDP (%)
1974 election	Switch to	1.3	0.3	0.2
	Remain	7.5	1.4	0.5
	Enter/re-enter	1.0	0.3	0.1
	Total	9.8	2.0	0.8
1979 election	Switch to	1.1	1.2	0.5
	Remain	7.7	2.3	0.4
	Enter/re-enter	1.5	0.5	0.4
	Total	10.3	4.0	1.3

Note: Percentage of total electorate.
Source: Harold D. Clarke, Lawrence LeDuc, Jane Jenson, and Jon H. Pammett, *Absent Mandate: Interpreting Change in Canadian Elections*, 2nd ed. (Toronto: Gage, 1991), 137, table 7.5.

effects, research shows that watching the 1979 debates had a minimal effect on individual voter behaviour and the election outcome.[82] If anything, it had a reinforcing effect on voters' pre-debate preferences.

The Progressive Conservatives attempted to use their strength on economic issues and focus on an array of related policy issues, while the Liberals chose to focus mainly on national unity, an issue over which they have always had an advantage. Although the national unity issue was mentioned twice as much by voters surveyed in Quebec, enough people mentioned it in English Canada to warrant inferring that the issue had some impact.[83] The Conservatives' advantage among voters switching on constitutional issues was offset by the Liberals' advantage in retaining their previous supporters as well as attracting new and transient voters concerned by this issue (see Table 5). Of those voters switching on economic issues, the Conservatives and NDP held an advantage, but the net effect was hardly decisive, since the Liberals acquired nearly half the votes of transients and new voters on the unity question.[84] The Progressive Conservatives' mortgage deductibility plan had little overall behavioural impact outside Ontario, a province with high home-ownership rates.[85] The energy issue, like mortgage deductibility, displayed a mixed pattern of small effects, but overall it was less favourable to the PCs.[86]

It was as if two separate elections had been fought. In Quebec, it was about national unity and a vote of confidence in Trudeau's ability to defend the interests of Quebec.[87] At 62 percent, not only did the Liberals receive their highest support in Quebec since 1940, but the voter turnout rate of 76 percent was

Table 5

Effects of issues in the 1979 federal election

Most important issue mentioned (voting pattern)		1979 vote		
		Liberal (%)	PC (%)	NDP (%)
All economic issues	Switch to	0.7	3.9	2.2
	Remain	8.0	6.2	3.2
	Enter/re-enter	1.9	2.2	2.7
	Total	10.6	12.3	8.1
Mortgage deductibility	Switch to	0.2	0.7	0.2
	Remain	0.9	0.8	0.5
	Enter/re-enter	0.4	0.4	0.5
	Total	1.5	1.9	1.2
All confederation issues	Switch to	0.8	1.3	1.0
	Remain	6.9	2.3	0.5
	Enter/re-enter	2.0	1.1	0.3
	Total	9.7	4.7	1.8

Note: Percentage of total electorate.
Source: Harold D. Clarke, Lawrence LeDuc, Jane Jenson, and Jon H. Pammett, *Absent Mandate: Interpreting Change in Canadian Elections*, 2nd ed. (Toronto: Gage, 1991), 139, table 7.6.

identical to the 1972 election – another time when French speakers' interests were perceived as being threatened.[88] English-speaking Canada, on the other hand, voted on economic issues, but not uniformly. In Ontario, Alberta, and PEI, the Liberals lost to the Progressive Conservatives. In Newfoundland, Nova Scotia, British Columbia, and Manitoba, they lost to the NDP, while in Saskatchewan, Liberal losses were divided between the NDP and Conservatives. The campaign was not overtly about class politics, but poorer regions and areas with more than 10 percent unemployment and a majority of rental accommodations switched to the New Democratic Party, while the economically better off chose the Tories.[89]

Although the Liberal Party had not issued any policy statements on women's issues during the campaign, it "made greater efforts to ensure the presence of a small but significant contingent of women in the House" than ever before.[90] While there is a tendency for political parties to recruit women for constituencies where their popularity is low – in "lost cause" ridings – Janine Brodie and Jill Vickers noted that "only the willingness of the Liberal Party to permit a small number of women to run in safe seats within its bastion of electoral strength –

Quebec – prevented the number of women in the Thirty-first Parliament from dropping dramatically."[91] Of the twenty-one seats contested by Liberal women, eight were in Quebec and six in Ontario. While incumbent Liberal MPs Iona Campagnolo, Coline Campbell, and Simma Holt went down to defeat, six of the ten women elected to the House of Commons in 1979 were Liberals (four incumbents and two from Quebec).[92]

Although the Liberals had won the popular vote (40 percent as compared with the PC's 36 percent), their lead was due to their Quebec landslide. Elsewhere, they placed second in four provinces and third in three.[93] While the PCs "received more votes and more seats than any other party in every province save three: Quebec, New Brunswick, and Newfoundland,"[94] they had not attracted many of the 2.3 million new voters who had come of age by 1979. That NDP and Liberal switchers constituted the largest component of the Conservatives' vote left the PCs extremely vulnerable to future desertion by these flexible partisans who comprised 15 percent of the total eligible Canadian electorate.

These independent-minded voters would shortly prove just how lacking in party attachment they were.[95]

Hiding the Charisma: Low-Bridging the Saviour

"The election was a defeat," conceded a member of Pierre Trudeau's staff in the aftermath of the 1979 campaign. "But," he continued, with a very Liberal determination to think positively, "it was not a catastrophe." When Prime Minister Joe Clark's team moved into the Prime Minister's Office (PMO) in June, a hand-lettered sign in their new quarters read "We'll Be Back." That defiant warning, which pithily expressed the arrogant self-confidence so long a hallmark of Canada's Liberal governors, was to prove prophetic. Only 273 days after the May 22 election, the Liberals had dismissed the vacillating Progressive Conservative government, recalled Pierre Trudeau from his attempted retirement as party leader, and mounted a winning campaign with a clearly articulated and carefully executed strategy. By February 18, 1980, the Liberal Party of Canada was "back" in power with comfortable majority control of the House of Commons, having rebuilt the party.

Rebuilding the Party

Pierre Trudeau gave a press conference in July, dealing with questions about his future with the cocky assertion, "My judgment, as of now, is that I am the best [possible leader of the Liberal Party]." Apart from that defiant appearance, he withdrew from the Ottawa scene to spend the summer engrossed in the favourite pursuits of his pre-political life: canoeing and travelling.[1] Once the Thirty-first Parliament convened – Clark had delayed its opening for over four months, while his fledgling cabinet prepared itself to govern – the Right Honourable Pierre Elliott Trudeau, MP, found himself having to face the House of Commons in the unaccustomed role of Leader of the Official Opposition. Not unexpectedly, his appearances there were infrequent (reporters calculated he was in the House only about one-fifth of the time it was sitting during October and early November), and his performance, apart from a powerful Leaders' Day speech scripted by his adviser Tom Axworthy, was widely described as lacklustre. Newspaper columnists and television analysts kept up a running series of sniping to the effect that the Liberal Party was in the process of withering away and that Trudeau was politically washed up. In the judgment of Richard Gwyn, "Pierre Trudeau will never again be prime minister. He has no real political future. He is an opposition leader on sufferance, occupying the post only until some Liberal with better long-term prospects replaces him."[2]

The probability that Gwyn was right – and the resultant precariousness of their own situation – reverberated throughout Liberal ranks, adding fresh fuel to the party's discontents. After years of being treated as ignorant foot soldiers, expected to mobilize during campaigns but to acquiesce between elections while their political betters went about the serious business of governing the country, Liberal partisans, who had remained publicly steadfast though privately seething during the government's deterioration in the late 1970s, now started to claim their right to be heard inside and outside the party's formal machinery. Throughout the summer of 1979, the party's national executive was the forum for a bitter battle between its anglophones, who wanted rid of Trudeau so they could rebuild the party under a leader more attuned to their concerns, and its francophones, who, though critical of Trudeau's deadening impact on the extra-parliamentary party, were determined to defend their blood brother against repudiation.

At the national executive's quarterly meeting, held at Toronto's Royal York Hotel in July, it was only the procedural dexterity of Jean Marchand, who was now a senator and a Quebec representative on the national executive, that postponed a crucial decision with which the anglos hoped to oust Trudeau. The question involved a usually humdrum decision, the timing of the party's next biennial membership meeting. But the party constitution required that, at its first conference after an election, there be a secret ballot on whether to hold a leadership convention. Since this automatic leadership review could be made to serve as an impersonal mechanism for forcing Trudeau out, most of the English Canadians on the executive wanted to hold the convention as soon as possible. The French Canadians wanted to wait at least until after the autumn of 1980 and the anticipated Quebec referendum campaign, so that Trudeau could lead the federalist counterattack against René Lévesque's separatist initiative. The July vote was a close shave: the loyalists won a reprieve until the next meeting in November. As they left the meeting, the insurgents had tears of thwarted rage in their eyes, but they maintained discipline and said nothing to the press.

Another challenge to the party establishment came from an independent initiative in Winnipeg in October 1979. The "Grindstone Group," an informal collective of party reformers that included activists from the extra-parliamentary wing, former ministerial assistants, and a few caucus members, had been periodically congregating on Grindstone Island near Kingston as a ginger group to talk about their party's need to reform.[3] The group members decided that, since the party leadership was resisting such discussion, they would organize their own policy conference to start the process of ideological renewal that they believed the Liberal Party should undertake before it could select a new leader. This is how Joseph Wearing put it:

> For Keith Davey and Jim Coutts, the point of winning is as self-evident as it is for the Montreal Expos or the Toronto Maple Leafs: but the Liberals gathered at Winnipeg greeted defeat almost with relief because of the chance it gave the party to redefine its goals. Concern was expressed about the power of the bureaucracy, the weakness of Parliament, and the diminishing relevance of political parties. Several participants argued that it was absolutely necessary for the party to decide on new directions *before* ministers again became the captives of their bureaucracies.[4]

These dissidents commissioned eight policy papers for discussion and invited some two hundred of the party's most energetic activists, including over two dozen MPs and former ministers, to a weekend thinkfest "to broaden the party process by generating fresh, forward looking ideas and initiatives that may serve to revitalize the Liberal Party." For two days and two nights, Grits in workshops, Grits in plenaries, and Grits in coffee shops let off intellectual steam in an orgy of collective self-criticism. They talked of their party's irrelevance ("People are smarter now [in the West]: you could fool them with Jimmy Gardiner's machine but not with Otto Lang's"[5]); policy incoherence ("Our position is about as attractive as a bucket of warm spit"); exhaustion ("We've used up our intellectual capital"); arrogance ("Cabinet has no respect for the value of other opinions"); and confusion ("Some of the people wanting to bell the cats [in the party establishment] are former cats themselves"[6]). As the meeting ended, there was the "sense that renewal had begun, that an agenda for the future was starting to take shape in areas such as individual rights, freedom of information, negative income tax, and proportional representation."[7] Whether uninvited or boycotting the event, conspicuous by their absence were the leader himself and his principal secretary, Jim Coutts; his senior policy adviser, Tom Axworthy; his former campaign manager, Keith Davey; and his Quebec lieutenant, Marc Lalonde.

Their absence spoke volumes about the party's disaffection from those it considered its ruling clique.[8] Having won the leader's job in the first place as an eloquent advocate of participatory democracy, Trudeau had fallen prey to oligarchy's iron law. In the less regimented atmosphere of defeat, Liberal activists openly expressed their poisonous hatred for his staff, who had given the leader advice they thought had run their party into the ground. They were less open in expressing their anger at Trudeau's own behaviour, a feeling they voiced mainly in whispers in the conference hotel's corridors and washrooms.

Although Trudeau had made some effort to attend party meetings across the country in the summer and early fall, his performances at these gatherings had been half-hearted. He balked at the pressure his staff put on him to sell himself to the "second-rate men of action," which was the way he described the people serving on the party's provincial executives.[9] For one important party gathering – a weekend meeting of British Columbia Liberals in Vancouver – he did not show up at all. Having sent word that he was suffering with the "flu," he was spotted by photographers that weekend entering a New York nightclub with a date. Even without this mishap, it was virtually certain that, despite the best efforts of Trudeau's staff and his francophone allies, the national executive would vote at its next meeting on November 24, to hold the party convention in the spring, with its automatic ballot on the leadership. Given the state of the troops' morale, it was clear that the executive's decision would be Yes and that the party's leader would have to suffer this humiliating rebuff.

When Trudeau pre-emptively announced his retirement on November 21, John Turner and Donald Macdonald were the potential favourites as successor. Don Jamieson, Allan MacEachen, Marc Lalonde, Jean-Luc Pepin, and John Munro all declined, while Lloyd Axworthy, Iona Campagnolo, Monique Bégin, and Gerald Regan each expressed an interest in running. But just as the succession seemed to be sorting itself out, Jim Coutts's craftily engineered, if unexpected, termination of the Clark government pushed the party's regeneration process into reverse.

The Defeat of the Conservative Government

When Progressive Conservative Finance Minister John Crosbie stood up in the House of Commons to read his "tough love" budget on December 11, 1979, key Liberals – particularly Coutts, MacEachen, who was still the Liberal house leader, and Lalonde, now the party's energy critic – knew immediately that the budget, which introduced a tax increase on petroleum products, tobacco, alcohol, and corporate profits, and that also increased unemployment insurance premiums, could be attacked with vigour as an affront to the ordinary voter.[10] Their view was confirmed after Crosbie's speech, when Liberal MPs dissected its provisions with officials and journalists in the Commons' lobbies and at the post-budget office parties. The Tories' proposed 18-cents-per-gallon increase in the tax on gasoline may have been fiscally sound in its conception as a way to finance the one election promise Joe Clark was determined to keep, that of giving a tax credit for mortgage payments and property taxes. But this backhanded way of penalizing working people to subsidize middle-class home ownership could be turned into a huge political mistake with a helping hand from the Liberals. It was a signal that Conservative times are hard times – tangible proof that although Clark might talk like a Red Tory, his finance minister was Bay Street's navy-blue tool.[11]

The next morning at their weekly caucus, the Liberals' determination to take action firmed up as the party's MPs, inspired by a brilliant speech given by MacEachen, admonished each other not just to vote against the budget of this heartless government but to stand together to bring it down. By the evening of Wednesday, December 12 at the annual Grit Christmas party, the exhilarating rush from freely flowing alcohol and the impending parliamentary battle created a distinct euphoria among the throng. For the first time in years, the Liberals as a collective felt they could agree on what the party stood for. It was as though the trauma and confusions of the 1970s, when the party was seen as corrupt by outsiders and riven by factionalism within, could be left behind. No matter how much personal success or power Liberals strove for and attained, most of them harboured the notion that they belonged to a reformist party historically concerned with social equity. In one stroke, the Tories had handed them back their identity and sense of purpose.

Rumours began to circulate the next morning on Parliament Hill that Clark and his cabinet did not realize how precarious was their hold on power. While the Tories had agreed to Thursday, December 13, as the date for holding the traditional vote of confidence on the budget, they neglected to make sure they could muster a majority of votes to defend it. Holding 136 seats, they were 6 short of a majority. With the Liberals at 114, the balance of power was shared between the Créditistes, who occupied 6 crucial seats, and the NDP, who had 26. Several Conservative MPs were away, and their sometimes ally, the Créditiste leader Fabien Roy, was abstaining from voting until the government made a commitment to allocate its proposed new gas tax revenues for energy projects in Quebec – a proposal Clark had rejected outright.[12]

The prime minister's thinking, heavily influenced by his election campaign chair, Lowell Murray, was based on the belief that – with Trudeau departing and the NDP eager to precipitate an election before the Liberal leadership imbroglio was solved – when the crucial vote came that evening, the Liberals would surely lose their nerve. Even if the Grits were brazen enough to engineer such a manoeuvre, the Tories believed they themselves would win the ensuing election. It would be like 1958 all over again, when Conservative Prime Minister John Diefenbaker followed his minority win of 1957 with a crushing majority victory by castigating the Liberals for their irrepressible arrogance in having questioned his right to rule.

Clark's advisers had declined to conduct polls since August, despite the warning from their pollster, Allan Gregg, that their support was softening. They further dismissed as an aberration the previous week's Gallup poll results, which showed the Liberals far ahead. Refusing to use a procedural gambit that would have postponed the vote of confidence and allowed time to manoeuvre, the Clark government rode into the valley of the shadow of death at eight o'clock on Thursday, prepared to meet its fate.

To help them on their way that night, the Liberals dragged onto Parliament Hill every caucus member but one, including an MP who had to come by ambulance from an Ottawa hospital. At 10:23 p.m., they had their reward.[13] The government went down to defeat by a vote of 139 to 133, and Prime Minister Joe Clark rose to announce he would seek out the governor general forthwith and ask for a dissolution of Parliament. The first step in the Liberals' return to power had been taken: the election was on. The second step was to resolve their leadership problem.

Throughout this drama in the Commons, Trudeau had been apparently unmoved. When the Liberals caucused on Friday morning to discuss what should be done about the party leadership in view of the impending election campaign, the retiring leader turned Delphic. When the possibility of his return was raised, he said, "the sovereign would have to ask me three times on bended knee," and requested that the caucus hold a secret ballot on the question. Some MPs interpreted his remarks to mean that Trudeau was unwilling to return to the fray. Others felt he was playing an elaborate game of tease. Still others saw him as uncertain about what to do and needing persuasion one way or the other. Allan MacEachen belonged to the last group. As one of the few left-wing, Pearsonian Liberals still on the public stage, MacEachen believed Trudeau's return was vital for his party's survival. When the caucus broke into regional components to discuss the leadership question, he had little difficulty persuading his fellow Maritimers of the need for Trudeau's return, but when the Grit parliamentarians reconvened as a caucus later in the afternoon, MacEachen discovered it was far from unanimous.

The tiny Western contingent was vehemently opposed to Trudeau's return, which would ruin the leadership hopes of Winnipeg MP Lloyd Axworthy and condemn the party's candidates west of the Great Lakes to almost certain defeat. The Ontario caucus was split: those MPs backing the still unannounced leadership campaign of Donald Macdonald balked, while those who had supported John Turner's aborted candidacy preferred to have Trudeau back in harness temporarily, if this would help get their man to reconsider and run at a later date. The Quebec caucus was solidly in favour of reinstating their champion, but Jean Marchand urged his confreres to abstain from the vote in the national caucus, lest its sixty-seven members be seen as using their majority to force Trudeau down the party's throat.[14] In the interest of national unity, he felt the decision should be left to the forty-seven MPs representing the rest of Canada.

Facing these strong cross-currents, MacEachen stood up to deliver what his colleagues would later consider the most brilliant speech of his career. Reminding his fellow caucus members that just two days earlier they had decided to do everything in their collective power to bring down the Conservative government, he called on them now to be consistent in their actions and true to their principles. Besides, they were assured a majority: Martin Goldfarb had conducted a quick poll at Coutts's behest that showed the Liberals enjoyed a twenty-point lead, and no party's pre-election support had ever fallen by more than 10 percent during the course of an election campaign since modern polling techniques had been inaugurated in the 1940s. What the party couldn't afford was to have its energies sapped by a bitterly divisive leadership race in the middle of an election campaign that had already begun. The speech proved to be a turning point. Member after member rose to speak in support of MacEachen's position, and by the end of the evening the caucus agreed (but without holding a secret ballot, which would have allowed the doubters to manifest their dissent) that Trudeau be asked to return as leader forthwith. The sovereign had bent his knee a first time.

To persuade a caucus that was experiencing the catharsis of a highly charged collective experience was one thing. To achieve consensus within the extra-parliamentary party's angry executive would be quite another. When the national executive convened in an emergency meeting on the morning of Saturday, December 15, most of its anglophone members were infuriated by the caucus decision, which they felt had been manipulated by Coutts through MacEachen to make Trudeau's return a *fait accompli*. They believed their rights, as laid out in the party constitution, had been violated. The only real power they could claim – control over the leadership renewal process – had been usurped. Knowing there was no way he could win unanimous support for Trudeau from this group, even in a voice vote, MacEachen made his arguments once more, relying on the francophone caucus chair, Jacques Guilbault, to make the case for Quebec, and trusting that some of his anglophone allies from the extra-parliamentary wing would see the light. Many expressed their determination that the "PMO in-group" be restrained from dominating the campaign and so controlling the Liberals' future.

While the national executive knew it had little choice but to fall into line, its invitation for Trudeau to return was accompanied by some strong recommendations:

> that the campaign co-chairman be chosen by the leader in consultation with
> the national executive; that the provincial executives be allowed to name five
> regional representatives to the national campaign committee; that the key
> personnel used to direct the party's advertising in the 1979 campaign (i.e., Jerry
> Grafstein) be changed; that the leader appoint two policy directors to the

campaign committee; that the youth and women's commissions each be asked to recommend a representative for the campaign committee; and that the campaign chairman in each province be appointed with the approval of the provincial executive.[15]

Faced with a possible executive revolt, Coutts accepted a participatory-democracy idea thought up by Tom Axworthy – an election platform committee that was representative of the party's main constituencies. Finally, a motion was put to the meeting that Trudeau be asked to return as leader: five were opposed, six abstained, but twenty voted in favour.[16] The sovereign had bowed a second time.

The party's chief power brokers briefed Trudeau on what had transpired, but Trudeau summarily rejected the suggestion that he would have to accept the conditions that the party executive wanted to impose.[17] They gave him the results of another secret Goldfarb telephone poll that confirmed the Liberals would win the election, doing as well with Trudeau in English Canada as they would with any other potential leader, and far better in Quebec. The overall message was, "the party needs you to win the election, Quebec needs you for the referendum, and the country needs you to hold it together." The "sovereign" had genuflected for the third time, but his subject still had to decide whether to comply.

Uncertainty still prevailed on Tuesday, December 18 when Trudeau entered the national press gallery's conference room to read a declaration. He had resolved to fight again. There was a battle in the offing, and he was ready to smite his enemies once more.

Organization

The national executive's determination to right the wrongs it perceived in the 1979 campaign did produce changes in 1980, the two most important being the creation of both a platform and a strategy committee.

The platform committee, consisting of forty members – half of whom were from the parliamentary wing, and the other half from the extra-parliamentary party – was "expected to publish, in pamphlet form, a comprehensive program drawn from the position papers of the caucus committees and the resolutions of the last policy convention."[18] The ad hoc group met on two successive weekends in late December and early January to hammer out their proposals. The assembled Liberals believed that the party could win the election, and since Trudeau had given his blessing to this ambitious platform-building process, they thought the ideas they adopted would soon become government policy. As a result, their discourse lost the air of futility that habitually clouded party policy discussions and took on the urgency of *realpolitik*.

Two substantial papers had been prepared. The first, a critique of the Crosbie budget, had been written by Nate Laurie, an economist who worked for Tom Axworthy in the Leader of the Opposition's Office (LOO), and this paper was adopted as the basis for a solemn campaign pledge to reduce the deficit. The second was an ambitious proposal to restructure the oil and gas industry, worked out by Marc Lalonde's caucus-and-party committee on energy, which he presented with all the force of his commanding personality. Western Liberals were able to amend a couple of measures that they considered particularly offensive, but they could not prevail against its startlingly interventionist thrust. Their fellow militants from Quebec and Ontario believed Canadians had to be protected from the world energy-supply crisis, even if this meant defying both the Americans and Alberta to do so.

After deficit and energy questions had been dealt with, reaching further agreement became more difficult. Lloyd Axworthy's plan for a massive housing program was accepted in principle but set aside, as was a proposal for a guaranteed annual income to complete the social security system. Both were deemed inconsistent with gradual deficit reduction. Tax reform, involving the review of tax expenditures and loopholes, was suggested and discarded for want of a hefty background paper. Tom Axworthy and Herb Gray tried to promote an industrial strategy, but the idea was blocked by Don Johnston and Roy MacLaren, both MPs with strong ties to the business community who argued against increased government intervention of any kind.

Although the platform committee did provide a forum for contrary views to be debated, it never released a report. The co-operative mood among the Liberals who were present was such that they simply assumed their ideas would become solid policy planks. The hand-picked participants experienced considerable frustration when they discovered later that they had not really been invited to participate in drafting an election platform, but merely to proffer advice for consideration by the strategy committee. Not having changed their manipulative spots, Trudeau's strategists felt it was merely necessary in order to motivate activists to work hard on election day to make a symbolic gesture to indicate that the extra-parliamentary party was being involved in drafting policy material for the leader's campaign speeches. In the end, all proposals were taken under advisement on behalf of the leader's real campaign group: Trudeau himself, Coutts, and the national campaign co-chairs, Lalonde and Davey.

Although many journalists were cynical about the actual effect it would have, the significance of the platform committee, according to one member, was that "for the first time, the extra-parliamentary people had participated in the development of policy for a campaign."[19] While not all of its policy proposals were adopted by the strategy committee, "all of Trudeau's policy announcements on energy, foreign ownership and western agriculture ... originated with the platform committee and none conflicted with resolutions passed at the 1978 convention."[20] This impromptu committee certainly had more impact than did the elaborate scheme the party's activists had devised for policy development in 1969-70.

Finances

Despite the fact that their campaign followed close on the heels of their 1979 defeat, the Liberals managed to find almost as much money to spend on their 1980 effort: $3.8 million in 1980 versus $3.9 million in 1979 ($8.7 million and $9.8 million, respectively, in 2002 dollars; see Table A.1, p. 285).[21] The number of individual and corporate contributions actually increased over the 1979 fundraising numbers (see Tables A.3 and A.4, pp. 288 and 289). On the expenditure side, the party spent only 84.6 percent of the statutory limit, while the Conservatives spent $4.4 million ($10.0 million) or 96.9 percent of their allowed expenditures.[22]

Strategy

Composed of five regional representatives, the strategy committee was Trudeau's attempt "to show that he had taken seriously the spirit of the national executive's recommendations and was not relying on the same old closed circle" to run the campaign.[23] In past campaigns, the national campaign committee had served mainly as an operational committee, with strategy being devised by the leader and his advisers. This time, the key campaign decisions were supposed to be made by a larger number of individuals. Trudeau was chair of both the campaign and the strategy committee; Al Graham, party president, and Jacques Guilbault, caucus chair, were co-vice-chairs of the strategy committee; Marc Lalonde and Keith Davey were campaign co-directors; and Gordon Ashworth, the party's national director, was named executive director of the campaign. The strategy committee also included Jerry Grafstein, still president of Red Leaf Communications despite being *non grata* to the national executive; Allan MacEachen, the platform committee chair; plus women and youth representatives.

The Liberal campaign planners worked out a dual strategy. Defensively, they would do everything possible to avoid issues that would call attention to Pierre Elliott Trudeau. Offensively, they would focus their campaign on the Progressive Conservatives' brief record in office, meaning they would concentrate their fire on the recently defeated Tory budget.[24] This approach was based on Goldfarb's findings that any mention of the national unity question reduced Trudeau's support in English Canada.[25] Although the constitution, language rights, and the need for a strong central government were important issues, the strategists "feared that the voters would hear other things, such as a celebration of 'French power' and Trudeau's arrogance. Liberal planners felt that anti-Trudeau feelings had been largely exorcised by the May defeat, but they did not want to take the chance of summoning that ghost again."[26]

To this end, the election strategy devised by Coutts and Davey attempted to keep the spotlight on Joe Clark's ineptitudes and away from Trudeau's personality. The party's asset in one election had become its liability seven months later. Known for his style and charisma, Trudeau would now be kept tucked away from public view. This contradiction was well expressed in Keith Davey's reflection on the 1980 campaign and contribution of a bridge metaphor to the vocabulary of Canadian politics:

> Our strategy also involved low-bridging Pierre Elliott Trudeau. Now that was tough, not because of Mr. Trudeau (in fact he helped us hammer out our strategy, and then he was a very effective team player). However, it was tough because of his celebrity status in the country. We were put under great pressure by the press and especially by what I chose to call the Pierre Elliott Trudeau marching and chowder society in this country. I guess I am a member but I had no idea the membership was as substantial as it is. I've never received, on a regular basis, as many phone calls from people I did not know – and the message was invariable, "Unleash this great man," which happily we did not.[27]

Leashed and "low-bridged," the gunslinger of 1979 morphed into a virtually invisible leader. At almost every rally, key Liberals would appear with Trudeau, who read his prepared speech, rarely deviating from the text. His speech was invariably about the Tory budget and its record of government, and it was given at every opportunity – despite demands from both the press and opponents for a new angle. "Often he virtually put his audience to sleep and received less applause at the end of the speech than he had at the beginning of it. Once he even personally apologized, thanking his audience for enduring his performance."[28] Campaign appearances were reduced to one per day, from the hectic pace of five or six per day in the 1979 election. From before Christmas until almost the end of the campaign, no press conference was held.

The success in executing this low-bridging strategy was due in good part to a change by Trudeau himself. When he fetched up in his office prepared to carry out the first tasks of the 1980 campaign, his staff found him energetic, responsive, and unusually co-operative. Trudeau was surprisingly willing to listen to the economic advice of Herb Gray, a nationalist whom he had once banished from his cabinet to the backbenches. In the closing weeks of the 1980 campaign, he made vigorous speeches promising an industrial strategy and a more interventionist approach to the auto industry and to foreign investment. He resolutely held his temper in public, ignoring hecklers' taunts, and he even gave in to his staff's demands that he appear at the traditional end-of-the-campaign party for the journalists travelling on his plane.

Integral to this muted strategy was the decision to prevent Trudeau from participating in the televised leaders' debate. In a role reversal from 1979, the Progressive Conservatives were now pushing for a debate, as they hoped it would bring the negative side of Trudeau's personality into the spotlight and give Clark an opportunity to demand policy details from the Liberals. So obvious was the Conservatives' desire for a debate that the Liberals were able to protract the negotiations in a teasing way: first they proposed several debates on specific topics among party "team members." When the networks demurred, the Liberals pushed for several changes in format before finally, on January 11, announcing that they would not participate in a debate unless they were granted a format that had already been rejected by the others.[29] Trudeau was again the only party leader who declined to speak to a meeting of the National Action Committee on the Status of Women. While he did agree to meet privately with NAC leaders, he showed there were limits to his self-restraint when he stormed out of the meeting saying, "you can't prove good faith with people who accuse you of being cynical."[30]

Policy

The five themes for the 1980 platform – regional equalization, economic development, a cut in government spending, more aid to individuals in lower income brackets, and a proposal for self-sufficiency in energy – were almost identical to those Trudeau had run on in 1968. But there was to be little elaboration of these policy statements: "Trudeau and the Liberals were after victory first, their ideas would come later."[31] The vagueness about how they would implement these commitments left little for the NDP or PCs to criticize.

Although Goldfarb's polling confirmed that Lalonde's energy policy would be useful in consolidating the Liberal vote in central and Atlantic Canada, Coutts was not convinced that Trudeau really had to announce a detailed energy position in order to win the election. They were ahead in the polls, so why should the Grits close off their options on energy if they really did not need to? For Axworthy and Lalonde, however, closing options was precisely the point. Trudeau had to announce the energy policy so that the Liberals would be obligated to act once they were elected. They were determined to get a formal commitment from the party leader and a formal mandate from the electorate.

After convincing Trudeau to accept this policy, Lalonde was angered to find that Trudeau's speech writers kept debating the pros and cons of his platform-committee-approved energy ideas. Lalonde reprimanded them like schoolboys and prevailed. Soon news services were flashing reports that Trudeau had promised in a speech to the Halifax Board of Trade on January 25 a comprehensive energy policy that included a "made-in-Canada" oil price, energy security, an expanded Petro-Canada, greater conservation, and stepped-up Canadianization of the oil patch.

Despite Lalonde's success in pushing his energy initiative, Coutts continued to argue against using the rest of the platform committee's polices. Goldfarb's daily polls showed that Liberal popularity fell every time Trudeau made speeches that went beyond scornful attacks on Joe Clark's pratfalls or the Conservatives' punitive budget. Coutts insisted that the only way to hold on to the Liberals' commanding lead was to continue their battened-down campaign; he was reluctant to take any more substantive policy positions, lest it give the other parties an opportunity to attack them.[32]

Following this strategy of evasion, the Liberals "were able to end the campaign with positive promises for the future, without having had to spend too much time defending them."[33] Speaking to a club of well-to-do women in Toronto, Trudeau pledged to increase financial supplements to poor pensioners. While the audience was not quite appropriate, "the strategy was exquisite: announcing the increase obviated the need to talk about women's issues.[34] Trudeau made a mistake in Saskatchewan by promising to double-track the CNR rail line from Winnipeg to Vancouver. This became the joke of the campaign in the West, where the shortage of hopper cars and poor port facilities in British Columbia were felt to be the chief obstacles to moving western wheat. In British Columbia, the Liberals promised support for a commercial seaplane designed in the province to be built on Vancouver Island. They also promised to expand port facilities in the north and to appoint an assistant deputy minister of fisheries who was to come from the West Coast.

National unity was the main issue that the low-bridging Liberals wanted to avoid. The other party leaders obliged them – in the interest of national unity – when put on the spot by René Lévesque. Just after the defeat of the Clark government, the Parti Québécois made public the question that it intended to put to Quebeckers in a referendum seeking a mandate to negotiate a new agreement with Canada. Although the PQ government promised to hold another referendum before attempting to change its constitutional status, Prime Minister Clark rejected this as "absolutely unacceptable," while Trudeau and Broadbent took the same position. This issue then resurfaced in mid-January with the release of the Quebec Liberal Party's position on the constitution – an event that potentially could have sabotaged the Liberals' hide-the-leader campaign strategy in that province. This *Beige Paper* did contain many positions that Trudeau could have endorsed, but its proposals on redistributing powers between the federal and provincial governments, and its calls for new binational institutions would have provoked sharp disagreement between Trudeau and Quebec Liberal leader Claude Ryan, the *Beige Paper*'s author and Trudeau's long-time critic. Despite this perfect opportunity for Clark and Broadbent to attack Trudeau by citing the positions of his provincial counterpart, all three leaders greeted the document in "as non-committal a fashion as possible," joining a "cartel of silence" on the matter for the rest of the campaign.[35] For fear of provoking quarrels among the pro-federalist forces in Quebec just before a referendum, Clark and Broadbent acquiesced in the Liberals' low-profile strategy.

Advertising

Although negative, the Liberal ad campaign did not attack Clark personally but rather his policy flip-flops and his budget. In TV spots that aired in Ontario, voices were heard predicting dire consequences from the Clark budget.

There was a striking difference between the advertising in English-speaking Canada, which ignored Trudeau, and the Liberal commercials in Quebec, where he was the French-Canadian hero. "The English advertising had used more image-creating tricks, a magician flipping over cards whose message changed every time, for example, and it did not show any Liberal personalities at all. The French advertising eschewed such tricks and focused completely on Trudeau speaking in a very relaxed manner in very familiar French."[36] The Liberal slogan in Quebec, "Une équipe pour ramener le bon sens au pouvoir," was a direct appeal for a team to bring common sense back to power.

This time the PCs were on the defensive, pleading that they had not been allowed a real chance to govern, and claiming it was unfair for their government to be judged after such a short period in office. With the slogan, "Real Change Deserves a Fair Chance," Joe Clark campaigned furiously and performed much more effectively than in 1979. He defended his budget, arguing that his decisions represented tough but necessary choices the Liberals were afraid to face. His speeches were laced with sarcasm for Trudeau, whom he accused of being unwilling to reveal his policies and displaying "a contempt for Canadian voters and for Canadian democracy" by aborting the leaders' debate. "They let Pierre Trudeau out for an hour each day and hope nobody will notice him," Clark mocked. "Last year it was the gunslinger – this year he's the fugitive."[37]

The PCs' advertising campaign attempted to revive 1979's popular antipathy toward Trudeau. One ad showed Trudeau displayed amongst former Liberal ministers whose pictures disappeared one by one, while the voice-over intoned, "Let's face it. If you vote Liberal, you're getting Trudeau and nothing else."[38] In Quebec the Tories could not afford to be openly critical of the French-Canadian leader, so they focused on constitutional change rather than economic or energy issues. The Progressive Conservative slogan in Quebec was, "Un Canada meilleur, ça se fait. Votons Conservateur, on va l'faire."[39]

All Clark could do was narrow the gap. The Conservatives' miscalculation was to have construed their support in the 1979 campaign "in positive terms, not realizing that it was much more a rejection of Mr. Trudeau than an endorsement of Mr. Clark."[40] The consensus among journalists seemed to be that the Conservative leader's problem was his person and not his policies. Other aspects of the campaign became insignificant compared to the question of image and the Tory leader's appearance of incompetence through losing control of Parliament. His dilemma was enhanced by lukewarm support from the seven provincial PC premiers. Despite concessions on federal policy supposedly given to Peter Lougheed of Alberta and Bill Davis of Ontario to assure their backing, Lougheed's minimal involvement and Davis's absence led a *Winnipeg Free Press* headline to read, "Premiers Make Themselves Scarce."[41] That Bill Davis's Big Blue Machine did not churn out much Tory support meant it was in Ontario that the Progressive Conservatives ultimately lost the election.

The New Democrats basically re-ran their 1979 campaign, focusing on how to achieve energy self-sufficiency, the impact of higher interest rates, the need for an industrial strategy and better social programs, and their being the only genuine alternative to the two old-line parties. The NDP gave much more emphasis to explicitly nationalist imagery, applying a "made-in-Canada" label to interest rate, energy, and employment policy. Ed Broadbent carried the full burden of the national campaign and remained the centre of the party's national advertising. Unlike the other parties, the NDP ad campaign was not negative. While it was critical of the Tories and Grits, its focus "was on the party leader speaking in very common-sense terms about particular issues of concern."[42] In the end, the NDP lost twelve of its thirty-two seats. According to Keith Davey, this was largely due to the Liberals' decision to "outflank the NDP on issues." Realizing the NDP was 1 percent behind the Tories in Ontario, the Liberals "came forward with a guaranteed income supplement, with our pricing policy on energy and in particular, for the first time in the history of the Liberal Party, we said something specific about foreign ownership (an issue in my judgement whose time has come even in the Liberal Party). And it worked. At least in the Atlantic it worked because the New Democrats lost both their seats. And they lost all three of their seats in northern Ontario."[43]

Media

There was no clear winner in the contest for media attention. The Liberals were able to hold their own, despite having lost their incumbency advantage, while the PCs were too new to benefit from one.[44] The treatment the Liberals received had less to do with their campaign performance than with the media's attempt to provide balanced coverage of the election.

Generally speaking, the 1980 election saw an overall slump in broadcast coverage, compounded by depleted editorial budgets and the sense that there had been too much electoral politics recently. A survey of six major English newspapers showed a modest increase in front-page election coverage since 1979,[45] but only 4 of the 102 daily newspapers in Canada supported the Liberals: the *Toronto Star,* the *Kitchener-Waterloo Record,* the *Owen Sound Sun-Times,* and *La Presse.* This last published an editorial called "Gouvernement Majorité Liberale," stressing that Canada needed "strong government and good leadership, commodities available only in the Liberal Party."[46] In contrast, the *Winnipeg Free Press* believed that "The Tories Deserve a Chance," the *Globe and Mail* argued that the Liberal platform was too skimpy and ambiguous, and the *Vancouver Province* supported the PCs because of the Liberals' "arrogance."[47]

Overall, the press in 1980 was slightly less hostile toward Joe Clark than it was to Trudeau. Negative coverage received by Clark focused more on his policies and mistakes in government than on his personal style, whereas for Trudeau "it seemed that virtually all of the pundits of the English press and most of the editorialists were against him."[48] In understanding why Clark received more negative press than Trudeau in 1979 and proceeded to win the election, while in 1980 he generally obtained better press but lost the election, Frederick Fletcher inferred "that Trudeau had built up a good fund of image capital which insulated him from the effects of ... bad press, and Clark's negative image was perpetuated in other ways than through the campaign coverage in 1980."[49]

The Liberals' strategic decision to run negative television ads on Clark and to bore the electorate rather than "rock the boat" created a malaise among many in the media. "Liberal strategists, in defence of their campaign, argued that Conservative experience had shown how unwise it was to make specific, highly visible promises that were part of a comprehensive, well-planned program."[50] Keith Davey later confided to an academic audience that they had had a more ruthless rationale:

> Winning elections is easy if the strategy works. You determine your best issue and you make that the issue of the election and sometimes you use surveys to help find out what your best issue is. Clearly in this last campaign our best issue nationwide was Joe Clark, so Joe Clark was what we wanted campaign '80 to be all about. And this meant keeping Joe Clark, a decent, honourable gentleman I know, centre stage. Now this may not be pretty. It may not be fair ... But our task was to win an election and I'm afraid sometimes we are as pragmatic as some of you fear.[51]

It was clear to most members of the media that the Liberals had mounted a shrewd and cynical exercise in image management, designed to manipulate the electorate's scorn for Clark's perceived ineptitudes and to evoke memories of their own reputation for managerial competence without arousing any more latent public distrust of Trudeau than was absolutely necessary.

The strategy succeeded brilliantly, and on February 18, 1980, Trudeau found himself once more at the Château Laurier for an election-night celebration. This time the ballroom thronged with Grits cheering their victory. Their leader's face was luminous with pleasure as he delivered his victory speech. "Welcome to the 1980s!" he called out as an opening, and the line met with an atavistic roar of a kind that had not been heard since 1968. Twelve years of overblown hopes and wrenching disappointments were forgotten. Trudeau had climbed into the Canadian pantheon with John A. Macdonald, William Lyon Mackenzie King, and Arthur Meighen, the only other prime ministers who had managed to rise from electoral ashes.

The Results: A Re-Coronation

Trudeau regained power with a popular vote only 1 percent less than in his coronation election of 1968. The voters returned the Liberals with 146 seats (and 44 percent of the vote), while the PCs received 103 seats (33 percent of the vote), and the NDP 32 seats (20 percent of the vote).[52] It was also Trudeau's greatest victory ever in Quebec, where he received 70 percent of the vote and, after a special by-election in the Frontenac riding where a Créditiste candidate had died in mid-campaign, seventy-four of the province's seventy-five seats. The election also marked the return of several prominent Liberals who had been defeated or failed to run in the last election, including Bryce Mackasey and John Roberts.

The Conservatives lost ground in every province except Newfoundland, due in part to the voting pattern nine months before. In 1979, new voters had supported the Liberals while the Conservatives had benefited from transient voters switching to the PCs. In 1980, the Conservatives were ineffective in mobilizing this 1979 vote as these transient voters, with little party identification or loyalty, switched back to their previous parties.[53] The decline in voter turnout also adversely affected the PCs, as "the proportion of the electorate moving from the Conservatives in 1979 to non-voting in 1980 was nearly as large as those switching from Conservative to Liberal."[54] The trend of increased voter turnout in Quebec continued from 56 percent in 1974, to 62 percent in 1979, to 68 percent in 1980. Another continuing trend was the more francophone a constituency, the larger were the Liberal gains from 1974 to 1980. Overall, the Liberal gains were largest among French speakers, and they came from the 1979 Conservative vote.[55]

The election produced a political situation in which the government had no representation west of Winnipeg and the opposition practically none in Quebec. The number of women in the House of Commons increased by four to a total of fourteen in 1980. The Liberal Party ran twenty-three women candidates in 1980 (an increase of two from 1979), the Progressive Conservatives ran fourteen (as they did in 1979), and the NDP ran thirty-three (fourteen fewer than in 1979). The success rates of the genders in the Liberals were not too far apart:

Table 6

Effects of issues in the 1980 federal election

Most important issue mentioned (voting pattern)		1980 vote		
		Liberal (%)	PC (%)	NDP (%)
All economic issues	Switch to	2.4	2.2	2.3
	Remain	9.5	10.3	4.7
	Enter/re-enter	0.6	0.9	0.2
	Total	12.5	13.4	7.2
Crosbie budget	Switch to	1.2	0.8	0.7
	Remain	3.8	4.4	1.5
	Enter/re-enter	0.4	0.6	0.1
	Total	5.4	5.8	2.3
Oil and gas prices, 18¢ tax	Switch to	1.2	1.1	0.8
	Remain	5.0	5.7	1.4
	Enter/re-enter	0.4	0.5	–
	Total	6.6	7.3	2.2

Note: Percentage of total electorate.
Source: Harold D. Clarke, Lawrence LeDuc, Jane Jenson, and Jon H. Pammett, *Absent Mandate: Interpreting Change in Canadian Elections*, 2nd ed. (Toronto: Gage, 1991), 142, table 7.7.

43 percent of women and 53 percent of male candidates were victorious. In the NDP, 6 percent of women and 12 percent of men were victorious, and in the PCs 38 percent of male candidates won compared to 14 percent of female contenders.[56]

As the election was precipitated by the defeat of the government's budget, most of the issues focused on the Conservatives' economic policies. Although it was commonly believed that the Crosbie budget and its gas tax were responsible for the Tories' loss, *Absent Mandate* shows that among the 13 percent of voters who defined the budget as the most important issue, support was almost evenly divided between the Liberals and Conservatives (see Table 6).[57] Similarly, the gas tax issue had a minimal effect, even though Trudeau had seized on its inequity as the basis for much of his campaign rhetoric. National unity, once again, was advantageous to the Liberals, but "most issues associated with the 1980 campaign had only the most limited ... impact on the results."[58]

Leadership was a different matter. While it had not been a major issue during the campaign, it gave the Liberals an even greater advantage than in the past.[59] Although Trudeau's popularity was lower than it had been in 1974, it was still higher than that of both his rivals, with Clark at his lowest rating ever. The Liberals enjoyed a three-to-one advantage among vote switchers who cited leadership as the most important election issue – an advantage that increased to five-to-one among voters who identified themselves as Liberals.[60] An effect of this magnitude would have been extremely difficult for the Conservatives to overcome, had even one or more issues worked more clearly in their favour.[61] Thus, while issue preference had been enough for the Conservatives to overcome the Liberals' leadership advantage in 1979, in 1980 it was not.

Joseph Wearing has posited for the inner life of political parties "a cyclical pattern of decay and renewal; the decay coming after a number of years in power and the renewal prompted by electoral defeat ... [when the] extra-parliamentary wing has subsequently become the source of new ideas and fresh faces."[62] Assumed in this view is the presence of an active, democratically motivated party base, a rank and file whose participatory energies, constrained by the oligarchs at the summit of the party structure, are waiting to be unleashed. The re-energizing of the Liberals' old leadership and its success at finding a progressive direction for itself without going through a period of grassroots resuscitation suggests that any resemblance between the Liberals and a European-style mass party is purely coincidental. The LPC was able to transform itself from above without paying heed to the putative need for resuscitation from below.

Seen from the perspective of 1980, the 1979 campaign was the first of a two-round bout. In the first encounter, Pierre Trudeau tried to defend himself on his exposed right but went down to defeat on points in the face of Joe Clark's dogged attack. When Clark tripped himself up, weaving around the political canvas with one policy change after another, and when the Liberals managed, by defeating his budget, to precipitate a second electoral encounter, Trudeau was able to fight a cautious round, relying on his more comfortable left jab to dispatch an opponent who was already staggering in the eyes of the citizen referees.

By February 18, 1980, it was obvious that the Liberal Party of Canada was really the Liberal Party of Pierre Trudeau. Once it returned to the task of governance, the reinstated government bore little resemblance to its previous administration. More from a change of heart in its leadership than from a change of role of its membership, the Liberal Party entered the new decade challenging the gospel of neoconservatism, asserting the need for a strengthened federal state, and directing the economy away from its continental drift. The Progressive Conservative Party, through its errors, had not held on to power long enough to redirect Canada's government. The Liberal Party, in its cunning, had regained power to reinvent itself in office.

John Turner
From Disappointment to Despair

The Dauphin and the Doomed: 1984
John Turner's Debacle

For the Liberal Party of Canada, 1984 was a year of opportunities – some of them grasped, but most of them missed. After leading his colleagues and the public through a guessing game about his political future that had gone on since his re-election in 1980, Pierre Elliott Trudeau finally consulted the stars on the night of February 29, 1984: "I listened to my heart and saw if there were any signs of my destiny in the sky, and there were none – there were just snowflakes."[1] He had concluded that after sixteen years of swinging from dismal failures to spectacular successes, the electoral fates would not smile on him again. By contrast, his successor as Liberal leader inherited a situation pregnant with possibility, but John Turner misread the meaning of the same snowflakes and led the Liberals to their worst humiliation since the conscription crisis of the First World War.

Prologue: The Prince, Fortuna, and Virtù

John Turner's drama took on classic proportions that highlighted the archetypal theme used by Niccolò Machiavelli to instruct his prince: how much Virtù can master Fortuna.[2] For Machiavelli, Fortuna represented the unexpected in politics, those uncontrollable factors and unforeseeable events that we now call luck, good or bad. Not that Fortuna was all powerful. The more a prince possessed Virtù – political knowledge, skill, prudence, strength of mind, good judgment, and wisdom – the more he could vanquish unreliable Fortuna.[3] The weak and imprudent leader who trusted in luck would suffer the malevolence of fate, but such an outcome is not necessary. The politician of supreme Virtù can exercise political control, carefully preparing for the future. By acting decisively and with foresight, the leader can change what the unsuccessful blame as the malignancy of fate into the determined execution of well-considered plans.

Fortuna's role is not entirely negative, because no potential prince can act unless given the opportunity to do so. The circumstances must be favourable for the would-be leader to get a start, but once Fortuna has smiled, what the leader makes of this opportunity is determined by his or her Virtù. When Pierre

Trudeau announced his definitive retirement, the immediate question was whether the succession offered some new prince a chance to show his Virtù. That opportunity was determined by the way Trudeau's last ministry had left the affairs of state, by the way the public perceived them, and by the way the Liberal Party related to them.

Trudeau's Last Ministry
Trudeau's 1980-4 government was everything his previous government had failed to be. Disregarding the uncertain mandate received in 1980 after a campaign that had "low-bridged" the Liberal Party leader in order to let the Progressive Conservatives defeat themselves without reactivating old anxieties among the public, the reborn Trudeau team had set out in the conviction that this was the last chance it would have to achieve its goals. Judged provocative and reckless by their detractors, and daring and courageous by their supporters, the team members implemented a clearly conceived strategy.

They played a crucial supporting role to Claude Ryan's No campaign in the Quebec referendum and, on May 20, 1980, helped to defeat the separatist option decisively. They then proceeded to engage in a bitter federal-provincial fight that resulted by 1982 in the patriation of the Canadian constitution, complete with a new Charter of Rights and Freedoms, plus a hard-won amending formula.

They unveiled the most interventionist economic strategy attempted by Ottawa in the twentieth century – the National Energy Program (NEP) – which challenged the dominance of the petroleum industry in Alberta and a powerful multinational oligopoly, and which provoked, as a by-product, a severe crisis in Ottawa's relations with Washington. They grappled with such historically intractable problems as western grain transportation (abolishing what to western farmers was the almost sacred Crow's Nest Pass rate), the Atlantic fisheries (implementing the Kirby Report, which recommended a comprehensive restructuring of the industry), civilian control of the intelligence service (pushing through the Canadian Security Intelligence Service Act), and East-West tensions (challenging Margaret Thatcher and Ronald Reagan's Cold War brinkmanship with the prime minister's bold peace initiative).

They held the line on social security programs and even expanded support for Canada's poorest citizens in the face of the growing appeal of neoconservative ideas, expressed most vividly by the popularity of "trickle-down" economic theories in Thatcher's United Kingdom and Reagan's United States.

Public Perceptions
Although these considerable achievements garnered a great deal of public support, the Liberals were strenuously opposed by the various powerful interests

Ottawa had confronted: big business, the western farmers, the provincial premiers, and their governments. The combination of Trudeau's abrasive personality and the controversial nature of much of his government's legislation soon relegated the Liberals to a poor second place in the polls, behind the Progressive Conservatives, who had become first in the public's voting intentions by mid-1981 under Joe Clark and remained comfortably in the lead under his successor, Brian Mulroney. After years of confrontational politics, the public had become fed up with the Liberals and their compelling leader. They were, in the words of the respected pollster Allan Gregg, looking for a "new man with a new plan."[4] While it was clear that the public wanted change, it was far from clear that the Liberal Party could satisfy this desire.

Party Responses

When champagne flowed in Calgary's Petroleum Club on March 1, 1984 at the news of Pierre Trudeau's retirement, relief also spread through the Liberal Party itself. Although the man who had won them four of the last five general elections and strengthened their grip in Quebec was still widely respected, there was a general recognition among Grits that they could not win again under this volcanic leader. For a decade, he had shown little more than reluctant interest in the health of the extra-parliamentary party, which had ossified under him. Worse, there was no obvious successor in his cabinet. The Liberal organization had been reduced to a handful of dogged loyalists scattered among a weakened party headquarters, the Senate, and the Prime Minister's Office itself. Most serious of all, Trudeau was leaving the party with limited electoral options. Because he had delayed his retirement decision so long, his successor as prime minister would be forced to call an election within eight months of being invested.

The succession involved three separate challenges: to take hold of the leadership of the Liberal Party and redefine its long-range goals; to take command of the Canadian government and implement new policies in the short term; and to go to the electorate and seek a formal mandate for a new government. The common thread in each of these three tasks was the need to represent the change so strongly desired by a majority of the public while demonstrating enough continuity to sustain the party's traditional base.

With the January 1984 Gallup poll showing Liberal support at 30 percent, compared to a 53 percent rating for the Conservatives, there was no question that Fortuna was offering a new contender very poor odds. Still, with 41 percent of the Conservatives' support motivated by hostility to the person of Pierre Trudeau, and 29 percent of it due to a generalized desire for change, the opportunity for a Liberal successor who could offer the promise of transformation was enticing.[5]

Act 1: From Dauphin to Leader

The Liberal Party's recent experiences with leadership renewal fell into two distinct categories. In 1948 and 1958 there had been a clear laying on of hands when the incumbent prime minister stepped aside (Mackenzie King, then Louis St. Laurent) and the long-acknowledged dauphin (Louis St. Laurent, then Lester Pearson) was duly crowned by the party establishment and endorsed by the partisan faithful. Since Pierre Trudeau had groomed no one to fill his shoes, it was natural for Liberals in 1984 to refer to the other model, that of 1967-8. When Lester Pearson announced his decision to retire, the party was well behind in the polls, facing a Progressive Conservative opposition with a new, apparently popular leader in Robert Stanfield. At that point, a pack of impressively experienced ministers had declared themselves candidates, only to be outshone by a relative outsider who took on the allure of party saviour. Pierre Trudeau's ideological mission regenerated enthusiasm among the Liberals who, excited by his charisma, grasped the reins of government once more and went successfully to the people in a snap election that returned them to power with a majority in the House of Commons. In 1984, all of these factors could be discerned, at least in potential – the cabinet candidates, the saviour from outside, the discussion of new directions, the renewed energy of the party, and the chance to rebrand the government before making an electoral appeal to the public – though their realization in practice was to fall far short of the standard set in 1968.

The pack of candidates who emerged from Trudeau's cabinet was experienced but not exciting. Donald Johnston had the most integrity in his advocacy of new approaches to old problems, but he was undynamic in their expression. John Roberts presented the most coherent and eloquent script for a "new Liberalism" but developed little support outside Toronto. Mark MacGuigan had difficulty squaring his fiscal conservatism with his social progressivism. John Munro's left-wing nationalism evoked almost no response, and Eugene Whelan's single-interest advocacy of farmers' needs was regarded mostly as comic relief.

Only Jean Chrétien demonstrated enough strength within the party's ranks to mount a credible campaign for the succession, but he nevertheless seemed a wild card. Since the Liberal Party had always alternated francophone and anglophone leaders, the principle of *alternance* was held against him by the party establishment. Although his frank expression of loyalty to the Trudeau record and his unashamedly patriotic appeals ("Canada is number one") had real resonance among delegates, his image as a somewhat folkloric French Canadian who seemed weak on policy undermined his campaign dynamic.

Four prominent Liberals outside the cabinet were eligible for the role of standard bearer. Donald S. Macdonald, the candidate who had been almost a sure bet to win the leadership, had Pierre Trudeau not returned from his momentary retirement in 1979, was politically immobilized as chair of a royal commission that he could not credibly abandon with its work unfinished. Iona Campagnolo, the incumbent president of the Liberal Party and a former minister in Trudeau's government, attracted considerable support among party activists because of her dedication, western roots, vivacious speaking style, and striking appearance, but she declined to stand. James Coutts, Pierre Trudeau's principal secretary from 1975 to 1981 and one of the shrewdest minds the party had ever attracted, still carried the burden of party hostility from the years when he had been identified as the backroom boy who had kept Trudeau isolated and inaccessible. He too decided not to run, despite a long-standing ambition to do so.

Given the political conjuncture, only the fourth "outsider" had a real chance to take on Fortuna. His name was John Napier Turner. As Walter Stewart described him,

> In appearance, he is perfect. Looking for the man to play the Senator from
> Rocky Ridge, central casting would bring him into the part without hesitation.
> It's all there – the trim, exercised body, still, at 54, the body of an athlete; the
> face, handsome enough for a shirt ad, but not weak, dominated by a firm jaw,
> an engaging grin and those remarkable eyes, baby blue one minute, icy grey the
> next. He has the voice, the carriage, the manners, the polish, the brains. He is
> bilingual, charming and hardworking. He chats as easily with tycoons as with
> janitors, smiles a lot, laughs a lot, and is guaranteed not to fade, rust or drip on
> the carpet.[6]

In one further respect John Turner fitted the Liberal Party's recruiting profile. In 1887, and again in 1968, when the party was in trouble in Quebec, it had chosen dark-horse candidates with real appeal among francophone Canadians: Wilfrid Laurier and Pierre Trudeau. In 1919, with class conflict growing in the shadow of the Russian revolution and the light of an industrializing capitalist economy, the Liberal Party had chosen Mackenzie King, an expert in mitigating labour-management tensions. Now in 1984, having fallen to third-party status in western Canada and having been spurned for years by corporate Canada, it made historic sense for the party once again to lead to its weakness by recruiting a figure in the business community who could claim Western roots.

Only in one major dimension did Turner not conform to the party's renewal formula. He represented a rejection of, not continuity with, the outgoing incumbent's record. Having resigned from Trudeau's cabinet as minister of finance in 1975 under a cloud that poorly concealed the two men's mutual antipathy, Turner had worked ever since as a corporate lawyer in Canada's financial capital, where he had ingested the laissez-faire ideology of big business as well as its emotional opposition to the Trudeau government's economic interventionism. Unlike Trudeau, who had been a severe critic of the Liberals but had joined the party to become a member of Pearson's government, Turner had left Trudeau's government to become the personification of its extra-parliamentary opposition, while remaining a member of the party. For almost a decade, this dauphin had been the undeclared leader of the discontented within the Grits' ranks.

Despite his muted disloyalty over the past years, he seemed so obviously the future winner in early 1984 that the party establishment flocked to support him even before he declared, on March 16, that he was indeed throwing his hat into the ring. On that day, flanked by seventeen ministers from Trudeau's cabinet and half the caucus carefully chosen to display a balance of old Liberals and new, male and female, anglophone and francophone, it appeared that Turner's dissociation from Trudeau could only help clinch his bid. Fortuna smiled, but enigmatically: Did he have the Virtù required to exploit this opportunity?

The successor to political leadership needs the capacity to be both an agent of continuity and an agent of change: an innovator will be accepted only after demonstrating knowledge and acceptance of the group's values.[7] So strong was John Turner's antipathy to the Trudeau legacy that he immediately made it clear, during the nationally televised press conference announcing his candidacy in Ottawa's historic Château Laurier hotel, that he was distancing himself from party dogma on bilingualism. Even though he was forced by the immediate outrage of Quebec Liberals and anglophone Trudeau loyalists to make subsequent "clarifications" of his position, he had managed in his first appearance to sow doubts about his leadership capacity. In other efforts to stake out positions attractive to new constituencies, such as westerners (on language policy) and those in business (on economic restraint), the question was whether these moves would be at the cost of losing support among the Liberals' traditional stronghold, especially now that the Conservatives were led by a Quebecker, Brian Mulroney.

Other questions were soon on observers' lips. Did Turner's difficulty in grasping the issues of the eighties, such as women's demands for equal pay for work of equal value, indicate that he had become rusty in the comfort of corporate boardrooms? Was his cautious campaign invoking the dreams of his own youth too much an appeal for a "better yesterday," in columnist Jeffrey Simpson's telling phrase, to offer the Liberal Party that renewed sense of mission it so badly needed? Did the small errors of his campaign – his refusal to resign his corporate directorships, his reviving the controversy about why he had resigned from the cabinet in 1975, the chaotic organization of his campaign headquarters in the early weeks – suggest that John Turner had lost his touch? These worries were expressed repeatedly through the media coverage of the fifteen-week Liberal leadership campaign. They were not entirely laid to rest even when Turner dropped his more right-wing themes in order to burnish his appeal to the Liberal delegates by affirming his commitment to their left-leaning social-reform values.

In the end, the delegates set aside their doubts about Turner's lack of passion, their worries about his political fumbles and his awkwardness on television, and their confusion about his real commitments and values. Liberal delegates considered him superior to Chrétien by margins of two to one on virtually all leadership criteria: his TV image appeal, his view on policy, his overall ability and competence, his ability to unite the party and make tough decisions, his appeal to different regions, his capacity to earn respect from international leaders. Only in one respect – who the delegates personally liked best – did Jean Chrétien outshine Turner by more than two to one. In sum, 63 percent of the delegates felt Turner was best able to help the party win the next election, compared to 19 percent for Chrétien.[8]

As convention delegates poured out of the Ottawa Civic Centre on June 16, 1984, having elected John Turner their leader on the second ballot (by a vote of 1,862 to 1,368 over Jean Chrétien), they had reason to be satisfied that the government party's second leadership renewal scenario had been followed in the main. The party's new standard bearer might have lost some of his gloss after emerging from exile, but he still had the demeanour of a prime minister and a winner. The party might not have been sure whether it had actually redefined its policy direction with Turner's ideas, but it had gained new energy from the delegate nomination meetings in the ridings and the candidates' tours across the country. Even if the public, for its part, had not developed any "Turnermania" similar to the outpouring of enthusiasm that Trudeau had generated in 1968, there had been enough excitement in the race, enough sympathy for the appealing Jean Chrétien, and enough sense of policy renewal conveyed by the five regional all-candidates' debates held in the run-up to the convention for Gallup to report in early June that the Liberals had climbed to a 10 percent lead over the Progressive Conservatives. Most voters expected Turner to produce the changes they wanted and, as a result, the Tories had lost the lead that they had held since 1982.[9]

The questions now centred on the new leader's performance as prime minister. Would he use the powers of his office to heal party wounds opened up during the leadership campaign? How would he manage the transition from party leader to prime minister? And what would he decide was the most opportune time to go to the public for a new mandate? Fortuna still seemed to be smiling. Turner now had to prove his princely Virtù in the office he had striven for all his life.

Act 2: From Leader to Prime Minister

The Turner team's difficulty in striking a workable balance between continuity and change was demonstrated vividly during the brief process of transition in the summer of 1984, when the newly crowned party leader became prime minister and formed his cabinet. Although he and his staff received briefings from the clerk of the privy council, Gordon Osbaldeston, and Pierre Trudeau's principal secretary, Tom Axworthy, the new team's arrival in office appeared more like the sweeping in of an opposition party than the maintenance of power by a political team that had merely changed leaders. The files of the PMO were considered tainted and packed off to the National Archives. The detailed transition books prepared for the new team by Tom Axworthy's staff to explain the problems of governance were ignored as suspect. The officers and staff in the PMO offered what they thought were their pro forma resignations; all but one waited in vain to be rehired. This dismissal of experienced staff indicated the new inner circle's near paranoia about maintaining any links with the Trudeau era.

Not adopting the Trudeau legacy in the new PMO was one thing. Not dealing effectively with rifts in the party was quite another matter. While observers were quick to note that Turner, visiting the House of Commons on June 21 (where he did not yet have a seat), led the standing ovation when Jean Chrétien returned to take his seat, tension remained between the two men.[10] Prolonged negotiations had taken place with "the little guy from Shawinigan," who was deeply wounded by his recent loss, but the compromise giving him symbolic but not real power in the Quebec party did not resolve the factional bitterness between his camp and the Turner forces. While Chrétien's showing at the convention could justify his becoming Quebec boss with control over patronage in that province, Turner preferred to reward Ouellet's loyalty than placate his chief and bitter rival.[11]

Though not vocally expressed, party unhappiness was ignored, with dire longer-term consequences. Little effort was made to recruit the best workers from the other leadership candidates' teams and so bind up party injuries by rewarding and exploiting their valuable capacities. The fissures of party disunity were underestimated, as the new party leader became absorbed by the process of cabinet-making.

One firm criticism that John Turner had levelled against the Trudeau government during his eight years in political exile was the excessive complexity of its cabinet committee system on the grounds that it had neutralized strong ministers and paralyzed the policy-making process. In an effort to signal that his new broom was sweeping in change, the newly installed prime minister made two recklessly bold moves. First, he pruned the cabinet from thirty-seven to twenty-nine positions. Though this gesture was meant to symbolize a concern for government austerity, it was interpreted as signalling continuity with the Trudeau era: twenty-four of the new Turner ministers had served in Trudeau's last cabinet and eighteen were left in the same ministries. The three senators who had provided Western representation in Trudeau's cabinet were dropped, and the number of women was reduced to two.[12] Of the five new faces at Turner's cabinet table, none had a national profile, since all had been elevated from the caucus. None qualified as one of the major figures from the business community or the West that Turner had promised to bring into government. At the same time, dropping incumbent ministers, some of whom had actually supported Turner's campaign, created dissatisfaction rather than solidarity in the senior ranks of the party.

Less politically damaging, but more expressive of Turner's weak grasp of governance problems, was his major reorganization of the cabinet committee system. In one stroke of radical surgery, two central organs of Trudeau's finely tuned system were amputated. Since the late 1970s, the Ministry of State for Social Development and the Ministry of State for Economic and Regional Development had acted as central agencies coordinating the decision-making process of most government departments. Turner gave little indication that the essential functions of these central agencies would be filled elsewhere in the government structure. His action was portrayed as a decisive step, but cognoscenti of government shook their heads, wondering why such a potentially disruptive reorganization was being made if there were at most a few summer months available to make it work before the next election.

While only close observers suspected that Turner's implementation of a decade-old personal agenda indicated that he had no clear strategy for government, it soon became plain for all to see that the new prime minister had no clear strategy for getting elected. Before he had secured himself in office and shown the country his capacity to govern wisely as prime minister, he plunged, exhausted and unprepared, into the next act of his drama of downfall. In circumstances that were fully under his control, he had neither assured continuity between the two Liberal administrations nor introduced convincing changes by the time he called an election on July 9.

Act 3: From Prime Minister to Campaigner

On the face of it, there seemed every reason for John Turner to delay his election call and enjoy his political honeymoon in the prime minister's residence until the autumn. For simple public relations reasons, taking a few months to act as head of government would have given the public a chance to firm up its image of John Turner as prime minister. He could have welcomed the Queen on her scheduled visit to the Maritimes and Ontario, greeted Pope John Paul II on the first papal visit to the country, congratulated Canadian medallists at the Summer Olympics in Los Angeles, cut ribbons, and announced projects. Meanwhile, the Turner team could have established control of the machinery of government and clarified the content of its policy agenda. Party wounds would have had time to heal, the troops time to rest, and the party cadre time to recover from the leadership campaign, collect funds, and prepare for the impending election.

And preparation was desperately needed. No planning had been done either at the general level of staffing the campaign headquarters or in such specific details as renting an airplane for the leader's tour. It was indicative of the extra-parliamentary party's disarray during Trudeau's last ministry that the election preparedness committee set up by Trudeau under the co-chairmanship – again – of Senator Keith Davey and Finance Minister Marc Lalonde had done next to nothing. First, it had waited for Trudeau's decision whether to run again or retire. Then it had procrastinated through the long spring leadership process, while the party chose which candidate would be prime minister.

Adding to the Liberal Party's planning difficulties was the power vacuum left unfilled after the sacking by party president Iona Campagnolo in the early 1980s of the party's national director, Gordon Ashworth, who was one of the few people in active party service with experience in running an election campaign. At the PMO, where Ashworth was taken in, election preparation had been initiated with a heavy emphasis on developing policy themes for a new Trudeau platform and on fleshing out a campaign research model produced by the party's pollster, Martin Goldfarb, to monitor public attitudes and link them to policy issues. Although Goldfarb had briefed the leadership candidates on his work, the new Turner group paid his ideas scant heed.

The new prime minister's staff did not ignore the old staff's material because it had arrived with its own coherent set of issues and techniques. Turner had taken various positions during the leadership campaign, moving from the political right to the centre, but without articulating consistent new policies for Liberalism. Even at a less lofty level, no slogan had been thought through, no logo designed, no ad campaign sketched out. In British Columbia, Alberta, and Saskatchewan there was virtually no party organization. As a consequence of the freeze on riding nominations decreed by what had become the Davey-Lalonde election unpreparedness committee, candidates had been nominated in only 40 of the 282 ridings, a figure that compared ominously with the Conservatives' 240 candidates and the NDP's 155 nominations already in place. For all these reasons, Jean Chrétien advised Turner to resist pressures to run, to strut his prime ministerial stuff, and to wait for a better moment later in the year.

Chrétien's was the minority position among the Liberals advising the new prime minister. Published polls had indicated that the Liberals had a 10 percent lead, but the party's private pollsters reported this support was soft. The Quebec caucus desperately wanted to seize the moment. An immediate election was also the advice of Minister of Finance Marc Lalonde. Economic prospects for the fall were poor, and if Turner found he had to bring in an autumn budget, he might run into difficulty. Senator Davey concurred: Turner could take the prize as front-runner.

Turner's accepting this advice indicated how his hubris had taken him to an overriding belief in the power of his own public persona. After all, he was devoting himself, a man of superior talents, to the mission of government. Deeds were not needed. His word alone should be enough to convince the public that he was bringing a new face to government. The very fact of his ascendancy would surely reverse years of discontent. He held Brian Mulroney in low regard, deeming him as lightweight in politics as he had been in business. When offered the choice between the untried Mulroney and the experienced Turner, surely the public would choose the better man.

In effect, John Turner consciously forfeited a situation of strength whose main variables were under his control and threw himself into Fortuna's hands on the assumption that his luck would hold and the Canadian public would endorse the Liberal delegates' recent decision. He took a weekend to fly to England and ask the Queen, who refused to visit any Commonwealth country while an election campaign was in progress, to postpone her visit to the fall. By the time he had returned to Ottawa, he had finalized his decision to ask the governor general to dissolve Parliament and issue the writ for an election. With his party leading in the polls, but "with several of its key members leaving political life, its election organization tired from a long leadership battle, and with few candidates nominated," the gamble was taken.[13] The outcome would depend on Turner's generalship, his campaign strategy and its policy expression, his performance on the hustings and on television, and the capacity of his new campaign organization. In each respect the prince blundered or was the victim of serious errors committed by the staff he had appointed.[14]

Campaign Generalship
Contrary to practice in every party, John Turner insisted that he would run his own campaign as if he were its democratic chief executive officer. Rather than perch on top of an organizational hierarchy that was managed for him by a designated chief of staff, he sat in the middle of a participatory circle, exposed not to the consistent counsel of his campaign staff but to conflicting advice coming from the many advisers whom he had chosen less for their experience or political astuteness than for their loyalty during his period in exile and their dissociation from the Trudeau regime.

Paradoxically, while Turner said he wanted to be open to advice, he established a campaign decision-making structure that inhibited the flow of information. William Lee, the manager of his successful leadership campaign, was put in overall charge of the election campaign and had to start from scratch to recruit staff. A complex policy structure was created to develop the party's platform. Regional co-chairs were appointed in such numbers that they made the campaign hierarchy top-heavy. These processes of decision making were too elaborate to produce either strategy or tactics expeditiously, but the lethargy that characterized the first three weeks of the Liberal campaign was due mainly to the prime minister's flat refusal to campaign during July. In waiting for Brian Mulroney to self-destruct, Turner lost control of the political agenda and let the media concentrate on the mistakes, small and large, with which he proceeded to oblige them.

Strategy

Although Turner structured his decision-making system so as to generate a plethora of advice, he had great difficulty resolving the contradictory counsel he received. One of his two competing pollsters, Angus Reid, warned him against becoming the candidate of continuity. On the other hand, Senator Jerry Grafstein, an old Turner supporter who had also worked actively in Trudeau's campaigns as the head of Red Leaf Communications, warned him against alienating the Liberals' traditional support base. Turner and his strategists had still not resolved the conundrum of how to accommodate the Trudeau legacy and at the same time turn the public's desire for change to his own advantage. His key advisers wanted him to swing back to the right and appeal to the West. Yet if he ran against his own party's record in government, the danger was that the voters might agree and reject the Liberal Party lock, stock, and barrel. Unlike Trudeau's better campaigns, which were directed according to a strategy hammered out by senior campaign officials, no strategic plan was finalized. With Angus Reid finding in his polling research that Turner was more popular than the Liberal Party and ahead of Brian Mulroney on such leadership criteria as experience, trustworthiness, and competence, the campaign centred by default on simply promoting the leader. No clear line of attack on the opposition leader was worked out. How Turner was to incarnate the public's desire for both change and strong leadership was not articulated for the guidance of the campaign organization.

Campaign Organization

William Lee had neither wanted Turner to call the campaign in the summer nor felt inclined to direct the operation himself. When Turner prevailed upon him to take on the formidable task of setting up and directing an organization with no time for preparation, he assumed that as campaign chairman he would have full operational control at the party's temporary campaign headquarters. But his authority was only partial. Even as Lee was setting up his office and worrying about installing electronic communications with the ridings, most of which still had to nominate their candidates, the new PMO was establishing another organization to direct the leader's tour by bringing in people who had become leery of Lee during the previous weeks of the leadership campaign. Torrance Wylie was recruited by the leader's principal secretary, John Swift, to provide counterbalance to Lee. Stephen LeDrew, who was put in charge of the leader's tour, was explicitly told to report to Swift, not to Lee. Although the chief players from the campaign headquarters and the PMO met every morning at eight to consult on decisions large and small, a gradual breakdown of relations between these two centres developed. Lee complained that a parallel campaign was being waged from the PMO, which in turn complained that Lee was withholding vital polling data. Other tensions developed, many focusing on the campaign chair.

Financing

As if the organizational woes of their competing campaign operations weren't enough, the Liberals had difficulty in mounting whatever William Lee and John Swift managed to organize owing to their sorry financial state. The two elections of 1979 and 1980 within one year had drained their coffers. Financial recovery had proven difficult, and the guardians of the party's purse strings were notoriously secretive. In 1982, the new president of the Liberal Party, Iona Campagnolo was unable to get an accounting of the party's finances. She was told only that it was $2.6 million ($4.3 million in 2002 dollars) in debt.[15]

The seven competitors for leader in the spring of 1984 had spent an estimated $5.86 million ($9.7 million), raising most of this money from sources that were not disposed to contribute again for the election.[16] Consequently, the party still found itself over $2.5 million ($4.1 million) in debt when John Turner took over.[17] Significantly, for the two elections in which the Liberals were soundly defeated, 1984 and 1988, their finances were in disarray. The Liberals' and Conservatives' declared election expenditures in 1984 were actually not very far apart (the Liberals spent $6.3 million versus the Conservatives' $6.4 million), but the Conservatives' revenue for the year was over $10 million greater. The Liberals raised only $13 million that year, compared to the Conservatives' $22.4 million, and the gap was to remain approximately the same in 1988.[18] During the 1984 campaign, the Liberals spent $5.3 million ($8.7 million) more than they received that year.

Policy

A leader-centred campaign requires that the leader have something to say. Neither John Turner's policy instincts nor his speech-writing infrastructure rose to the occasion in 1984. Instinctively heading for what had traditionally been Conservative turf, John Turner spoke like a corporate manager. He sounded the chords of fiscal responsibility, describing the need to eliminate waste from government and, above all, emphasizing the need to reduce the federal deficit. Ignoring the fact that his party had won four out of the five previous elections by appealing to an evolving social-democratic coalition of francophones, ethnic minorities, the poor, women, youth, and the aged, Turner took the "high road" of responsible leadership, pledging not to bribe the public with promises to spend its money as Brian Mulroney was doing. This did not stop him from making many old-style promises of his own, particularly in the West, where he announced a number of emergency measures to combat a prairie drought. He did pledge that his commitment to capitalism would not be at the expense of his support for social programs, but he did not clarify how he would square this particular circle. In shying away from Trudeau's issues of social justice, economic sovereignty, and energy self-sufficiency, he failed to remind traditional Liberal voters why they should stay in his fold.

While no one else could be blamed for his failure to articulate his overarching vision, the weak content of his major speeches resulted from a breakdown of the policy process in the PMO. Although Torrance Wylie, Senator Michael Kirby, and Tom Axworthy, three policy wonks from the Trudeau era, were hastily recruited to produce solid theme texts for the leader's use, their material arrived late and was so inadequate that Turner's scripts were mainly produced on his plane by one staff person scribbling valiantly without research support. A large youth-apprenticeship program; grants for young entrepreneurs; a doubled tax write-off for capital losses; a tax credit for living in the North; a new organization – Small Business Canada – to harmonize programs for small entrepreneurs; a dozen commitments on women's issues: it was a scattershot production that did nothing to clarify the confusing personal message that Turner was transmitting through his own performance.

As for the task of communicating the party's admittedly vague policies to its candidates across the country, William Lee took this responsibility away from the veteran Audrey Gill and handed it to Gordon Kaiser, a lawyer who had been active in the Turner leadership campaign as its policy director. Although he had no experience in the job, Kaiser threw out the large briefing books that had already been prepared by Gill and her staff. Following the many days of inaction that ensued, Marc Lalonde in exasperation sent out to candidates a policy briefing book prepared by his office in the Department of Finance. Later still, John Turner's final leadership campaign brochure was sent out masquerading between new covers as a policy agenda, but after a month of campaigning, it was too little and too late to be of use to the candidates in the field. With relations testy between the PMO and campaign headquarters, crucial correspondence addressed to the prime minister was not forwarded to the party office. As a result, a number of questionnaires sent by interest groups for policy responses languished unanswered in a huge pile. This accounted for further bad press when, for instance, a South Asian group announced the Liberal campaign was the only one not to have responded to its questions.

The Leader's Performance

During the leadership campaign, Turner had brushed aside criticism of his policy vagueness by maintaining that he would be judged by his actions, not his words. The first act of his election campaign was to announce at a press conference, in accordance with an agreement made with the former prime minister, that seventeen members of Parliament were being appointed to various positions ranging from senator to judge to ambassador. At one stroke, Turner tarred himself with the same invidious brush of patronage politics with which his predecessor, in a rash of appointments made during his last weeks as prime minister, had been painted. Turner had been induced by Trudeau to sign an agreement to appoint these outgoing members of Parliament at the time the next election was called (on the politically dubious grounds that Turner needed these MPs to maintain his majority in the House), but he failed to put these appointments into perspective for the public. Offered the chance to dramatically reject the Trudeau style (as his campaign manager had advised), Turner instead implicitly associated the new regime with the old, causing voters to question just how new the new Liberal leader was. Dwelt upon by the media for lack of other campaign news, exploited by his opponents, who worked it into a major campaign issue, Turner's patronage appointments became a symbolic hot button, indicative of the norms of public life being degraded by the same man who proclaimed it his mission to restore integrity to public life.

This major error in the opening moments of the campaign reminded reporters of the repeated slips and clarifications that had characterized Turner's leadership campaign and alerted them to further pratfalls. Turner proceeded to oblige them with the help of his party colleagues. Jeffrey Simpson describes one jocular moment in which Turner "patted party president Iona Campagnolo's rear end (to her everlasting credit she returned the gesture). CTV captured the incident on film but considered it incidental. When Turner repeated the gesture, this time to [Quebec Liberal candidate] Lise St. Martin-Tremblay, CTV reckoned it had a story. Instead of apologizing immediately, Turner laughed off the whole affair, an indifference that compounded the damage."[19] In full view of a television camera, Turner turned a chauvinistic quirk that lingered from his boardroom days into a major public incident. Brian Mulroney had committed a far worse breach of decorum by saying to reporters, about the appointment to an ambassadorship of the old Liberal Bryce Mackasey, there was "no whore like an old whore." But unlike Mulroney, who had swallowed his pride and apologized to the public, Turner stubbornly refused to address his unacceptable behaviour, sloughing off the incident for several weeks, until just two days before his appearance at a leaders' debate on women's issues. (In tribute to the bum-patting incident, the media christened Turner's tour plane *Derri-Air*.)

Other errors, such as his claim that Mulroney would fire 600,000 civil servants when there was only a total of 500,000 in the federal government's employ, kept undermining Turner's original asset: his reputation for competence. In another gaffe, he alleged that Manitobans "were leaving the NDP government [province] at a rate of 2,000 a month and was forced to recant when it was revealed that the population of Manitoba had actually been growing by some 1,000 people a month in the past year."[20] Far from displaying his Virtù, Turner's performance indicated his incapacity to make issues work for him and prevent problems from working against him. While he needed to reject the style but not the popular policies of Pierre Trudeau, he was in fact rejecting the policies while endorsing the patronage style and was becoming an object of public derision in the process. Rather than offering the public a new man with a new plan, he appeared in the relentless spotlight of daily campaign coverage to be an old man with no plan at all. At no moment was this ineffectiveness transmitted to the public more immediately and dramatically than in the first two of the three national debates Turner had accepted to hold with the other party leaders.

The Television Debates

In a situation in which both Turner and Mulroney were running their first election campaigns as party leaders, a televised debate offered voters a direct chance to observe and assess these newcomers' political skills. In a devastating set of back-to-back debates in the third week of the campaign, Turner laid out his weaknesses in full public view, first in French on July 24 and then in English the next day. No precedent required the Liberal leader to engage in more than one debate, and in 1980 Pierre Trudeau had refused to participate in any such event. Presumably confident in his Paris-learned French and his Rhodes-scholar-certified intellect, Turner had accepted the challenge to a French-language debate with the colloquially bilingual Brian Mulroney. Where Turner was stiff, Mulroney was fluent. Where Turner spoke in generalities; Mulroney spoke with well-rehearsed sincerity and concern for Quebec's specific political problems. Mulroney affirmed his affinity with Quebec; Turner communicated his distance in both time and space.

Since these two untested leaders had not yet been brought into well-defined focus, the public was looking for indicators, not just of their ability but of their humanity. In his English-language debate, John Turner proceeded to forfeit what had been meant to compensate for his lack of campaign organization – his claim to superior leadership qualities, such as decisiveness and intelligence. In sharp contrast to Mulroney's ease, he appeared frozen and nervous, referring to his notes and pronouncing with a rehearsed air formulations that had nothing special or personal to say to Canadians. Asserting confidence but communicating unease, he showed neither the intellectual dexterity nor the combative quality that voters could remember in the performances of his predecessor.

Indeed, Turner let his challenger dominate the bulk of the debate. At one point he attempted to rally with a counterattack that handed the patronage issue to the Conservative leader, who proceeded to put him totally on the defensive. Claiming he had "no option" but to accept the deal that the former prime minister had imposed on him, Turner let himself be branded as the errand boy of Pierre Trudeau – in no way a break from the Liberal past. The entire exchange lasted only a couple of minutes but political observers felt they were two of the most electrifying minutes in the short saga of televised political debates. Raising the patronage issue to challenge Mulroney would, for the rest of the campaign, be known as Turner's "big mistake."[21] On the third Wednesday of the campaign, he was exposed for all to see on the TV stage and was politically finished. He had faltered in full public view, in good part because his cumbersome campaign organization continued to give him conflicting advice. During the last-minute preparations for the debate, Keith Davey was urging him to sound like a Trudeau-style reformer while William Lee was still telling him to distance himself from the Trudeau record.

While the 1979 debate had occurred in the latter stages of the campaign, when voters had largely made up their minds, the 1984 debates occurred early in the campaign, so they had a much more dramatic effect. "Polls taken immediately after the French debate showed a swing of 10 to 12 percent from the Liberals to the Conservatives in Quebec."[22] The results were similar in Ontario after the English debate.[23]

As dismal as Turner's performance was in the first two debates, the 1984 election presented him with a small opportunity to redeem himself, thanks to the dogged efforts of women's groups to organize a debate addressing women's issues. Having triumphantly emerged from the constitutional struggles of the early 1980s with a prohibition on gender-based discrimination enshrined in the Charter of Rights and Freedoms, the National Action Committee on the Status of Women (NAC) "was sufficiently strong to enable it to organize a nationally televised leaders debate on 'women's issues.'"[24] Entirely attributable to the increased media coverage of women's social concerns, the NAC debate, which was scheduled near the end of the campaign on August 15 and was covered by the press as a news event, forced the leaders to expand on their party's agenda.[25] Although Turner did apologize for the "fanny patting" incident during the women's debate and was considered by many to have performed best, it was too late: the public had already made up its mind.[26]

Nearly two-thirds of adult Canadians tuned in to at least one of the three debates, with 5.4 million watching part of the English debate, 2 million viewing the French debate, and nearly 5 million taking in the bilingual debate on women's issues.[27] Subsequent research confirmed that the timing of the 1984 debates – "early in the campaign when Turner strategists felt (wrongly) that they would do the least damage"[28] – accounted for their great influence.[29]

Advertising and Polling: "Organizational Paralysis"

The public learned only indirectly of the organizational paralysis on the policy side of the campaign, but the tension between William Lee and Senator Jerry Grafstein's advertising group was played out in full view, thanks to the protagonists' internal memoranda being leaked. In previous campaigns, Grafstein had enjoyed a free hand in setting up Red Leaf Communications as the Liberals' umbrella advertising group. This time, Lee insisted on exercising his dubious authority and demanded a full accounting of Grafstein's efforts. The ensuing bickering delayed the production of the campaign's television commercials, whose impact was blunted by the bad publicity this internal feud had generated.

Another conflict arose between an old hand at Liberal campaigns, the pollster Martin Goldfarb, and a new figure brought in from the Turner campaign, Winnipeg pollster Angus Reid, who was an associate of Turner's leadership campaign co-chair, Lloyd Axworthy. Goldfarb's elaborate issue-monitoring model was set aside by the new PMO in favour of his western rival, but, with his reputation and, more important, rich future government contracts at stake, Goldfarb fought for his turf. As a result, the campaign had two pollsters giving two sets of interpretations of their somewhat differing data.

Turner was unable to resolve such bitter infighting and personality clashes in time. Whatever was going on behind the scenes, the campaign's evident chaos in the field made this organization the most incompetent that observers could recall. Events were poorly planned, failing to display Turner to best advantage. Crowds were small and the ridings he visited were often neither key constituencies nor those where he owed the local candidate a favour. Bickering seemed contagious. On "Derri-Air," a small DC-9 where the leader's group was in full view of the press, the disarray had reporters agog. In the crucial campaign for Metro Toronto, no one seemed to be in charge to pull the organization together. Open disputes between the supporters of John Roberts and those of David Smith, who had replaced Roberts as political boss of Metro, came to the surface in nomination struggles through the northwestern ridings of the city. Around the country, half of the provincial chairs selected by Keith Davey had been replaced, and the newcomers had to start from scratch.

Media Coverage

The cumulative press impact of John Turner's repeated gaffes and the organizational shambles in his campaign office was devastating. If the party could not put together a well-organized campaign, if it could not deal with the issues of the day, if it could not coordinate its personnel, and if the leader could not provide the campaign with the direction it so desperately needed, it was bound to sacrifice that aura of competence on which its electoral success had been premised for decades. The Liberal mystique had disintegrated within days of the campaign's launch, thanks to the gleeful efforts of the media to report that the white knight had fallen off his horse. Keith Davey wrote an angry letter to the Toronto Globe and Mail complaining of its "yellow journalism" and accusing this prestigious flagship of the Thomson press empire of being "just another Thomson newspaper."[30] Elizabeth Turner, the prime minister's daughter, vented her rage at the media in general by screaming "Screw 'em all," in their earshot.[31] Lloyd Axworthy complained that while Turner and the Liberal organization had been subjected to highly exacting scrutiny, Mulroney and the Conservative machine had been treated uncritically.[32] It was true that the press gallery was reporting with unprofessional alacrity every quirk of the prime minister, from the way he licked his lips to how he harrumphed and cleared his throat after attempting a joke. Displaying the pack mentality so often seen in election campaigns, the press had ganged up on the faltering colossus. Like a band of tormentors, the reporters watched out for every error or mannerism that could be added to their repertoire of Turner gaffes. The Ottawa bureau chief for the Toronto Star later acknowledged that the reporters were tougher on the Liberals: "With Turner, we always went after him as a group. We smelled blood and we attacked. With Mulroney, we attacked at the end, but at the end people had already made up their minds."[33]

The Conservative dominance of editorial endorsements observed in 1979 and 1980 continued in 1984 and was now supported by the francophone press.[34] Although the Toronto Star half-heartedly supported the Liberals on its editorial page, Montreal's La Presse, which had endorsed the Liberals on its front page in the last four federal elections, chose not to endorse any party. The 1984 election also saw an acceleration of the trend toward adversarial, personal journalism,[35] which meant a shift in coverage away from direct reporting of leaders' statements toward more assessments of their performances and an increase in attention to party strategies and organizational problems.[36]

Major features of the media's campaign coverage were the unprecedented use of public opinion polls, the extremely negative coverage of Turner and the Liberal Party, and the centrality of the leaders' debates.[37] With polls setting the tone (they were featured in 33 percent of the lead television items and 25 percent of front-page news stories), much of the coverage during the campaign focused on the horse-race element of the campaign, having a devastating effect on the Liberal Party in light of its organizational and financial problems.[38] As Keith Davey put it, "poll after poll from all kinds of media outlets told of our plight in excruciating detail. Every time we got up off the floor the next poll would knock us back down."[39] By mid-August, the media was declaring the election over, then focusing on the magnitude of the Tory landslide and the date of the next Liberal leadership convention.[40] The 1984 National Election Study found the media presentation of the leaders was reproduced among those surveyed, "with a generally positive attitude toward Mulroney and a generally negative attitude towards Turner."[41]

Unfair though this treatment seemed – an extraordinary 85 percent of Turner's media coverage was negative – the Liberals had only their leader to blame, for he had utterly failed to address the press corps' changed nature.[42] Having been described for years in flattering terms by reporters who built up his myth as dauphin-in-exile, he was unnerved by their switch to a more critical stance once he re-entered the political ring. The pathetic spectacle that Turner made on the evening news and in the morning papers showed the prince at Fortuna's mercy, having lost all control of how and what he was communicating to the public. The reality of Turner the politician so clashed with the previous image the same media had sustained that reporters could barely disguise their contempt.

The Liberal imbroglio's impact on public opinion was extraordinarily swift. By the end of July, the Liberals had already lost their lead and were heading for a rout, leaving Brian Mulroney and the Conservatives as the only alternative. The patronage issue continued to haunt the Liberals. Canadian Press reported on July 31 that the salaries and expenses for the twenty-three MPs appointed to patronage jobs would be around $4 million in the next year. Rubbing in the salt, constitutional experts contradicted Turner's claim that, had Trudeau made the appointments himself, it would have posed a "constitutional" danger.[43] Responding quickly to its disappointment with Turner, the public reverted to its basic attitude as revealed in poll after poll over the previous two years, identifying the need for change with support for the Progressive Conservative Party.

By mid-August, 49 percent of the support the Liberals had commanded in June had turned elsewhere.[44] Their coalition crumbled as the party lost popularity among every group of its supporters. Highly educated and affluent voters, who had moved to the Liberals in June, moved back again to the Conservatives. Research showed it was the debates that had crystallized the party leaders' images with the public by showing Turner insensitive to the needs and aspirations of Canadians. Though he had been considered the best candidate for prime minister in June by a margin of two to one over Brian Mulroney, by mid-August it was the Tory who was preferred for prime minister by a margin of two to one.[45]

Nowhere was the turnaround more devastating for the Liberals than in Quebec. A Southam Press poll published in June indicated that the Liberal Party still enjoyed 61 percent of the public's support in Quebec. By all indications, Brian

Mulroney would lose the seat he was contesting in his home riding of Manicouagan. With the departure from the scene of the compelling Pierre Trudeau, however, the Quebec electorate had become volatile, as it had been in earlier times when the overwhelmingly popular leaders Premier Maurice Duplessis and Prime Minister Louis St. Laurent had died or retired.

Turner made further errors about Quebec, managing to deepen the doubts about his commitment to the defence of the French language and culture that he had provoked on the first day of his leadership campaign. He showed how badly he misunderstood the significance to Quebeckers of the referendum's defeat in 1980 and their humiliating exclusion from the federal-provincial constitutional accord in 1981 by declaring he would not negotiate a deal with the separatist government of René Lévesque for Quebec to sign the 1982 constitution. He even attacked the Conservatives for running three candidates who had supported the "Yes" side in the 1980 referendum campaign. At a time when Quebec wanted to heal its wounds from the referendum and constitution struggles, Turner scratched off its scabs. When he accepted Brian Mulroney's challenge to debate in French on television, he gave the untried Conservative leader a windfall chance to present himself as Quebec's new champion. Identifying himself with Quebec's interests and preaching reconciliation, the boy from Baie-Comeau reached out to assume the mantle of Quebec's federal champion made available by Pierre Trudeau's retirement.

Bitterness persisted between supporters of Jean Chrétien and André Ouellet, the Turner chief in Quebec. The allegedly invincible Big Red Machine turned out to be non-existent. No theme was declared for the provincial campaign. No signs appeared. On July 16 *La Presse* ran the headline: "Pas un seul candidat Libéral au Québec." The Quebec City daily *Le Soleil* exemplified the switch by the Quebec media from the losing to the winning horse. Having supported Joe Clark over Brian Mulroney during the Conservatives' leadership campaign of 1983, and having supported Turner over Chrétien in the Liberals' race the following year, *Le Soleil* nevertheless shifted to Mulroney as its favourite for the 1984 general election. The Conservatives and Mulroney were ready to seize the chance that Turner had handed them in Quebec when he chose to run against the Liberals' record and threaten to tear down what Trudeau had built.

Turner raised concerns, and Mulroney soothed fears. Brian Mulroney, like John Turner, had directed his life toward the goal of becoming prime minister. Like Turner, too, he had been frustrated in an earlier attempt to win the leadership of his party. But unlike Turner, he left nothing to chance when Fortuna finally chose to smile on him. Indeed, the Progressive Conservatives in 1984 were a study in contrasts with their foes. The campaign organization had been put in place months before the electoral call, staffed by professionals who were experienced in electioneering, and animated by a team spirit that resulted from bringing together talented organizers from all factions of the party. Mulroney's tour had been given a dry run while the Liberals were choosing their leader. No detail had been left untested: the visual effects, the leader's speeches and themes, the way that he and his wife functioned together, holding hands as they walked to the podium for a speech.

The numerous members of the cast were rehearsed and practised until their performance was letter and gesture perfect. Policy positions were worked out and held in readiness. Most important of all, a strategy was fashioned from exhaustive survey research and shrewd analysis of its implications. Mulroney carefully avoided the traps set for him by the Trudeauites. Whether it was supporting the medicare system, defending French language minority rights, or supporting Trudeau's world peace initiative, Mulroney refused to be tagged as a reactionary right-winger, sticking so close to the ideological centre that he could have passed for a Liberal himself. When Turner did try to focus on Mulroney's credibility and the costs of the Tories' promises, his criticisms were paid scant attention, being "mentioned only in 2.6 percent of television media attention and 2.5 percent of front-page stories in the daily newspaper samples."[46] Having striven to reassure Canadians that a Progressive Conservative government would not attack the basic policy achievements of the Trudeau era, the Conservatives' task was to identify John Turner with all the unfavourable characteristics Canadian voters associated with the polarizing personality of Pierre Trudeau and, at the same time, sell Brian Mulroney as prime ministerial in quality and an agent of change.

Mulroney and his well-practised team stuck to their strategy and, campaigning hard, kept the media busy but at arm's length. He attacked Turner's patronage appointments extravagantly as a national scandal. He excoriated the Liberals' handling of the Canadian-American relationship, grossly exaggerating the ill will between Reagan and Trudeau. He lavished promises along the road. He conjured up the prospect of a brand-new era of federal-provincial harmony and Canadian-American reconciliation that would dawn upon his election. He obfuscated difficult issues. He brushed aside contradictions in his own positions. And he gave only three television interviews. Meanwhile, Tory ads, closely coordinated with intensive polling and Canada's most ambitious direct mail campaign to date, reinforced the message that only Mulroney could bring peace and prosperity to the post-Trudeau period. In English Canada, the focus was on Mulroney's emerging star quality.[47] Returning to the "time for change" theme, the PCs ran a series of commercials in which Mulroney expressed concern about an issue and closed by saying "You help me and *we* will solve this together."[48] By the end of the campaign, the Conservative leader was, Richard Gwyn observed, "looking and sounding prime ministerial while saying nothing. He's promising what amounts to Liberalism with a Fresh Face."[49]

In Quebec, Mulroney courted the francophone vote by pledging to negotiate a constitutional veto for Quebec.[50] Mulroney's ads and speeches in Quebec stressed his Quebecker heritage and avoided directly attacking Trudeau's legacy.[51] He flattered the nationalists and received enthusiastic support from the Parti Québécois' political machine. He also flattered the provincial Liberals, many of whom, including their leader, Robert Bourassa, were happy to settle a grudge with the federal Liberals who had treated them with so much scorn over the Trudeau years and had been responsible for their defeat in the 1981 provincial election.

The NDP, for their part, fought for survival. At the onset of the campaign, the NDP stressed the essential similarity of the two major parties and their leaders – dubbing them the "Bobbsey Twins of Bay Street, Chin and Twin, and the Corporate Clones."[52] But once the Liberal lead dissolved, its second wave of commercials tacitly admitted that there was going to be a large Conservative majority, freeing voters who wanted to oust the Liberals from having to vote Conservative and stressing that ordinary Canadians would need active representation in a House dominated by Conservatives.[53]

What had happened? According to Alan Frizzell and Anthony Westell, "the party [had] shot itself, with some help from journalists who were extraordinarily interested in its problems with patronage, organization, and campaign difficulties."[54] The Liberals' rout was ensured when they blew the media campaign: "They lost the contest to control the agenda, they lost the battle of leader image, and the party organization was portrayed, accurately, as in disarray."[55] No doubt Turner faced a new and far more probing media, but "the inappropriateness of the Liberal campaign for a modern, media-oriented contest was in stark contrast to the slickness of the Conservative organization."[56]

Rearranging the Deck Chairs

With their organization in a state of collapse, their strategy incoherent, and their leader in desperate straits, a consensus emerged among Turner's campaign advisers that William Lee had to go. Although opinions differed about whether he was actually responsible for all the ills attributed to him, Lee had become the scapegoat. Denied his leader's full confidence, Lee quit along with four key members of his staff. Keith Davey, who had been advising Turner from the wings, was put in full charge of the campaign organization on August 4 with a mandate to redefine the campaign strategy, revive the organization, and restore morale throughout the party. Even this, as the *Halifax Chronicle-Herald* pointed out, was not done easily: "clumsiness and distemper marked the retrieval of Senator Davey from the ashcan of politics."[57]

This desperate purge provided a further revelation of Turner's ineptitude, negating what was left of his whole effort to dissociate himself from the Trudeau era whose excessive backroom power had long been exemplified by none other than Keith Davey himself. The change came too late to resolve the backbiting that had developed in Quebec between Trudeau and Turner loyalists. Nor could the promotion of Keith Davey stop the policy conflict that broke out when party president Iona Campagnolo publicly disagreed with Turner, as did his wife, Geills, on Canada's support of a nuclear freeze.

Despite these obstacles, Davey did manage to stabilize the campaign's thrust, restore morale in the campaign team, enhance the effectiveness of the tour, and, most important, steady the leader enough for him to deliver his speeches effectively and gain more respectful press attention. By the final fortnight of the campaign, John Turner seemed to have hit his stride, even generating reports that his campaign was catching fire with its new strategy.

Davey had prevailed upon the prime minister to rebuild his links with the Trudeau legacy by reactivating a left-of-centre reform appeal to the old Liberal coalition. Turner pledged he would maintain the thrust of Trudeau's peace initiative. He wrote a letter to Soviet First Secretary Konstantin Chernenko and appointed retired diplomat George Ignatieff as Canada's ambassador for disarmament. He announced a multifaceted program of women's issues. He endorsed the notion of a minimum tax on the rich and started questioning Brian Mulroney's honesty by branding him a "let's-pretend Liberal." He claimed Mulroney had made 338 promises that would cost over $20 billion, and castigated the Conservative leader's last-minute accounting as a snow job deceiving the Canadian public. Having ruled out negative advertising as unacceptable at the beginning of the campaign, Turner concurred when the Davey-Grafstein team decided to put commercials on the air that enraged Conservative supporters by their negativism: a supermarket cart, for instance, being heaped by a Mulroney-like shopper with packages that were identified as Tory promises but bore no price tag until, at the cash register, the shopper was forced to admit he could not pay. These last-minute slashing ads by Red Leaf were ineffective, most likely because they reeked of despair.[58] The wheel had come full circle when Keith Davey prevailed upon Pierre Trudeau to make a formal appearance on behalf of the Liberals in an uncrowded hall in Montreal. "Requested in panic, given with reluctance, crafted in indifference," his speech was in Jeffrey Simpson's words, "a loon's cry before the terrible storm."[59]

Was the impact of the Davey rescue operation further to discredit Turner, who had made so much of his own integrity, only to switch from a right-wing to a left-wing position in a desperate effort to save himself?[60] Or had it rescued the Liberal Party from oblivion on the right in order to end the campaign at least in a position consistent with its previous principles in the centre? These questions would only be answered after the immediate post-mortems had been carried out.

The Results: Opposition Leader or Albatross

Falling from 49 percent support in the polls on July 9 and a ten-point lead over the Conservatives to 28 percent of the vote on September 4, 1984, must be seen as the worst electoral disaster in the long history of the Liberal Party of Canada. It went from holding 146 seats (52 percent of the House) to 40 seats (14 percent of the House) and saw twenty-five cabinet ministers go down to defeat. In the Atlantic provinces, the Liberals fell eleven points in the popular vote, from 45 percent in 1980 to 34 percent, retaining only seven of the region's thirty-two seats. In Quebec, the party fell thirty-three points in their traditional stronghold, receiving 35 percent of the vote and seventeen seats, losing fifty-six to the Progressive Conservatives. In Ontario, a loss of 12 percent of the vote left them with fourteen seats, thirty-eight less than they won in 1980 and just one seat more than the NDP obtained. In the West, where Turner had promised to restore Liberal strength, the party lost 7 percent of the popular vote, declining to a negligible 17 percent. It won only two seats, with Lloyd Axworthy retaining Winnipeg-Fort Garry, which he had won in 1979 and 1980, and with Turner picking up Vancouver-Quadra, which he contested in a symbolic gesture of solidarity with the West.[61]

The 1984 election recorded the largest voter shift since the beginning of national polling in Canada.[62] It smashed familiar voting patterns, with the Conservatives winning in every province in terms of both the popular vote and the seats won in the House of Commons, "a feat not achieved even in the great Conservative landslide of 1958."[63] One group of scholars has suggested that the reconfiguration of the electoral landscape that took place in 1984 was so cataclysmic that it marked the end of the third, pan-Canadian system of party politics that had prevailed since the days of John Diefenbaker and Lester Pearson and signalled the transition to a fourth party system.[64]

The important issues in the campaign varied greatly from region to region. Following the recession of the early 1980s, the 1984 campaign saw a move away from the national unity and resource issues of the late 1970s to a general concern with economic issues, particularly unemployment.[65] Issue effects for these themes were all substantially tilted in favour of the Progressive Conservatives, including the issue of leadership, which had played to the Liberals' advantage throughout the Trudeau years.[66]

Leadership turned out to be critical, since both John Turner and Brian Mulroney had been chosen by their parties because of their perceived electability.[67] The passing of the torch from Trudeau and Clark brought not only changes in personalities but differences of style and emphasis that affected the public's perceptions of the parties themselves.[68] Although the Turner succession had induced a temporary revival of the Liberals' fortunes, these gains dropped away early in the campaign. Turner's campaign blunders, patronage appointments, repudiation of Trudeau's legacy, and rehabilitation of Keith Davey all worked to Mulroney's advantage. Leadership was a particularly important factor among Liberal voters who switched to the Conservatives, with the massive swing in Quebec largely attributable to a disproportionate number of Quebeckers citing leadership as their most important election issue (see Table 7).[69]

By the final stages of the campaign, the Tories had consolidated a coalition of voters that eliminated many of its earlier differences from the Liberal Party. Through the course of the campaign, the Conservatives' gender gap closed, and support from all linguistic groups shifted from the Liberals to the Conservatives, as Tables 8 and 9 show. In this landslide, the Liberals lost votes to the Tories among all social sub-groups, although this effect was less evident among the elderly, the less well educated, and residents of the Atlantic provinces.

The Liberal Party had lost touch with its basic electoral coalition and could only hope that if the voters had been volatile in 1984, they could be volatile once more and return to its fold, as they had after Conservative leader John Diefenbaker won a similar landslide victory in 1958. The Liberals could do little but wait for the new government to falter.

The Liberal Party did enter opposition with some assets, whose husbanding could determine whether it would be able to turn its bleak situation to advantage. When Liberal senators appointed by Trudeau were added to the small group of Liberal members of Parliament, the party's caucus could be seen to boast considerable organizational and policy-making talent. The extra-parliamentary party was far more substantial, legitimate, and active than it had been in the late 1950s after the rout of 1958. It provided the potential vehicle for recruitment of new blood and the forum for debating issues around which new political content would have to be defined for Liberalism in Canada.

The party's liabilities were nevertheless substantial. The organization had been shaken to its core. Its troops were in shock; its technology was behind the times;

Table 7

Effects of party leaders in the 1984 federal election

Leader personality as most important factor in voting decision (voting pattern)	Liberal (%)	PC (%)	NDP (%)
Switch to	0.4	4.0	0.3
Remain	1.7	3.3	0.7
Enter/re-enter	0.5	2.1	0.2
Total	2.6	9.4	1.2

Note: Percentage of total voting electorate.
Source: Harold D. Clarke, Lawrence LeDuc, Jane Jenson, and Jon H. Pammett, *Absent Mandate: Interpreting Change in Canadian Elections*, 2nd ed. (Toronto: Gage, 1991), 137, table 7.5.

Table 8

Voting intention by gender in the 1984 federal election

Poll		Men (%)	Women (%)
4-12 July	PC	46	39
	Liberal	41	50
	NDP	10	8
	Other	3	3
1-7 August	PC	53	49
	Liberal	31	34
	NDP	15	15
	Other	1	2
19-22 August	PC	58	54
	Liberal	25	30
	NDP	15	14
	Other	2	2

Note: Percentage of decided voters.
Source: Alan Frizzell and Anthony Westell, *The Canadian General Election of 1984: Politicians, Parties, Press and Polls* (Ottawa: Carleton University Press, 1985), 94, table 6.

Table 9

Voting intention by language spoken at home in the 1984 federal election

Poll		English (%)	French (%)	Other (%)
4-12 August	PC	48	27	29
	Lib	39	63	60
	NDP	12	3	7
	Other	1	7	4
1-7 August	PC	54	45	37
	Lib	27	42	56
	NDP	18	8	6
	Other	1	5	1
19-22 August	PC	57	57	44
	Lib	25	31	34
	NDP	16	7	20
	Other	2	5	2

Note: Percentage of decided voters.
Source: Alan Frizzell and Anthony Westell, *The Canadian General Election of 1984: Politicians, Parties, Press and Polls* (Ottawa: Carleton University Press, 1985), 94, table 7.

its fundraising capacity was inadequate; its debt remained large. Factionalism, the bane of opposition parties, broke out, particularly in Quebec, where disciplinary levers could no longer be pulled to keep order and maintain an electorally crucial facade of unity.

For those who saw John Turner as the LPC's main liability, his winning the Vancouver seat of Quadra was the worst news of the night on September 4, because it ensured he would hang on as party leader. He had caused the electoral catastrophe by his astonishing lack of political Virtù. Uncertain of where he stood, unsure in his political instincts, uncomfortable with the attacker role required of an opposition leader, he now appeared to be the party's albatross. Those who saw Turner as an asset pointed to his sense of personal mission to rebuild the Liberal Party, his general decency, and his determination to transcend his personal humiliation and fight his way back to power. It remained an open question whether the downed giant could acquire in opposition the Virtù he had so obviously lacked during his painful summer as prime minister.

To outside observers, it seemed that now, more than ever, Turner was in the hands of Fortuna. It would take many mistakes on the part of Brian Mulroney's Progressive Conservatives and an equally unskilled performance by the New Democrats' Ed Broadbent for him to find the fates smiling his way again.

Election or Referendum? 1988
Disoriented in Defeat

It was a curiosity of Canadian politics in the 1980s that John Napier Turner, once thought to be the most conventional of politicians, turned out to be the least conventional of leaders. For in the two elections he fought at the head of the Liberal Party of Canada, he did the completely unexpected. In June 1984, with all the advantages of office at his disposal, Turner seemed poised to win the election he had set for September 4, but the newly minted prime minister managed to sabotage his own campaign and produced his party's worst defeat ever. In October 1988, with all the disadvantages of being the least respected of the three party leaders, with only 11 percent of the public feeling that he would make the best prime minister, Turner seemed poised for annihilation. Yet the man who had been written off as a political loser single-handedly executed such a reversal of his standing by mid-campaign that, for a few heady days, a Liberal victory seemed in the cards. That he went down to defeat for a second time despite his Herculean effort showed the extent to which he had failed to accomplish the primary goal he had articulated in 1984: rebuilding his own party. At the end of the 1988 campaign, the Liberal Party was bereft of direction, depleted in its organization, and devastated in its former stronghold of Quebec.

Turner's Electoral Challenge
When the election writ was issued on October 1, 1988, the leader of the opposition faced three near-impossible tasks. First, he had to prove that the decentralization he had brought to the organization of the Liberal Party could be electorally effective. To achieve this he needed to win the active political support of the two most powerful Liberal politicians in the country: Quebec Premier Robert Bourassa and Ontario Premier David Peterson.

Next, he had to remind voters of their earlier scorn for a Progressive Conservative government that had wallowed in scandal and incompetence for its first two-and-a-half years in office but had then seized control of the public agenda through increasingly capable management in its final nineteen months.

Finally, he had to convince the public that he was a politician who could lead Canada back from the historical brink at which it stood, as citizens debated whether to ratify a watershed economic integration agreement with the United States. For this he had to establish his leadership of the opposition by neutralizing the campaign on his left flank of the New Democratic Party, which had been riding high in the polls.

This was a formidable set of executive assignments for a man whose performance as Leader of Her Majesty's Official Opposition in the four years since he had lost the previous election had been most notable for its almost uninterrupted record of pratfalls. Opposition party leaders typically control few of the factors affecting their fate. But even in the one domain where Turner was supreme and to which he brought firm convictions – the principles guiding the Liberal Party's internal organization – it was by no means certain when the writs were issued that what he had wrought since 1984 would stand the test of electoral fire.

The Organizational Conundrum

Due to the overwhelming impact that leaders in Canada have on the parties they command, understanding John Turner's notion of the Liberal Party is the key to explaining what the party became under his tutelage. In his political exile from 1975 to 1984, Turner had criticized Pierre Trudeau's centralized, pan-Canadian way of operating the party and favoured a return to the regionally based system used during the second, brokerage party system, when the accommodative Liberals were led by William Lyon Mackenzie King and Louis St. Laurent.[1]

For a defeated prime minister to turn for help to the extra-parliamentary party was not unusual, given that Wilfrid Laurier and Mackenzie King had done the same in 1911 and 1930, respectively. For Turner to hark back to a regionally based formula that was fifty years out of date, however, was something else again. During the decade from 1958 to 1968 when Lester B. Pearson was leader, the Liberal Party had been rebuilt according to the centralized management principles of Walter Gordon, the successful business consultant whom Pearson had recruited to modernize the party's organization and reshape its policies. This was a time when Quebec especially, and the English Canadian provinces to some extent, went through a "province-building" process that saw their economic and administrative powers develop at the expense of the federal government's. With the provincial Liberal parties taking regionalist stands that increasingly challenged the federal party's positions, Walter Gordon and Keith Davey, then the Liberals' national director, had moved to become independent of their provincial cousins' organizations.[2]

This process of federal-provincial differentiation had continued during the Trudeau regime. Even if he had wanted to build his federal party on regional foundations, Pierre Trudeau would have found few powerful, provincially based chieftains to aid his cause. During his incumbency, the Liberals lost power in the six provinces whose governments they held in 1968: New Brunswick in 1970, Newfoundland and Saskatchewan in 1971, Quebec in 1976, Nova Scotia in 1978, and Prince Edward Island in 1979. With Ottawa as the sole remaining source for partisan patronage, the federal party naturally had become the dominant force in Liberal circles at the end of the Trudeau years.

The strong ideological component in Trudeau's vision of federalism had a particular impact on the Liberals' fortunes in Quebec. His dogmatic anti-nationalism made him the committed foe not just of separatism in Quebec but also of the somewhat nationalistic "neo-federalism" espoused by the provincial Quebec Liberal Party (PLQ). First as a polemicist and then as an MP and a rookie minister in the mid-1960s, he had fought Quebec's demands for special status. As prime minister in the 1970s, he had mocked Premier Robert Bourassa's ambivalent federalism. As constitution-maker in the early 1980s, he had repudiated the punctilious neo-federalism of the PLQ's austere new leader, Claude Ryan, thereby fracturing the tenuous solidarity between federal and provincial Liberals that had been cobbled together during the "No" campaign against the referendum over sovereignty-association in 1980. Despite their defeat of separatism, the federal and provincial Liberal parties in Quebec had emerged from the Trudeau era deeply alienated from one another.

This same period had also radically changed the federal party's organizational structure. Far-reaching reforms to Canada's election-expense legislation in 1974 had created a new legal context for federal parties. Although they remained private associations operating by rules sanctioned in their own constitutions for such activities as candidate nominations, parties now were publicly accountable bodies whose legislative research activities, constituency offices, and riding campaigns were largely financed by the federal state. What was initiated at the federal level soon spread throughout the provincial political systems so that, by the early 1980s, provincial parties had also been transformed from private clubs of partisan activists into legally bound institutions financed in large part by the same taxpayers whose votes they courted at election time. As a result, the Canadian party system was firmly institutionalized, and Canadian parties were clearly differentiated by statute between their federal and provincial levels.

So when John Turner promised to a meeting of federal Liberals in Calgary on January 18, 1985, that he would rebuild the federal party on the basis of strong provincial party foundations, he was operating in a context fundamentally different from the situation in which Mackenzie King had found himself in 1932, when he had created the National Liberal Federation as an umbrella organization of the nine provincial Liberal associations.[3]

Nevertheless, one of Turner's prime organizational preoccupations as opposition leader was to invest what resources he could muster to support his Liberal counterparts in their provincial election campaigns. He believed that the route back to federal power led through recapturing power in the provincial capitals. For instance, he designated Sheila Copps, a young MP who had previously been a member of the Ontario legislature, to liaise with Queen's Park and establish closer co-operation between the federal and provincial Liberal opposition caucuses. By mid-1985 Turner could exult in renewed provincial Liberal strength throughout English Canada: from gains in Newfoundland (15 seats from 8), to the election of two Liberals to the territorial legislature in the Yukon, to strong provincial by-election performances in British Columbia, Saskatchewan, and New Brunswick, to the swearing in of David Peterson's minority Liberal government in Ontario in June.[4] The provincial co-operation strategy served a second, if less overtly expressed, goal: Turner's own struggle to secure his confirmation as leader by the federal party's next convention.

> As the Liberals approached a convention in 1986 at which delegates would vote
> on whether they wished to hold a leadership contest, it was clear that discontent
> with Turner was widespread. Chrétien retired from Parliament, distancing himself
> from Turner and possibly preparing to challenge his leadership. Keith Davey ...
> published a book in which he politely but pointedly drew attention to Turner's
> failings. Marc Lalonde, who had been Trudeau's first lieutenant and a leader in
> Quebec but who had supported Turner as the successor, now published an open
> letter in which he called for a review of the leadership, in part because the party
> was millions of dollars in debt.[5]

As none of the provincial leaders to whom he offered electoral support had ambitions for his job, identifying himself with their causes could do him little harm, particularly when their fortunes were on the rise. When the party's biennial convention was held in November 1986, this strategy proved to have been astute. Having control of the party machinery, Turner's loyalists managed to engineer a far higher level of delegate support for the leader than continuing dismay with his generally poor political performance had led observers to expect. Surprisingly, 76.3 percent of Liberal delegates voted "No" on their mandatory secret ballot about whether to hold a leadership convention (and have Turner's position contested). The covert campaign to oust Turner by the faction supporting Jean Chrétien, his chief rival for the leadership in 1984, had been warded off.

The euphoria induced by this apparent endorsement of Turner's leadership was short-lived, for he had little to show for the two years that had passed in terms of concrete financial and organizational restructuring. The party was still deep in debt, as his leadership failings and anti-free-trade stance had dried up corporate donations.[6] Although large amounts of money were being raised, the expenses of the national organization were rising so much faster than its income that staff reductions were required at the national office.[7] As a result, the Liberals had little choice but to finance their next campaign in part with loans secured by expected official reimbursements for campaign expenditures, and with what the *Toronto Star* of May 19 called "a series of unique fundraising efforts," including the sale of bonds and "victory certificates."[8]

The leader's own office was in a state of continual turmoil. Turner never found a principal secretary strong and experienced enough to bring order to his affairs. Members of his staff kept resigning and emerging from his office to recount, to an avidly listening press, new horror stories about what was to be christened John Turner's "reign of error."[9]

More important to many Canadians, both in the Liberal Party and the mass media, was Turner's continuing failure to resolve the ideological uncertainties he had created when he rejected Trudeau's federalist legacy in 1984. Though his caucus had been reduced to the manageable size of forty, he proved unable to discipline the various factions still stirring within it and to meld them into a coherent team united behind his leadership. The caucus was wracked with dissension over such fundamental and divisive issues as the testing of cruise missiles and the negotiation of an economic treaty with the United States. His endorsement in June 1987 of Brian Mulroney's Meech Lake Accord on constitutional decentralization exacerbated the dismay of the party's Trudeau loyalists who "saw it as a reversal of the policies for which they had stood and fought: "One Canada" with a strong central government and two official languages."[10]

Battered by these problems of leadership, organization, and policy, the chances of the Liberals getting their electoral machine onto a winning footing seemed best if Turner abdicated.[11] Four Liberal provincial premiers (Robert Bourassa, Joe Ghiz, Frank McKenna, and David Peterson) all rallied to their beleaguered leader's side, but as late as April 1988, twenty-two of the thirty-nine Liberal caucus members took part in an abortive mutiny, drafting letters urging Turner to step down and make way for a more effective leader.[12] Their petition, made public on April 25, emphasized Turner's perceived inability to win the next election and his support of the Meech Lake Accord.[13] Turner's reputation only slid further when a Gallup poll reported that Liberal support would rise if he undertook to step down as leader.[14]

The Liberals had done reasonably well in the public opinion polls because of the many failures of the Conservative government, but Turner's third-place standing among the party leaders was a strong disincentive to potential recruits to the party. Though a search for big-name candidates had been entrusted to Paul Martin Jr., a Montreal business executive and candidate of potential star quality himself, few strong figures emerged to contest and win constituency nominations, with the notable exceptions of auto-parts magnate Frank Stronach and provincial cabinet ministers Doug Young (New Brunswick) and Gilles Rocheleau (Quebec).[15] Displaying a stance strikingly similar to that of his predecessor, whose attitudes to party matters he had so noisily repudiated, Turner adopted a laissez-faire stance to recruiting.

What made contesting a Liberal nomination even less attractive to established public figures was the prospect of having to spend well over $30,000, with little assurance of success against possible single-issue or "ethnic" rivals who could capture ridings by enlisting hundreds from their organization or their particular ethnic community in the party's local riding association.[16] With Turner adopting a hands-off, this-is-democracy-at-play attitude toward the nomination process, the party was unable to resolve the tension between its old English- and French-Canadian bases and the new multicultural forces that were demanding admission into its ranks.

By the summer of 1988, the Liberals' situation looked disaster-bound. Although the party was still wallowing in what was reported to be a $5 million debt ($7 million in 2002 dollars),[17] Turner had to fire his Quebec fundraiser, Senator Pietro Rizzuto, for leading the caucus mutiny against him. With campaign preparations still in their early stages, Turner acted as though Mackenzie King's decentralized party federation was alive and well and would come to his rescue. He turned to his provincial counterparts and asked them for organizational help. Since Turner's own leadership was a factor dragging the Liberal cause down, the success of his risky gamble hung largely on whether his policy positions could galvanize the various provincial Liberal organizations into action.

Policy without Presence

Policy confusion had been a continuing problem for Turner ever since he had returned to politics in 1984 and shown his grasp of current issues to be shaky. Whenever caucus members squabbled over a question, the media reinforced the impression that the Liberals were hopelessly divided on the major issues. Even active and experienced party loyalists could be heard bewailing their party's intellectual void. The reality was somewhat more complex.

True to his promise to hand the party back to its members, Turner had stood back while its activists designed their own policy-making process and brought in their own ideas. As those who were active on policy issues tended toward the nationalist left of the party's ideological spectrum, Turner, in effect, let his policy agenda be rewritten by those who theoretically should have been most alienated from his pro-business stance in 1984. They consulted policy experts; they organized three regional thinkers' conferences; they established a platform committee to draft position papers that dealt with the broad spectrum of public policy concerns. Working with Brooke Jeffrey, the director of the Liberal caucus's research bureau and her dozen staff people, they prepared forty separate policy positions for the campaign. Each policy was supported by an extensive background paper that analyzed the government's record and the New Democratic Party's position on the issue, explained the principle on which the Liberals stood, and outlined what action a Liberal government would take. An outside expert, the political scientist Robert Jackson, was hired to liaise with the leader's office and monitor this policy work. David Husband, an economist with finance department experience, was engaged to cost each proposal professionally and prepare a careful document to describe how the party would pay for all its campaign promises. The publication of *What a Liberal Government Would Do for You* was designed to boost party morale.[18] Turner had learned from his 1984 trauma, when he had started his campaign with no policy weaponry, to equip himself with more than enough ammunition.

What went wrong this time was both the strategy of how to use policy in the campaign, and its tactical execution. In an action that indicated how rooted Turner was in the politics of the brokerage party system, the Liberals unveiled their forty policies as an election manifesto on September 28, just before the writs were issued. Admittedly, there were advantages to this pre-emptive strike. Turner could make the point that he had a comprehensive set of policies ready for the campaign. He was able to give his candidates solid material with which to prepare their campaign appeals. Alas for him, the electronic media, which have trouble transmitting more than a single idea in a thirty-second clip, could not cope with such a cornucopia of ideas that had not been predigested into a simple theme featuring a few easily grasped issues, and wrapped around a catchy slogan.

Turner's strategic decision to release frequent and detailed policy statements but to hold back until late in the campaign the explanation of how the Liberals would pay for their promises went off track from the very beginning. When his child-care policy was released in Montreal on the first Wednesday of the campaign, bad tactics and poor communications between the leader's office and Lucie Pepin, the caucus member responsible for the issue, led to a damaging debacle for the badly briefed leader in front of the press. After a few more such incidents, the collective journalistic mind had clearly decided that the Liberals had no policies and could still not do anything right.

This also seemed to be the view of two influential party insiders. In their book *Marching to a Different Drummer*, which was infelicitously published in the midst of the campaign, former Trudeau adviser Tom Axworthy and former Liberal pollster Martin Goldfarb argued that "the party was on the brink of oblivion, having been unable to establish a compelling, policy-oriented identity in the eyes of the voters."[19] Although in press interviews they retracted some of their criticisms of the leader, whom they now felt had got back into step with the party, this manifestation of disharmony was damning.[20]

Though Turner continued to release policy positions in his daily speeches (half of the forty planks were formally announced in this way), the media seemed interested only in his flag-waving attacks on the Conservatives' free trade agreement. By mid-campaign, Turner's handlers decided to give the media what they apparently wanted. The leader would no longer try to remedy the party's perceived weakness in policy. For the duration of the campaign, Turner would lead to his strength as champion of the anti-free-trade cause.

Presence without Policy

Taking a nationalist position was not an obvious stance for a politician whose leave from politics had been spent in the private sector, serving the continental interests of Toronto's corporate community. His former business allies and present political enemies could never quite bring themselves to believe that the John Turner they thought they knew had defected to the nationalist camp out of conviction. Several key Liberal policy planks had come under fire from the business community, leaving Roger Hamel, head of the Canadian Chamber of Commerce, wondering if "Mr. Turner just doesn't care about the community anymore."[21] After all, Turner had always been close to his American counterparts, both in politics and in business. He had been well known as a strong critic of Trudeau's more nationalist acts – from the Foreign Investment Review Agency of 1973 to the National Energy Program of 1980. He had been invited by George Shultz, who later became the American Secretary of State, to join the board of the giant US engineering firm Bechtel. For many years, one of his closest advisers had been Simon Reisman, the man Prime Minister Mulroney had appointed in 1985 to be Canada's chief free trade negotiator.

But something had indeed happened to change Turner's mind on the question of free trade with the United States. Unlike many politicians who took positions on the issue, he had grasped the broader implications of the Canada-United States Free Trade Agreement (FTA). Immediately following the publication in October 1987 of the FTA's main provisions in summary form, he came to the firm conclusion that it was a bad deal; Canada's negotiators had given up too much and got too little in return. More seriously, it would imperil the country's survival as the autonomous state he thought it had become in the golden age of his political heroes, Mackenzie King and St. Laurent.

From the time the text of the FTA was made public, John Turner and his trade critic, Lloyd Axworthy, established a confident leadership of the anti-free-trade position, thereby making NDP leader Ed Broadbent and his trade critic, Steven Langdon, appear to be less clear-headed and decisive. Whereas the NDP

talked about abrogating the deal should they come to power after it was implemented – an action that could involve serious retaliation by the United States,
the Liberals insisted an election be held on the issue and vowed to "tear up" the
document if they won. Representatives of the Pro-Canada Network, a coalition
of church, labour, women's, cultural, environmental, ethnic, elderly, and Native
groups who were against the FTA, found the Liberal caucus more responsive
than the NDP to their briefings.[22] John Turner, the nervous achiever who had
always tried to do what the elites with whom he associated expected of him, had
turned into a champion of the people.[23] He was defying the business establishment from which he sprang with a calm self-assurance he had never achieved at
any other time in his life.

Although Turner spoke consistently and strongly against free trade throughout the early months of 1988 and although he had presented a coherent alternative to the deal negotiated by Mulroney's government, his low ratings in the
public opinion polls had prevented the Liberals from causing the Conservatives
much grief on the issue. Faced in the summer of 1988 with the muffling of the
one issue that had explosive potential with the public, the Liberals decided to
use the majority they commanded in the Senate to block the FTA's implementation. As party leader, John Turner announced in August that he had instructed
Liberal Senators not to consider the government's proposed implementation
legislation until the Canadian people had been given a chance to vote on the
issue. With one brilliant stroke, Turner had used the politically discredited Senate to make two politically credible points: the FTA put Canada at risk, and the
public must pass judgment on it before the agreement became law. With the
public favouring a let-the-people-decide position by a two to one margin, Turner
breathed life into a moribund issue, dramatized its importance to the country,
and forced the government's hand. While alienating traditional Liberals in the
West, for whom free trade had always been a party cause,[24] Turner was able to
revive his appeal to one of the two branches of the traditional Liberal vote – the
coalition of working people, women, disadvantaged, elderly, and ethnic voters
who looked to government for economic security. Having already lost the support of the other branch – the high income earners who made up the business
and professional class and who populated the suburbs of the large metropolises
– Turner was at least making a bid to wrest the anti-business, social-democratic
centre-left away from the NDP. This was the broad mainstream of middle- and
working-class voters who had prudential concerns about the maintenance of
the country's social programs, who appreciated the quality of Canadian life, who
believed it to be threatened by further Americanization, and who wanted Canada
to play a role on the world stage as mediator of conflicts and provider of aid to
the third world.

For a week or so in the late summer, as the nation's open-line radio shows debated the pros and cons of the Senate action (denounced haplessly by NDP leader Ed Broadbent as undemocratic), Turner caught the public's attention. The Conservatives initially delayed calling an election in the expectation that the issue could not be sustained, and, as time passed, the Tories did seem to regain control over the public agenda. Premier Robert Bourassa's endorsement of the FTA offset Turner's impact on Quebec opinion. Guided by expensive polling data, the Conservatives tried to distract lingering public concerns about free trade by launching new initiatives in environmental protection and housing, and so reworking their image as a government willing to intervene on the public's behalf.[25] When Prime Minister Mulroney finally called on Governor General Jeanne Sauvé to precipitate the election campaign on October 1, it seemed that the free-trade genie had been safely coaxed back into its bottle, and that John Turner's political chances remained bleak.

Finances

By the mid-1980s, a revenue sharing program ensured that the Liberals' national headquarters received a steady stream of income from their better off provincial and territorial associations (PTAs). Whereas the lucrative fundraising opportunities presented by direct mail had been the exclusive preserve of these PTAs since they first launched such programs in 1981,[26] they now split this revenue evenly with the federal party, which also received a further 25 percent of all revenue raised by constituency associations and the PTAs. In 1986, the party created a financial management committee that, apart from having a "general responsibility for the LPC's finances, prepared and implemented long-range financial plans and operating budgets, and allocated available financial resources."[27] As the revenue subcommittee of the financial management committee, the former treasury committee continued to raise funds "to finance the operations of the national level of the Party, including national election campaigns."[28] The chair of the revenue committee was to be "appointed by the Chief Financial Officer subject to the agreement of the Leader and the President of the Party."[29] This centralization of the federal party's financial organization was a long overdue step enabling the party to regain control of its finances from the leader.

Various methods were developed during Turner's tenure to help pay down the party's significant debt from the 1984 election campaign. One such effort was "Project 200," which was set up to solicit 200 donations of $25,000 ($35,000 in 2002 dollars) each from large corporations.[30] Although this project was a failure, the Liberals' next effort launched in 1985 was at least a modest success. Modelled after the Progressive Conservatives' "The 500," which offered successful business people privileged access to the federal leader in return for a generous donation,[31] the Liberals' "Laurier Club" succeeded in raising $416,312 ($584,086) for the 1988 campaign.[32] Most successful of all was the series of leader's dinners, which netted $2.2 million ($3.1 million) in revenue for the 1988 election year,[33] and which remains a mainstay of Liberal fundraising efforts to the present day.

The federated structure of the party continued to be a problem through the late 1980s because the PTAs did not wish to lose control over their hard-earned funds. The national executive finally forced a change in 1987 by using the tax credits provided in the election expense legislation. Requiring all contributions for tax receipts to be issued from the national headquarters following their deposit, it then returned funds to the PTAs to cover their centrally determined budget.[34] In an effort to control costs, budgets were cut drastically at all levels, staff was fired, and the Ottawa headquarters relinquished an entire floor of office space.

Despite this drastic reorganization, increased centralization, and decreased autonomy for PTAs, the Liberal Party's financial difficulties continued into the 1988 election. In Toronto, the prominent billionaire businessman Gerald Schwartz took charge of fundraising, pleading with executives that, while they might not like Turner's position on free trade, they should still shell out generously, lest the socialist NDP sneak up the middle to exert a controlling voice in a minority government. He was only partly successful. The number of corporate donations to the Liberals in 1988 fell to less than half of what the Conservatives received, although their average size was slightly larger (see Table A.4, p. 289). As a result of those difficulties, the party did not come close to its statutory limit on campaign expenses (see Table A.1, p. 285), spending less than the NDP and over one million dollars less than the Conservative Party's $7.9 million ($11.1 million).[35] Beyond intra-party organizational problems, the issue remained John Turner, whose unpopularity and uncertain leadership dissuaded many from donating.

The Campaign Organization

Not only was Turner low in the popularity polls as the campaign began, but his organization was generally third in quality compared to the well-financed professionalism of the Conservatives and the experienced discipline of the New Democrats. This is not to say that the Liberals presented the same chaotic face to the public that they had shown in 1984. The men and women around Turner who staffed the central campaign were certainly conscious of what errors they needed to avoid, though how much they could achieve without a substantial organization of their own in each province remained to be seen.

In Ottawa the co-chairs of the overall campaign structure, Senator Alasdair Graham and André Ouellet, kept the tempers and turf-fighting natural to any fractious organization within bounds. John Webster, a novice, was proving to be an effective campaign director. Peter Connolly, Turner's controversial principal secretary, continued as chief of staff on the tour, acting as gatekeeper to the leader. The equally controversial Senator Michael Kirby headed the national strategy committee and controlled the flow of speech ideas to the leader's tour. He applied opinion data received from pollster Martin Goldfarb to determine the political impact of the party's proposed policies and, along with policy consultant George Radwanski, worked to translate them into one-liners for the leader. (To the *Wall Street Journal*'s jeremiad against Canadian free trade opponents who were described as wanting to become the Argentina of the North, they had Turner quip, "Don't cry for me, *Wall Street Journal!*")

In contrast to 1984, when communications between campaign headquarters and individual candidates' campaigns were sorely lacking, in 1988 the caucus research bureau staffed a policy hotline to provide candidates with answers to voters' questions and devised replies to the myriad questionnaires with which special interest groups inundated riding offices. The introduction of a new communication technology, the fax machine, helped to keep the riding campaigns informed of the leader's daily positions more easily and economically than ever.

David Morton, vice-president of Quaker Oats of Canada, took over from Jerry Grafstein as the head of Red Leaf Communications, the party's advertising consortium. For the 1988 campaign, Red Leaf created strong but subtle commercials bringing to a wide audience the Liberal message about free trade's threats and Turner's commitment to Canadian sovereignty, the most dramatic of which was an ad showing an American free trade negotiator erasing the Canada-United States border, and a Canadian negotiator acquiescing.[36] (The French language commercials produced in Montreal studiously avoided mentioning either John Turner or free trade.)

The normal tensions that plague the crisis-management climate of campaign structures broke into open view in mid-October, when a CBC broadcast elevated an apparently deliberate leak from the leader's tour group into an explosive story alleging that yet another coup against John Turner was being hatched by none other than his campaign strategists. Based on two real facts – Michael Kirby had brought gloom to party headquarters in the shape of Martin Goldfarb's latest disheartening poll data, and the strategy committee had debated what to do should Turner's acute back pain cause him to step down – the highly embroidered story devastated party morale for a precious week.[37] Whatever the media might suggest, the party was stuck with its leader, for better or for worse.

The Leader in the Campaign

That anything involving John Turner could be for the better seemed close to impossible as the two televised debates approached in late October. Having made the mistake of agreeing to debate in French with the bilingual Brian Mulroney in 1984, an encounter that put him on the defensive and precipitated his electoral downfall, Turner was stuck with the precedent and could hardly back out of a repeat engagement. It looked as though the French debate on October 24, would prove an unpropitious prelude to the following day's donnybrook in English. But Turner surprised first French Canada and then the rest of the country by outperforming Mulroney on both occasions. In the French debate he was both more at ease with himself and his material and in better humour than Mulroney, who appeared evasive and defensive. While the 1984 debates were crystallized by Turner's "big mistake," this time around "Mr. Turner went on the offensive over Conservative appointments and alleged abuses of power."[38] To their own astonishment, Quebec editorialists declared Turner the debate's winner, spurring him on for the next day's three-hour rematch in English.

When the three party leaders convened for their second encounter, Turner managed to accomplish two objectives. First, he effectively branded Ed Broadbent a pacifist by linking him to the NDP's unpopular defence policy, which promised withdrawal from the joint Canada-United States North American Aerospace Defense Command (NORAD) and the North Atlantic Treaty Organization (NATO). This reminded Atlantic Canada, where military bases formed a crucial component of Ottawa's income-support system, that it was the Liberals, not the NDP, who understood their employment needs.

Then, as political scientist Robert Young graphically described it,

> With less than 15 minutes left in their last head-to-head encounter, Chick Turner started to jab desperately on the trade issue. Mr. Mulroney, doubtless to the dismay of his corner-men, neither clinched nor danced away, and the two heavyweights stood toe-to-toe, punching and counter-punching, slugging it out in a sheer test of power and commitment which enormously enhanced Turner's stature, punctured the prime ministerial balloon of inviolability, and left Ed Broadbent looking like the kid peeking over the fence at the big guys.[39]

In the context of the low esteem in which he was widely held, the fact that John Turner proved in these exchanges to be both coherent and persuasive had a powerful impact on the millions of Canadians who watched all or part of the six hours of debates. When the polls judged him winner of the English debate as well, his standing increased with the millions of other voters who heard about the debates or saw short clips from them repeated in news reports.

Suddenly, the inevitable Tory majority was in doubt. Turner "said nothing which had not been said many times before, but he said it with enormous conviction."[40] He had made Liberals feel good again about being Liberal, and those activists who had been sitting out this campaign because they couldn't stomach the leader or his organization or his platform now turned out to drum up public support. Jean Chrétien re-entered the fray and started making pro-Turner speeches. Public opinion polls recorded steep gains for the Liberals and precipitous losses for the Conservatives. Environics, the polling organization used by the *Globe and Mail,* quickly proclaimed the Liberals to be in first place with the prospect of winning a majority.[41] In Quebec, the old tribal voting question was raised: if the rest of Canada appeared to be going back to the Grits, would Quebec swing behind Turner in order to remain on the winning side?

In his exchange with Mulroney, Turner did more than just reverse his standing in the polls. He succeeded in transforming a normal election campaign into a virtual referendum. The millions of upbeat pamphlets distributed by the government in praise of free trade had not satisfied the public, 70 percent of whom wanted more concrete information about the deal. A Gallup poll released on October 25, showed widespread public support for a debate devoted solely to the issue of free trade.[42] Turner had finally managed to wrest control of the campaign agenda from the Conservatives and turn it to the one issue on which he was the most credible leader. The question now became whether he could maintain the referendum atmosphere for the campaign's remaining four weeks.

Advertising As the Ultimate Weapon

When Gallup announced on November 7 that the Liberals had leaped to 43 percent in the polls while the Conservatives had fallen to 31 percent and the NDP to 22 percent, Liberal insiders knew that their chances of pulling off an electoral upset had actually diminished. Not only were these figures out of line with what their own pollster, Martin Goldfarb, was reporting – the Liberals and Conservatives were running neck and neck – they set the Liberals up to appear to be losing rather than gaining momentum once more accurate polls were published, as they were on November 10 when Environics showed the Liberals and Conservatives at 37 and 35 percent.

Worse still for the Liberals, Turner's triumph in the debates and the apparent Liberal leap in the polls shocked both the Conservatives and their business allies out of their complacency. The Conservative strategists decided they had to go for broke. They unleashed their leader, Brian Mulroney, his trade negotiator, Simon Reisman, and his senior economic ministers, John Crosbie and Michael Wilson, in a campaign of political attacks that branded Turner a liar and even a traitor. The eminent Justice Emmett Hall was persuaded to issue a statement that Canada's public health care system would not be jeopardized by the trade deal.[43] The Tories cancelled their bland and ineffectual commercials in favour of a counterattack that took a leaf from George H.W. Bush's contemporaneous campaign for the US presidency. South of the border, the Republicans were proving that vicious ads could persuade the public if they were repeated frequently enough. Since the TV advertising time allocated to the governing party was far greater than the quotas for the other parties, and since the Tories had plenty of money left in their campaign war chest, they were able quickly to order a television commercial onslaught aimed at "bombing the bridge" – destroying John Turner's reputation and credibility.

At the same time, the Conservatives' allies in the business community swung into action. In 1983, the Canada Elections Act had been amended with Bill C-169, forbidding any "election advertising by citizens or groups"[44] for fear that a disproportionate amount of money would be spent by third parties in campaigns. In 1984, the Alberta Court of Appeal determined that such constraining of citizen spending infringed the right to free speech enshrined in the Charter of Rights and Freedoms and was therefore unconstitutional.[45] Taking advantage of this ruling, corporate Canada poured millions of dollars into advertising to defend free trade.[46] Spending by business in favour of the Free Trade Agreement in the 1988 election was estimated at $13 million, "the largest lobbying and public relations effort in Canadian history."[47] At the core of the pro-free-trade campaign was the Canadian Alliance for Trade and Job Opportunities (CATJO), which reported $5.24 million ($7.35 million in 2002 dollars) in election spending.[48] Corporate donations to the trade lobby far exceeded companies' political donations. Canadian Pacific donated $74,300 ($104,243) to the Conservatives, $79,500 ($111,539) to the Liberals, and $250,000 ($350,750) to CATJO in order to support free trade. Imperial Oil made no contributions to political parties but contributed $259,000 ($363,377) to the trade alliance. Other companies that donated over $200,000 to CATJO included Alcan Aluminum, Shell Canada, Noranda, and the Royal Bank.[49] Some firms extended their campaign to the workplace by pressing their employees to vote Tory, even suggesting their jobs were at stake.[50]

A final category of non-party spending during the election campaign included advertising by government departments. Since the Progressive Conservatives were in power, they were able to use the public relations budget of the Department of External Affairs to publicize the putative virtues of free trade. Government ministries are perceived as separate from the governing party, and therefore the estimated $24 million ($33.7 million) they spent on advertising during the campaign was not regulated as part of the Conservative campaign, even though every word and image favouring free trade was boosting the Tories' chances.[51] Faced with this sustained barrage by superior firepower, John Turner proved unable to stay the course by playing a lethal David to the free trade Goliath. Rejecting advice that he should supplement his flag-waving attacks on free trade by explaining his alternative solution, he kept to his one-dimensional line that Canada's survival was at risk. Turner carried on his single-issue campaign in an emotional bubble while infighting broke out among his staff. He strongly rejected the idea of retaliating with a "negative" response to the commercials that the Tories unleashed, and he disallowed a plan for a mass rally in Toronto's Maple

Leaf Gardens, but he was indecisive in explaining what he would do instead. As the last two weeks of the campaign ground on, he still failed to broaden his attack beyond its narrow, one-note range. With the leader's national campaign faltering and the party's standing sinking at the rate of 1 percent per day, Liberal riding campaigns reaped the whirlwind Turner had sown during the previous four years, when he had failed to restructure his party.

The Results: Redemption through Referendum

When the first results came in from Atlantic Canada on election night, Liberals could hardly contain their joy. A breakthrough in the Maritimes, where they almost tripled their seats from seven to twenty, seemed momentarily to prove the wisdom of Turner's return to the King/St. Laurent model of the decentralized party. In Newfoundland and Nova Scotia, healthy provincial organizations had been able to capitalize on Turner's articulation of the region's concerns about the impact of free trade. In New Brunswick, where the provincial Liberals had recently won all the seats in the legislature, Premier Frank McKenna had gone one step further. His organization had responded to Turner's call for help by taking over the federal Liberal campaign lock, stock, and barrel. Camille Thériault, a member of the provincial legislature, was made chair of a campaign committee that consisted of exactly the same people who had run and won the provincial campaign in the fall of 1987. With McKenna personally making the major campaign decisions, this group had raised money, recruited candidates, and activated riding organizations, all to telling effect. The Liberals won five of the province's ten seats. In Prince Edward Island, the federal Liberals were overwhelmed with assistance from Premier Joe Ghiz's troops.

The positive results in the Atlantic provinces were the exception, as the returns from central and western Canada soon showed. By the end of the evening, the Conservatives had won 169 seats and 43 percent of the popular vote, the Liberals 83 seats and 32 percent of the vote, and the NDP 43 seats and 20 percent of the vote.[52]

From the electorate's point of view, 1988 was an issues-based election. Those citing the party as the most important factor influencing their voting decision were more likely to mention an issue rather than refer to the party's "general approach to government" as the reason for their choice; and even for those declaring leadership as most important, over 70 percent said that the leader's issue positions, rather than his "personal qualities," motivated their choice.[53]

With free trade dominating the campaign, it is no surprise that 82 percent cited the FTA as the most important issue, followed by social issues and the environment, which were each cited by only 2 percent of the voters.[54] Among voters who switched their intentions because of free trade, the pattern worked against the PCs, with 8 percent switching to the Liberals and 5 percent toward the NDP – compared to 5.5 percent for the Tories.[55]

As the Conservatives received only 43 percent of the popular vote, opponents of free trade have argued that 57 percent of Canadians voted against the proposed deal with the United States.[56] The authors of *Absent Mandate* determined, however, that "the pool of those who were motivated to vote because of free trade was split almost evenly, with 15.6 percent voting Conservative and 16.3 percent voting for either the Liberals or the NDP," which indicates that "no policy mandate for the Free Trade Agreement emerged from the voting in the 1988 Canadian federal election."[57]

Leader personality effects were unusually low in the 1988 election, being cited substantially less often as the most important factor motivating voters than in any recent election (see Table 10).[58] Mulroney's leadership edge was insignificant in comparison to 1984. Indeed, all of the leaders' popularity standings had reached a nadir, with Turner becoming the least popular Canadian leader in twenty years.[59]

The debates played a crucial role. While supporters of all the parties were willing to admit that Turner won the debates, the resulting surge in the polls did not translate into any long-term gains for the Liberals.[60] It did, however, increase the morale in the party at the campaign's mid-point by drawing support away from the NDP and by threatening to change the course of the election.[61] The effects were not lasting because the voters "were influenced by the arguments presented on either side, first by those of the anti-free-trade camp and later by those of its opponents."[62] The debates reinforced the existing impression that the electors held of the leaders' characters. Turner's nationalistic stance produced a short-lived bandwagon effect in Quebec; it also led to strategic voting outside Quebec, "which effectively rendered the New Democratic effort impotent and insured a Tory victory on the plurality split of the vote."[63] While there

Table 10

Effects of party leaders in the 1988 federal election

Leader personality as most important factor in voting decision (voting pattern)	Liberal (%)	PC (%)	NDP (%)
Switch to	0.2	0.5	0.8
Remain	0.6	1.8	0.5
Enter/re-enter	–	0.2	–
Total	0.8	2.5	1.3

Note: Percentage of voting electorate.
Source: Harold D. Clarke, Lawrence LeDuc, Jane Jenson, and Jon H. Pammett, *Absent Mandate: Interpreting Change in Canadian Elections*, 2nd ed. (Toronto: Gage, 1991), 137, table 7.5.

were considerable movements in opinion and vote intentions over the course of the campaign, it appeared ultimately that the campaign had made no difference: the distribution of vote intentions among committed voters in the last days of the campaign closely resembled that of existing partisan identification at the outset.[64]

Although the Conservatives retained a majority of the seats, both opposition parties gained support from dissatisfied Conservative voters from the 1984 election switching to the Liberals and the NDP. Overall, 7.9 percent of those who had voted Conservative in 1984 switched to the Liberals, while 4 percent of Tory voters from 1984 defected to the NDP (see Table 11). By contrast, only 4.7 percent and 1.5 percent of Liberal and New Democratic voters from 1984 switched to the Tories in 1988.[65] The gender gap in Conservative support rose from 3 percent to 9 percent, with women who were moving away from the Conservatives more likely to end up with the NDP than the Liberals.[66]

The Conservatives were far more successful in courting new voters than either of their rivals, capturing the support of 41 percent of them, compared to 28 percent for the Liberals and 29 percent for the NDP.[67] A more attractive Liberal leader would have likely produced very different results with first-time voters, both because new voters in 1988 identified more with the Liberal Party than with any other, and because they were more hostile to free trade than any other voter cohort.[68] Unfortunately for the Liberals, however, John Turner was also more unpopular with new voters than with any other segment of the elector-

Table 11

Vote switching between the 1984 and 1988 federal elections

	1988				
1984	PC (%)	Liberal (%)	NDP (%)	Other (%)	Did not vote (%)
PC	33.2	7.9	4.2	2.5	3.2
Liberal	4.7	13.7	1.9	0.7	2.0
NDP	1.5	2.0	10.0	0.2	0.5
Other	1.0	0.2	0.3	0.4	0.2
Did not vote	2.2	2.1	1.1	0.4	3.8
					100.0

Note: The entire table adds to 100 percent. Individual rows or columns do not.
Source: 1988 re-interview of 1984 National Election Study sample; Harold D. Clarke, Lawrence LeDuc, Jane Jenson, and Jon H. Pammett, *Absent Mandate: Interpreting Change in Canadian Elections*, 2nd ed. (Toronto: Gage, 1991), 134, table 7.3.

ate.[69] As Jon Pammett remarked, leadership, "while not looming large in an overall interpretation of the 1988 election, did play an important role in drying up a possible reservoir of Liberal votes and salvaging them for the Conservatives."[70]

Another factor working against the Liberals was the participation of Robert Bourassa, the Liberal premier of Quebec, on what for them was the wrong side of the federal election campaign. Bourassa had several motivations. Partly it was to repay Prime Minister Mulroney for securing the Meech Lake Accord on the constitution, which accepted his demand for Quebec's recognition as a distinct society. Partly it was gratitude for the massive amounts of federal money that had poured into Quebec since 1984. Partly it was to defend the free trade agreement, which was strongly supported by Quebec's business community, opinion leaders, and political elite as a godsend for the province's economy.[71]

While Bourassa could take much of the credit for the federal Liberals' worst Quebec defeat in their history, Turner deserved much of the blame for letting his fortunes in Quebec depend on its premier's whims. Back in 1984, Turner had deliberately repudiated Trudeau's federalist legacy of resisting both separatism and neo-federalism. Though forced to make some "clarifications" vis-à-vis the Quebec situation in an attempt to mollify the Trudeauites, Turner had remained a consistent supporter of provincial rights. In 1987 he had believed assurances by Raymond Garneau, his Quebec lieutenant and finance critic, that Bourassa would reward Turner's present political support for the Meech Lake Accord with future electoral support. Having failed to rebuild a federal party apparatus in Quebec, even though his party president, Michel Robert, was a Quebecker, Turner left himself with no option should his strategy fail. Without an effective organization of its own, the federal Liberals in Quebec went down like ninepins, with even Garneau falling victim to the Tory sweep. Contrary to some analysts' view that Turner misread the country by not playing the unity card, national unity was a losing issue for the Liberals in Quebec, just as it was in the rest of Canada.

It was understandable that Turner's anti-free-trade position harmed the Liberals in Quebec, where all but the major trade and farmers' unions favoured the FTA. It was less clear why the provincial Liberal Party in Ontario proved incapable of delivering even half of Ontario's seats. Certainly Premier David Peterson offered considerable moral support to the federal leader during the campaign. He cut short a trade-promotion trip to Asia to campaign for a number of federal candidates – in particular his own brother, Jim, who was running in the Toronto riding of Willowdale. He invited John Turner to a well-publicized meeting with his caucus, whose members campaigned actively for their federal counterparts. But the Queen's Park Liberals did not make up for the inadequacies of the federal party's weak organization, even though many of them were seconded to bolster its staff.

While various factors, such as the nomination imbroglios, which gave the electorate the impression of a party riven with conflict, can be cited in explaining the Liberals' poor showing in central Canada, it can also be argued that no organization could have withstood the sustained punishment the Liberal leader had to take from the NDP on the left and the alliance of big business and the Conservative Party on the right in the closing weeks of the campaign. In an age of TV politics, it would have taken a brilliant political performance by the leader, as well as impeccable organization, for the Liberals to withstand the combination of negative news reports (Ed Broadbent attacking John Turner's credibility) and negative commercials (Conservative ads impugning Turner's integrity). In the end, the Liberal campaign of 1988 faltered after a weak beginning and an astonishingly strong middle period. The organization required to squeeze the extra few hundred votes it needed in every riding was simply not there.

Liberal gains in Manitoba did show that a strong regional figure in the person of Lloyd Axworthy could successfully affect a local campaign. The federal party also profited from the provincial Liberals' electoral success earlier that year: the five seats the Grits won on November 21 were all in the city of Winnipeg, where the provincial Liberals had just made an electoral breakthrough. Further west, the pathetically weak provincial organizations could hardly have done much to bolster the federal Liberals. The West's alienation from the Liberal Party, which began in the 1950s, was so entrenched by the 1980s that it was hard to imagine what strategy could reap an electoral harvest from such barren political soil.

With more money, more experience, and better organization than the Turner camp, the Progressive Conservatives' campaign was a testimonial to media management and the effective use of polls and advertising to identify and then attack their opponent's weaknesses.[72]

As the Liberals shifted in 1989 from electoral post-mortems to renewing their leadership after John Turner announced on May 3 that he would step down as party leader, two somewhat contradictory conclusions were drawn about his time at the helm of the Liberal Party. On the one hand, it was thought that he could retire with honour, ennobled by having fought free trade with tenacity in what he himself called the cause of his life. On the other hand, he was seen as likely to go down in Liberal annals as the man who single-handedly brought his party to the brink of disaster, then twice led it over the edge. It was too late to point out the danger of trying to return to the formulae of the golden age of Liberalism, given that permanently changed conditions made the past impossible to replicate. It was still too early to tell whether internal factionalism would become linked with provincial regionalism in a syndrome that would perpetuate the federal Liberals' new loser-party status.

The tragedy of John Turner lay in his inability to comprehend the nature of the political change that had engulfed him. While losing the Liberal Party's century-long hold on Quebec, he had failed to rebuild its base in the West. Business lawyer though he had been, he even managed to deepen his party's alienation from the business community that had begun under Lester Pearson and worsened steadily under Pierre Trudeau. He had not even been able to convince broad sections of his own party that free trade was fatal for his beloved Canada. Having achieved a personal redemption – the courage he showed in the campaign was everywhere admired – he left his party disoriented in defeat.

Jean Chrétien
Power without Purpose

Yesterday's Man and His Blue Grits: Backwards into Jean Chrétien's Future

While Jean Chrétien had been "first in the hearts" of the delegates who chose John Turner as party leader in 1984, he was far from being the sentimental favourite when he finally achieved his long-standing ambition to lead the Liberal Party of Canada at its June 1990 convention.[1] The little-guy-from-Shawinigan-turned-corporate-lawyer may have had a superior organization and sounder finances, but his rival contenders had stolen the limelight during the 1990 leadership campaign. Sheila Copps, the politically dynamic daughter of a former mayor of Hamilton, had wowed Quebec Liberals with her bilingual support for the constitutional recognition of Quebec's distinctiveness. Paul Martin, son of the eponymous Mackenzie King-era social reform minister from Windsor, was the preferred choice of the business communities of Montreal and Toronto, thanks to the blessing of his mentor, Paul Desmarais of Power Corporation, and his successful record as CEO of Canada Steamship Lines. Where Copps and Martin had proven articulate rivals, one slightly to the left and the other slightly to the right of the ample Liberal middle, Chrétien appeared to have lost his grip on the policies, unable to express either values or ideas. Like Turner before him, he had managed, while working in the private sector as leader-in-waiting, to lose his appeal with English Canada and, worst of all, with his own province.

After almost thirty years of dogged service in the Liberal Party, the gold that Chrétien finally grasped turned to dross on the very day of his election to the leadership, June 23, which was also the deadline for the provinces to ratify the Meech Lake Accord. In 1987 Prime Minister Brian Mulroney and the ten provincial premiers had struck an agreement at Meech Lake in order to bring Quebec into the 1982 Constitution with "honour and dignity." The accord was controversial for the restraints it placed on Ottawa's ability to use its "spending power" in areas of provincial jurisdiction and for giving provinces a role in selecting senators and Supreme Court justices. But no provision proved more divisive amongst Liberal partisans and ordinary Canadians alike than Meech's recognition of Quebec as a "distinct society" within Canada.

Hoping to win support for their leadership bids in Quebec, candidates Martin and Copps threw their support behind Meech from the outset of their campaigns and spoke clearly in favour of recognizing Quebec as a distinct society. Chrétien, on the other hand, was stubborn in his opposition to the deal, following Pierre Trudeau's lead in condemning the "distinct society" notion as antithetical to his absolutist "a province is a province is a province" conception of Canada. As the country fell deeper into crisis and the deadline for Meech's ratification approached, Chrétien began to have second thoughts about opposing a deal that might lay Quebec's discontents to rest. Early in June, he expressed his hope that the accord would be ratified, even as he continued to call for changes to it in his public statements. He seriously undermined his credibility in his home province by remaining undecided during the final, frenzied days of federal-provincial negotiations to ratify Meech. Finally, on the stage of the national convention in Calgary where he had just been elected leader, he hugged Clyde Wells, the Newfoundland premier who had just killed the accord by refusing to submit it to his legislature.

The repercussions from this provocative gesture were immediate. Two members of his parliamentary caucus, Jean Lapierre and Gilles Rocheleau, branded Chrétien a traitor and quit the party before the convention even adjourned in order to join Lucien Bouchard, the Chicoutimi lawyer who had himself quit Brian Mulroney's cabinet to establish a dissident Bloc Québécois of sovereigntist MPs.[2] The once-popular "p'tit gars de Shawinigan" had become a pariah in his home province. Francophone Quebeckers shunned his outstretched hand in airport cafeterias and accosted him with insults in the street.

Chrétien's trauma as an outcast in his own society was partly linked to his party's ideological divisions. Squaring Trudeau's hard line on the constitution with Quebec's demands for greater powers was far from being Chrétien's only policy dilemma. The question of free trade had left the party deeply divided since John Turner had fought the 1988 election promising to tear up the Canada-United States Free Trade Agreement (FTA), even though many in his party supported further continental economic integration. Equally difficult was bridging the gap between the party's "business Liberals," whose top priority was reducing the federal deficit, and its "welfare Liberals" who wanted to maintain universal social-welfare programs at any budgetary cost. On breaking issues such as George H.W. Bush's Gulf War against Saddam Hussein, Chrétien was split within himself, reversing positions often enough to become a national joke.

Without a seat in the House of Commons for six months after his election as leader, Chrétien seemed to be in shock and to have lost his fabled common touch. His handlers gave him long speeches to read from a teleprompter, suppressing the spontaneity and folksy humour that had once been his endearing hallmarks. Unable to communicate either his own ideas or those of his staff and refusing to take voice lessons to improve his delivery, he appeared completely incapable of projecting to the public a Liberal alternative to what many party activists considered to be Brian Mulroney's implacably neoconservative agenda – devastating the industrial sector via the FTA, shifting the tax burden from corporations to individuals with the Goods and Services Tax (GST), "downloading" the responsibilities of the federal state to the provinces, and curtailing its social services via spending cuts. With their new leader appearing so weak at the starting blocks, Copps and Martin kept their organizations at the ready in case a Chrétien collapse or a caucus coup should precipitate another leadership contest. Personal tensions between Copps and Martin, between Chrétien and Copps, and between Martin and Chrétien kept the rivals' supporters in the party continually at odds. Although the 1988 election had more than doubled the size of the Liberal caucus from forty to eighty-three, morale among its members was low.

Having been out of power for almost six years by the time the leadership convention to replace John Turner took place in 1990, the Liberals seemed to have developed a losing-party syndrome, a set of self-perpetuating characteristics that had caused it to blow the previous two elections: weak leadership, debilitating factionalism, policy confusion, and organizational disarray.[3]

Filling the Leader of the Opposition's Office (LOO) with loyalists such as Eddie Goldenberg, Chrétien's personal adviser of long standing, did little to sweep out Turner's old disorder. The LOO remained in an organizational uproar. The extra-parliamentary wing, which had not been revitalized by Turner, was not reanimated by his successor either. The party's debt of several million dollars remained on the books because business was so in thrall with the Mulroney government's American-style conservatism that the Liberals' entrepreneurial friends had not been able to raise the kind of corporate cash needed to return the party to solvency. The vicious circle created by these mutually aggravating factors was perpetuated by a press gallery for whom Chrétien had become "almost a non-person, written off by many and ignored by the rest."[4] It was not only passionate Quebec nationalists who had bolted the party in disgust. Two respected policy activists – the lobbyist Rick Anderson and the political scientist Blair Williams – also quit, in their case to join Preston Manning's emerging right-wing Reform Party. With such substantial figures abandoning ship, a wreck seemed imminent.

The Pre-Campaign: Subverting the Syndrome

Two and a half years later, by January 1993, Chrétien was still not taken seriously, but his party was nevertheless poised to win office. Not only had Mulroney made himself and his government irremediably unpopular; Chrétien had made significant progress in turning each of his liabilities into assets. He recruited his old friend Jean Pelletier, the former mayor of Quebec City, to take charge of the

LOO. At the same time, three other Liberals were brought in to burnish Chrétien's image and bolster his policy positions. Peter Donolo, a bright and energetic young Liberal, was put in charge of communications; Jean Carle, a convert from the Turner camp, was made director of organization. Chaviva Hošek, a former president of the National Action Committee on the Status of Women (NAC) and a former Ontario minister of housing in David Peterson's government, was taken on to direct the party's policy research. A professional management team was hired to bring the party's debt under control and reassure its creditors. Old loyalists such as John Rae, executive vice-president of Desmarais's Power Corporation, remained in the background, ready to manage the leader's campaign. Young loyalists such as Dominic LeBlanc, son of Trudeau's regional minister for New Brunswick and future governor general, Roméo LeBlanc, remained active in the party, and senior caucus members André Ouellet and Senator Joyce Fairbairn were named co-chairs of the planning committee for the next election.

In 1988, the appointment of a new president and a new chief financial officer for the party had brought about some much-needed changes in its budgetary affairs. National headquarters was given exclusive use of revenue from corporate donations solicited by the revenue committee, nation-wide direct mail, the Laurier Club, and the leader's dinners. The provincial and territorial associations (PTAs) and ridings were assigned local sources, such as door-to-door canvassing, smaller businesses, local events, and local direct mail.[5] With less financial overlap between national headquarters, the PTAs, and riding associations, each division was better motivated to seek out its own donations.

Although its finances were improving, the party was still $3.8 million ($4.4 million in 2002 dollars) in debt when Jean Chrétien became leader.[6] The situation was not helped by the $10.85 million ($12.68 million) spent by candidates during the leadership race to succeed John Turner. The party's 1991 reform commission concluded that the problems that began following the passage of the Canada Expenses Act in 1974 were still present: "decreasing level of funds ... and dependence of the Party on corporations."[7] The party's problems were relative, though: by 1993 the Liberal Party had the lowest deficit of the three major parties.[8]

"All parties need money," Jean Chrétien was to say in 1993, and never more so than during an election campaign.[9] "It is possible to lose with money, [but] it is impossible to win without it."[10] With order re-established in the parliamentary party, Chrétien quietly courted the business community with the short-term goal of getting its cash and the longer-term goal of gaining its confidence. Corporate contributions increased 12 percent in 1992 to $8 million, while, significantly, donations to the Progressive Conservatives fell slightly.[11]

Before forking over their cash to the Liberal Party, however, business, like other potential supporters, wanted to know where it stood on the major issues.

To provide an answer, Chrétien put Hošek in charge of a process to redefine the party's ideology, starting with a thinkers' conference on the model of the Liberals' famous Kingston meeting of leading intellectuals in 1960, which had helped Lester Pearson work his way back to power.[12] Held in Aylmer, Quebec, in November 1991, the weekend seminar was designed to infuse the party's policy activists with intellectual substance. The roster of speakers was ideologically balanced, from the alarmists on the right, who emphasized the country's economic straits, to the activist left, who called for a reaffirmation of the welfare state and its cultural institutions. The overall message lay somewhere to the left of centre, as defined by Lester Thurow of the Massachusetts Institute of Technology: government had to be active in the new age of tougher global competition.[13] The media saw the conference as sending the "clear message that the Liberal Party had put its welfare-statism and nationalism behind it," citing as evidence such pronouncements of Chrétien's as "the old concepts of right and left do not apply to the world of today and tomorrow," and "protectionism is not right-wing or left-wing; it is simply passé."[14] The Chrétien party was not going to resist globalization but embrace it, and such left-leaning nationalists as Lloyd Axworthy would have to concur or quit.[15]

Whereas the party leadership was signalling to business that the high-spending days of the Trudeau era were over, delegates who came to debate policy at the party's biennial convention in April 1992 seemed to be cut from the same left-Liberal cloth as their predecessors. Apart from a few off-the-wall resolutions (oxygen was to be recognized as an exportable resource for countries with tropical rain forests), the consensus on social policy questions was decidedly left of centre. On constitutional reform it reflected Copps's and Martin's neo-federalist views with a nine-point position that accepted the recognition of Quebec's distinct-society status.[16] To get more feedback, Chaviva Hošek toured the country twice with Paul Martin and consulted party activists on proposed Liberal policies for the next campaign.[17] By July 1992, a binder of two dozen papers – reflecting key ideas from the Aylmer meeting, the convention, the caucus's own policy committees, and the party activists consulted by Hošek – had been readied to introduce newly nominated candidates to the Liberals' positions.

Attracting good candidates was critical. The recruitment process within the Liberal Party had come under intense pressure in the 1980s, particularly in urban areas where ethnic groups had learned how to capture riding nominations by mobilizing thousands of their community members. The bitterness of many nomination fights and the damaging allegations made by the losers had jeopardized the party's capacity to assemble a credible roster of candidates.[18] The ethnic activist who could deliver a nomination did not generally provide the high-profile material Chrétien needed for his cabinet, yet prospective candidates who might have made good ministers were repelled by the prospect of

waging nomination campaigns that could cost tens of thousands of dollars, require many months of slogging, and still offer little assurance of success.

In contrast to Turner's passivity in the face of this dilemma, Chrétien took
decisive action. The party amended its constitution at its 1992 convention to
give the national campaign committee (appointed by the leader) carte blanche
to "adopt and publish rules regarding the procedures to be followed in the nominations of candidates."[19] Using – some felt abusing – this authority, Chrétien's
provincial campaign chairs exercised draconian control over the nomination
process, sometimes recommending that the leader impose a candidate over the
heads of a constituency's rank and file. At the cost of considerable unhappiness
on the part of aspirants who were shouldered aside, Chrétien's people helped
position prominent citizens in winnable ridings across the country. Six women
were appointed as candidates, along with stars such as Art Eggleton, former mayor
of Toronto; Douglas Peters, retiring vice-president and chief economist of the
Toronto-Dominion Bank; Anne McLellan, former dean of the University of
Alberta law school; Robert Blair, president of Nova Corporation; Marcel Massé,
former senior federal civil servant; and Michel Dupuy, a former ambassador.
Once the press gallery had duly rapped Chrétien on the knuckles for his anti-
democratic propensities, it proceeded to take note of the Liberal team's high
quality and then to take the party's chances more seriously.[20]

In courting the female vote, the Liberal Party had taken affirmative action
steps in the early 1990s, guaranteeing that women would be co-chairs of important national policy committees, including the National Campaign Committee,
which established guidelines for candidate selection.[21] Although two other parties had female leaders in 1993, most "feminists" did not view either Conservative leader Kim Campbell or NDP leader Audrey McLaughlin as politicians who
represented the aspirations of their movement. Judy Rebick, president of NAC,
said at the time of Campbell's election as PC leader that "women like [Campbell]
are going to become our most bitter opponent,"[22] while Rebick's successor as
NAC president, Sunera Thobani, told reporters that the NDP was ignoring the
concerns of women just as the Liberals and Conservatives were.[23] The NDP nominated far more women (113) than any other party in 1993, but only one, the
leader, was successfully elected.[24] Of the fifty-three women elected to the House
of Commons, thirty-six would be Liberals.[25]

Opinion polls, which consistently showed the Progressive Conservatives at
historic lows and their leader even more unpopular, were a tonic for Liberal
solidarity. Dissension among the MPs declined. In contrast to Turner, Chrétien
had proven a healer in caucus, more ready to listen to his colleagues, better able
to sustain their morale and to delegate responsibility. Copps and Martin now
sublimated their ambitions, partly because they had been co-opted by the leader –

Copps was made deputy leader, and Martin co-chair of the platform committee – and partly because self-interest dictated that they present a united front to win power and so have a shot at the leadership next time round. Chrétien made André Ouellet, a former opponent as Turner's supporter, his key constitutional spokesman, representing the federal Liberals on the Bourassa government's Bélanger-Campeau commission of inquiry on constitutional affairs and the Mulroney government's similar Beaudoin-Dobbie commission.

Notwithstanding these moves, and his very vocal support for the failed 1992 Charlottetown Accord that attempted to redress Quebec's constitutional grievances, Chrétien's home province remained hostile territory. With no social base in the province left to the party – big business, labour unions, and new social movements found their allegiances elsewhere – it was extremely difficult for Ouellet to recruit high-quality candidates. Premier Robert Bourassa maintained close ties with the Mulroney regime, and the francophone media continued to treat Chrétien as a pariah.

Beyond Quebec, Chrétien's major liability in early 1993 was his low credibility as a leader. He had turned inward, stricken by a health crisis (requiring a difficult lung operation) and a family disaster (his adopted son, an Aboriginal, was found guilty of sexual assault after a painfully long trial). But as the months passed, his confidence gradually rose. With Margaret Thatcher ousted in the UK and George Bush on the run in the United States, the neoconservative wave of the 1980s was demonstrably receding. Chrétien withdrew as much as he could from the public eye so that the Tories would have no target to attack while they concentrated on the process of their own self-destruction. When the electorate rejected Mulroney's Charlottetown Accord in the referendum held on October 26, 1992, it looked as though victory was assured for the Liberals with their 28 percent lead in the opinion polls.

Within weeks, however, the Liberals' best-laid waiting game seemed to have come to naught. In February 1993, Mulroney announced his resignation, and the Conservatives quickly rallied round Kim Campbell, a dazzling political newcomer who was not just a feisty intellectual from the West but a forty-something woman of Bill Clinton's generation, able to champion Mulroney's policies while distinguishing herself from Mulroney's persona.

Even at Campbell's moment of triumph in June 1993, when she became party leader and prime minister, the Progressive Conservatives stood at only 21 percent in the polls, compared to the Liberals' 43 percent. The disapproval rating for the GST remained almost 80 percent, opposition to free trade was over 50 percent, dissatisfaction with the federal government stood at 75 percent, consumer confidence was low, and feelings about the economy were bad.[26] Canadians hated the PCs and liked the Liberal Party, but they loved Campbell and had more negative than positive feelings about Chrétien. The Liberal leader's challenge was to change public rejection of the Conservative record into support for himself, the least popular of the party leaders.

When Kim Campbell launched her summer prime ministership by courting photo opportunities at PC barbecues from coast to coast and eclipsing the Liberals in the media, Chrétien kept his nerve, waiting for her honeymoon to end and the real campaign to begin. He would then have a chance to challenge the Progressive Conservatives on a level electoral playing field. Showing a new resolution, he rallied his caucus by chiding its more anxious members as "nervous Nellies" and set off to try out his campaign technique in British Columbia, where the local media operated independently of the national news services.

Gaffes, Goofs, and Godsends: The Battle of the News Clips

The shape of the election campaign was visible from its first day, September 8, when Prime Minister Campbell, in conceding that employment rates were unlikely to improve before "the turn of the century,"[27] offered Chrétien a foil for his main message: "For us, the goal is to create jobs in 1993, right now, and we'll start in November."[28] The pattern had been set: Campbell would make a gaffe that she would be forced to correct, thereby giving Chrétien the chance to make an immediate, often humorous reply that would transmit his message of hope.

The Liberal game plan for the news media was modelled on the Democrats' 1992 presidential campaign in the United States, in which Republican communications were closely monitored in a "war room," enabling Governor Bill Clinton to respond nearly instantaneously to President Bush's statements. A high-tech Liberal war room of half a dozen led by Warren Kinsella monitored the Tory campaign.[29] At 5 p.m. on September 23, to take one example, the Kinsella team alerted Peter Donolo that Campbell had said, "You can't have a debate on such a key issue as the modernization of social programs in forty-seven days."[30] He faxed the wire story to the Liberals' press room in Vancouver so that the reporters covering Chrétien there could attend his impromptu news conference in time for the evening news and hear him respond, "In my judgment it is almost contemptuous. It's not [showing] a great respect for the electorate."[31] When the Conservatives unveiled their first commercial slogan, "It's time," Chrétien appeared on TV news the same night crowing, "It's a fantastic slogan. Yes, it's time for a change. It's time to get the truth. It's time to throw them out." In the face of this derision, the commentator reported, "The Conservatives may find it's time to change their slogan."[32]

Chrétien enhanced the impact of his campaign by making fun of the Conservatives without attacking them in the aggressively partisan style with which, according to the party's pollster, the Canadian public had become increasingly disenchanted. Rather than denouncing Conservative policies, Chrétien would hold up an empty blue binder in a mocking gesture that suggested to his audience that the Conservative campaign had no substance. When Campbell waffled over the government's bookkeeping methods, Chrétien jumped on this as proof that her government's books were in a mess.[33] When Campbell tried to escape Mulroney's shadow, he feigned sympathy: "Poor Brian. Just think how disappointed he must be that the woman he took and made her prime minister won't even mention his name. What ingratitude! But don't worry, Brian, I won't let people forget you."[34] Attacking the Conservative decision to buy helicopters for sophisticated antisubmarine warfare, he wondered if they were designed "to protect us against North Koreans coming up the St. Lawrence."[35]

Marketing Integrity: The Strategy of the Plan

When Chrétien said, "It will be like the good old days. Canadians will be working again,"[36] some commentators felt he had made a major mistake, calling attention to his weakness – his unflattering label as "yesterday's man." But his appeal to nostalgia at a time of economic distress and political anomie was deliberate. The old days had been better days for most Canadians. For those who could remember them, the Keynesian 1960s and 1970s had been decades of increasing prosperity and economic security.

Unveiling a political manifesto on Day 8 of the campaign was old-fashioned, equally deliberate, and equally risky. When Turner attempted this in 1988, the strategy had proved disastrous, but Chrétien's advisers knew from their polling and focus group analysis that the public was more skeptical than it had ever been of all politicians, their self-serving motives, and their unkept promises.[37] Remembering the fiasco of Turner's inadequately prepared positions, they had instructed Hošek to turn her policy material into a coherent campaign platform with each promise carefully costed. The 1993 document, *Creating Opportunity: The Liberal Plan for Canada,* was more than just a detailed presentation of the party position. It was a brilliant prop – unveiled by Chrétien at a press conference broadcast live on CBC Newsworld.[38] For a leader who was short on intellectual agility but long on political experience, the document signalled – as the leader repeated ad nauseam in TV interviews and on the hustings – that he was the man with a plan. He told voters they could accost him at any time after the election and ask which of the promises he had kept. The document had been professionally edited with the kind of graphics and sidebars more typical of a sleek corporate report than a partisan campaign document. The media covering its release were briefed at a "lock up," a session that gave reporters enough time to appreciate the high quality of the research and careful budgeting between its glossy covers. Once the figures and the logic had proved to be solid, the implicit messages of what quickly came to be known as the "Red Book" were that the Liberals were competent and the party was accountable.

Beyond its symbolic value, the platform positioned the Liberal Party flexibly on a middle ground that appeared responsible in relation to the deficit problem while still appealing to the party's traditional left-of-centre constituency. On the hard, macroeconomic issues, the document took the position developed by Douglas Peters while he was still chief economist at the Toronto-Dominion Bank: the deficit could not be solved by reducing inflation to zero as the Progressive Conservatives and the Bank of Canada's over-zealous governor had insisted, but was related to four other factors – economic growth, employment, interest rates, and the debt – which had to be handled together as a complex whole. As Paul Martin expressed it to a seminar of CBC reporters on September 18, the twin spectres of the national debt and high unemployment could not be traded off one against the other. The root cause of both was the same: the economy had fallen behind. Appearing on a CBC Town Hall debate on September 20, Martin asserted that unemployment and the deficit were caused by economic decline and insisted that "economic growth is not a matter for market forces alone." If the private sector was to be the motor of the economy, government had to play a positive role by reducing the cost of capital through lowering interest rates and inflation. Taxes were not to be used to fight the deficit because companies could not pay more. Monetary policy should not be used to prop up the dollar or to achieve zero inflation, which in reality meant a pernicious deflation of the economy. The role of a Liberal government would be to help change the culture of the private sector, pushing it toward innovation by linking business to university researchers, for example.

Creating Opportunity had two policy ranges to propose. In the short term, funds for housing rehabilitation and a $6 billion infrastructure program – to be launched in co-operation with the provinces and municipalities – would provide immediate economic stimulus and raise consumer and business confidence. In the longer term, the deficit would be reduced by requiring new government projects to cost less than programs that had been cut. The price tag for the infrastructure program, for instance, would be lower than the Conservatives' helicopter program, which would be cancelled. Rejigging the unfair and overly complex GST, enhancing education and job training, introducing a youth service and an apprenticeship program, providing capital for small and medium enterprises where levels of Canadian ownership were high and female participation significant, diffusing innovation through a technology network, and converting military industries to peaceful purposes – these policies rounded out the Liberals' economic policy. Chrétien's personal stamp on the economic platform was its overall prudence: the deficit would be reduced over three years to 3 percent of GNP.

On softer, social-policy issues, the Red Book emphasized the decidedly Liberal values of human dignity, justice, fairness, and opportunity. On the environment, industry was to be greened with rules to address ozone depletion, national parks were to be expanded, and the treaty on the Law of the Sea implemented. When it came to social programs, the platform spoke of a "society of reciprocal obligations in which each of us is responsible for the well-being of the other."[39] Equality of social conditions was the objective. Health care was to remain universal, portable, comprehensive, publicly funded, and publicly administered in keeping with the principles of the Trudeau-era Canada Health Act. Prenatal nutrition programs for expectant mothers living in poverty (an idea taken from former Conservative Finance Minister Michael Wilson's prosperity action plan) addressed both the needs of children and the need to save future medical costs.[40] The public was to be made safe from crime through gun control, a tightening of the Young Offenders Act, and, above all, by alleviating poverty, which had been increased by the Conservatives' cuts in social programs and was presented as a basic cause of crime. Immigration was a dynamic force to be fostered with careful selection programs. Aboriginals were to get "head start" programs and support in achieving self-government. National identity was to be nourished with support for the CBC and cultural development policies.[41] Political institutions would be reformed, starting with Parliament, and lobbying would be brought under public control. Finally, a Liberal foreign policy would emphasize peacekeeping, the United Nations, Canada's sovereignty, and an arm's-length relationship with the United States.

These policies could as easily have been expressed in the 1960s and 1970s by the Pearson/Trudeau party in its more generous moments, but Chrétien's stamp of businesslike caution could be seen on the social policy side with his caveat that the day-care plank was conditional on the economy achieving real growth of 3 percent. His political shrewdness was evident in the omission of constitutional reform proposals from the Liberal platform. Chrétien believed – and his polling confirmed – that the public was sick of constitutional wrangling. Government was central to the Liberal vision, but it would have to live within its means, as it had in the good old Mackenzie King and St. Laurent days of the second party system.

On Day 19 of the campaign, September 26, a major survey by CBC's *Sunday Report* showed the Liberals at 36 percent compared to the Conservatives' 31 percent. The Liberals had achieved the magic quality of momentum.[42] Equally important, the Liberals appeared to be winning control of the agenda. The survey reported a "massive" shift on what the public considered to be the major issue of the election. Now 36 percent believed it to be unemployment, not the deficit, and the Liberals were thought best able to deal with the problem by 32 percent of respondents, compared to the 17 percent who chose the Conservatives. Two obstacles still remained in the Liberals' path. They were in third place in Quebec at 24 percent, compared to 45 percent for the Bloc Québécois and 27 percent for the Conservatives. And 40 percent endorsed Campbell's leadership, compared to 28 percent who favoured Chrétien's. Coping with the leadership question would be the task of the campaign's next phase.

Making the Man Prime Ministerial

On Sunday, October 3, viewers of the French-language debate saw a Chrétien who had given up the brawling ways of his youth. Where Campbell was aggressive, the Liberal tried to stay above the fray. Never interrupting, he appeared calm and low key, turning aside Bloc Québécois leader Lucien Bouchard's attacks on his constitutional position by insisting that the public wanted politicians to focus on creating jobs. He was playing the statesman, a man with dignity enough to pass as prime ministerial. Eventually drawn out on his basic themes, Chrétien gained points when he described himself in an exchange with Lucien Bouchard as a "proud Quebecker, a proud francophone, and a proud Canadian."[43] While journalists were reluctant to declare a winner in the French debates, he benefited from having performed better than expected, thus improving his position slightly.[44]

The next night on English-language television, Chrétien turned in another adequate performance. Although he did not win the debates by being the most articulate, he conveyed his positions with enough coherence to reassure voters – who had long since indicated they wanted to vote Liberal – that he was sound enough to cope with the top job.[45] The research organization Insight Canada found that 36 percent of respondents felt Chrétien gave the best performance in the debates, compared to 9 percent who chose Campbell, placing her fourth out of the five leaders. A significant 20 percent were not impressed with any of the leaders.[46] A week after the debates, 31 percent of the public felt that Chrétien would make the best prime minister, compared to Campbell's 24 percent support.[47] In Quebec, the turnaround was even greater as Chrétien rose from 13 percent to 20 percent, while Campbell fell from 44 to 19 percent.[48]

By this time the Liberals' advertising group, Red Leaf Communications, was airing its commercials. The creative team, consisting mainly of political neophytes working out of Vickers & Benson (a Toronto ad agency with strong Liberal ties), decided to reverse its original, poll-driven strategy of emphasizing the party and hiding Chrétien. Defying the notion that people vote for parties rather than leaders, Red Leaf decided to focus its small budget on commercials that featured Chrétien talking quietly about his policies and reflecting on his campaign: "I have the plan. We will make a difference."[49] These were accompanied by ads fighting his "yesterday's man" tag. Day 2 of the commercial campaign saw him looking vigorous and energetic, talking about job creation, while Day 4 had Chrétien showing the Liberal flag in Quebec.[50]

Although the Liberals were outspent three to one by the Conservatives, Insight Canada's tracking polls indicated that their ads bested their rivals' in effectiveness by a factor of two. A sample of viewers rated Liberal ads better than Conservative ads on several scales: "most interesting," 30 vs. 15 percent; "most believable," 28 vs. 14 percent; "most informative," 28 vs. 16 percent; "make most sense," 32 vs. 17 percent; "deal with issues important to you," 33 vs. 15 percent.[51]

But if Chrétien's image problem had been largely rectified by the end of the fourth week, this was as much due to chance as to his cunning media campaign and Campbell's pratfalls. In large part, Chrétien's luck lay in his timing. He had been dismissed for so long by the national media (one columnist opined, "Chrétien mangles his syntax in both official languages while his words echo the concepts and values of the seventies"[52]) that reporters found themselves compensating for their past condescension.[53] Outstanding facilities provided by the Liberals in their campaign bus helped create a positive mood in the press entourage. Chrétien, whom veteran journalists remembered as affable, communicative, informal, and helpful a decade earlier, turned out to be more accessible than Prime Minister Campbell and more capable, humorous, and likeable as a politician than younger reporters had expected. In contrast to the many scandals they had revealed about the Mulroney regime, they could find no skeleton in Chrétien's closet. They knew that when he had moved into Stornoway, the official residence of the Leader of the Opposition, and found the kitchen cupboards to be bare, he had bought china with his own money. Campbell received substantially more press coverage than Chrétien,[54] but of all the stories written about the Conservatives during the campaign in *La Presse*, the *Globe and Mail*, and the *Toronto Star*, 42 percent were negative, compared with 32 percent being negative for the NDP, and only 26 percent for the Liberals.[55]

After Audrey McLaughlin publicly declared the Liberals would get a majority, further boosting the Grits' momentum, Chrétien seemed to lead a charmed life. Every tactic the Conservatives employed served only to boost his popularity, including the commercials that played on his facial deformity and which produced an immediate outcry: "One of the two ads aired combined close-up photographs of Chrétien focused on the partially paralyzed left side of his face ... while off-screen voices described his job-creation policy as a joke, suggested he wasn't with it, had lost touch with reality, and so on. The last voice on this ad said: 'I personally would be very embarrassed if he were to become prime minister of Canada.'"[56] In the 1988 election, that kind of negative advertising would scarcely have raised an eyebrow. After four more years of politics characterized by overt government manipulation, and after two weeks of Liberal commercials boosting Chrétien's prime ministerial qualities, the media were ready to play up the public's outrage. Although the Liberals had themselves pointed out his facial distortion in their own commercials in Quebec ("Drôle de tête. D'accord. Mais quelle vision!"[57]), Chrétien's tear-jerking plea about the Conservative ads – "They try to make fun of the way I look. God gave me a physical defect and I've accepted that since I was a kid" – was given generous treatment in the news.[58]

In a time of deep voter cynicism, this populist from rural Quebec turned out to have experience and savvy. He was not too aggressive compared to Campbell, whose style was belligerently partisan, not too scary compared to Preston Manning and his Reform Party's fierce commitment to wrestle the deficit down to zero, and not too charismatic compared to Lucien Bouchard's unabashed determination to lead francophones to the promised land of an independent Quebec. Chrétien was a team player, appearing at rallies with his candidates from the region, not as a superior like Campbell, but as a leader in touch with his associates. When he made mistakes, such as attending a $1,000-per-person event that promised donors special access to him – after having given a speech promising to restore integrity to government – he addressed the problem directly by answering reporters' questions and then joking that the only person with preferential access was his wife, Aline.

Having successfully navigated the debates and beaten off the Conservatives' final attack, the last phase of Chrétien's campaign shifted to the regions where he was weakest. In British Columbia and Alberta, where the new Reform Party was surging, he urged voters not to waste their votes in protest but to elect Liberals so that the West would be represented in the cabinet. "I want Western Canada to be on the inside."[59] In Quebec he insisted that "le vrai pouvoir" (the Bloc Québécois's slogan) meant having the province's representatives in the government rather than on the opposition benches, a not-too-subtle reference to the power of government to dispense patronage and public works. As the Quebec press published polls indicating that Chrétien might lose in his own riding, he returned to Shawinigan to remind his electors that he was their favoured son and would bring the benefits of the prime minister's good offices to them if elected.

The Results: Opting for the Safe Change

Chrétien's success was historic, but even more so was the spectacular and unprecedented thrashing of the Progressive Conservatives at the hands of voters in every part of the country. In the Atlantic provinces, where the Liberals already controlled every provincial legislature, the party carried every seat but one. It was an indication of the extent to which the Conservatives had alienated the Maritimes, dependent as they were on federal funding to maintain the quality of social services and to enable the private sector to create jobs. In Ontario, the Liberals managed a similar feat by winning all but one seat. Free trade, the GST, and a Bank-of-Canada-induced recession had devastated its manufacturing economy, notwithstanding the panacea the Conservatives and the economics profession had promised once the Free Trade Agreement with the United States was signed. Comparatively speaking, the Liberal breakthrough in the West was just as spectacular: 45 percent of the vote and twelve seats in Manitoba; 32 percent of the vote and five seats in Saskatchewan; 28 percent of the vote and two seats in the Territories; 25 percent of the vote and four seats in Alberta – the first time that the Liberals had carried a constituency in that province since 1968.

Never before had a governing party been so decisively rejected by the electorate as in 1993. Along with a sharp decline in voter turnout from 76 percent in 1988 to 70 percent, the 1993 election was marked by massive voter volatility – so much so that political scientists R. Kenneth Carty, William Cross, and Lisa Young reported that "in an analysis of more than 300 national elections across a century of democratic experience in thirteen countries, the European scholars Stefano Bartolini and Peter Mair did not find a single case in which the electoral volatility was as high as in the Canadian election of 1993."[60] An extraordinary 40 percent of the electorate shifted their support to a different party, thanks in part to the arrival on the scene of Reform and the Bloc – two new regional parties that destroyed the electoral coalition that Mulroney had constructed between Quebec and the West.[61] The Liberals' success, on the other hand, could be seen in their retention rate. Seventy percent of their 1988 voters remained with the party, compared to 22 percent remaining with the Conservatives and 26 percent with the NDP.[62] The Liberals also gained significantly from vote-switching, securing 25 percent of the Conservative voters and 11 percent of the NDP voters from the 1988 election. Those who abandoned the Liberal Party this time spread themselves fairly evenly among the other four parties.

Despite the appearance of five new leaders on the federal political scene, leadership had even less of an impact than in 1988,[63] continuing the trend of declining leader importance that had begun with the departure of Trudeau in 1984 (see Table 12).[64] Even among those who indicated that the leader was the most important factor affecting their decision, their stances on certain key issues outweighed the value of the leaders' personal qualities. Eleven percent of overall Liberal support came from those who held negative views of the other parties, but only 6 percent from those with negative perceptions of other leaders.[65] While Jean Chrétien performed well during the campaign, he attracted few voters on the strength of his personality alone.[66] Four percent of the party's supporters voted Liberal for Chrétien's positive leadership traits while 23 percent voted for economic issues and 41 percent decided because of the party's overall positive image.[67]

Unemployment was the key to the Liberal victory – 12 percent of voters for whom unemployment was the main concern supported the Liberals, while the remaining 10 percent with the same concern spread their support among the

Table 12

Effects of party leaders in the 1993 federal election

Voting pattern	Liberal (%)	PC (%)	NDP (%)	Reform (%)	BQ (%)
Switch to	1.7	0.3	0.1	0.6	1.4
Remain	1.7	0.3	0.1	–	–
Enter/re-enter	0.4	0.1	–	–	–
Total	3.8	0.7	0.2	0.6	1.4

Note: Percentage of voting electorate.
Source: Harold D. Clarke, Lawrence LeDuc, Jane Jenson, and Jon H. Pammett, *Absent Mandate: Interpreting Change in Canadian Elections*, 3rd ed. (Toronto: Gage, 1996), 131, table 6.3.

four other parties (see Table 13). It was a strong enough issue for 6 percent to switch to the Liberal Party and 9 percent to remain with them. On the second most important issue, deficit reduction, Reform had a small advantage (4 percent) over the Liberals (3 percent).[68] If the meaning of the election could be deduced from voter attitudes, "the Liberal Party won a mandate limited to increasing employment and fostering economic growth, while no party received a mandate for deficit reduction or cuts to social spending."[69]

The 1993 electorate was characterized by extremely high levels of cynicism and dissatisfaction. The electorate voted for change, and each party represented dramatically different alternatives.[70] The collective decision to opt for Jean Chrétien's Liberals was the "safe" choice – an acceptance of the party's declared intention to tackle economic problems in "a measured, gradualist manner rather than with radical surgery."[71] "Yesterday's man" knew Canadians wanted to return to yesterday's Canada.

It had taken until the end of the campaign for Chrétien to overcome his personal deficit. It would take still longer for him to deal with his Quebec problem, although he had made considerable progress in his home province. Liberal support there had risen from 23 percent at the beginning of the campaign to 33 percent at the end, when his party won nineteen seats. Outside the anglophone area of West Montreal, the Liberals had done better than most expected, coming second in forty-four ridings and re-establishing themselves as a substantial force. Being endorsed by two senior members of Robert Bourassa's provincial government (Health Minister Marc-Yvan Côté and Security Minister Claude Ryan),[72] having his infrastructure program applauded by the mayors of Montreal and Quebec, turning in a decent performance in the debates, and getting his own message across through the party's commercials had led to a steady rise in Chrétien's popularity throughout the campaign. He had not been able to counter the nationalist protest vote in the wake of the 1992 referendum on the

Table 13

Effects of issues in the 1993 federal election

Most important issue mentioned (voting pattern)		Liberal (%)	PC (%)	NDP (%)	Reform (%)	BQ (%)
All economic issues	Switch to	9.2	2.1	1.2	10.1	5.2
	Remain	13.7	6.0	2.7	0.7	–
	Enter/re-enter	2.5	0.7	–	1.6	0.7
	Total	25.4	8.8	3.9	12.4	5.9
	Issue voters only	17.1	6.0	2.6	8.4	4.0
Unemployment	Switch to	6.4	1.1	0.8	3.9	3.3
	Remain	9.3	2.4	2.4	0.1	–
	Enter/re-enter	1.5	0.3	0.1	1.1	0.2
	Total	17.2	3.8	3.3	5.1	3.5
	Issue voters only	11.8	2.4	2.0	3.5	2.5
The deficit	Switch to	1.0	0.8	0.3	4.0	1.0
	Remain	2.2	2.9	0.1	0.6	–
	Enter/re-enter	0.6	0.2	–	0.5	0.3
	Total	3.8	3.9	0.4	5.1	1.3
	Issue voters only	3.1	2.7	0.4	3.9	0.4
All other issues	Switch to	2.7	0.2	0.7	2.1	1.6
	Remain	2.8	0.9	0.8	0.1	–
	Enter/re-enter	0.9	0.1	0.1	0.6	0.1
	Total	6.4	1.2	1.6	2.8	1.7
	Issue voters only	3.5	0.5	0.9	1.6	1.1

Note: Percentage of voting electorate.
Source: Harold D. Clarke, Lawrence LeDuc, Jane Jenson, and Jon H. Pammett, *Absent Mandate: Interpreting Change in Canadian Elections*, 3rd ed. (Toronto: Gage, 1996), 141, table 6.7.

Charlottetown Accord, but he did so well on election day that Quebeckers started to re-evaluate the man they had come to despise.

The Birth of a New Party System?

Like the election of 1896, the 1993 contest produced a stunning defeat of a Conservative government and a fundamental realignment in Canadian politics, so much so that one highly regarded group of scholars has called the 1993 election "one of the greatest democratic electoral earthquakes ever recorded."[73] R.K. Carty, William Cross, and Lisa Young contend that the 1993 election rang the death knell of the third, pan-Canadian system of party politics, which had prevailed since the days of Diefenbaker, and that it heralded the birth of a fourth, balkanized system in which elections are fought on local issues by different constellations of political parties in each of five regions: the provinces of Ontario and Quebec, the Atlantic, the Prairie provinces, and British Columbia.[74]

According to the Carty group, Canadian party politics "collapsed" in the early 1990s because the three old "pan-Canadian" parties, which had played a major role in bridging Canada's linguistic, ethnic, and regional cleavages since the end of brokerage politics in the 1950s, had failed "to accommodate the forces of political, social and governmental change" that were sweeping across the country.[75] As a result, voters in three regions (Quebec, BC, and the Prairies) almost completely abandoned the Liberals, Conservatives, and New Democrats in favour of two regional upstarts (the Bloc Québécois and the Reform Party), which, to win votes, exploited Canada's regional divides instead of bridging them.

For the Progressive Conservative and New Democratic parties, the new regional realities of Canadian electoral politics brought them to the brink of oblivion. Both lost their official party status in the House of Commons (set at a minimum of twelve MPs), with the Conservatives sliding from 169 seats in 1988 to just 2 in 1993 and the NDP falling from 43 seats to 9. As for the newly elected Liberals, their legitimacy as a national party was not unscathed either. Just as the other parties had been reduced to regional bases, the Liberal Party's reliance for their parliamentary majority on one hundred seats from one province suggested it was "a party of Ontario with small pockets of support tacked on across the country."[76]

In addition to having been reduced to narrow regional bases, the Carty team argue that technological and demographic changes altered the way that the parties conducted their campaigns. New means of communicating political messages enabled them to target sectional voter bases rather than a single, pan-Canadian electorate as in the past.[77] In fragmenting their electoral appeal, the parties were responding to an increasingly informed and democratically demanding electorate whose identities were constructed more around special interests than national themes. Regionalized parties exploiting technologies of fragmentation had combined unwittingly to create elections in which there was "no national political debate" any more.[78]

The unprecedented results of the 1993 federal election provided strong evidence for the Carty team's proposition that Canadian politics entered a new, regionally balkanized phase on the evening of October 25, 1993. But compelling as their thesis seemed, a full assessment had to await more elections in order to confirm that 1993 was something more than an aberration.

Regardless of how its results are theorized, the importance of the 1993 election lay in the questions it raised about the future of the country. Did the devastation of two national parties by two new regional formations herald the beginning of the end for Canada? Or did the fact that the other national party, the Liberals, won a clear majority with representatives elected from each province and territory indicate that Canadian federalism had been given a reprieve from sea to sea to sea? If neoconservatism had really been rejected, had it been replaced by the humanistic welfare liberalism of the Pearson/Trudeau years, by a leaner, meaner neoliberalism adapted to tough economic times, or by some tough-love blend of the two ideological variants? In the longer run, the nature of Chrétien's liberalism would depend on two factors largely beyond his control: the willingness of the Quebec public to remain within the Canadian state would be decided in that province, not in Ottawa, and the capacity of the private sector to produce enough jobs and tax revenue to sustain an advanced social structure would depend on North American free trade delivering prosperity not just to the United States, but to the territory to the north as well. Only time would tell whether blue Grits was the appropriate diet for feeding the continuing demands of Canada's political economy.

Securing Their Future Together 1997

The Liberal Party's campaign in 1997 stands as one of the most puzzling in the annals of Canadian electioneering, for although Jean Chrétien and his team pulled off the historically rare triumph of returning to power with a second majority government in a row, this feat was treated by most observers as tantamount to a failure.[1] Viewed from outside the frenzy of the struggling combatants, the enigma of the Liberals' campaign can be broken down into six queries.

- Why, when the Liberal government had coped brilliantly with the heavy fiscal legacy it inherited in 1993, did it bring its mandate to a close under increasing public discontent?
- Why, when the leader's team of managers had been so capable both in campaigning in 1993 and in governing thereafter, did they show no flair for political generalship when it came time for re-election?
- Why, when the government, and especially its finance minister, had already redefined liberalism for the 1990s, was the party's policy direction anything but clear?
- Why did the long-underestimated but shrewd Jean Chrétien seem both overconfident and underachieving when he returned to the hustings?
- How did the media, which consistently indicated Chrétien would win handily, help facilitate the Liberals' slide?
- How did the well-prepared and competent campaign organization fail to achieve some of the party's most basic objectives?

Answering these questions should help us understand the evolving character of the Liberal Party of Canada as it struggled to hang on to its historic role as the country's "government party" during what seemed to be a historic period of transition in the country's party system.

The Record

In the summer of 1995, as they contemplated the approaching second anniversary of their electoral triumph, the prime minister and his entourage had good reason to be happy. In Parliament they were in politicians' heaven, since no party offered an immediate threat to their hold on power. The Official Opposition, the Bloc Québécois (BQ), was a separatist party with no pan-Canadian mandate. The Progressive Conservative Party (PC), the only rival that could expect to replace the Liberals because of its deep roots in every province, had been reduced to two seats, leaving in third place the upstart western Reform Party with fifty seats, and in fourth a shattered New Democratic Party with nine seats. The impending referendum in Quebec was heralding the federalist side as being in a good position to beat the sovereigntists.

Despite having performed lamentably as Leader of the Opposition up until the 1993 election campaign, Jean Chrétien had been transmogrified by power into an effective head of government. His staff was loyal and sage. He ran a competent cabinet judiciously, giving his ministers free enough rein to let them get on with the job of managing their departments and doing their best to implement the many promises made during the previous campaign in their famous Red Book.

One of these promises – bringing the escalating deficit and runaway national debt under control – had been taken on as an overriding goal by the finance department. However reluctantly, the government as a whole then bent to the dictates of deficit cutting and succeeded in carrying out more drastic amputations of government programs than their Conservative predecessors had dared attempt. More astonishing still, in cutting the various social and cultural programs that had been the Liberal Party's greatest pride and his own father's enduring political legacy as a welfare Liberal, Finance Minister Paul Martin had become the governing party's most popular member.

A striking confirmation of Martin's magic was the friendly attitude that English Canada's "national newspaper" adopted toward the party of whose policies it had long been a relentless critic. In the *Globe and Mail*'s eyes, the Chrétien government had become "responsible, frugal, and in control," its character pragmatic and prudent, its integrity high since by being productive, fiscally responsible, and hard-working it was "rapidly fulfilling its promises."[2] When the government published *A Record of Achievement: A Report on the Liberal Government's Thirty-Six Months in Office,* the *Globe* gave the Liberals' unabashedly inflated self-evaluation more space than the opposition politicians' much steelier critiques.[3] The view cumulatively established in the chief organ of Canadian capitalism suggested that the Liberals were unbeatable and that they deserved to be re-elected. Not only had Chrétien done well as prime minister, he had performed satisfactorily at G7 meetings and in other capacities abroad. Only he could speak for Canada.[4]

The Liberal government had indeed proven generally competent, with only two ministers having to resign over issues that exuded not even a whiff of scandal. While a formal inquiry into military misdemeanours during the armed forces' peacekeeping mission to Somalia in 1992 caused it prolonged embarrassment, the general impression the government had created by 1995 was one of success. Luck helped: the decline of interest rates allowed it to accelerate its deficit-reduction schedule so that the finance minister could validly claim to have gone beyond the Red Book's target of reducing the deficit to 3 percent of GNP.

Although the Chrétien team had run a down-to-earth government of the type to be expected from an experienced group, it also committed two major blunders, first in Quebec and then in the media. Ever since Jean Chrétien had misjudged the constitutional mood of Quebec in 1990 when he opposed the Meech Lake Accord, his political nose for his home province had been unreliable. As prime minister, he was still so traumatized by his vilification in the francophone media and the hostility expressed to him on the street that he rarely ventured into the province and, when he did so, the Prime Minister's Office (PMO) did not alert the press, lest this give reporters another chance to vent their scorn on him. His poor feel for the Québécois political sensibility was demonstrated for all to see by his insouciant handling of the 1995 referendum on Quebec sovereignty, a campaign that was directed so badly by the federalist forces that it came within 50,000 votes of losing.

A year later, in a televised "Town Hall" meeting orchestrated by the CBC, he took a verbal beating from the well-primed audience, one member of which flailed him for having broken the Liberals' 1993 campaign promise to replace the much-reviled Goods and Services Tax (GST). Overnight Chrétien's image was transformed. The straight-shooting patriot of unblemished integrity had become just another evasive politician, alternately defensive and aggressive, charming and pitiable, denying the fact that was patent to all: he had broken the promise he had made to eliminate the roundly hated sales tax.[5] As speculation in the media turned to the next election, Chrétien looked out of his depth, his skills rusting. How else to explain his incapacity to reframe the image of broken promises into one of contracts kept, the appearance of failed generalship into one of effective leadership? Part of the answer lay in the team he had around him.

The Tacticians

The prime minister's entourage was seasoned and smart. From his octogenarian mentor Mitchell Sharp, whose long and distinguished career in public life had spanned the prime ministries of Mackenzie King, St. Laurent, Pearson, and Trudeau, to Peter Donolo, his youthful communications manager, Chrétien's principal advisers had been with him through the worst times in opposition and turned out to be adept at handling the best times of running a majority government. They kept him out of trouble, rallied the caucus and cabinet behind Paul Martin's tough-love deficit cutting, and helped orchestrate a very substantial record of achievement across the whole range of government policies and ministries. But they were not exempt from that most common malady of the powerful – hubris.

Excited in the early days of 1997 by their continuing high poll numbers, and heartened in the weeks that followed by the Bloc Québécois's self-destructive leadership campaign to replace Lucien Bouchard (who had moved on to become the premier of Quebec), the Liberals decided to precipitate an early election despite three obvious reasons for patience. First, there was the "Peterson factor." In 1990, David Peterson, the Liberal Premier of Ontario, basking not just in his legislative majority and high poll numbers but in the psychic high that power engenders, called a surprisingly early election only to be soundly punished by the voters for provoking an unnecessary campaign. Second, there was much unfinished business. The government's battle to reduce the national deficit was progressing but was not won. In a year it would be on the point of balancing its books and would be on much firmer ground for seeking a mandate to implement a new program. Finally, there was the question of sovereignty. Since the Parti Québécois's threatened next referendum could only be held following a new provincial election, and since Premier Lucien Bouchard would not want to issue the writs before the next federal election, holding off the national campaign would prolong the period during which the PQ would be forced to make federalism work in Quebec, raising the chances that Bouchard might run into political difficulties of his own making.

Overconfidence, which had brought the Chrétien team to the brink of disaster in the October 1995 referendum, still prevailed in the PMO in the early months of 1997 when it was felt that the newly shortened seven-week campaign period would favour a cautious front-runner's return to office. The BQ's disarray also promised Liberal gains in Chrétien's home province.[6] Besides, why wait for the opposition to get more press, or for the media to get tougher?

The decision may have been wily, but its execution was wobbly. In the spring of 1997, campaign preparations had been going on for many weeks. Nominations were held. Candidates were appointed in specific ridings where Chrétien wanted a female or minority representative. Constituency workers were trained. Policies were prepared. In response, the opposition parties had geared up their own pre-writ activities. The preparatory process developed such a momentum that its creators seemed unable to stop it. Not even an act of God – the rising waters of the Red River that threatened to flood Winnipeg and southern Manitoba – was enough to give the Liberal high command serious pause. It simply flew the

PM out to Winnipeg to throw a sandbag onto a dike for the TV cameras on Saturday, April 26 in time to fly him back to Ottawa so he could call on the governor general the next day and start the race. But when quizzed by the media about the reason for holding an election after just three and a half years in office, the prime minister looked unsure of himself. "We are in the four year [sic], and I believe it is important that we take the summer to prepare for the launch of the new government in September," he offered, implying that an election was a disagreeable diversion from the more serious business of continuing to govern.

No sooner had Chrétien given his campaign such a lacklustre launch than he became embroiled in Western anger at this intrusion of politics into Manitoba's calamity. Then, when he took to the hustings, he gave confusing signals. Despite claiming credit for three years of tough deficit cutting and government restraint, he dropped one spending promise – $200 million for AIDS research – followed by another – a commitment not to cut the Canada Health and Social Transfer to the provinces by the further $2.1 billion envisaged for the next two fiscal years. Voters presumably were to be grateful not to have more pain indirectly inflicted on them via reductions in their provincial social services.

While producing these manifestations of traditional campaigning, Chrétien was being kept in a cocoon by his advisers. CBC's "National Magazine" was refused a conversation with the Liberal leader, although the other party chiefs were lining up at interviewer Hana Gartner's studio door. Chrétien's isolation was so complete that it was not until the last day of the campaign's first week that Canada's great man-of-the-people politician was to be seen glad-handing with voters.

But the greatest confusion of all in these early days was the bizarre spectacle of the Reform Party calling a press conference so that its leader, Preston Manning, could brandish before the media a leaked copy of the Liberal platform. The Liberals had lost control, ironically enough with that part of their campaign agenda generally most amenable to complete management, the articulation of its policy.

The Platform

There is nothing new in an electoral organization being deeply divided over how to present its platform. Whatever the party's ideology, there are bound to be partisans who lean more to the left arguing with fellow workers who lean more to the right, activists versus minimalists, idealists confronting pragmatists. There is nothing new, either, in compromises having to be made in the interests of presenting a united front to the public.

Those Liberal insiders, such as MP John Godfrey, who argued that the party should champion some real nation-building projects, were deriving their proposals from poll data showing that the public wanted some sense of vision from its politicians. Their aim was to reassemble the lower-to-middle-class coalition of the Trudeau years who had been repelled by the Liberals' drastic cuts in social and economic programs but who might be lured back by the promise of new social initiatives. Those arguing for a minimalist program of staying the course of restraint believed that their party should appeal to the wealthier and more conservative voters across the country who had already been attracted by the Liberals' deficit-cutting achievements. With the prime minister's concurrence, these tactical realists purged the visionaries' prose from the party's platform, leaving behind a document that was as long in verbiage as it was short in content.[7]

Many are the times that the Liberal Party has successfully campaigned on the left, only to govern on the right. The question facing the Liberals in 1997 was whether to try to repeat the stunt. The political context created a delicate problem. In 1993 the Red Book had been a serious exercise in policy analysis that provided intellectual context, reasoned analysis, and specific promises, all of which were carefully costed and professionally packaged. The platform's actual exploitation had centred less on the party leader explaining the policies than on his brandishing the slickly designed book as a talisman, constantly asserting that he wanted the public, whose cynicism about politicians' unfulfilled promises had been mounting, to hold him accountable for carrying out its undertakings.[8]

These commitments amounted to governing along the two putatively parallel, but actually diverging, tracks of fiscal caution and economic stimulus. Upon taking power, the Chrétien team proceeded to implement its promises up to the point that their inner contradiction appeared. Once it finally understood the full implications of the burgeoning national debt, it could no longer stay on both tracks. To reduce the deficit required cutting programs, not expanding them. Paul Martin's mildly restrictive 1994 budget was followed by draconian ones in 1995 and 1996. Cutting 45,000 jobs from the civil service and $16.5 billion from program spending was simply not compatible with the 1993 campaign's commitment to create jobs and improve social services. With another election in the offing, the finance minister delivered a budget in the spring of 1997 in which the second track was officially rehabilitated. Now the deficit would continue to come down as a portion of gross domestic product, but certain new expenditures put some rouge back on the cold blue face of the Grit government.

The Liberal Plan – 1997: Securing Our Future Together: Preparing Canada for the Twenty-First Century was a carefully compiled text. The presentation was so similar to its 1993 model that it was quickly dubbed "Red Book II." Much of the analytical material had been pulled from *A Record of Achievement,* which had put the most positive spin possible on how the 1993 promises had been implemented. Cutting and pasting many items from the 1997 budget into this document created the impression that the government party was simply filing a report to its stakeholders about its performance. As for the new promises, many were put forward tentatively: their implementation would depend on provincial agreement and participation.

The document was coherent. The promises were costed in an appendix. As an exercise in political positioning, it seemed to have the political wisdom of King Solomon. The government would stay the course in bringing the deficit down to zero. Once a surplus was achieved in the government's accounts, one-half would be used to pay down the national debt or cut taxes or both; the other half would be used to enhance social programs targeted for children in poverty, the health care system, and job creation. In one stroke, Red Book II made Reform and the Progressive Conservatives on the right seem recklessly irresponsible in calling for premature tax cuts, and the NDP on the left hopelessly idealistic in urging increased government spending. No figures seemed necessary to justify such an eminently sensible solution. All that was needed was for this program to be communicated.

Interestingly, however, the story of *Securing Our Future Together* was all show, no tell. Despite being released twice – once by Preston Manning in his scoop, and next by Jean Chrétien at its official unveiling – the document disappeared from public view. Its circulation was perfunctory. It was available on the party's new website, but the few who had access to the Internet in 1997 could hardly be expected to wade through its 102 dense pages. And its propositions seemed to be the last thing that the party leader wanted to discuss, even though almost all the concrete proposals that might prove embarrassing to him either on the campaign trail or when returned to power had been deleted. He who campaigned in 1993 urging voters to hold him accountable for his platform wanted neither to discuss the original document nor to elaborate on the new one lest, perhaps, it perpetuate the impression that his government had broken more promises than it had kept. On the one occasion that Chrétien did highlight a campaign promise – pharmacare, the idea of a national prescription drug insurance program – questioning reporters found him to be unsure about the costs of such an initiative, how much provincial governments would contribute, or when it might be implemented.

The Leader

The pharmacare incident exemplified the Liberals' new proclivity for turning their assets into liabilities. Even though their cautious policy was consistent with the spirit of the times, it seemed of little value in their campaign. The Jean Chrétien who had surpassed expectations as prime minister became a salesman who managed somehow to diminish his product, a generally inferior campaigner who appeared to have lost the self-confidence, the charm, and the common touch that, until recently, had endeared him to his party and the country. His engagements were confined to events from which the public was generally excluded. If a protest or a demonstration developed at a campaign stop, the visit would be cancelled from his schedule or postponed in order to keep him away from the protesters.[9] Requests for media appearances were routinely turned down, with ministers from the "auxiliary team" being dispatched to take Chrétien's place on the nation's airwaves.

The one rendezvous that Chrétien could not miss was the leaders' debate. This nationally televised event had become too entrenched in the public's consciousness for the Liberal leader to avoid it, as had last been done by Pierre Trudeau in 1980. Similar in format to the debates of 1993, two hours were allotted to the debate in each language, with the speaking order for opening and closing statements determined by a draw.[10] In the first encounter, staged in English on May 12 and moderated by Ann Medina of the CBC, Chrétien looked uncomfortable, reading his opening statement somewhat haltingly and answering questions posed to him by the journalists in a flat, unforceful style. He blamed the opposition parties for having precipitated the early election. He emphasized the party's fiscal achievements and the need for a "balanced approach" to government,[11] and he woodenly apologized for the government's cuts to social programs. In their respective opening statements, Alexa McDonough sold the NDP as the only "left party," Preston Manning billed Reform as a "fresh start," Gilles Duceppe offered the Bloc as a "voice for Quebec," and Jean Charest of the Conservatives stressed tax cuts and their "health care guarantee."[12] It was national unity, however, that became the most heated issue of the evening. In the cut and thrust of the leaders' exchanges, Chrétien defended himself reasonably well, even demonstrating some energy when attacking Gilles Duceppe: "You are not interested in any solution because you are a separatist."[13] While Chrétien held his own, Charest's heart-on-sleeve avowal that he had made a commitment to his children to "pass on to them the country [he] received from [his] parents" drew the only round of applause from the studio audience.[14] The next day Charest was declared the winner by most of the media.

In the next evening's debate in French, Chrétien was more confident, counterpunching with some assurance. Even though he had nothing memorable to say, his stance was more statesmanlike. While refusing to get into slanging matches with his opponents, he was still able to convey both his negative message (Quebec's economic problems were caused by the political instability resulting from the threat of another referendum) and his positive message (the government's tough fiscal management was working, having produced low interest rates).

When cornered by the difficult question about how he would respond to Quebeckers voting by 50 percent plus one in favour of a clear question on sovereignty, he was taken off the spot by the debate's moderator, Claire Lamarche of

TVA, collapsing to the floor in a faint. The next morning, most of the press declared the French debate a draw.[15]

About one-half of the electorate watched at least part of one of the 1997 debates, with viewership being slightly higher in Quebec (55 percent) and Ontario (54 percent) than in the Prairie or Atlantic provinces (41 percent).[16] Overall, Charest came out of the debates in an improved position, with greater visibility and a more positive image. Perceptions of Chrétien appeared little changed – which was perhaps the best outcome that could be expected for an incumbent.[17] While respondents in all regions clearly saw Charest's performance in the debates as best, "polls measuring vote intention barely moved following the debates, nor did more general approval ratings of the leaders or opinions about who would make the best prime minister."[18] The exception to this trend was in Quebec, where an Environics post-debate poll saw support for Charest's Conservatives shoot up to 36 percent, putting it ahead of the Bloc, which had been reduced to 27 percent.[19] In terms of overall "debate effects," however, surveys showed little variation between the viewers and non-viewers of the debates in voting choice, leading Lawrence LeDuc to argue that, "as was the case in 1993, one might conclude that the debates had some effect on the image of the leaders but little on voting behaviour."[20]

Claire Lamarche's collapse has also been used as a symbol of the decreasing number of women on the Canadian political stage.[21] In the 1997 election, Janine Brodie noted that the federal parties were virtually silent on gender issues. Indeed the two major parties felt it was "so irrelevant that they could refuse to debate women's issues as they had in the two previous federal campaigns without paying any electoral penalties."[22] Despite women's efforts to put gender onto the political agenda, their issues received almost no attention during the campaign. The National Action Committee on the Status of Women (NAC) tried to sponsor another debate, as it had in 1984, but, with the exception of NDP leader Alexa McDonough, none of the major party leaders attended. Hedy Fry, the minister responsible for the status of women, was scheduled to attend on behalf of the Liberals but cancelled on short notice. While the debate had been televised on a major national network in 1984, in 1997 NAC was only able to have the debate carried by CPAC, a cable channel catering to political junkies.[23]

Being saved by the bell during the French-language debate was not the only example of Chrétien's luck during the campaign. His good fortune often took the form of his opponents' mistakes, which were frequent enough to buoy up the plodding Liberal campaign and keep it out of trouble. After a dismal first week for the Liberals, former Quebec premier Jacques Parizeau gratuitously entered the campaign by publishing a book in which he stated he would have made a unilateral declaration of independence following a successful referendum result in 1995. The pandemonium this embarrassment caused in the Bloc Québécois' own halting campaign gave the Liberals a reprieve for several days. When they were again in trouble following the debates from which Charest had emerged as the media's articulate, passionate, and youthful darling, the PC leader himself offered his foe an opportunity: "Mr. Chrétien seems not to originate from Quebec. [His policies] demonstrate that he is from Ottawa."[24] Pumping up his moral indignation, Chrétien tried to turn this rather banal criticism into a blood insult as he had done in 1993 when the PCs ridiculed his facial features. This was an ethnic slur, Chrétien expostulated, and completely unacceptable. "It's been done to me several times. It's hard to take ... because I was elected nine times by Quebeckers in a riding that is 98 percent francophone."[25]

His enemies' attacks had a tonic effect. When in the second week Charest charbroiled the Liberal Party's platform at a barbeque, Chrétien used humour to dismiss this as "childish" behaviour showing that they were "the same old Tories – just like Mulroney: they're cooking the books again."[26] Attempting to offset Charest's success in handling the national unity issue, Chrétien became more aggressive. He accused his opponent of leading a one-man parade, of hiding his party, of taking different stances in different regions, of opposing the Liberals' tough gun-control legislation.

To Preston Manning's attacks, Chrétien made some effective ripostes. When the Reform leader implied the prime minister was too old, Chrétien responded, "I'm old enough to know how divisive and irresponsible this brand of politics is and I'm old enough to know how it hurts our country. And I'm old enough to know it's wrong – absolutely wrong – to pit region against region."[27] When Reform tarred Chrétien in a TV commercial with the same brush as Lucien Bouchard and Gilles Duceppe, he felt personally insulted but claimed the high road in response. He excoriated regional divisiveness: Manning was the prince of darkness, appealing to a nostalgia for a time that never was.[28]

In the panic of the campaign's last week, when the Liberals knew from their pollster that they faced the real possibility of coming back as a minority government, Chrétien pleaded for strong government so that Canada could stay the course of deficit reduction, saying that Canada had "built an example for the world."[29] Revving up tired rhetoric of this kind confirmed how unfocused his campaign had been. His advisers had not seemed able to decide what image to project. The campaign had produced a confusion of Chrétiens – some negative, some positive. The competent statesman at international summits and the captain of the Team Canada trade-promotion missions was little to be seen. Instead viewers were reminded more of his referendum persona, the inarticulate, insecure, out-of-touch leader who was graceless and testy under pressure. He may have seemed to some to be mature, "a man among the girls and boys" during the debates, but he also appeared, in Charest's simple epithet, "disconnected."[30] The Liberal ads presented him close up as an average, hard-working man competently doing a tough job because of his long experience. But the *petit gars de Shawinigan* seemed so discombobulated that he staged his own nomination in St. Maurice surrounded by all seventy-four other Quebec candidates, as if he needed their protection to run in his home riding.

The Liberals wanted him to be the agent of hope, the leader of the people unifying regions. Ironically, there was a good deal of truth to these desired projections: Chrétien could be optimistic and express positive messages; he had been a very strong party leader with a firm grip on such key inner-party functions as its nomination process. However, he ended the campaign a moral loser, his standing diminished everywhere except in Quebec, where it was too low to fall much further.

Chrétien's passive approach of waiting for situations to arise before dealing with them was exemplified by the hoary issue of national unity. Although the political situation in his home province was the chief reason he had precipitated the early campaign, and although the BQ campaign obliged him with a series of disasters – its new leader was untried, his tour was accident prone, and the separatist camp was openly squabbling over fundamental policy issues – he was unable to exploit this disarray. The Liberals even helped the BQ remedy it. At the outset, national unity was the principal issue the Liberals wanted to avoid, lest it remind the public of their fumbled referendum performance and give the BQ a way to rally its soft supporters. National unity could also play into the hands of Reform, which needed a new issue, since the Liberals had appropriated fiscal restraint as their own. No sooner had Jacques Parizeau caused consternation among the sovereigntists by admitting his intention to declare Quebec's independence unilaterally following a Yes vote than Chrétien weighed into the brouhaha, labelling all sovereigntists as anti-democratic and claiming that Parizeau's avowal of premeditated unconstitutionality justified Ottawa's decision in September 1996 to seek the Supreme Court's opinion on the legality of separation.[31]

Having coaxed the national unity génie out of its bottle, Chrétien proved unable to turn it to his own advantage during the debates. It was Charest who occupied the attractive middle ground between the tough federal line and the sovereigntists. Claiming he could sell reconciliation to both camps, he struck such a chord in the francophone media that his popularity rocketed. Although Chrétien had been saved during the francophone debate from having to declare himself on the validity of another referendum vote, he hesitated to accept a reprise engagement that necessarily would focus on national unity, since both Duceppe and Charest had been counting on the French debates to increase their standings in Quebec.[32]

When the debate was restaged on May 18, Chrétien remained ambiguous about his position. It was only a few days later, and in a carefully chosen venue (an interview on the francophone news service RDI), that he stated clearly that a majority Yes vote of 50 percent plus one would not be enough to legitimize Quebec's separation.[33] The statement had been considered, and so, presumably, were its consequences. In an apparent effort to shoot down the Charest rocket, Chrétien offered the BQ – aided by Premier Bouchard who denounced Chrétien as an "adversaire de la démocratie" – a perfect target against which to mobilize its supporters. With his deliberately staged intervention, Chrétien managed to polarize the francophone vote at the expense of the Progressive Conservatives, but without great benefit to his own fortunes. *Le Devoir* expressed outrage at Ottawa's interference. Even *La Presse*'s moderately federalist columnist Lysiane Gagnon criticized Chrétien's statement. With its ascribed role as historic national conciliator and as the bridge between the two founding peoples, the Liberal Party of Canada (LPC) showed in the crunch that it preferred to have separatists rather than rival federalists elected in Quebec. It was willing to risk the possibility of having Gilles Duceppe as leader of the opposition rather than Jean Charest, even though the latter's support had been crucial in saving the last referendum debate, and his contribution would be essential once again if there were another.

The Chrétien group was equally ineffective on the national unity question in responding to attacks from the Reform Party. While Preston Manning's aggressively anti-Quebec stance did give Chrétien the opportunity to present himself as the incarnation of national unity, tolerance, and acceptance of Quebec as a distinct society, Reform maintained the offensive. Whatever Chrétien's counterattacks, they failed to put the Western populist on the defensive, guaranteeing Manning his goal of making Reform the second party in the House and himself leader of the opposition.

Failure to control the national unity issue illustrated a broader problem: the Liberals' incapacity to work out a general strategy for their electoral battle. Since Chrétien and his intimates prided themselves on their rejection of grand schemes in favour of an incrementalist, nuts-and-bolts approach to politics, whether in governing or in campaigning, it is not surprising that no strategy document was communicated to the party as a whole. The campaign was designed mainly to avoid mistakes and seemed in the end to be largely improvised, responding to attacks more than delivering a specific message.

Beyond the national unity confusion (the Liberal Party stood for national reconciliation but was taking a tough stand on Quebec), Chrétien and his team talked tough economically (discipline was needed to stay the deficit-reduction course) and soft socially (child poverty was their prime concern). Having been unable to give a reason for precipitating the campaign in the first place, Chrétien nevertheless ended it by talking vaguely about "a Liberal vision for a better future."[34] Government can be a force for good, he repeated, yet the Liberals had cut back the federal government more drastically than any of their predecessors.

The leader himself was tightly scripted in his public performances, but was meant to show his passionate love for Canada. He was offering hope for Canada, but there were no grand plans in Red Book II. Chrétien was a strong leader, but he let his ministers speak for him whenever possible. These contradictions did not escape the deeply skeptical pack of reporters covering the campaign.

The Media

Even if the Liberals had managed to develop an effective campaign strategy with a clear message, they would still have suffered from a number of handicaps in communicating it to the public. They could not enjoy the benefit-of-the-doubt treatment that had been the corollary of the media's merry destruction of the Progressive Conservatives' campaign in 1993. Nor could they count on the generally favourable treatment they had benefited from in government. Once campaigns begin, newspaper, radio, and television editors consciously attempt to achieve balance among the contesting parties. Less overt is their tendency to hold the likely victor to a higher standard. Promises made by Alexa McDonough did not rate as careful a vetting as statements made by Chrétien, since there was no chance she would ever be put to the test of implementing her policies. The Liberal communications chief summed up the dilemma nicely: "Being a front-runner is always trouble; being an incumbent front-runner is double trouble."[35]

Still further trouble resulted for the pan-Canadian centrist Liberals trying to compete with parties that appealed to different regions' senses of alienation. Speeches claiming credit for cutting the deficit did not have the same hot-button newsworthiness as anti-Quebec statements made in the West by Reform or attacks on Chrétien's broken promises made in the East by the PCs and the NDP. Without being overtly hostile, the Liberals' coverage in print and on television was palpably unfavourable. In quantitative terms, the Liberals were given slightly more television exposure than any other party, getting 16.3 percent of the items on CBC's The National, as compared with 14.7 percent for Reform, 11.8 percent for the BQ, 9.5 percent for the PCs, and 8.3 percent for the NDP.[36] However, 62 percent of the items reporting on the Liberal Party could be considered unfavourable, compared to 24 percent that were neutral and 14 percent that were favourable.[37] Similarly, while the Globe and Mail gave almost as much front-page coverage to the Liberals as to the other four parties combined, quantity did not make up for quality. Fifty-five percent of these items were unfavourable, compared to 30 percent that were neutral and a mere 15 percent that were favourable.[38]

The leaders' sound bites had fallen to below ten seconds in 1993, and in 1997 they clocked in between two and three seconds in 1997, leaving the bulk of the content of television news items to the editorial whim of the reporter. In one of its series of "Reality Checks," the CBC on Day 13 of the campaign had Neil

MacDonald appraising Chrétien's record of new job creation with the dismiss-ive comment, "Chrétien is right, if you're interested in one meaningless, raw number."[39] CBC television news's comment on the Liberals' campaign at mid-point was that it was "plodding and predictable, and above all as safe as possible. Factory tours are safe – Chrétien does a lot of them,"[40] implying that he feared interrogation from the media and the voters. Emphasizing Chrétien's reluctance to engage in contact with the media or the public, the same broadcast treated its viewers to an image of Chrétien waving goodbye from inside his campaign bus. The clip was the message: the Liberal leader in an enclosed, protected, and inac-cessible space leaving the scene of the photo-op.

Chrétien's advance men must have felt that the CBC was dedicated to un-masking their best laid plans, rather than to delivering the message they had worked to set up. This pattern was set by its treatment of the prime minister's visit to the dike-building operation to save Winnipeg from the rising Red River. Rather than just showing him participating in the effort by tossing a sandbag, it aired the prior few seconds, which caught Chrétien's question to his handlers: "What do you want me to do with this [sandbag]?"[41] The message, of course, was that Chrétien's demonstration of concern was staged and opportunistic.

All the Liberals could do in the face of media cynicism was buy space for their own commercials to be broadcast unmediated by journalistic spin. Here too the governing party's apparent advantage proved of minor value. Although the elec-tion legislation formula gave the Liberals 118 minutes of commercial media time during the campaign period, compared to 51 minutes for Reform, 43 for the BQ, 34 for the PCs, and only 26 for the NDP, an Alberta Court of Appeal ruling removed the cap so that each party could buy extra time if they wished. Given the regional concentration of the other parties, the Liberals felt at a disadvan-tage, since they were constrained to buy commercial time on the national net-works, whereas their opponents could produce and air cheaper regional ads that targeted the key issues in the areas where their prospects were best.[42]

Chrétien had governed as if taking a cue from former Ontario Premier Wil-liam Davis's winning formula: "bland works." Applying the same approach to their ads, the team at Red Leaf Communications had Chrétien make such com-forting, non-controversial, and sunny remarks as "This country is much stron-ger than it was a few years ago," or "People in this country are starting to dream again." As a mild counterattack on the right, he said in another ad, "Over and over I ask Canadians what is important to them – a strong economy or a tax cut before they can afford one. They told me a strong economy."[43] The blandness of the ad-vertising reflected the campaign organization's obsession with minimizing risk.

In the Quebec media, the Liberals' treatment was mixed both in quantitative and qualitative terms. The Liberals had received the most coverage of all the parties on Radio-Canada's *Le Téléjournal,* while in *La Presse* they came third, judged in terms of content. On *Le Téléjournal,* 39 percent of the Liberals' coverage was unfavourable, 49 percent neutral, and only 12 percent favourable, whereas in *La Presse* 50 percent of the front-page coverage of the Liberal Party was neutral, 33 percent favourable, and 17 percent unfavourable.[44] The Liberals nevertheless suffered from the same media cynicism as they had received in English Canada. At the end of the first week, *Le Téléjournal* showed Chrétien signing autographs in a crowded market, but the reporter went on to say that his advance men had come earlier in the week to remove all the "For Rent" and "For Sale" signs in this usually deserted site.[45] At least the Liberals could console themselves with the fact that their treatment had not been as bad in the hands of the francophone media as in the rest of Canada; but this was largely because the Bloc's pratfalls had drawn reporters' gleeful attention away from the duller, safer Liberal campaign.

Organization

However inept the leader's tour appeared, the Liberals' electoral organization was a formidable machine both for raising money and for spending it. In 1997, for the first election since 1979, the Liberals received more corporate and individual contributions than did the Progressive Conservatives (see Tables A.3 and A.4, pp. 288-9). Two years after the election, Elections Canada reported that the Liberals' revenues of $13.76 million ($15.21 million in 2002 dollars) far exceeded those of any other party; the Progressive Conservative and Reform parties raised approximately $5.8 million ($6.4 million) each, and the NDP raised $6 million ($6.6 million).[46] The Liberals had apparently managed to improve the financial state of their party with the same alacrity they had shown in bringing order to the nation's finances.

But by 2005, the Gomery inquiry into the federal sponsorship program uncovered evidence of serious funding irregularities during the 1997 election campaign. Marc-Yvan Côté, the Liberals' top organizer for eastern Quebec, confirmed that the party's provincial wing used illegal funds to finance its campaign activities.[47] In his testimony, Côté said he had received $120,000 cash from the Liberal Party's Quebec director-general, Michel Béliveau, who admitted to soliciting illegal donations from a friend of Chrétien, Jacques Corriveau, who later made millions from sponsorship subcontracts.[48] Côté used the money to support several needy candidates in eastern Quebec.[49] Allegations of wide-ranging corruption within the Liberals' Quebec wing were substantiated by Benôit Corbeil, who confessed that, in the 1997 election, he had accepted money – fronted by the former head of Groupaction Marketing Inc., Jean Brault – from his predecessor as director-general of the party and distributed it to organizers in the ridings of successful Liberal candidates Denis Coderre and Yvon Charbonneau.[50]

In March 1997, long before being willing to admit that an early election was to be called, the Liberals mounted campaign colleges around the country, providing election seminars complete with a checklist of riding-readiness deadlines (between March 17 and April 24) for candidates and their chief constituency personnel to meet. Party organizers were in the field to help ridings in difficulty. Advice was offered on fundraising and technical services, and a logo and other paraphernalia from national headquarters were provided to demonstrate visual consistency between the candidates' local efforts and the national campaign. Ottawa could produce for each constituency a whole brochure for distribution, complete with a photograph of the candidate with the leader; also available were draft letters that candidates could send to voters concerned about specific issues, such as gun control. Candidates turned to the national campaign office for political-cum-legal advice on how to deal with such dirty tricks as billboards linking Liberal MPs with killers who had been let out of prison or the National Citizens' Coalition commercials attacking Liberal MPs' generous pensions.

An almost daily fax from Ottawa, "Talking Points," provided the ridings with a continuous digest of information based on the party's platform and the government's record to use at all-candidates meetings and for media interviews. To help ensure that the 301 local campaigns sang from the same hymnbook, lines were prepared to help candidates respond to the other parties' stances and explain Chrétien's statements. However brazen, the message would be consistent from coast to coast: the government that had made deep cuts to the provincial health and education programs faxed its candidates the message that "we have been remarkably successful in bringing spending and the deficit under control. We have initiated the biggest spending cuts since the end of the Second World War. Ensuring a continued commitment to fiscal responsibility, all spending commitments in the Liberal platform fall within the framework of existing deficit reduction targets. This is necessary to ensure the sustainability of key social programs like health care."[51]

Partisanship exceeded the bounds of the acceptable when one Talking Point referred to Jean Charest as "the separatist who shamefully questions the birthright of those who disagree with him," necessitating an apology when the text was leaked to the media.[52] The regional organization in the provincial capitals and the national organization in Ottawa strove to maintain the morale of the troops on the ground and to keep the local campaign "on message." The problem in the ridings – as in the country as a whole – was to know what that message was. "It is a challenge to pinpoint one specific strategy," observed one rural Ontario campaign worker who served on her MP's re-election committee. "Throughout the election, the strategy was not set in stone, but [was] rather flexible, to deal with any issues that arose daily or weekly."[53]

The Results: Restrained Rebellion

While the 1997 election was supposed to be a cakewalk for Chrétien, it ended up being more of a cliffhanger, as he won only the smallest of parliamentary majorities after attracting just 40 percent of the popular vote. The Liberals did have the highest voter retention rate among the older parties, holding on to 63 percent of their 1993 support, though this figure compared poorly to the BQ and Reform's retention rates of 78 percent and 80 percent respectively (see Table 14).[54] The Liberals were also at a disadvantage when it came to vote-switching. Of the 1993 Liberal vote, 11 percent switched to the PCs, 7 percent went to the NDP, and 8 percent went to Reform in 1997.[55] Some 9 percent of 1993's Liberal voters did not return to the polls at all.[56]

Despite the saturation media coverage given to the leaders, leadership remained low on the voters' list of factors influencing their voting decision. Only 20 percent picked leadership as their number-one factor, while 58 percent picked the "party as a whole" and 22 percent chose "local candidates."[57] Issues played a similar role in 1997 as in the 1979 and 1980 elections, since there was no single dominant issue but rather sets of issues that surfaced at various times during the campaign.[58] All in all, 24 percent of voters believed the most important election issue was employment, 13 percent chose national unity, 10 percent mentioned the debt and deficit, and 10 percent chose social programs.[59] The dominance of the employment and debt-and-deficit issues had declined since 1993 when 44 percent and 18 percent, respectively, cited these issues as the most important. In contrast, the weight of those citing national unity as most important issue increased by 9 percent from 1993 and social issues by 6 percent.[60]

Table 14

Where the vote went in 1997

1997	1993 behaviour							
	Liberal (%)	PC (%)	NDP (%)	Reform (%)	BQ (%)	Other (%)	Did vote (%)	Not yet eligible (%)
Liberal	63	15	13	8	2	19	26	24
PC	11	51	4	2	7	10	11	16
NDP	7	5	59	9	2	7	6	6
Reform	8	20	9	80	2	8	10	10
BQ	1	1	–	–	78	3	7	11
Other	1	–	2	2	–	15	2	3
Did not vote	9	8	13	6	10	38	38	31

Source: POLLARA Perspectives Canada Survey, The Canadian General Election of 1997, 228.

Before the campaign was launched, the Liberal Party's pollster, Michael Marzolini, had warned that the voters might rebel against an early election call. Once the results came in on the evening of June 2, it was apparent that this predicted rebellion had taken place, but in a peculiarly restrained form in which the government party was chastised without being dismissed. Periodic opinion polls suggesting the Liberals would be returned with at least a comfortable minority may well have created among voters an understanding that they could register their displeasure without worrying that the consequence of their actions would be to defeat the government. Considering the results region by region confirms that 1997 was more like a series of regional by-elections than a general election: citizens could reflect their provinces' priorities, confident that it would still be the Liberal Party that ran the country. The results varied enormously from region to region, less because of variations in the voters' socio-economic characteristics than because of these regions' differing political agendas and issue priorities.[61]

The Atlantic provinces had voted massively in 1993 for the Liberals because they made job creation the top issue and for the security of being on the winning side, but Liberal rule resulted in radical cuts to social programs and the virtual closing of the fisheries. In 1997 Atlantic Canada clearly felt betrayed and refused to heed counsels of prudence. In a panic during the fifth week of the campaign, the Liberals managed to persuade their three Maritime premiers – Brian Tobin of Newfoundland, Frank McKenna of New Brunswick, and John Savage of Nova Scotia – to rally to their cause. As the *Halifax Chronicle-Herald* put it on May 27, "Premiers swarm Charest ... Atlantic Canada's Liberal premiers on Monday accused federal Tory leader Jean Charest of wanting to cut $100 million annually out of funding for health, education, and social services." Charest counterpunched, attacking the premiers as "liars" and "stooges," but this outburst served only to tarnish his image in New Brunswick and Newfoundland where the premiers were popular.[62]

This Liberal attempt at damage control down east did not save the party from the public's wrath. Nor did it soften scorn for the prime minister, who had been insensitive enough to express sympathy with the plight of the chronically unemployed in the area by saying that he too had been unemployed – for a month after he finished law school when his wife was pregnant. As one Nova Scotian put it, "What he said is enough to make me sick ... If he really wants to know what unemployment is, let him walk in my shoes for a long period of time."[63]

For his part, Jean Charest ran his Atlantic campaign to the left of the Liberals (although he ran on their right in the rest of the country), attacking their cuts to government services. He was rewarded with thirteen seats – enough to regain official party status for the Progressive Conservatives. Atlantic Canada awarded the same prize to the NDP under Alexa McDonough, the former provincial party leader in Nova Scotia, who found willing listeners to her call to "wake up the

Liberals" and "send a message to Ottawa." It was in her home province that the Liberals received the clearest message, falling to zero seats from a full house of eleven in 1993 and from their highest vote in forty years (52 percent) to third place and their lowest vote on record (28 percent). New Brunswick brought the next worst result for the Grits who lost six of their seats and 23 percent of their 1993 vote, coming second in votes and seats after the PCs. They fell even further in Newfoundland's popular vote, from 67 to 38 percent, and lost three of their seven seats, but they managed to stay one seat and one percent ahead of the second-place Conservatives. Prince Edward Island's results suggest that part of the Liberals' fall from the voters' good graces elsewhere in the East had to do with public anger at Liberal provincial governments. Charlottetown was the only Atlantic provincial capital not under Liberal control, and the federal Liberals kept PEI's four seats for a third time in a row – their single holdout against the Maritime tide. Not protecting social programs and not keeping its election promises to create jobs had deeply hurt the Liberal Party in the Atlantic region, where one of its kept promises – reducing the deficit – had seriously hurt them.[64]

The eastern Canadian vote constituted the Liberal Party's most dramatic rebuke on election night. Having generally been acknowledged in media editorials as the best party for the country, it was not seen by the eastern voters as best serving the interests of their region. The Tories and New Democrats, in contrast, campaigned specifically to defend the interests of the Atlantic region and carried off twenty-one of its thirty-one seats.[65] Still, the results were less a calamity than a correction. The previous election had given the Grits 97 percent of the area's seats for just over half the popular vote. In 1997 they received a more appropriate one-third of the seats in return for one-third of the votes. Yet even this second-place position was tenuous, since almost half the Liberals' Atlantic seats were held with margins of less than 5 percent (see Table 15).

Quebec had appeared in the spring to be fertile ground for solid Rouge gains, and the Liberals had exerted themselves with determination during their campaign; Chrétien initially spent more time in his home province than in any other, even though he remained widely unpopular among francophones. The party was considered to have fielded a good slate of francophone candidates. Indeed, the strength of the Liberal team was the leitmotif of their approach. Finance Minister Paul Martin, of whom Quebeckers were twice as likely to have a good as a bad opinion, was used throughout the province, as were caravans of ministers in the "auxiliary team" who went out on six or more daily tours into different regions of the province. The slogan was "agir ensemble" ("acting together") and, together, Chrétien's ministers came to Montreal to let the city know how many goodies the government had provided during its previous mandate.[66] Even anglophones such as Allan Rock dropped in to extol the virtues of his tough gun-control legislation.

Table 15

Percentage by which the Liberals won/lost in all ridings, 1997 federal election

Province		Total won	0-4.9 (%)	5.0-9.9 (%)	10.0-14.9 (%)	15.0+ (%)
Ridings won	PEI	4	2	1	1	-
	Newfoundland	4	2	-	1	1
	Nova Scotia	0	-	-	-	-
	New Brunswick	3	1	-	2	-
	Quebec	26	3	2	6	15
	Ontario	101	5	2	11	83
	Manitoba	6	-	1	1	4
	Alberta	2	2	-	-	-
	Saskatchewan	1	-	-	1	-
	BC	6	-	2	1	3
	Territories	2	-	-	-	2
	Total	155	15	8	24	108
Ridings lost	PEI	0	-	-	-	-
	Newfoundland	3	-	2	1	-
	Nova Scotia	11	3	4	1	3
	New Brunswick	7	1	2	1	3
	Quebec	49	2	10	5	32
	Ontario	2	1	-	1	-
	Manitoba	8	2	-	1	5
	Alberta	24	-	2	2	20
	Saskatchewan	13	-	2	3	8
	BC	28	-	6	3	19
	Territories	1	-	1	-	-
	Total	146	9	29	18	90

Source: Tabulated from election results in the *Toronto Star,* June 3, 1997, and the *Globe and Mail,* June 3, 1997.

This concerted effort had not prevented Jean Charest from appropriating national unity as his issue during the leaders' debates, inducing the Liberals to polarize the Quebec electorate with a tough stance on this issue so as to push soft nationalist voters away from the Conservatives and into the Bloc's arms. Far from responding to the Liberals' preferred pan-Canadian issue of economic management, the largest number of Quebec voters seems to have decided how to vote on the basis of which party would best defend the regional interests of Quebec in Ottawa.

The BQ did suffer a setback due to its close association with the increasingly unpopular PQ government in Quebec City. It fell 11 percent from its 1993 results and dropped ten seats, thus losing its status as official opposition. It nevertheless retained a commanding majority of the province's seventy-five seats. Charest's 22 percent of the vote yielded only five MPs for the Conservative caucus, and, after all their exertions, the Liberals raised their vote only from 33 to 36 percent. But this was enough to win twenty-six seats (seven more than in 1993) giving them, in the East, roughly one-third of the seats for one-third of the votes. While the Liberals won by large margins in their urban stronghold, they lost heavily elsewhere: of the forty-nine seats where they were defeated, only two were lost by less than 5 percent, with most being lost by over 15 percent. Condemned by the concentration of their vote in the Montreal area to remain in second place in the province, the Chrétien Liberals had little prospect for returning to their historical norm of winning four-fifths of Quebec's seats.

Ontario had replaced Quebec as the Grit fortress, making it possible for Jean Chrétien to boast about being the first Liberal since Louis St. Laurent to deliver back-to-back majorities. The heartland of the country was nursing no particular grievances against Ottawa, so there was no major Ontario flashpoint to prevent the Liberals from repeating their coup of 1993, when they had captured all but one of the province's seats in exchange for about half of its votes.[67] Their vote dropped four points to 49 percent, but their sweep of the province was still overwhelming. Eighty-three of the Liberals' 101 seats were won by over 15 percent margins (see Table 15) – enough to deny the Reform Party legitimacy as anything more than a voice of Western protest, and enough to stymie Charest's attempt to come within challenging distance of the government party. Economic optimism was a factor in this large Liberal vote, as was approval for the government's success in tackling the deficit, imposing gun control, and encouraging job creation.[68]

In Ontario, Chrétien attacked Charest more aggressively than he criticized Manning, but it was Premier Mike Harris who clinched the Ontario election for the Liberals by rejecting the notion of constitutionally entrenching Quebec's status as a distinct society. Even though this was Chrétien's position, it was also Charest's. In undermining Charest, Harris was implicitly supporting Manning, and so helping ensure that his province's right-wing vote was divided evenly between Reform and the Progressive Conservatives at 19 percent each. (In twenty-five constituencies the combined Reform and PC vote would have beaten the Liberal candidate.) Survey data show that those who identified themselves provincially as Conservatives in Ontario voted 30 percent for the Liberals, 29 percent for the Conservatives, 1 percent for the NDP, and 25 percent for Reform.[69]

Ontario's results were consistent with the electoral trend to regional protest. The major issue in the province in the spring of 1997 was the severe cut in public services (especially the threatened closure of hospitals) executed not by the federal Liberals but by the Mike Harris Conservatives in Queen's Park. To the extent that they were protesting, Ontario voters were objecting to the Conservatives in what the columnist Dalton Camp called a "mid-term assessment of Harris."[70] They also acted differently from other regions, but with their customary Ontario twist. It was the national economy, national programs, and national unity (based on a traditional accommodation with Quebec) that dominated the province's electoral discourse. The Liberal policy on these issues was seen to be in the province's interest, in contrast with Jean Charest's platform (cloned from Harris's Common Sense Revolution) and Preston Manning's perceived anti-Quebec bigotry. Voters in Ontario were concerned with the threat posed by the Bloc Québécois.[71] In the face of a threat to Ontario mainstream values, many New Democratic sympathizers seem to have voted strategically for the Liberal Party in order to shut out Reform, though this left the NDP with just 11 percent of the ballots.[72]

The voters' behaviour in the Prairie provinces was as distinct as every other region's. In Manitoba, prophecies of a "Griterdammerung" were not fulfilled, as the natural catastrophe in the Red River Valley did not turn into the anticipated political catastrophe. Despite the flood, despite the four Western premiers' publicly denouncing the Liberals for undermining health care, and despite the aggressive Reform campaign, the Liberal vote fell only 10 points from 45 to 35 percent. Massive flood relief funds channelled into the province by Chrétien's seasoned cabinet minister, Lloyd Axworthy, plus some eight thousand troops dispatched to help build dikes and guarantee security had shown the federal government in a favourable light. As a result, the Liberals held on to six of the province's fourteen seats, with the remaining eight being split among the NDP (four), Reform (three), and the PCs (one).

Farther west, the Grits did much less well than they had expected. In Saskatchewan, they fell from first place (five seats) to third (one seat). In only three of the other thirteen ridings did the Liberals finish in second place. Since Premier Roy Romanow fully supported Chrétien's statement that 50 percent plus one is not enough for future Quebec secession referenda, the Saskatchewan vote can also be seen as an expression of protest, "a rejection of the national party and the governing party," as David Smith put it.[73] Editorial comment during the campaign emphasized the province's tradition of protest: as the Regina *Leader-Post* reflected, the province sends "voices to oppose the central government rather than be a part of it ... This is truly the Saskatchewan way."[74]

In Alberta, the birthplace and stronghold of Reform, the Liberals went from a poor second-place position (25 percent of the vote) to a poorer second-place position (24 percent of the vote). They only managed to salvage two of their four seats (with margins of under 5 percent). If Chrétien's 50-percent-plus-one statement had been aimed at challenging Reform's primacy on the national unity question in the West, there is no evidence it succeeded. The pronouncement received no editorial or news coverage comparable to its treatment in the Ontario and Quebec media. Instead, Alberta's media presented the campaign as a battle between Manning, the hometown boy, and Chrétien, the man from Ottawa. When on May 27 the *Edmonton Journal* wrote, "the Reform Party's platform on national unity is a genuine contribution to the debate on the issue," it was evident that Chrétien's attacks on Manning for divisiveness had fallen on stony ground in the West. Quebec's disproportionate influence in Ottawa is a long-standing western grievance, and Manning's promotion of equality among the provinces was an attractive position for those in a relatively prosperous Alberta, who were enraged that Ottawa paid it so little heed. Far from being intolerant bigots, Reformers were seen in the region as intelligent federalists. In the words of the *Edmonton Journal* on the morning after the balloting, "the election made Canada better ... Her Majesty's Loyal Opposition will be formed by a party committed to federalism." Its perceived treatment by Ottawa was a sore point that mattered.[75]

Receiving proportionally fewer seats than votes on the Prairies has been the fate of the Liberal Party for half a century, and 1997 was no exception. The Liberals may have been down, but they were far from out. Canada's national party still harvested one-quarter of the ballots cast in protest country.

British Columbia also proved frustratingly resistant to the Liberals' charms. As in other regions, editorialists commended them for their fiscal management and national unity positions while nevertheless favouring a protest vote. Thus the *Vancouver Sun* could write on May 30, "Canada needs a party that represents all regions and can steer a middle course ... when it comes to national purpose, Liberals are best," and at the same time could promote Reform as "a Western-based party willing and able to give voice to Western grievances and aspirations. That is no small thing in a country that has been constantly governed by parties rooted in Central Canada and, for the last 30 years, obsessed with Quebec."[76] The Liberal Party, in other words, was good for Canada, but Reform was better for BC. And since the former was going to win in any case, British Columbians could vote for the latter, however flawed, without fear of repercussions.

The Liberals had hoped for a share of the thirty-four available seats proportional to the 30 percent of the vote that they could expect, but this kind of equity eluded them once again. Chrétien's effort in the final days to persuade British Columbia to be "part of the solution not part of the problem," and his appeal "to the good side of people" – in contrast to Reform's attack on Liberal MPs for being soft on crime – had little impact. Compared with the 1993 results, their vote edged up one point from 28 percent, but their catch remained constant at six seats. Reform had outfought them with a classic Western protest campaign that brought in 43 percent of the votes and, thanks to the electoral system, 74 percent of the seats.

The first-past-the-post, single-member ridings may have favoured Reform in BC and Alberta, the Bloc in Quebec, the NDP in Nova Scotia, and the Conservatives in New Brunswick, but on balance, thanks to Ontario, it had benefited the Liberals the most. They formed a majority government because they managed to make the winner-takes-more principle work for them once again. The corollary: the pan-Canadian Grits had morphed into a "party of Ontario" whose national vocation had been undermined for the second time in a row.[77]

Throughout the 1997 campaign there were two "bedrock attitudes": that Jean Chrétien would make the best prime minister, and that the Liberals would win the election.[78] In understanding the election results, one must keep in mind that the latter attitude was both an electoral asset and a liability to the Liberals. As a Liberal asset, it prevented the PCs or Reform from picking up any bandwagon effect, but as a liability it also diluted the imperative to vote Liberal in order to elect a Liberal government. People believed the Liberals would be re-elected no matter how they voted individually.[79]

Tables 16 and 17 best illustrate this phenomenon. While each region in Canada identified the party that had catered to local sentiment as the "best party to represent your regional interests," every region identified the Liberal Party as the "best party to represent national interests." In truth, more than half of Canadians wanted the Liberals to win, felt the Liberals ought to win, believed the Liberals would do the best job, assumed they would win regardless of their individual vote, and so proceeded to vote for their local favourite.[80]

Table 16

Best party to represent your region's interests

	Liberal (%)	PC (%)	NDP (%)	Reform (%)	BQ (%)	Other (%)	Don't know (%)
Atlantic Canada	29	24	32	5	–	2	9
Quebec	35	13	2	–	43	–	7
Ontario	58	12	8	10	–	1	11
Prairies	20	9	15	48	–	1	7
British Columbia	19	3	21	47	–	1	8

Source: Michael Marzolini, "The Regionalization of Canadian Politics," in *The Canadian General Election of 1997,* Alan Frizzell and Jon H. Pammett (Toronto: Dundurn Press, 1997), 195, figure 1.

Table 17

Best party to represent national interests

	Liberal (%)	PC (%)	NDP (%)	Reform (%)	BQ (%)	Other (%)	Don't know (%)
Atlantic Canada	45	19	15	6	-	1	14
Quebec	53	19	5	2	10	1	10
Ontario	56	11	5	14	-	2	12
Prairies	43	10	7	27	-	1	12
British Columbia	49	6	10	23	-	2	10

Source: Michael Marzolini, "The Regionalization of Canadian Politics," in *The Canadian General Election of 1997,* Alan Frizzell and Jon H. Pammett (Toronto: Dundurn Press, 1997), 196, figure 2.

The Confirmation of the Fourth Party System?

Did the campaign, which started with only one really national party and ended with none, turn the Liberals into the country's fifth regional formation? Certainly Chrétien's boast from 1993, that he had a caucus with members from every province of the country, now had to be adjusted to every "region" of the country. But the party was still competitive from coast to coast: it had run second in every region outside Ontario, coming second in 104 of the 146 ridings it lost.

Despite the best efforts of Jean Charest and Alexa McDonough to rebuild their shattered parties, the 1997 campaign reinforced rather than changed the political landscape that the 1993 election had altered so dramatically. The two, new regional parties that had filled the void left by the collapse of the Mulroney Conservatives' electoral coalition between Quebec and the West showed that they were going to stay, while the two parties they had displaced were still shadows of their former selves.[81] There seemed to be little doubt now that the 1993 election had fundamentally transformed the nature of party politics in Canada, as R. Kenneth Carty, William Cross, and Lisa Young argue.[82] A fourth, balkanized party system in which elections had degenerated into "a series of regional competitions, each with its own issues," seemed to have dawned, for better or for worse.[83]

With the Office of the Leader of the Opposition occupied by Reform, the geographical balance in the House had shifted westwards. The Bloc Québécois had lost seats and votes, but the sovereigntists remained a coherent force, facing the Liberals with the prospect of another referendum to come. Ideologically, the 1997 Parliament was somewhat more evenly balanced than its immediate predecessor. With a majority of the members of the NDP and PC caucuses hailing from the have-not Atlantic provinces, these parties could be expected to make the case for sustaining social programs. And with these partisan groups restored to official parliamentary status, the new Liberal government could expect to be under more substantial pressure from the left to abandon its deficit-cutting obsession in favour of genuine two-track support for economic development and social programs.

Apart from having a severely reduced majority and apart from their reliance on Ontario, the Grits thus found themselves in a dream position for a second time in a row. They had lived up to the title of their campaign platform, *Securing Our Future Together,* in the sense that they had secured their own future. They were able to take the summer, as Chrétien had anticipated, to prepare for the launch of the new government in the fall. The campaign had shown that this new government would be much like the old. Its vision would be limited by the imperatives of fiscal prudence, its administration would be cautious, and its handling of Quebec problematic. Without any clear guidelines emerging from Red Book II, and with ambitious candidates to succeed Chrétien already starting to plan their leadership campaigns, it remained to be proven how secure Canada's future would be – together or divided.

The Liberal Threepeat: The Multi-System Party in the Multi-Party System

For both observers and participants, the first federal election campaign of the new millennium was a dispiriting affair, an intellectually barren contest in which the four challengers were as uninspiring as the aging defender who precipitated the premature contest and posed its only significant issue – whether, in his arrogance, Jean Chrétien had overreached himself and would self-destruct. However uninteresting this phoney war may have been in its own terms, the 2000 election has double value for students of the Canadian polity.[1]

On one level, the restoration of the same constellation of players to the federal stage as in the previous election provided important material for analysts of the Canadian state. The Liberal Party's "threepeat" guaranteed the political economy would continue to be guided by a hybrid paradigm that could be labelled either "Jean Mulroneyism" or "Brian Chrétienism," with its commitment since the mid-1980s both to liberalizing trade and to reconciling fiscal prudence with social liberalism.

On another level – which will be this chapter's main concern – the campaign's electoral politics illuminated some of the features of Canada's evolving party system, highlighted in the ambitious study by R. Kenneth Carty, William Cross, and Lisa Young, *Rebuilding Canadian Party Politics,* which presents a number of analytical categories and challenging hypotheses through which the changes experienced in the recent past can be scrutinized.[2]

In their study of the 1997 election, Carty, Cross, and Young argued that three crucial factors distinguished the emerging fourth party system from its precursors. Foremost among these was the "pronounced regionalization of party support," which had fragmented "national party politics into a series of distinctive regional party systems."[3] Second, they pointed to the growth of public cynicism about politics and politicians during the 1990s, which had led to demands for more openness and grassroots participation.[4] Third, they feared that, by allowing the parties to target "relatively small groups of voters with specially tailored messages," the emergence of new communications technologies imperilled the "national political debate" that characterized the third, pan-Canadian party system.[5]

The Liberal Party's behaviour in 2000 presents a major exception to the Carty group's arresting thesis – whether it had to do with change in the party system, change in the nature of the parties themselves, or change in the manner in which they waged their campaigns. The 2000 campaign showed several things:

- Liberal Party behaviour while in office remained a mix of managing regional issues and declaring national objectives.
- The regionalism demonstrated in the party's electoral activity was more reminiscent of its traditional behaviour than prophetic of systemic change.
- Issues of leadership did not suggest that the party system had changed gears.
- The use of policy programs by the Liberal Party (and its opponents) was consistent with behaviour in the third party system.
- Far from regionalizing the campaign, the communications media helped foster some national political debate, albeit of a distressingly superficial quality.
- Even the new technologies of individualized communication failed to denationalize the campaign and, in the Liberal Party's case, actually worked to support the diffusion of its pan-Canadian message.

The Liberal Party in Office

Come election time, the party in office occupies a position decisively different from that of its opponents because it has wielded the levers of power by passing legislation, appointing officials, taking decisions, responding to crises, and representing the country in international affairs. Whether its record as a government plays to its advantage or not becomes evident at election time, when the media give its opponents' attacks full exposure for several weeks. What distinguished the Liberal Party of Canada (LPC) from its rivals was the extent to which its use of government power helped it when preparing for or fighting campaigns: the 2000 election marked the eighteenth out of twenty-seven elections since 1900 in which the Liberal Party was seeking re-election. Having recaptured power in 1993 and renewed his mandate in 1997, Jean Chrétien had given his supporters reason once again to be known as the "government party."

In the third party system (1963-93), the parties' focus shifted from the brokerage of regional interests that had characterized the second party system (1919-57) to a politics that was elite-driven and national.[6] Having lost the function of inter-regional accommodation to federal-provincial diplomacy, parties in the third system engaged with pan-Canadian issues aimed at consolidating the nation from coast to coast to coast. For Carty, Cross, and Young, the fourth party system has lost this focus on bold nation-enhancing projects. Key to this part of their argument was the Liberal Party's failure to offer pan-Canadian governance, having "lost credibility as a national party" because of its dependence since 1993 on Ontario for the vast majority of its seats.[7]

There is considerable substance to this view. Having come to power during a phase of retrenchment, the Chrétien government completed the fiscal self-disciplining that Brian Mulroney had initiated. Cutting federal spending, privatizing Crown corporations such as Canadian National Railways, shrinking the size of the civil service, deregulating the application of environmental controls, devolving federal programs to provinces, and uploading federal powers to institutions of continental and global economic governance, such as the North American Free Trade Agreement (NAFTA) and the World Trade Organization (WTO): all this combined to reduce the size, visibility, and functions of the federal state.

Beyond these government-reducing actions, the Liberal government was described as having "no discernible agenda" a year into its 1997 mandate.[8] Apart from managing the various files that crossed his desk – replacing the Navy's ancient helicopters, dealing with victims of the tainted blood scandal who had contracted hepatitis C, addressing the exhaustion of the fish stocks on the East Coast and their predation by American fishermen on the West Coast – Jean Chrétien's governing style seemed inspired less by the big vision model of Pierre Trudeau than by the cautious formula practised with even greater success by William Lyon Mackenzie King: never do today what can be put off till tomorrow.

For all his blandness, Chrétien had never repudiated the activist role for government that typified the third party system. When under attack for irregularities in the administration of Human Resources Development Canada's billion-dollar Transitional Jobs Fund, he defended himself without embarrassment. Mistakes are made in any big organization, he insisted, but the important point was that his government was trying to help create jobs in areas with unacceptably high levels of unemployment and poverty. Government activism became even more attractive to the Liberals starting in 1998, when an unexpectedly buoyant economy replaced the need for deficit cutting with the prospect of surplus spending. Emboldened by a Supreme Court ruling that appeared to legitimize the federal government's spending power in areas of provincial jurisdiction, Ottawa spawned pan-Canadian programs such as the National Child Benefit, the Millennium Fund to give scholarships to one hundred thousand students for their post-secondary education, the Canadian Foundation for Innovation to encourage research and development, and the Canada Research Chairs to establish two thousand professorships in Canadian universities.

There is no question that the "selective activism" of Paul Martin's fiscal policy was different from the blithely deficit-growing approach of Pierre Trudeau's finance ministers.[9] Nevertheless, the Chrétien Liberals practised fiscal prudence with both a pan-Canadian and a regional face. On the nation-building front, the 1999 Speech from the Throne undertook to double parental leave offered under the Employment Insurance program. The 2000 budget reindexed the tax system and enriched the Child Tax Credit, confirming that the government party was firmly wedded to Canada-wide policy initiatives. The run-up to the election also showed the Liberals to be as adept as ever at responding to regional interests.

Regionalism, Liberal Style: New Politics or Traditional Behaviour?
At first glance, the contrast between the national character of electoral politics waged under the third party system and its regional nature in the 1990s is striking. From the 1960s to the 1980s, federal partisan politics consisted of a battle between the Liberals and the Progressive Conservatives for power, with even the New Democrats campaigning nationally in the hope of holding the balance of power in the event of a minority government. Albeit competitive and antagonistic, the third party system operated under a general agreement about the legitimacy of the welfare state, official bilingualism, and equalization between regions.

The 1993 debacle shattered this national consensus, with "regionally based parties increasingly acting as representatives of regional interests within the national political arena."[10] Since the Liberals were the only party able to compete aggressively across the country in both the 1993 and 1997 elections, they provided strong evidence for testing the regionalization hypothesis: they resorted to different strategies and messages for each regional campaign in 1997 as they struggled to deal with the different electoral permutations they faced in each area.

In Atlantic Canada in 1997, the Liberal Party had the familiar challenge of facing the Conservatives and the NDP. In Quebec, it had the novel problem posed by an avowedly separatist Bloc Québécois holding a majority of the province's seats. In Ontario it faced a disappearing left and a right split equally between the PCs and Reform. To the west of Ontario it had to face a resurgent regional force in the shape of the Reform Party, which had marginalized the PCs and was even eroding the NDP's prairie populist appeal.

Because the basic partisan challenge facing the Liberal Party in each region in 2000 was essentially the same as it had been three years earlier, its approach to campaigning in the various regions should have validated the Carty thesis. On the eve of the election, the *Globe and Mail* confirmed that the Liberal Party had developed a regional *strategy* for the campaign: "The Liberals are pinning their hopes for a majority on capturing virtually every seat in Ontario, picking up seats in Atlantic Canada and Quebec, and keeping their losses [in the West] to a minimum."[11] In other words, the Liberals did their electoral calculus region by region. But this was a practice as old as federal politics.

As for their regional *tactics,* the Liberals certainly deployed their leader with a careful eye on the regional payoff that would accrue from his appearances. In a five-week campaign, Chrétien spent only parts of nine days campaigning west of the Ontario-Manitoba border. On each of the two days Chrétien visited Alberta (restricting himself to the city of Edmonton, where two Liberal MPs were in tough re-election battles) he visited two other provinces as well. He visited British Columbia, Canada's third-largest province, just three times, sticking to the cities of Vancouver and Victoria where there were Liberal votes to be found.

Calculating how to get the best return for the leader's time is not, of course, new to the fourth party system. What differentiates the fourth-party-system thesis is its insistence on the parties – including the Liberal Party – tailoring different messages for specifically targeted regions. The Grits' 2000 campaign provides ample evidence for testing this proposition.

The Atlantic Provinces

In the 1997 election, the Liberals' challenge in the east had come from the left, as the NDP and the Tories successfully tapped discontent over the Chrétien government's cuts to Unemployment Insurance benefits for seasonal workers and other job-destroying austerity measures. Together, the NDP and PCs had defeated twenty of thirty-one Liberal incumbents. In 2000, the Liberals adopted a three-pronged strategy to bring Atlantic Canada back into their fold. They recruited star candidates such as then Newfoundland premier Brian Tobin and former Nova Scotia finance minister Bernie Boudreau. The prime minister apologized personally to Atlantic Canadians for the hardships the region had suffered from Ottawa's deficit-cutting exercise. And policy grievances were addressed by the full restoration of Employment Insurance benefits for seasonal workers in Paul Martin's October 18 mini-budget and by promises of increased funds for regional development made during the campaign.

Atlantic Canadians were fully aware that the Liberals promised goodies such as money for economic development in order to save their parliamentary majority. An opinion piece in the *Halifax Herald* observed, "Truth is, the Liberals will perhaps need us, like never before, to return to power with a majority government for the third election in a row."[12] Maritimers understood the courting being pursued by the Liberals and expressed it as a delicate twist of irony that the Atlantic provinces seemed better treated by Ottawa when they shunned the Liberals than when they embraced them.

Quebec

Jean Charest had rallied both soft federalists and soft sovereigntists to capture 22 percent of the votes and five seats in 1997, but this revival did not outlast his abandoning federal politics to command the Quebec Liberal Party. Since Joe

Clark had resumed the federal party's leadership, Conservative support in the province had collapsed, leaving the Liberals optimistic that they could make gains in a polarized, two-party fight with the sovereigntists. Their strategy was to proceed along the double track of headhunting and policy making. On the recruiting rail, the Liberals enticed from political retirement Serge Marcil – one of two former provincial Liberal ministers to run – and seduced three Progressive Conservative MPs who had won seats in Parliament in 1997 to switch sides.

The Liberals' chief personnel problem could not be resolved by their long-practised art of elite co-optation among francophones, because it resided in the boss himself. Jean Chrétien was perhaps more unpopular than ever among vast reaches of Quebec francophones, who were ashamed of his coarse manner and embarrassed by his frequent demonstrations of linguistic ineptitude.[13] They were regularly reminded by sovereigntists and by a congenitally nasty pack of reporters in the francophone media that he had "betrayed" Quebec by supporting Pierre Trudeau's constitutional reforms in the early 1980s and by opposing Brian Mulroney's attempt to reconcile a disaffected Quebec with the Meech Lake Accord at the end of that decade.

Deeply hurt by the antipathy of his own people, the prime minister had taken the policy battle into his enemies' camp. During his second term in office, Chrétien maintained the tough approach he had adopted in the aftermath of the 1995 referendum with such bold actions as the Clarity Act, which spelled out under what referendum conditions the government of Canada would countenance a province's secession from Confederation. Sensing that support for sovereignty was in a free-fall, Chrétien dared Lucien Bouchard to hold another referendum after the Quebec premier had made pro forma gestures of support for the Bloc Québécois in the early part of the campaign. When Bloc leader Gilles Duceppe decided to play down sovereignty, however, in order to position his party as a defender of Quebec's interests, Chrétien backed away from his confrontational tactics, saying "the people of Quebec don't want to visit the dentist one more time."[14]

Figuring Quebeckers would prefer Santa Claus to root canals, the Liberals borrowed a strategy used in the first, second, and even the third party systems – courting winnable ridings with old-style election goodies. For example, commitments to spend $357 million on building two bridges and 14 kilometres of freeway in the suburban riding of Beauharnois-Salaberry helped the Liberals unseat prominent BQ MP Daniel Turp.[15] Extensive media coverage of allegations involving the Prime Minister's Office (PMO) feeding federal funds to cronies' projects in Chrétien's own riding, Saint-Maurice, helped to make the point that the way to get goodies from Ottawa was to elect a Liberal. No targeted advertising was needed when the media could much more credibly make the case that the Rouges were an old-fashioned, pork-barrel party.

Government projects affording political favouritism turned out to be only part of the story. In 2005, testimony from the Gomery inquiry into the federal sponsorship program revealed that underground financing was again a prominent feature of the Liberal party culture in 2000. According to Benoît Corbeil, director-general of the Liberal's Quebec wing from 1998 to 2001, a parallel campaign operation was underway in Quebec during the 2000 election, run by 30 so-called "fake volunteers," who supplied key ridings with extra campaign workers and resources.[16] Jean Chrétien's riding (Saint-Maurice) was among those that benefited from special attention, as were those of successful candidates Denis Coderre (Bourassa), Raymond Lavigne (Verdun), and Hélène Scherrer (Louis-Hébert).[17] Corbeil also revealed that illicit donations of substantial sums were funnelled to the party by Jean Brault, president of Groupaction Marketing Inc.[18] This firm made millions of dollars in sponsorship contracts to implement Jean Chrétien's strategy of visibility in Quebec, which, in Corbeil's blunt words, was aimed to "annihilate the Conservative Party in Quebec, to unite all of the federalists in Quebec under the Liberal banner, and to ensure that the Liberal Party became synonymous with Canada in the province of Quebec."[19]

Ontario
The Liberals' golden goose presented the party with a delightful challenge: how to hold on to their 101 seats and even capture the remaining 2. The principal reason for their all but clean sweep in 1997 had been the even split on the right end of the political spectrum. This self-defeating situation had been at least temporarily rectified by Reform's partly successful effort to "unite the right" by transmogrifying itself into the Canadian Alliance and choosing in Stockwell Day a younger, more telegenic leader than Preston Manning. Aided by a press corps excited by the prospect of having more confrontational politics to report, and boosted by the new *National Post,* a newspaper created by the media mogul Conrad Black to further his right-wing agenda, the Alliance had managed by October to raise its popularity in Ontario to 25 percent, while the PCs had sunk to a bare 9 percent.[20]

Not only was the right-wing vote unlikely to split so self-destructively again in Ontario, it was about to be courted by a revitalized party with a brand new leader whose political future depended on making a significant breakthrough in central Canada. Faced with this threat to its main power base, the government party did what only a party in power can do. Before calling the election, it moved to address its Ontario problem through public policy. On September 11, 2000, the prime minister and the provincial premiers signed a Health Accord that pledged to increase federal transfers from $15.5 to $21 billion by 2005-6. Shortly afterwards, Finance Minister Paul Martin's October mini-budget pre-empted the Alliance's major policy appeal by promising sweeping tax reductions and allocating $10 billion toward reducing the national debt – outclassing the Alliance plank on this issue by a cool $4 billion.[21] Just two days before the election call, Jean Chrétien appeared for a photo-op in front of Toronto's skyline with the premier of Ontario and the mayor of Toronto to announce a $500 million contribution to a tripartite infrastructure project to revitalize the city's waterfront – and, no doubt coincidentally – support the city's pending bid for the 2008 Summer Olympics. Whatever the understanding may have been between the normally Ottawa-bashing Mike Harris and the prime minister, the fact is that the Ontario premier did not provide Stockwell Day with the subsequent political support on which his electoral chances depended.

The Social Democratic West (Manitoba and Saskatchewan)

However undifferentiated "the West" may seem in central and Atlantic Canada, the four provinces could be grouped more appropriately for Liberal strategists into two pairs. In Manitoba and Saskatchewan the NDP was in power provincially and the LPC still accounted for a quarter of the federal vote. On the right, the PCs attracted enough votes in Manitoba to prevent Reform from dominating the stage after the 1997 election, but it had fallen below the 10 percent mark in Saskatchewan.

In Manitoba in 1997, the Liberals had lost half of the dozen seats they had carried in 1993. But with six seats and 34 percent of the vote, they had edged out the NDP (four seats and 23 percent of the vote), Reform (three seats and 24 percent of the vote), and the PCs (one seat and 18 percent of the vote). In 2000 the Liberals failed to persuade Glen Murray, the mayor of Winnipeg, to run federally and fill the giant hole created by the left-Liberal Lloyd Axworthy, the only member of Chrétien's cabinet to retire from politics before the campaign. Counting on attracting NDP voters, the Liberals conducted an urban campaign and hoped for the best.

Saskatchewan had been barren territory for the Liberals since 1958, when John Diefenbaker swept into power in a landslide victory. Exceptionally in 1993, they had taken five seats and 32 percent of the vote in a three-way split with the NDP and the new Reform Party, but they had fallen back to their more normal quarter of the vote in 1997, only keeping the urban seat in Regina held by Ralph Goodale, Chrétien's minister of agriculture. In a bid to woo the supporters of the NDP provincial government, Chrétien was thought to have solicited Roy Romanow, the retiring NDP premier, to run for his team. If he did, he failed.[22] However, the party did manage to persuade a sitting Saskatchewan NDP member of Parliament, Rick Laliberté, to change uniforms and join the Liberal team.

The Socially Conservative West (Alberta and British Columbia)

In Alberta and British Columbia, where Reform had become dominant in 1993, the Liberals were in an even more unpromising situation. Their gun-control law was widely unpopular in rural areas, where it had become a symbol of how disconnected from western sensibilities the Ontario-dominated Grits were. The mini-budget's promises of tax cuts did little to change the mood in western Canada, where many accused Martin of simply trying to steal the Alliance platform. Health care remained a particularly contentious issue in the region, as the Alberta government continued to attack the federal Liberals on the topic. The provincial health minister, Gary Mar, accused Chrétien of posing as the saviour of medicare despite his transfer cuts being the reason for Bill 11, Alberta's controversial health care privatization legislation.[23] The message that federal funding cuts had led to the parlous state of Canadian health care resonated strongly throughout the West.

Many journalists in the region argued that the Liberals had written off western Canada in their pre-election manoeuvres in order to focus on other parts of the country where they had a better chance to augment their seat total. Political scientist Roger Gibbins pointed out that they had gone to great lengths to recruit Brian Tobin to captain the campaign in Atlantic Canada, but they had not found a similar leader in the West. "A good election outcome for the Liberals would be to have roughly the same number of seats, perhaps a few less than they have right now," he maintained.[24]

Early expectations of expanding their six-seat caucus of British Columbian MPs proved vain. The problem was not just that in 1997 Reform's 43 percent share of the vote had allotted them twenty-five of the province's thirty-four seats. Stockwell Day's by-election campaign in the Okanagan Valley following his victory in the Canadian Alliance leadership contest had increased the Alliance's popularity in the province to the point that several BC provincial Liberals, including the MLA in Day's riding, had endorsed the new party. In an attempt to maintain unity within the local Liberal Party on the eve of a provincial election call, its leader, Gordon Campbell, forbade all members of his caucus and staff from involving themselves in the federal election, warning darkly that "if someone has time to work federally they should probably think about working federally full time, and get out of provincial politics."[25]

The federal Liberals' strategy was to focus on the metropolitan areas of Vancouver and Victoria, whose multi-ethnic population would be more receptive to Liberal policies than to those of the Canadian Alliance, and whose traditional NDP voters might be persuaded to abandon ship out of fear of Stockwell Day's social values. As in Quebec, the Liberals targeted winnable ridings with goodies in return for their electoral support, although Chrétien's BC lieutenant, Environment Minister David Anderson, didn't seem to be so sure about the strategy. On the one hand, the minister said, "I have absolutely no expectation of announcements during the campaign. If anyone is voting Liberal to get largesse I think they should reconsider their reasons for voting." On the other hand, he insisted that, "If re-elected, I look forward to fighting for Victorians to make sure our national plan pays local dividends."[26] Notwithstanding his strategic confusions, Anderson flew in to his Victoria riding a week before the writs were issued to announce a further $27.7 million to help mend leaky condos, in addition to the $75 million federal contribution made the previous June. In the first week of the campaign, the prime minister announced a grant to be matched by funds from the other levels of government for rebuilding Vancouver's public transit system, Translink.[27] Such old-politics gestures led the *Vancouver Sun* to encapsulate the Liberals' BC campaign as "Vote Liberal – it's the only way we'll get any good stuff for this riding."[28]

Advertising for the Regional Vote
For policy platforms to contain specific promises responding to local demands was neither new nor is it claimed as a defining characteristic of the fourth party system. What is meant to distinguish the new system from its predecessors is the parties' use of the mass media to send *different* messages to different parts of the country. "Campaign communication at the outset of the fourth party system is no longer national in scope, but rather is targeted by region and a host of socio-economic factors."[29]

Evidence for this proposition was provided to Carty et al. by the Liberal Party itself in 1997 when "for the first time" it "used regionally targeted advertisements" that responded to "different opponents attacking them on different issues, and from different directions, in each region."[30] Given the need to wage war on separate electoral fronts, "it quickly became apparent to the campaign's leadership that one set of national advertisements would not suffice. The party needed to tailor its advertisements to an electoral context of different opponents and different salient issues in each region."[31]

Although the Liberal Party faced the same variety of partisan battles in the 2000 campaign's various regions as it had in 1997, its advertising this time was almost entirely pan-Canadian in content, even when its delivery was in regional markets or via specialized media. (In Quebec, as has long been the custom, Liberal advertisements were designed for the province by an agency within Quebec. French-language advertisements in the 2000 campaign played to Finance Minister Paul Martin's popularity, featuring him walking side by side with the prime minister.)[32]

For the rest of Canada, advertising was created by Red Leaf Communications, the Liberals' consortium, which again was led by the Toronto ad agency Vickers and Benson. In contrast with the other parties, which bought commercial time in selected regions, most of the Liberals' advertising was paid for by the national campaign and was purchased for showing nationally. A health care advertisement released on Day 3 of the campaign featured the prime minister saying, "Someone in Newfoundland, if he gets sick, should not worry if he would be better off in Ontario or British Columbia."[33] The advertisement stressed that, irrespective of what province or region they lived in, Canadians have the same social rights. The message was pan-Canadian.

Two variations of a "feel good" ad were produced to inform the public about the LPC's accomplishments. One boasted about Canada's economic growth during the previous three years. It showed multi-ethnic Canadians of all ages interacting in happy places, such as a park while calm, uplifting music played, and it included endearing scenes with a naked baby tottering along a pristine beach and an older couple sharing an apparently worry-free laugh. Statistics declaring Liberal achievements scrolled across the bottom of the screen. Ending with the words, "All this because of your hard work," the commercial suggested that the governing party respected Canadians, understood their desire for tax reduction, and would manage the budgetary surplus responsibly. The Liberals' last ad, which aired just before and just after Stockwell Day's fifteen-minute infomercial on the final weekend of the campaign, emphasized the contrast between the two parties while warning voters about Joe Clark's claim that he would form a coalition with the Bloc Québécois in a minority government. Showing a number of Canadians in a variety of settings, the ad told Canadians not to take risks with other parties but to choose a strong, proven team.

Liberal advertising was "regional" in only two restricted ways. The first was in a series of national attack ads, which highlighted the role Stockwell Day had played in introducing legislation allowing for a form of private health care in Alberta. One featured ordinary Albertans expressing apprehension about health care and the provincial government's controversial Bill 11, which was passed on Day's watch as Alberta's treasurer. The ad ended by asking Canadians, "Does Stockwell Day's Reform Alliance speak for you?" The subtext was pan-Canadian: medicare should be maintained from coast to coast to coast.

The Liberals also produced and aired a few commercials for regional audiences. One ad that was broadcast exclusively in British Columbia attacked certain Alliance candidates, such as Keith Martin for his stance in favour of "profit-driven health care." It would have supported the fourth-party-system thesis, except that it concluded with a provincial variant of Red Leaf's mantra: "Does Stockwell Day's Reform Alliance speak for BC?" In effect, it gave a regional twist to the Liberals' pan-Canadian theme.[34] A similar ad attacked Day's belief that abortions, even in cases where women had been victims of rape or incest, should not be publicly funded unless the pregnancy threatens the life of the mother. Crafted to appeal to voters in urban areas where incumbent Liberal MPs were fighting tough re-election battles, it was aired only in British Columbia and Alberta.[35] In addition, the national campaign designed a commercial featuring Justice Minister Anne McLellan and other Liberal candidates for broadcast in Alberta. For Saskatchewan, Red Leaf created an ad featuring Ralph Goodale on the need for the province to have strong representation in the federal government.

The importance of having MPs in the government was also the gist of radio commercials produced for the Atlantic provinces. The Liberals did prepare some separate communications directed at specific ethnic groups, but these were mainly translations of one of the national commercials into Italian, Filipino, or Chinese. One Liberal candidate in Toronto, Allan Tonks, used his own funds to purchase $10,000 worth of television time mainly on multi-ethnic CFMT's Italian programming to explain that he was the "real" Liberal in the riding where he was challenging the independent ex-Liberal MP, John Nunziata.[36] Such individual advertising, while rare, had occurred throughout the third party system.

The only instance that fully fit the Carty model was a response ad in Chinese that was aired in Vancouver, Calgary, Edmonton, and Winnipeg to exploit Alliance candidate Betty Granger's apparently racist outburst about an "Asian invasion" of Canadian universities.[37]

With the exception of these few provincial and ethnic commercials, the LPC made no systematic effort to produce messages specially tailored to appeal to voters in one part of the country or another. In short, while the Liberals in 2000 did not completely contradict the Carty team's claim that parties were using television "as a primary tool in their efforts to send targeted messages to particular voting groups," the extent – and therefore the significance – of this phenomenon in 2000 was minor.[38]

The LPC also failed to take advantage of the explosion in specialty TV channels to appeal to "discrete groups of voters" by creating ads containing "campaign messages designed specifically for the targeted group."[39] Carty, Cross, and Young reported that parties see specialty TV as the "wave of the future, and foresee producing a much larger number of advertisements, with each one tailored to a particular audience targeted through the television specialty channels."[40] While the Liberals aired some advertising on specialty channels during the 2000 campaign, they simply played the same ads they had produced for broadcast television. This may have represented a missed opportunity for tailoring their appeal to certain demographics, but given the resources necessary to make special ads for the minuscule audiences that most specialty TV channels attract, the party figured that its time and money would be better spent on pan-Canadian commercials.

Looking at the LPC's use of advertising in the 2000 campaign, it seems that little had changed since its halcyon, pan-Canadian days. Wherever they were in the country, Canadians watched essentially the same messages from the Liberals, who showed little inclination to deliver substantially different targeted messages to particular subgroups of voters. Pan-Canadian appeals were implicitly judged to be just as effective in the regions as any regional message might have been. In sum, national messages prevailed over regional targeting in the Liberal campaign.

Leadership and the Fourth Party System

Apart from noting that the new parties had charismatic leaders, the fourth-party-system thesis does not pay much attention to political leadership as a factor differentiating the new era from the old.[41] This is curious, since André Siegfried declared back in 1907 that Canadians "vote as much for the man who symbolizes the policy as the policy itself."[42] Almost a hundred years later, leaders remain the central elements in political parties, symbolizing their political history, policy, goals, and even character. It follows that the Liberal Party's position in the emerging party system can hardly be analyzed without considering the nature of its leadership, whether in personal or systemic terms.

Appraising the leadership persona of Jean Chrétien is a difficult task for analysts. His performance in public view has been uneven, varying from dismayingly inept, particularly when he was leader of the opposition, to unapologetically insensitive, as in his flippant response to the human rights abuses committed by police at the 1997 Asia-Pacific Economic Cooperation (APEC) conference in Vancouver. Beyond being generally difficult to understand in either official language because of his neurological speech impairment, he often appeared disoriented and confused.

However disconcerting his verbal deficiencies, analysts resisted taking him seriously at their peril. On his watch, the Prime Minister's Office had become a more exclusive centre of government power than ever.[43] Within the caucus, Chrétien was seen as more autocratic than his predecessors. Whereas Pierre Trudeau respected a backbencher's right to dissent even on so fundamental an issue as his beloved Charter of Rights and Freedoms, Chrétien severely punished disloyalty, even if it was trivial. Within the extra-parliamentary party, his power of appointment in constituency nominations was enhanced by amendments made to the party's own constitution.

While adamantly insisting on his prerogatives as leader, Chrétien also showed great political shrewdness. He refrained from egregious patronage, having placed career diplomats, rather than partisans, as ambassadors in the key Canadian embassies in Washington, Paris, Rome, and London. Surprisingly for a politician known to be vindictive toward the disloyal and particularly resentful of those who challenged him for the party leadership in 1990, he was able to coexist with an avowed rival for his job who was more popular with both party and public. But when Paul Martin's supporters met to strategize before the party's March 2000 convention in anticipation of the leader's presumed imminent retirement, Chrétien defiantly fought off his "lame duck" label. He rallied party militants to the electoral barricades, insisting he would lead them on a populist campaign to stop the country's Americanization, preserve medicare, and build a compassionate society.[44] Following Martin's failed palace coup, journalists reported the two men did not speak, except at formal events. Nevertheless, these "two scorpions in a bottle" continued to run the government as a businesslike team.[45] Martin, described as the most powerful finance minister of the century, was given free rein to bring in his pre-campaign mini-budget and went on to play a major role in the campaign itself, making many appearances in Quebec and in the West to compensate for Chrétien's personal electoral deficiencies.

Emblematic of the leader's omnipotence in relation to his party was his decision, in the face of his caucus's nervousness, to call an election after just three years and four months of his 1997 mandate had elapsed. Not only was Chrétien unchallengeable in power, he was secretive in his exercise of it. Even in the Liberal Party's Ontario office in Toronto, where the crucial part of the campaign would be run, the staff was kept completely in the dark about the election timing until ten days before the writs were issued. These indications of Chrétien's omnipotence show the Liberal Party to have been a significant exception to the trend identified by Carty, Cross, and Young that, in the fourth party system, parties are becoming more member-driven in response to the public's demands for a more democratic and participatory politics.

The Campaign

Chrétien may have clung to his leadership to stave off a challenge from inside the party, but what energized him into fighting form was the outside challenge that came from the rebranding of the Reform Party as the Canadian Alliance and from its new, more socially conservative leader. The prospect of polarizing the election's discourse around the question of values led Chrétien on June 3, 2000, to a meeting of centrist and social democratic NATO leaders in Berlin, where he articulated his claim to be offering Canada its version of a "third way" government, "The Canadian Way in the 21st Century." Referring obliquely to the "forces of darkness" in an obviously intended, if quickly denied, reference to the Canadian Alliance, he repositioned himself as the defender of the generous state, apparently relishing the prospect of doing battle with Stockwell Day. Minutes after the writs were dropped in October, Chrétien declared outside Government House, "This election offers two very different visions of Canada, two crystal clear alternatives."[46] On October 31, in Week 2 of the campaign, the Globe and Mail's headline – "Alliance supports two-tier health care" – was manna from heaven for the reborn crusader. Chrétien immediately responded to the headline by asserting, "Never, never, never we will let the Alliance destroy [health care]."[47]

Chrétien seemed to have luck on his side again when the *Globe* published information obtained from a Canadian Alliance "secret document." The "Policy Overview" was intended to be used by Alliance candidates to help them answer questions and debate issues. It stated that the Alliance would hold a referendum on an issue if 3 percent of voters signed a petition, it would consider bids for the sale of CBC television, and it would make Natives on reserves pay sales taxes.[48] This document seemed to give substance to Chrétien's claim that the Alliance, under Day's leadership, harboured a secret agenda that contained views diametrically opposed to those of most Canadians.

Kind though it had been thus far in the 2000 campaign, Fortuna alone could not defend Chrétien from four opposition parties and their leaders who were hoping to draw blood. Chrétien's vulnerability was painfully evident in the television debates, when he was reduced to a new kind of *primus inter pares*: he was the prime target for each of the other party leaders. During the French-language debate in Week 3 of the campaign, with Alexa McDonough and Stockwell Day too inarticulate in French to be effective and Joe Clark punching only slightly harder, Bloc leader Gilles Duceppe led the assault, attacking Chrétien for cuts to health care, mismanaged funds, and even his commitment to Quebec. Chrétien had the difficult task of responding to the criticisms without appearing defensive. He adopted a dignified, prime ministerial pose and stressed the Liberal Party's vision of balance between social spending and tax cuts. He conceded that his government had made some deep cuts, but argued that they were necessary to repair the economic damage he inherited from the Conservatives under Mulroney. Chrétien also emphasized the Liberals' past experience in government, in contrast to the PC's and NDP's weak federal standing, the Alliance's newness, and the BQ's sovereigntist irrelevance.

The next day's debate in English was harsher, because all four opposition leaders joined in the attack. Accusations of arrogance and corruption were not the worst of the personal opprobrium heaped on the prime minister. He was also "accused of lying, of being a hypocrite, gutting health care, misrepresenting his opponents' policies and calling an election to prevent Liberal rival Paul Martin from ousting him."[49] Chrétien's objective was to ensure that he did not make any gaffes, while also remaining prime ministerial. Although he did not "win" the debate, he was able to avoid committing major errors. Stockwell Day's attempt to appear prime ministerial failed, but his energy and confidence succeeded in making Chrétien seem worn out. On the defensive during most of the debate, his one-liners were flat at best and he was unable to launch a successful offensive. As Edward Greenspon put it, his "inability to defend the very defensible must drive Liberals to total distraction."[50]

Given the five parties' needs to direct their appeals to their regional bases, the debates could have revealed the fourth party system's new dynamic. While the nature of the French-language debate necessarily geared itself to the regional interests of Quebec, the English language debate paid almost no attention to regional divides within the rest of Canada. The journalists' five question topics – justice, public finance, health care, federalism, and leadership – did not specifically raise the problems of different regions in the country. Had it been Chrétien's desire to speak to different regions, he could have reached out to them by making promises and slipping in references to local Liberal accomplishments in his answers, but he did not. The only times that the regions entered the debate was when the province of Alberta was invoked in relation to health care and when Stockwell Day attacked the Liberal leader for having dared Quebec to hold a referendum. If Canada had truly entered a new political era in which regions took precedence over national messages, this would have been reflected in the debate. It was not. As a result, this pre-eminent moment of the campaign's communication with the electorate turned out to be more nationalizing than fragmenting.

Back on the campaign trail, Chrétien downplayed concerns about his leadership by emphasizing the experience and competence of his team, which he claimed was best suited to lead the country: "As you all know a government is not a one man show," he said, adding, "History shows that the best governments are those with the best teams."[51] With the media digging deeper into the allegations of corruption concerning the prime minister's own riding, Chrétien attempted to relieve concerns about his long stay at the head of the party by raising the possibility of retirement – "In the third year, or something like that, I will decide if I still want to do it or not." He then immediately cast doubt on this hypothetical scenario by adding, "At this moment I intend to serve my mandate that I'm seeking from the people of Canada."[52] This "vote for me and I may retire, but then again I might not" message was unlikely to reassure those voters who were becoming uneasy about voting Liberal. It was certainly not enough to shake the opposition or the press from pursuing the corruption question.

When it was revealed in the media that Chrétien had called the president of the Business Development Corporation about a loan it was considering for one of the prime minister's constituents, Stockwell Day alleged that the prime minister had engaged in a criminal act. When Day and Clark continued this vein of attack even after the federal ethics counsellor had cleared him of inappropriate behaviour, Chrétien brought out the blameless-victim defence he had used with diminishing effect in the previous two campaigns. "Mr. Clark and Mr. Day have overstepped the accepted bounds of fairness and decency, which have been our tradition in Canadian elections. Instead, they have sought to destroy my reputation and in so doing have demeaned the political process." In an end-of-campaign interview with CBC TV's Rex Murphy, he took another run, with comically infelicitous syntax, at the same wounded-warrior defence: "I have been in public life a very long time and my name is very important and to attack my integrity *after a long career based on nothing* – it was very sad, but for me it was a sign of desperation."[53]

Jean Chrétien is clearly the most important party leader in the period following the breakdown of the third party system, yet his behaviour hardly corresponded with what one might expect of the fourth system outlined by Carty, Cross, and Young. On the contrary, his qualities connected more with each of the previous systems. The incessant reporting of probable corruption regarding federal grants in his constituency may have enraged the opposition parties and the media, but clientelism and patronage echoing Macdonald or Laurier elicited no apologies from him. His tendency to reach into the ranks of provincial premiers past and present as recruits for his cabinet smacked of Mackenzie King's brokering regional differences within the bosom of the federal cabinet. His championing of national values mirrored Trudeau's style in the third system when parties presented "consistent and coherent messages to voters in all corners of the country and ... inevitably reinforced the long-standing importance of the party leader's appeal in electioneering."[54] As for the more democratic, pluralistic, grassroots-centred style of the fourth party system, Chrétien seemed in his autocratic practices to be its antithesis. While he was adept at responding to local demands in proportion to their electoral needs, the entire thrust of his personal campaigning was pan-Canadian. Indeed, the overwhelming focus on the leader by the media was itself a nationalizing rather than a balkanizing force.

The Use of Policy by the Liberal Party

For Carty, Cross, and Young, policy is the central indicator of change from the third to the fourth party systems. Beyond a greater diversity among the political parties and a highly regionalized political climate, they found better educated and more participatory voters pushing the parties to produce more substantial platforms and demanding a new level of accountability of their representatives. The Liberals' 1993 campaign platform exemplified this new paradigm. Their "Red Book" allowed "the party leader to offer voters a checklist – a kind of political guarantee – for which, he promised, a Liberal government could be held accountable. In doing so, the party was signalling that it understood growing voter mistrust and that Liberals could offer a real response to meet it,"[55] although Carty, Cross, and Young acknowledge that "the party's membership played no direct role in deciding what would be included" in either the Red Book or its less meaty successor platform in the 1997 campaign.[56]

The Liberals' platform statement for 2000, *Opportunity for All: The Liberal Plan for the Future of Canada,* confirmed the Liberal Party of Canada's (LPC's) nonconformity with the new campaign behaviour identified by the Carty team. At thirty pages in length and small in format, it was so much less weighty than its two predecessors that it was quickly dubbed the "Red Leaflet." Developed following informal consultations with cabinet, caucus, and the extra-parliamentary party by a small group led for the third time by Chaviva Hošek in the PMO, the brochure was as slight in substance as it was light in the hand. Apart from recycling as electoral promises the content of the federal-provincial health accord in September ("we will invest $500 million for health information technologies") or the 2000 budget ("the Liberal government is doubling maternity and parental benefits from six months to one full year"), the planks were notably pulpy. A new Liberal government would:

- champion community action on illness prevention, health promotion, and wellness
- work with partners from across the country to enable citizens, experts, and officials from all orders of government to engage in a dialogue on the opportunities and challenges facing our urban regions
- increase access to capital through the Business Development Bank of Canada and the Farm Credit Corporation.

More important than the substance of policy as a litmus test for the new party era is its function as a yardstick for accountability. Far from being marketed as a symbol of accountability, however, the Liberals' 2000 platform document followed in the footsteps of the 1997 Red Book II and barely made an appearance after its launch in Week 2 of the campaign. Following some desultory media discussion, the Red Leaflet and the party's brochure on its corollary, the October mini-budget, virtually disappeared from the news.

From the beginning of the campaign, the Liberals presented the election as a choice between their values and the radically different ones represented by the Canadian Alliance. Since the media bought into this view of the election as an ideological polarization – marginalizing as a result the other parties outside Quebec – the Liberal Party's specific positions on policy questions for which it was to be held accountable became largely irrelevant.

While this decline in accountability as the central focus of the campaign might be thought to weaken the Carty, Cross, and Young argument, the switch of campaign discourse to a debate over values presented a more substantial counterfactual. Carty et al. hold that the balkanization of campaigns following the collapse of the third party system had been so great that they had lost any semblance of a "national discussion of politics."[57] To the extent that the campaign in 2000 became a polarized fight over values, it was certainly a national discussion. However much its discourse may have degenerated into personal attacks on the integrity of Chrétien and slurs on the religious views of Day, there was no denying it was a national, rather than a regional, contention.

The fourth-system thesis maintains not only that "the parties' policy positions are increasingly influenced by their membership" but that they are "tailored to specific segments of the electorate."[58] As with the earlier versions, the Red Leaflet bucked this putative trend, showing a strong desire to present the Liberals as a national party with policies designed to serve all Canadians across the country. As its introduction proudly stated, "Our vision sees a strong national government as essential to serving the broader public interest," and "Canada needs a vision for the future that recognizes a national perspective and the aspirations of all Canadians." As the Liberals' effort to control the political discourse, their policy platform was presented as a national, pan-Canadian document. Naturally, some promises in the Red Leaflet applied specifically to some regions (such as the anti-gang law for Quebec) or interests (such as Native peoples) rather than to others. But the platform was a single compendium prepared to be read in all parts of the country and by all interests. For their part, the media reinforced the role of party policy in helping foster some national political debate.

The Media of Communications and the National Political Debate

In the third party system, according to the Carty team, "television initially had a nationalizing effect on campaign communication in that it encouraged and facilitated the simultaneous delivery of the same partisan message to Canadians from coast to coast."[59] If Canada had shifted to a fourth party system, one could expect that the mass media would now treat federal election campaigns as multiple regional contests rather than as single, overarching competitions, and so would focus on regional issues as they went about setting the daily agenda for their readers, listeners, and viewers.

In fact, the press coverage of the 2000 campaign was far more national than regional, thanks in good part to Conrad Black's new *National Post,* whose unashamedly right-wing bias had helped turn the Reform Party's slow transformation into the Canadian Alliance and its subsequent leadership race into a months-long media obsession. By the time the writs were issued, the electronic media supported the Liberals' claim that the 2000 election campaign consisted of a pair of two-party contests between the Liberals and the Bloc Québécois in Quebec and between the Liberals and the Canadian Alliance in the rest of Canada. On the CBC's initial election broadcast, news anchor Alison Smith lumped the PCs, the NDP, and the Bloc together as "the other three parties."[60] Verbal marginalization heralded quantitative discrimination. Compared to the 1997 campaign, the media in 2000 gave much more coverage to the Liberals and the Alliance than to the PCs, the Bloc, and the NDP. CBC's *The National* in 2000 gave the Liberals and the Canadian Alliance roughly three times as much attention as they gave the three other parties; in 1997 the equivalent CBC coverage favoured the Liberals and Reform by just 30 percent.[61]

Canadians spend more time watching TV news coverage of elections than partisan advertising during commercial breaks, so how campaigns are presented on the news has a huge influence on voters' decisions. Thanks to cost cutting in the media, which reduced the resources they devoted to local and regional news coverage, television news coverage in 2000 was more centralized than in 1997, causing a greater focus on the national campaign in general and the leaders' tours in particular. For example, in September 2000 the CBC effectively cut its locally produced television news in half, which meant it focused less on the local and regional aspects of federal campaigns than before. Similarly, the other television networks aired more and more segments produced by national reporters for their local suppertime newscasts. Regardless of what network viewers watched, they would have seen the same pictures of the leaders' tours on every channel, since the major television networks pooled their camera crews to cover the leaders' tours, as they had done in 1997.[62] Meanwhile, radio and newspapers, which had both been hit by deep cuts, increasingly turned to wire services for their stories.

Instead of national issues being displaced by regional ones, the 2000 campaign saw local issues becoming national. In their watchdog mode, the press was on the lookout for inconsistencies in the parties' messages, so a faux-pas by a low-profile candidate fighting a losing battle for election could be deemed newsworthy nationwide. For example, when Alliance candidate Betty Granger (running in Winnipeg South Centre) made some unfortunate comments about people of Asian descent to a political science class at the University of Winnipeg, it became an issue that the Liberals exploited in their national campaign. Faced with four opponents with regionalized support bases, the Liberals profited from the "nationalizing effect on political communication" that television had had in the third party system, thus enabling them "to set a national agenda" and "to present a common front to all voters." As in the third party system, "all Canadians, regardless of their location ... were provided with a base of common political information."[63]

It would be inaccurate to affirm that there were no regional issues in the campaign. It is also true that some of the national issues were more or less important in different regions. Employment Insurance was only a serious concern in Atlantic Canada; organized crime was a major issue only in Quebec; and farm subsidies were only salient in Saskatchewan and Manitoba. Since pan-Canadian policies such as gun control tend to evoke different responses in different regions, the Liberals' success in turning the campaign into a question of "values" helped them avoid taking stances on potentially divisive issues and so present themselves as the most "national" of the parties. In sum, the media helped the Liberals make "a mass appeal to the Canadian electorate through network television" – this is precisely the characteristic of media campaigning in the third party system.[64]

New Technologies and the Liberal Party's Pan-Canadian Message

Since television broadcasting is the communications medium that differentiated campaigning in the third party system from that of the second, it is not surprising that it continued to infuse politics in the 1990s with a strongly nationalizing character. If there is a medium or media to set the fourth party system apart from the third, it is the microprocessor-based World Wide Web, e-mail, and the cellular telephone. Given the fragmentation of the fourth party system into "a series of regional competitions, each with its own issues,"[65] Carty, Cross, and Young point out that these new instruments allow political parties to target "relatively small groups of voters" with "specially tailored messages ... in specific areas of the country."[66]

There are solid theoretical and empirical grounds for the Carty group's fears about the national campaign dialogue of the third party system being undermined when the parties can "deliver different messages to voters in different regions or provinces, and do so without the transparency and accountability inherent in the traditional media."[67] For print, radio, and television, the cost of producing content is high. A small amount of content must be distributed to vast audiences so that the media companies can recoup their investment. The production and distribution costs for new media, however, are much lower, so it is feasible to produce content for viewing by very small audiences. New communications technologies give political candidates an opportunity to engage in direct, private communication with voters, without being distorted or monitored by the media. Combining "more sophisticated polling techniques providing the party with detailed information on subsets of voters" with e-technology gave them the capacity to engage in private, customized communications with a much larger number of small groupings of voters than ever before at much lower costs.[68] The issue is whether the parties were making use of this technology effectively to address relatively small groups of voters with specially tailored messages.

World Wide Web

Carty and colleagues see the Web as one of "three computer-based technological advances that parties are using to communicate with targeted groups of voters," and they quote the former national director of the Liberal Party, who viewed "the technology as essentially an extension of direct mail, in that the message can be tailored to the demographics of the likely user group."[69] Since the cost of producing and distributing content is very low on the Web, it is ideal for sending messages that may be tailored to a nearly endless number of socio-demographic characteristics. In particular, the parties believed that the Web offered a unique opportunity to reach young voters, since young people accounted for a disproportionate number of Web surfers.[70]

Parties could enhance their credibility by posting background and supporting materials on their websites so that people interested in these issues could find details. Since every bit of information on the Web is available to anyone anywhere with an Internet connection, it is an excellent tool for making party politics more accessible and transparent. This possibility also supported the general distrust of elites and the demands for more grassroots participation putatively characterizing the new party system. With these two functions in mind, we need to examine the two kinds of websites deployed by Liberals in the 2000 campaign – the national site and individual candidate sites.

On October 22, the day of the election call, the Liberals replaced their old, rather stodgy website with a more up-to-date version that greeted surfers with a picture of the prime minister energetically working a crowd. The site contained information on the leader's tour, copies of the policy platform in a number of formats, biographies and pictures of all the party's candidates, and a number of self-serving press releases generated by the campaign war room. During the campaign, press releases and a new picture of the prime minister looking his best were added daily. Interestingly, the national site was not used to target the Liberals' message to youth or any other particular group. Youth issues did not appear among the nineteen policy fields listed as "Your Issues" on the home page – a compendium that included seniors, women, Aboriginals, and Canadians with disabilities.

Consistent with the fourth-party-system analysis, the Liberal website did increase the transparency and the accessibility of the campaign. Candidates reported that they often referred individuals with detailed policy questions to the national website, where an abundance of information on policy matters could be found.[71] But neither the Liberals nor any other party made significant use of multimedia capabilities in presenting this information, which led one observer to describe the various party websites as "banal, offering up little more than brochure ware."[72] Missing another opportunity offered by e-technology, the Liberals failed until just before election day to include a facility on their website for supporters to make secure online donations via credit card.

Since candidate websites are aimed at narrow audiences – the electors in a riding – they are ideal for sending targeted messages. If different issues and messages are dominating the campaign in different parts of the country, this phenomenon should be reflected here. Although the Liberal Party provided templates for candidates along with tools for helping them construct their own sites, most were as primitive in 2000 as in 1997, featuring a picture and a biography of the candidate, the campaign office's street and e-mail addresses, and, sometimes, a schedule of events. Very few of them referred to policy beyond the occasional hyperlink to the electronic version of the Red Leaflet on the party's national site. Most incumbents chose to highlight their parliamentary record, while most challengers concentrated on their accomplishments in the community. Only 29 percent of Liberal candidates nationwide had campaign-relevant websites, from a high of 44 percent in Atlantic Canada to a low of just 6 percent in Quebec. Even though nearly half of Canadians were then online, compared to just 10 percent in 1997, 71 percent of Liberal candidates did not make the effort to create websites. Many probably felt that few people would visit them, so if they had one at all, they decided to create only the most rudimentary sites. The low number of visits reported on most sites with visible hit counters seemed to confirm this theory, but candidate websites were exceptionally difficult to locate.[73]

Contradicting the ideas of most theorists, Warren Kinsella, a communications adviser to the Liberal Party, reported that the Web was used in the 2000 campaign to "ensure consistency of message" across the country, and not to appeal to narrow audiences.[74] Although the economics of the Web allow for content to be created for and distributed to narrow audiences, the fact that all Web content was universally accessible meant that if blatantly contradictory messages were put online by candidates in different parts of the country, it would be much easier to detect than if the message was delivered using local media or conventional door-to-door methods.

Voter-Tracking Software
With recent advances in computing power, it became possible to use statistical data to isolate small pockets of potential supporters within a riding. This was the promise of voter-tracking software, which Carty's group saw as another of the "computer-based technological advances that parties are using to communicate with targeted groups of voters."[75] By combining data from the electronic version of the Elections Canada voters list with codes obtained from Statistics Canada, which provide a socio-demographic snapshot of every postal code in the country, voter-tracking software could identify clusters of individuals in a riding whose demographic characteristics predispose them to support one party over another. Party workers could then concentrate their campaigning on the individuals whom the software identified as being most receptive to their party's message, and they could customize their communications with these voters so as to appeal to their likely interests, as deduced from the demographic data. And as the party's database of demographic information grew with every campaign, information collected during previous campaigns could be used to give candi-

dates a running start in the next campaign by speeding up the process of identifying support within a riding.[76]

Although the data-processing power of the ManagElect software created for the Liberals was tremendous, the system was only used to track a riding's party supporters and to mobilize these supporters on election day. The electronic version of the Elections Canada voters list was merged with an electronic version of the local telephone white pages to generate a database containing the name, address, and telephone number of every registered voter in a riding. This information was then printed and distributed to street and phone canvassers, who marked the party affiliation of the voters they contacted on computer-generated lists. Party affiliation information was then re-entered into the computer using a barcode scanner, and a new list of committed and potential Liberal supporters was generated for use on election day. Party scrutineers used these lists to keep track of who had voted during the day. Should supporters fail to materialize at the polls, volunteers could mobilize the vote by phoning the electors identified on the list.

In practice, the effectiveness of this operation was hampered by inaccuracies and omissions in the voters list and in the electronic phone book data. In the Liberals' urban riding of Willowdale, whose electronic behaviour was monitored for this study, the system administrator for the voter-tracking software estimated that only two-thirds of the records in the database were accurate enough to be useful to the campaign.[77] The ManagElect software had the capability for creating new fields in the database and thus exploiting information from commercial databases to identify potential voters and the issues they were interested in, but using these features was both difficult and unnecessary. It was difficult because it was costly to acquire the data and time-consuming to analyze it; both time and money are in short supply in a campaign. It was unnecessary, because campaign volunteers, who are familiar with the riding, have an intuitive sense of where their supporters reside.

Assuming that candidates did make use of the software's power to identify individuals who were likely to support them, there was little time in the campaign to respond by sending these individuals information on the issues that interested them. Preparing literature on specific issues and mailing it out to interested individuals was not feasible in a thirty-five-day campaign.[78] Nor were the data collected during the previous federal election campaign useful either, both because of difficulties in importing this information and because the data quickly go out of date, since people in an urban area move with great frequency.[79] The unpredictable timing of Canadian elections and the strict limits on campaign spending also reduce the effectiveness of this software – unlike in the United States, where election dates are fixed and campaign financing mushrooms despite all attempts at its regulation.

Electronic Mail

The Carty team made three observations about the uses of e-mail in campaign communications with voters. First, they anticipated that bulk, unsolicited e-mail (popularly known as "spam") could well replace conventional bulk mail for sending specific messages to specially targeted groups of potential supporters. For example, parties could purchase an e-mail address list from an ecological citizens' group and circulate to these individuals information on how they proposed to protect the environment. Second, they noted that e-mail was an effective way for citizens to engage in a dialogue with candidates and parties. During the 1997 campaign, thousands of e-mail messages were sent to parties, which welcomed the opportunity to communicate "with real voters about issues that they are concerned about."[80] Finally, e-mail, like the other new communications technologies, allowed parties to engage in private communications with voters, away from the watchful eyes of the press.[81]

For all its alluring promise, there were many practical barriers that prevented the effective exploitation of e-mail as a campaign tool. The largest was finding accurate e-mail addresses for a targeted population. A party or a candidate could purchase lists of e-mail addresses from Internet service providers or other commercial sources and then send a uniform message to all electors, but this option failed to capitalize on the ability e-mail gave senders to customize their communication. In the 2000 federal campaign, spam was not used as a substitute for bulk mail by the LPC or by any Liberal candidate.

In one simple test of citizen dialogue during the campaign, two e-mail messages were sent to addresses provided by each of the five national parties on their websites explicitly to encourage questions and comments from the public. The Bloc answered both queries within an hour, the NDP replied to one query after two weeks, while the PCs, the Alliance, and the LPC did not manage to respond at all. As far as democracy-enhancing interactivity was concerned, the parties seemed to have given a very low priority to interacting electronically with the voters. Canadian parties also failed to make use of the e-mail addresses that fell into their laps when they received messages from the public by adding them to their mailing lists for sending out partisan newsletters and press releases – as is common practice in the United States.[82]

Nor was the Internet much used by voters, who seemed to send few e-mails to candidates. During the course of the campaign in Willowdale, only about thirty e-mail messages were received from constituents. Ten people sent good wishes, eight volunteered their time, and the rest asked general questions about party policy and the candidate, Jim Peterson, the incumbent secretary of state for financial institutions.[83] Since the most common way of finding candidates' e-mail addresses was from their websites, which were very difficult to find, candidates might have received more e-mails if more people had known where to send them. Since the parties hardly used e-mail, its capacity for sending communications unde-tected by the press remains valid in theory but moot in practice.

One further function of e-mail is its use for internal campaign communica-tions. In the 2000 campaign, the Liberal Party's national headquarters sent talk-ing points, polling results, and other information to local campaign staff via the Internet in an effort to keep them "on message" and informed about develop-ments in the national campaign. Such messages were relatively infrequent, how-ever, averaging less than one per day; and the use of e-mail to send this information merely displaced the role played by fax machines in internal cam-paign communications since the late 1980s.[84]

The Liberals also failed to maintain an electronic mailing list either for their members or for interested citizens. The party could have got more mileage out of its press releases by judiciously sending them to Liberal partisans or to inter-ested citizens, as do most candidates for high office in the United States. Nor did the Liberals send press releases or other information to journalists by e-mail.[85] For the first time, Liberal and Alliance campaign buses were equipped with data ports at every seat, where journalists could access the Internet from their laptop computers, and all CBC reporters were issued Blackberry wireless e-mail de-vices. Yet the parties failed to take advantage of this technology to get their mes-sage out to the reporters. For example, the Liberal war room could have easily sent some damaging information about the Alliance to a reporter on the Stockwell Day tour via e-mail, but this opportunity was not exploited. Instead, party war rooms bombarded newsrooms with faxes, and journalists on the tour with the leader were handed sanitized versions of these faxes by campaign staff.

Wireless Communications
Wireless technology has significant implications for the fourth-party-system thesis. Pagers, cellular telephones, and wireless e-mail devices have become an indispensable tool for party operatives and for political reporters by making information available anywhere in an instant. There are pedestrian uses for this technology in all aspects of a campaign, but its greatest significance is for the entourage accompanying the leader's tour, which used to be isolated from the rest of the campaign while it was on the road. Information on the activities of other parties and other breaking news formerly could only be learned in detail at the end of the day as the tour staff retired to a hotel for the night. Today, the leader, the leader's staff, and the media covering the tour are con-tinuously updated on developments elsewhere in the campaign by various elec-tronic devices.

The speed with which electronic messages travelled back and forth fostered the emergence of campaign war rooms, which responded instantly to every move of the other parties. When information took longer to travel across the country, such war rooms were neither possible nor as valuable. This instantaneous electronic communication across the country created a "ping-pong effect" in the campaign's daily routine. Whereas in the past a leader could respond to another leader's charges or missteps only the next day, by 2000 there were three, four, or even five cycles of exchanges in a single day. One result was to make the campaign much more acrimonious.[86] In the words of Roy MacGregor, "a leader barks in Saskatoon and the sound has not even faded when another leader yelps back in Halifax," and "very often by the time a day comes to an end the reaction has so far outstripped the original news that no one can even remember where the day began."[87]

That all these exchanges of invective between leaders were considered newsworthy by media nationwide only served to increase the amount of coverage the leader and the leader's tour received, compared to the coverage that might be given to regional issues. Furthermore, the emergence of the war room increased the importance of the parties' national offices in campaign communications, which meant there was even less opportunity for the media to focus on local issues and messages.[88]

In sum, the Liberal Party, along with its opponents, failed to make effective use of the new communications technologies, even though they were potentially conducive to targeting relatively small groups of voters with specially tailored messages. At the same time, they were forcing parties to be consistent in their messaging, since contradictions could be easily spotted when information was available anywhere in an instant. Despite these technologies' successful use in the United States, the unpredictable timing, short duration, and strict spending limits in Canadian elections were frustrating their use north of the border. The Internet had not yet arrived in Canada as a powerful political tool.

The Results: A Mandate for the Status Quo

"No one has more at stake in the result than Jean Chrétien," warned Peter Mansbridge somewhat lugubriously on the CBC TV news on October 29. "It was his decision – and his decision virtually alone – to call the election ... No one has bothered to hide the fact that many in his own party are skeptical and worried that, on election day, the Liberals won't be able to match their current standing in the opinion polls." At the end of a gruelling campaign in which a beleaguered and seemingly failing prime minister had sustained continual political attacks and been dubbed "King Lear" in the media, he vanquished his foes outside his party and confounded his critics within it. He returned to Ottawa virtually impregnable. Beyond the question of their leader's personality, the Liberals were felt to have done a good job in managing the economy by 59 percent of the electorate, especially in creating jobs and reducing the national debt.[89]

Overall, they had managed to maintain their control of the political centre, with caution as their watchword.

The results comfortably met the party's own goals. In the Atlantic provinces they picked up eight seats, going from four seats to five in Newfoundland, from zero to four in Nova Scotia, from three to six in New Brunswick, and again carrying all four in Prince Edward Island. In Quebec they picked up eleven ridings – four from the Conservatives, thanks in good part to former Tory MPs André Harvey, David Price, and Diane St-Jacques, who all ran successfully as Liberals – and seven from the Bloc, which fell to parity in seats with the Liberals at thirty-seven each. Despite Duceppe's solid campaign, his moral support from the ever-popular Premier Bouchard, and his material support from the Parti Québécois organization, the BQ faltered. In what had become a two-party race, the Liberals took 44 percent of the provincial vote, which meant 90 percent of the ethnic vote, 80 percent of the anglophones, but just 35 percent of the francophone voters (though this was up from one-quarter in 1997).[90]

While the Liberals carried off moderate gains in Quebec, they held their ground in Ontario, knocking off the Conservatives' sole MP and the independent Nunziata, while losing only one riding to the NDP in Windsor and two seats to the Alliance in eastern Ontario. That they kept one hundred seats as the core of their parliamentary majority was in large measure thanks to the Canadian Alliance's failure to unite the right: twenty-four Grit seats were won from the vote being split between the Alliance and the PCs.[91]

The Liberals' net loss of one seat in Ontario was duplicated in Manitoba, where they retained five seats and so kept ahead of the NDP and Alliance, which took four apiece, leaving one seat to the Progressive Conservatives. Further west, the pickings were very slim. Like Manitoba, Saskatchewan has fourteen seats in Parliament, but the Liberals won only two of them, having kept Goodale's and gained Laliberté's – which meant they could claim to have doubled their Saskatchewan representation. In Alberta the Liberals also took two, holding on to their 1997 gains. In BC, the Alliance picked up two more seats, one from the NDP and the other from the Liberals, whose caucus fell to five of the province's thirty-four constituencies. They also picked up Yukon's single seat.

Overall, Jean Chrétien returned to Ottawa with 173 MPs, eighteen more than he had elected in 1997 thanks to two percent more of the vote. This gave him a resounding mandate for sticking to the status quo, as he had proposed in the Red Leaflet. It suggested, as well, that the party system's alleged transition from its third to a fourth phase was stuck in neutral.

The Persistence of the Old Party Systems

Combined with the results of the 1993 and 1997 elections, the evidence produced by the Liberal Party's successful electoral outing in 2000 did not confirm a general transformation in either the nature of Canadian parties or their campaign practice. Far from showing a failure to accommodate the forces of political, social, and governmental change, the Liberals proved once more to be masters at responding to the electorate's broad desire for balance and moderation. Confronting party competition, the LPC enhanced its dominance of the political stage in the face of the concerted fire of its four opponents. Far from having to "wrestle with the problem of finding a way to reposition the party as the core of a new national party system," the Liberals had remained, as in 1993 and 1997, the sole credibly national player, albeit dependent on their quasi-monopoly in Ontario.[92]

Not only had the "old" Liberals succeeded in the new party system better than their rivals, they achieved this feat by notably old-fashioned means. While denounced in the media for practising first-party-system clientelism, Maritime and Quebec voters rewarded them for a campaign laced with patronage-style promises, whether Employment Insurance for the seasonal fishery workers in the Atlantic provinces or bridges for the riding of Beauharnois-Salaberry. In BC, David Anderson's riding was helped by a direct promise. And running a campaign against Alberta was a tactic that echoed Mackenzie King's second-party-system campaign in 1940 against the Quebec government of Maurice Duplessis. Even the Liberals' use of new technology was for traditional purposes: to enhance communications within the campaign organization, but not to displace its fundraisers or communicate tailored messages to select groupings.

As for general campaign practice, the 2000 campaign suggested that the national consensus, which characterized the third party system, was being reconstructed. In Quebec, the BQ shied away from sovereigntist talk. In the rest of Canada, Stockwell Day made every effort – including holding up his awkwardly lettered "NO TWO-TIER HEALTH CARE" sign during the leaders' English debate, routinely speaking some French at press conferences, fielding visible-minority candidates, and abandoning his party's flat tax proposal – to move toward the liberal mainstream in his effort to attract central Canadian voters. Both these new parties judged their campaigning by an old-politics standard: Duceppe prided himself on his well-run, disciplined campaign, just as Day apologized for a poorly organized, incoherent one. Parties, as the Carty group reminds us, adapt to the successes of their opponents. The 2000 campaign showed the four smaller parties adapting to the Liberals' national focus rather than the Liberals adapting to their challengers' regionalizing practices.

Paul Martin
Saved By the Far Right

Disaster and Recovery: 2004
Paul Martin As Political Lazarus

The 2004 election campaign was about succession, not success.[1] How would Jack Layton, whom the New Democratic Party had recently plucked from Toronto's City Hall, lead it on the hustings? How would Stephen Harper make the transition from running the Alberta-based, right-wing Alliance Party to speaking for all Canadian conservatives after its merger with the PCs? Who would end up wearing the mantle as defender of Quebec's interests? And – the central issue for this chapter – how would Paul Martin manage the double-edged task of sustaining the Liberal Party of Canada's (LPC's) hegemony over federal politics while bringing it the renewal that he had promised during his determined campaign to oust Jean Chrétien from the Prime Minister's Office?

Renewal has seldom troubled new Liberal leaders. Five men have taken over the party leadership while their caucus faced the government from across the aisle in the House of Commons. Alexander Mackenzie (1873), Wilfrid Laurier (1887), William Lyon Mackenzie King (1919), Lester Pearson (1958), and Jean Chrétien (1990) had ample opportunity to redefine their party while learning the ropes as Leader of the Official Opposition. Nor had the first two occasions when Liberal leaders changed while in power proven problematic. Louis St. Laurent had carried on in 1948 as Mackenzie King's anointed successor and, embodying continuity rather than change, won two more majority governments before going down to defeat in 1957. Having won a highly competitive leadership race in 1968, Pierre Elliott Trudeau so incarnated fresh air in his personal style and philosophy while also winning his party's loyalty that he quickly turned Pearson's minority into a majority government without having to attack his predecessor in order to prove he was different. The transfer from Chrétien to Martin in 2003 took neither of these successes as its model.

It was the example of John Turner, who shattered the Liberal temple by shaking its pillars to the ground in 1984, that Paul Martin found himself following. Indeed, the parallels between the two aspirants were eerie. As successful former ministers of finance who had left the cabinet following bitter personal breaks with their prime ministers, each had become the toast of the business community and the darling of the media. As dauphins-in-exile, each had rallied supporters who split the party into feuding camps. Once crowned leader after their prime minister's belated announcement of retirement, both swept into Ottawa as if the Opposition had just defeated the government. They purged incumbents connected to the old regime, which they disowned by announcing major restructurings. Then, supremely confident in their own electoral superiority, they rejected counsels of caution, preferring campaigning to governing. Unable to change their organizational approach while trying to please everyone, they blundered on the hustings, giving mixed ideological messages and managing thereby to enhance their enemies.

It was the difference in his Conservative opponent that saved Paul Martin from suffering Turner's fate. In 1984 Brian Mulroney had been the more "liberal" of the two leaders, more clearly offering the public continuity with the outgoing Trudeau record on bilingualism and social policies. Twenty years later, the Liberals' challenger came from the far right, not from the centre, thus allowing Martin to adopt the campaign strategy of his ousted nemesis, Chrétien. Like his predecessor, he could provide bland, left-leaning policy rhetoric while demonizing his opponent. With the media communicating deep concerns about Stephen Harper's social conservatism, the voters ultimately had second thoughts about dismissing the government party, however unworthy of office it might have seemed.

To understand how Martin turned what was generally expected in the fall of 2003 to be the most boring of Canadian elections (because it would return the Liberals with an even larger majority) into one of the most exciting campaigns ever (in which their impending defeat was only averted on the weekend before the vote), we need to investigate the following five issues:

- How did the dynamic of Martin's ascent to power establish the conditions for his near loss of it?
- How did his handling of the prime minister's job lead him to call a premature election?
- Why were his campaign's organization, strategy, and platform so nearly disastrous?
- Why did the media first act as enemy and then as ally to reinforce his message?
- How did the campaign in the regions confirm continuity rather than change in the Canadian party system, and what do the results suggest about the ongoing evolution of the Canadian party system?

Paul Martin's Ascent to Power and the Conditions for Trouble

Always close to his Liberal cabinet-minister father and namesake who had run unsuccessfully for the party's leadership against both Pearson and Trudeau, Paul Martin Jr. went into politics to avenge these paternal failures by becoming prime minister himself. He had won the nomination in the safe Montréal riding of LaSalle-Émard in 1988[2] and, rookie though he may have been, was attractive enough as a successful, bilingual businessman that he might well have won the party's leadership in 1990 had Jean Chrétien not already secured effective control over its organization following his own defeat by Turner in 1984.

Biding his time on the assumption that his turn would come in due course, Martin accepted Chrétien's assignment of co-authoring the party's winning platform in 1993 and went on to become the country's most successful finance minister. Even though he cut federal spending programs more drastically than had ever been tried before, he managed to remain the most popular member of the government, a reality that contributed to sustaining the prime minister's ambivalent animus against him. For his part, Chrétien was neither inclined to forget nor to forgive. He did not forget that, during a candidates' policy debate in 1990, Martin's supporters had shouted "vendu," implying that he was a traitor to Quebec on the white-hot issue of the year, the Meech Lake Accord. And he did not forgive Martin's obvious ambition to succeed him. Nevertheless, Chrétien gave Martin such sustained support in his deficit-slashing mission that their prime-minister-and-finance-minister partnership proved the most productive in Canadian history. The volatile mix of political solidarity and personal antipathy remained stable during Chrétien's first ministry.

Following Chrétien's second majority election in 1997, Martin's advisers began to become impatient. At the party's 1998 convention, they kept a low profile, not running insurgent candidates for the executive.[3] But by the following year, they launched a quiet campaign to take over the party organization. In the summer, Martin organizer Karl Littler concluded from a study of Liberal Party membership rules that capturing riding presidencies was the key to establishing control. Starting at the riding level, John Webster and Michele Cadario began working with friendly MPs. By September, these covert activists had taken over the party's Ontario executive at its provincial convention,[4] a pattern that was repeated over the next two years in all provinces outside Quebec, where the organization remained under Alfonso Gagliano's patronage-fuelled control until it fell to the Martinites in December 2002.[5]

By February 2000, one month before the party's looming national convention, everything seemed to be falling into place for Paul Martin to realize his ambition once the prime minister made his expected announcement of retirement. On March 10, just days before the delegates gathered in Ottawa, Martin's backers met at the Regal Constellation Hotel near the Toronto airport to review their situation.[6] When the press reported this gathering as a meeting of conspirators plotting against the party's leader, Chrétien reacted with typical spitefulness. Although Martin gained control of the party's national executive that month, Chrétien spiked their guns by pre-emptively calling another election, winning a third majority, and postponing the inevitable.

The pressure that was building up on Chrétien from the rebels within his caucus and the party's extra-parliamentary wing was exacerbated from the outside by the media's periodic reports of polls suggesting strong public support for his replacement by his finance minister. Furthermore, his chief contender's grip on the party apparatus meant that Martin's minions could skew the delegate-selection process to ensure their supporters would be elected when convention delegates were being chosen to represent the ridings at the party convention. By 2002, the Alberta, British Columbia, Ontario, and Quebec wings had changed the rules for recruiting new members to the party. Riding presidents, who were now mostly in Martin's camp, would be given 100 membership forms at a time, whereas others could only get five. In British Columbia, a further restriction favouring the Martin team required names of new party recruits to be submitted prior to getting the requisite forms. (Martin's rivals Sheila Copps, John Manley, and Alan Rock complained so vigorously about these rules' unfairness that they were modified in Ontario the following January, but complaints continued to be voiced that those opposed to Martin were not receiving even their five forms upon demand.)

Once it became clear that so many Martin delegates would converge on the Liberals' long-postponed convention in February 2003 that they would pass the party's constitutionally required resolution calling for a leadership convention (and in so doing indicate no confidence in their leader), Chrétien announced his intention to retire at a caucus meeting in Chicoutimi in August 2002.[7] But ever ornery, he declared he would hang on for eighteen more months, giving himself time to leave a more progressive legacy and keep Martin champing at the bit.

By this time, however, the prime minister had made the serious error of firing his finance minister. Whether or not he had engineered his own dismissal from cabinet,[8] Martin's departure from the government on June 2, 2002, left him free to pursue his leadership campaign without being constrained by the norm of cabinet solidarity. With alacrity, he accepted high-profile speaking engagements around the country. He burnished his international bona fides by accepting the invitation of the Secretary General of the United Nations, Kofi Annan, to co-chair, with former Mexican President Ernesto Zedillo, a study on how private enterprise might rescue the Third World from its poverty. He conferred with such public figures as Michael Ignatieff about the direction that Canadian foreign policy should take, and he commissioned papers from scores of policy analysts on the host of issues for which he needed to prepare positions.

The conclave to choose the party's new leader – finally held in Toronto's Air Canada Centre on November 14, 2003 – was as bereft of surprise as any American presidential convention whose outcome had been determined long in advance. Potential candidates John Manley and Alan Rock had already thrown in the towel, complaining of the rigged process and leaving a valiant Sheila Copps to deny Martin victory by acclamation.

After thirteen years of autocratic rule, the new prime minister's promise to do politics differently by reducing its "democratic deficit" was attractive both to activists and journalists. His charm (however forced), his ideas (however focus-grouped), and his eloquence (however scripted) seemed to respond to the general public's desire for change. On his left, the NDP presented no serious threat, as it languished at well under 20 percent in the polls despite having chosen the ebullient Jack Layton as its leader. Meanwhile, the Alliance Party had just staged a reverse takeover of the Progressive Conservatives. The new Conservative Party of Canada (CPC) still had a bruising leadership campaign of its own to endure, so it was unlikely that Martin would have much to fear on his right. In sum, Martin's crown seemed to be fashioned out of pure political gold. That his prospects for an increased majority soon turned bleak had much to do both with the manner of that crown's winning and the manner of its wearing.

A Hyperactive Prime Minister and His Premature Election

In the cliché of the time – and Martin's highly programmed discourse was replete with clichés – the new prime minister hit the ground running. He appointed a new cabinet. He restructured the government. His caucus changed the standing orders of the House of Commons to allow for more free votes. He took legislative action to deliver on some of his commitments. The governor general read his Speech from the Throne, and his minister of finance delivered a budget. He welcomed Kofi Annan in Ottawa to signal his support for enhanced international co-operation, and he was welcomed by George Bush at the White House as a token of his determination to improve bilateral relations. And, of course, he staffed the Prime Minister's Office (PMO) with the men and women who had brought him to it. Each of these facets of the prime minister's activities had its darker side.

The new cabinet sent out a message of renewal without assuring that change would happen. It was no surprise that – beyond his leadership rivals Allan Rock, gone to the United Nations as Canada's ambassador, and John Manley, who had refused the Washington embassy – notable Chrétien supporters were out: David Collenette, Sheila Copps, Stéphane Dion, Elinor Caplan, Jane Stewart, Martin

Cauchon, and Don Boudria. While these firings guaranteed deepened dismay from the party's defeated wing, the newly anointed could hardly hope to make their mark before a spring election. Pierre Pettigrew, the new minister of health, quickly came to grief by stating the obvious, if politically incorrect, truth that part of the public health system was delivered through private practice. John Godfrey was named parliamentary secretary co-chairing a task force on Canadian cities. "Designed more for appearances than performance," wrote one commentator later, "that group ... made the machinery of government appear impossibly complex and hopelessly unmanageable.[9]

Martin also significantly restructured government to create a new Department of Public Safety and Emergency Preparedness. He split the Department of Human Resources Development Canada into two ministries and separated foreign affairs from international trade. The changes were rushed through without proper consultation with the civil service, leaving bureaucrats stranded, not knowing how to adjust their work. Signalling his intention to improve Ottawa's relations with the Bush administration, he established a new secretariat to coordinate federal and provincial activities in Washington, he created a special cabinet committee on Canadian-American relations, and he appointed a parliamentary secretary to work with him on that issue. He set up new cabinet committees, several of which he intended to chair himself, such as the Cabinet Committee on Aboriginal Affairs, and the Cabinet Committee on Security, Public Health, and Emergencies. Each of these administrative changes had a rationale, but, as had also been the case with John Turner's attempt to put his own imprimatur on government just before the 1984 election, they were the kind of changes that take a few years, not a few weeks, to implement. They also demanded far more of his hands-on time than he seemed willing to spend during a pre-election period.

Taking legislative action, producing a Speech from the Throne, and coming up with the 2004 budget so that he could keep some of his commitments were obviously worthy measures. But the relatively picayune nature of the actions in the House, the vagueness of the speech, and the small down payments that the 2004 budget made toward its more grandiose spending promises confirmed that Martin was not really planning to govern. It was his impending election campaign that this frenetic hyperactivity heralded.

Nothing in the measures to revamp the PMO necessarily spelled disaster. Unlike John Turner, who had not frequented the corridors of power for nine years when he became prime minister, Martin's year and a half sabbatical had been more like a busman's holiday, keeping him from getting rusty. Because he had been so focused on preparing for victory (unlike Turner who had a big-time business lawyer's load to demand his attention), his extensive consultations had yielded coherent plans that he started to implement immediately. Where

Martin mimicked Turner to a fault, however, was in the spirit his staff brought to their mission and the way he structured his relationship with them.

It was natural for Martin to bring his own people to the PMO. Many of them had been at his side as political aides in the Department of Finance or virtually there through quarterbacking his covert mutiny from the offices of Earnscliffe, a prominent Ottawa lobby company. What was neither necessary nor politic was the way they ran the PMO and guided the prime minister. Like the Turnerites before them, they made no attempt to reach out to their leadership rivals' capable personnel, who were made to feel defeated, ousted, and unwelcome. When Turner's people took over the PMO, they threw out the briefing books that had been prepared for the transition. Unable to contain their triumphalism in their turn, Martin's people had all references to Chrétien wiped from the government's website the day they arrived.

Like Turner, Martin preferred a horizontal decision-making style. As minister of finance whose year-long job had been the preparation of one complex budget, he had revelled in chairing lively debates animated by his political and bureaucratic staff. The transition to being prime minister, a position in which he had constantly to confront dozens of critical problems, did not move him to change this way of operating. Whereas Trudeau and Chrétien had started their days by meeting the clerk of the privy council (the bureaucratic head of the civil service) and the principal secretary (the head of his political staff), Martin, like Turner before him, began his work by meeting the clerk plus half a dozen people from the PMO. These backroom boys and girls had much more recent political experience and were more closely connected to the federal government than Turner's staff had been, but with every opinion around the table seeming to have equal weight, Martin's behaviour continued to reflect their anti-Chrétien obsession. While they had Martin preach the gospel of democracy in public, they continued to practise the same centralized control from behind closed doors that had won him the ultimate prize. He talked about doing politics differently, but they kept power where it had always been, in the hands of the prime minister – and themselves in his office. This management style was put to its first major test, and found terribly wanting, when political disaster struck on February 10, 2004.

There was little that was new in Auditor General Sheila Fraser's report on the irregularities of the Chrétien government's Quebec sponsorship program. Moneys unaccounted for and excessive rake-offs by communications firms profiting from their political connections had been detailed the previous autumn in her interim statement without eliciting much reaction. Instead of treating this new document as unfortunate history that needed further investigation and eventual discipline by a commission of inquiry (thus burying the problem at least until the election was over), Paul Martin turned "Adscam" into an issue in order to prove that he represented a different kind of politics – the kind he had made so many speeches about. With mad-as-hell outrage, he mounted a frenetic media campaign, declaring on national television and radio his indignation at what had been revealed and his determination to punish the perpetrators.[10] Although his caucus pleaded with him to stop keeping this scandal in the news by appropriating the issue (because the public was not distinguishing between the new and the old Liberals), Martin continued his cross-country campaign talking to media in British Columbia, Saskatchewan, and Manitoba. His unilingual anglophone staffers were no less eager to add fuel to the fire. With not-for-attribution phone calls to journalists, they eagerly contributed to a not-so-implicit blame-Chrétien campaign by talking about the program's "political direction."[11]

At the same time that a parliamentary committee chaired by a Conservative started hearings, Martin appointed Mr. Justice John Gomery to chair an independent commission of inquiry. He then deepened the attack on Chrétien's administration by summarily removing Alfonso Gagliano, the former minister in charge of the sponsorship program, from his ambassadorship in Denmark without compensation. Next, he fired Jean Pelletier, the CEO of Via Rail and formerly Chrétien's principal secretary, without obvious evidence of criminal behaviour, let alone due process. Acting as if an opposition party had come to power determined to vilify its defeated enemy, Team Martin managed in the process to raise doubts about its own integrity, given that its captain had been finance minister during the sponsorship program and that, as Chrétien's most senior Quebec minister, he could hardly have been unaware of what was happening. Unable to declare closure on their feud with their departed predecessors, the Martinites exacerbated, rather than healed, the party's internal divisions. Moreover, by so gratuitously castigating the Chrétien record, they burned their own bridge to claiming credit for over ten years of government achievements, many of which were Martin's own doing in Finance.

This dubious exercise in protesting its innocence boomeranged on the Martin team and created a more persuasive reason for voters to abandon the Liberals than any argument the newly elected leader of the Conservative Party of Canada could possibly have made. Within four weeks, support for the Liberal Party of Canada had fallen from 48 percent to 35 percent in the polls.[12] In the wake of this disaster, a consensus outside the PMO held that Martin should postpone his election plans, get on with the business of governing that had been laid out in the throne speech and budget, consolidate his identity as Canada's spokesman by attending summits on the international stage, and – not least important – give the public time to get over its anger about "Adscam." But the Martinites had long set their hearts on holding a quick election. The earliest date that was politically acceptable was April, lest the West protest it had been deprived of the five extra seats that redistribution would then give it. They *said* they needed a "mandate" to implement their demanding program, but what they *meant* was that they wanted an election to clear out the hostile Chrétienites from caucus and to elect new stars with whom they could replenish the cabinet. There was apparently to be no closure with his nemesis until Martin had won his own majority in Parliament.

Whereas Turner in June 1984 had been elected leader only eight months before having to call a new election, Martin had almost two years from when he was elevated. But his inner circle did not lack time as much as flexibility. Having decided on an early election, it seemed unable to realize it was no longer unbeatable. Consider these major problems:

- Unlike Martin, Harper had reached out to his contenders for the leadership, Belinda Stronach and Tony Clement. For his new party in Ontario, the one province that the Liberal Party needed for its majority, he was projecting a perhaps uncharismatic but certainly unscary image that seemed to belie the moralistic and dogmatic social conservatism associated with his Western supporters' hostility to granting rights to homosexuals and allowing abortions.
- Martin's honeymoon with the media had ended. Reporters were not giving the new prime minister any less cynical treatment than they had given the previous one.
- Martin had spent the months since coming to the PMO making promises in every region and for every imaginable issue, such as giving hundreds of millions to support HIV/AIDS alleviation programs in Africa, so there would be little new policy for Martin to announce during the campaign to provide a positive message.
- Once campaigning started, the media would give equal time to the other parties, which would concentrate their attack on the incumbent Liberals. Martin would be constantly forced to defend such contradictions as the one between his pledge to create a more democratic politics and his actual record in manipulating the nominations of his own candidates.

The Liberals were vulnerable to public criticism over Martin's management of the party's nomination process. But the main reason that should have caused them to delay the planned election was the impact that the issue would have on internal party morale. Like every political party, the Liberals needed their rank-and-file members to turn up at riding campaign offices and volunteer to canvas voters, put up signs, and carry out the myriad other chores required for a winning local campaign. However, the well-publicized examples of strong-arm tactics by Martin's team taking Liberal riding nominations out of the hands of the local constituencies had shown that Martin's commitment to democratic practice was selective.

Under amendments made to the party's constitution in 1992, the leader had the power to impose a candidate on a riding notwithstanding the riding's own democratically expressed will. Also under Chrétien, the leader's provincial campaign chairs had acquired powers that allowed them to protect a sitting MP whom they wanted to keep, or to favour a contender whom they preferred to win. As part of his advocacy for local democracy, Martin had affirmed at an earlier stage that he would not automatically have incumbents protected unless they were strong, female, or from visible minorities. He would nevertheless appoint candidates with these qualities to make his team more representative of Canadian society's diversity.[13]

How these principles were actually applied was strongly influenced by the Martinites' continuing vendetta against their vanquished rivals. Most notoriously, Sheila Copps, who was not just a woman but the only Chrétien minister with hard-earned credibility in the cultural and anglo-nationalist communities, was exposed to a bitter fight for her nomination. Martin supporter Tony Valeri took this nomination from her, thanks to dirty tricks that loose nomination rules did not prevent (or so it was widely reported). Nor did strength and ethnicity provide protection for male incumbents. Chrétien's minister of energy, the Sikh Herb Dhaliwal, was shoved aside, and two substantial Chinese Canadian candidates were frustrated by Martin's appointment of Bill Cunningham, his WASP BC organizer, as the party's candidate in Burnaby-Douglas. Buttressing the prime minister's power of appointment was his command of patronage. The MP John Harvard was persuaded to free up his seat by the promise of being appointed lieutenant governor of Manitoba.[14] The MP for Brampton-Springdale was similarly bought off with the promise of an appointment.[15]

Even if Paul Martin did not get personally involved in riding contests, his associates could generally manipulate the process to get the candidate they wanted. A Manley supporter, Andrew Kania, was displaced in favour of a glamorous female Asian, Ruby Dhalla, in the Brampton-Springdale riding. Despite claiming its commitment to gender equality, the Martin team dissuaded a prominent woman from running in Ottawa South to favour the Ontario premier's brother, David McGuinty.

In some cases, the PMO could get its way without manipulation. Where Martinites already controlled a riding association, they could produce an uncontested victory for their candidate without engendering more dissension.[16] In such situations, more provocation was not needed to encourage non-Martin supporters to abandon the campaign. Thirty-six sitting MPs did not run again. Anger was so high in some cases that whole riding association executives moved to support another party.

Neither this rank-and-file alienation over present nominations nor public disaffection following the previous sponsorship scandal deterred the Martin machine. Although polls through April predicted the Liberals would achieve no more than a minority government, a blip suggesting they were back in majority territory momentarily gave them the figures they needed. On May 24 Paul Martin promptly announced that an election would be held in thirty-seven days. It would not be easy for him. His tacticians were untried. His platform was insipid. And the media were loath to extend him the benefit of the doubt any more.

Organization, Strategy, and Tactics

The structural shape of the campaign had been devised months earlier, when polls commissioned and analyzed by Martin's chief strategist, David Herle, suggested that the future campaign should exploit his boss's extraordinary popularity. Perhaps deluded by the near-unanimous delegate support they had bought for their leader's coronation at the Air Canada Centre (thanks to their $10 million organizational effort), the Martin group did everything it could to differentiate itself from the party it had taken over. A new party logo was designed, although even it was barely discernible with Martin's face dominating the candidates' signs.

The campaign's organizers were talented and experienced. Martin's senior strategist since 1990, Mike Robinson, had run the debate preparation for Turner. Terrie O'Leary, who had played an integral part in Chrétien's tour in 1993, acted as Martin's special assistant as she had from 1990 to 1998. Media spokesman Scott Reid had been politically involved through the 1990s. Along with other leading lights, such as campaign co-chair John Webster, national party director Michele Cadario, chief of staff Tim Murphy, communications director Steve MacKinnon, and Ontario director Karl Littler, the group was accustomed to campaigning together, many having been with Martin at the Department of Finance, and all having worked on the recent leadership campaign. Equally important, this triumph had left them in firm control of the party apparatus so that there were no tensions between the PMO and the campaign office as there had been under Turner.

But their various organizational assets had their darker sides. Having successfully placed their man in the PMO through ruthlessly squeezing out his rivals and recruiting instant Liberals from ethnic groups, they were poorly equipped to rally the rest of the party faithful. And, having made their mark in Ottawa as high-profile lobbyists, they were unable to resist the lure of media fame themselves. In striking contrast to the discretion of Jean Chrétien's team – John Rae, Eddie Goldenberg, Gordon Ashworth, who kept themselves invisible as they managed the campaign – Martin's handlers eagerly joined the pundits on television or radio programs to spin their party's situation. But given its rapidly deteriorating condition, their words were not always helpful to the cause. David Herle admitted to being "nervous" about running a national campaign for the first time and conceded he had made "rookie" mistakes in alienating the Chrétien wing of the party. He accepted full responsibility for "failing to reach out to those Liberals who remained faithful to former Prime Minister Jean Chrétien throughout last year's bitter leadership race."[17]

The deleterious impact on campaign morale of such poor judgment was aggravated by poor discipline elsewhere in the party. Hélène Scherrer, the Quebec campaign's co-chair, frankly expressed her dismay that Paul Martin was not a very good politician: "I don't think [Martin is] a good politician, in the sense that he can't attack the others and be demagogic ... It's hard for him in an election campaign that is being fought below the belt. He is not good when it comes to playing that game ... He wants everybody to love him."[18] Scherrer's musing precipitated an admission one week later that the campaign's message was failing, and that a new strategy would have to be adopted to address Canadians' distrust of Martin.[19]

This self-destruction by the team leaders was aided by those it had alienated. Brian Tobin, the former Liberal minister of industry whom Finance Minister Martin had forced out of the party leadership race even before he officially declared his candidacy, by blocking the funding Tobin needed for a high-tech economic policy, told the press before Week 1 was even over that the Grits were heading for a minority.[20] MP Carolyn Parrish was quoted as calling the campaign a "comedy of errors."[21] And, in a presumed act of sabotage, someone helped connect a key journalist to a conference call organized so David Herle could give the straight goods to all the Ontario candidates. This covert access yielded a front-page story in the *Globe and Mail* blaring, "Liberals are in a spiral," the words having come straight from no less authoritative a source than the campaign director's own lips. The report characterized the call as sounding "desperate," and revealed some MPs' discomfort with the negative ads that would begin airing later that day.[22]

Having publicly admitted to failure in reaching out to the Chrétien camp, Herle supported two efforts to heal the rift. The first, hosted by Senator David Smith and the party president, Mike Eizenga, in mid-April, provided leading disaffected Liberals with a chance to vent. However, their advice – to postpone the election but specify a date for June 2005 – went unheeded. The second, in Week 3 of the campaign, was a forum Herle used to try to bring the party's factions together. When he told those in attendance he expected to win one hundred seats in Ontario, they realized they were being used so that he could spin the signal through the media that reconciliation had been achieved.

Detached from this organizational disarray in Ottawa, but driven by its focus-grouped thinking, the leader launched his campaign, veering away from the continentalist right, where he had dug in as finance minister to satisfy the business community's demand for deficit reduction, and where he had originally positioned his government by making overtures to the Bush administration. No sooner was the writ issued than Paul Martin shifted to the nationalist left. Distancing himself from a US model of society, he identified himself on Day 2 with that most Canadian of values, health care, and attempted to convey as much emotion over hospital waiting lists as he had over the sponsorship scandal, if with no greater success. It was no accident that Martin chose social policy for his first message. Months had gone into preparing its priority in his platform.

Platform As Positive Policy Message

To understand the political impact of the Liberals' 2004 campaign, it is necessary to distinguish the printed message from its messenger. The message was coherently, if numbingly, presented in the form of a traditional platform document. The messenger, Paul Martin, had considerable difficulty exciting the public with its contents on the campaign trail. *Moving Canada Forward: The Paul Martin Plan for Getting Things Done* was a document modelled on the Red Books produced in the three Chrétien campaigns, although in this case it was the product of the Martin leadership process, whose extensive pre-convention consultations generated a series of four connected documents.

First had come "Making History: the Politics of Achievement," the vague, committee-written, cliché-filled but comprehensive and politically flexible speech that Martin gave to the Air Canada Centre crowd on November 14 after it had been warmed up by the real excitement of hearing the rock star Bono. Whereas Bono had spoken from his capacious Irish heart about the specifics of Africa's HIV/AIDS crisis, Martin spoke in platitudes. "Bono cares," he intoned, in lieu of specifying any details about his third-world policy, "We care." This feel-good appeal to each constituency within the party made few commitments beyond suggesting that issue after issue was important, crucial, or urgent, and that Canada had a historically transformative opportunity to confront it. Though it contained few actual commitments, it did provide the framework for the later iterations of Martin's program.

Next came the greater specificity of the new government's Speech from the Throne. Whereas the convention speech contained two economic promises and seven concerning the democratic deficit, the throne speech made forty-five, including $4 billion to be spent on the environment and $2 billion on health.

Then Finance Minister Ralph Goodale's budget laid out the dollar amounts that Parliament would be invited to spend on itemized programs. In some cases these were extraordinarily small down payments: of the $5 billion promised for child care, only $91 million would be spent in 2004 and $93 million in 2005. Of the $4 billion nominally committed to the environment, only $250 million would be spent in 2004, with a minuscule $10 million allocated for the following year.

Moving Canada Forward reworked these three statements, presenting a document similar in format and in style to the earlier Red Books, which looked like corporate annual reports. Heavier in motherhood declamations about the importance of education, or health, or prosperity, or peace than in hard policy content, it nevertheless managed to make thirty-five promises (fifteen of which reprised commitments from the Speech from the Throne) that were printed in twenty-one coloured boxes and grouped in four main sections:

- "A Strong Start" reduced the seven promises from Martin's campaign text to one on eliminating the democratic deficit.
- "Strengthening our Social Foundations" provided a medley of admonitions and statements of good intent concerning such areas as hospital waiting lists, child care (recycled from the 1993 Red Book), pharmacare (recycled from 1997), and the cities. Since all these fell under provincial jurisdiction, the text was replete with caveats about the negotiations and co-operation that would be needed with the provinces and/or the Native nations.
- "Building a 21st Century Economy" reiterated the real action taken in the budget, such as GST relief for municipal governments, but the rest of the text was notable mainly for its celebration of the Chrétien government's economic triumphs achieved when Martin had been holding its purse strings.
- "Canada in the World: A Role of Pride and Influence" stood out for its vacuity. For all its claims about the country's unique international mission, it managed to mention neither the United Nations nor the United States. (Martin's convention speech had given a prominent role to improving relations with Washington.) Iraq was only mentioned in terms of reducing its debt.

The turgid, campaign-speak style and the many promises recycled from the Chrétien era deprived *Moving Canada Forward* of any sense of vision. Leaning to the right on fiscal prudence but to the left on social programs, it fitted the mould of the party's past ambivalent pitches. Worthy, but weak in its sentiments, it should nevertheless have provided plenty of material for the leader to use on the road.

Martin As Messenger

At first glance, it was a puzzle that Paul Martin, Ottawa's undisputed policy wonk, should appear so bereft of vision. The problem lay, undoubtedly in part, in his exhaustion from already having spent much of his prime ministerial energy out-side the capital promising goodies for every region. In doing so, he had seriously depleted his supply of policy ammunition. The problem also lay partly in his handling of the sponsorship scandal, which had brought him to an emotional precipice, as he faced the humiliation of jeopardizing the Liberal Party's domi-nant position, inherited from Chrétien. In part, his apparently compulsive need to please all constituencies made it hard to determine what a re-elected Martin government would actually do. For instance, the platform took a multilateralist position, promising more money for the military to bolster its peacekeeping capacities, but his minister of defence, David Pratt, had made it very clear that Canada would support Washington's controversial National Missile Defense scheme, which was presumably just a first step toward Canada's forces integrat-ing via an extended NORAD in US Northern Command, the Pentagon's newly created continental defence organization.

Worse, it was hard to credit his new, slightly anti-American stand. Having long sniped at Chrétien for not getting along with the Bush administration, and having made much of his own capacity to reconcile with the White House both in his convention speech and in reorganizing the government to integrate better with American security policy, he had already made a well-promoted trip to Washington to signal his pro-American bona fides. At the beginning of the cam-paign, however, here he was suddenly tweaking a feather from the eagle by mor-alistically asserting the superiority of Canada's social values.[23]

Martin might have managed the transmogrification from flinty-eyed neocon to warm-hearted liberal had he still been enjoying his honeymoon with the media. When heavy-handed, inaccessible, touchy Chrétien was in the PMO, the media had not portrayed Martin as disloyal, conniving, and heavy-handed himself (for example, in the party's delegate selection process) but as a rebel with a cause. The press gallery could easily still have celebrated his conversion, burbling about how this tough-minded business-executive-turned-politician had found his real ideological roots as son of the Paul Martin Sr. who had championed generous social programs in the 1950s and 1960s. But as soon as the media lost Chrétien to kick around and Martin had shown his political incompetence in the sponsor-ship scandal, he lost the journalists' respect.

It was the "boys on the bus" whose reportorial eyes had turned flinty as they prominently reported Jack Layton's attacks on the contradictions between the prime minister's present promises and his past actions, and relayed to the public Gilles Duceppe's sustained barrage over Martin's possible involvement with Adscam. Appropriating a role for itself as truth squad, for instance, the CBC on Day 3 responded to Martin's promise to fix the health care system by reminding its viewers that it was his 1995 budget that had caused most of the damage in the first place.[24] Anti-Martin commentary was not restricted to the public broadcaster. Although the Liberals scored high in "mentions" in the print media over the campaign – 80 percent of all articles referred to them – 22 percent of these were negative. By contrast, 69 percent of all articles mentioned the Conservatives, but only 12 percent of these were negative.[25] More important, the bulk of the negative coverage for Martin occurred in the first three weeks, when the Liberals' negative mentions exceeded those of all other parties combined.[26] In the campaign's opening phase, the Conservatives won what was known as the ballot box question, turning the election into a referendum on Liberal rule with their "Demand Better" slogan.

Paradoxically, the Martinites' disowning of Chrétien over Adscam prevented them from claiming ownership of Martin's great economic achievement as finance minister – eliminating the budgetary deficit and presiding over robust growth rates that improved Canada's economic position to the point where it was the only G7 country to enjoy both fiscal and trade surpluses in 2002. This record was well presented in *Moving Canada Forward,* but Martin's attempt to assert it fell on deaf ears. His defence of health care cuts on the grounds that, "If we had not taken the action that we did in 1995, we would be Argentina today," had no resonance with reporters.[27] Nothing positive that he tried seemed to work for him, whereas what others did worked against him. The storm of criticism that greeted Ontario Premier Dalton McGuinty over his broken promise not to raise taxes (his budget, which was unveiled just days before the federal campaign began, introduced a health care premium) rubbed off directly on his federal cousins. In Ontario, their support immediately fell to 36 percent,[28] and around the country their opponents gleefully charged that Martin's "Fiberals" could not be trusted to keep their new promises either.

Nor did the Liberals' ad campaign work any better. Their much-ballyhooed attack on the Conservatives proved counterproductive. On Saturday, May 22, the day before the campaign was launched, full-page advertisements appeared in newspapers across the country with side-by-side photographs of both Paul Martin and Stephen Harper in business suits, managing to make the Conservative leader look just as respectable as the prime minister, if considerably younger and certainly not scary.[29] Beyond the visual, the Liberals' negative campaign suffered from the same credibility gap as their positive message: it was disingenuous to allege that Harper would endanger the country's social fabric by cutting taxes – "Stephen Harper's number one priority is tax cuts" – when this was exactly what Martin had boasted about doing throughout the previous decade. Did the attack ads represent an implicit admission that the government had little record to defend? Were they aimed to divert attention from Adscam? The media raised these queries while describing the pre-campaign television commercial that gave partial quotes from what Harper had said in the past and referred viewers to a website that would give them the full text. This multimedia

ploy seemed ineffectual and was pulled within a week. The *Globe and Mail* called
the early attack ads "unprecedented," and characterized them as a "last ditch
effort" to unite the fractured party.[30]

It was not necessary for the media to allege desperation on the Liberals'
part. David Herle himself openly admitted as much on Day 19 (June 10), when
his most negative ad was released. "The Stephen Harper We Know" threw everything at the new leader: Iraq, abortion, environmental degradation, and
separatism, all under the guise of Harper's alleged secret agenda. On Day 24
(June 15), "Conservative Economics" alleged Harper would introduce US-style
tax cuts and alter the country's social fabric. In an effort to show guilt by association, it invoked the records of former Ontario Premier Mike Harris and
former prime minister Brian Mulroney, to suggest that Harper would create a
new fiscal deficit.[31]

Had Harper been a real Mulroney clone, Martin's fate would have been sealed.
Not only was Mulroney in 1984 strongly identified with his province as a boy
from Baie Comeau on Quebec's North Shore, but he had campaigned from the
political centre, thereby making it impossible for Turner, the corporate lawyer
from Bay Street, to polarize the election on a left-right basis. Fortunately for
Martin, many members of Harper's Conservative caucus had impeccable credentials as social conservatives.

The Media: From Enemy to Ally

Fortunately, too, for the new prime minister, the Conservative leader was
declared by the pollsters to have the magic quality of *momentum* as early as
Week 2,[32] inducing the fickle press corps to shift their baleful scrutiny to the one
whose election now seemed likely. With the polls in Week 3 suggesting Harper
would win at least a minority, reporters were no longer willing to give him the
free ride he had been accorded when he was just another opposition leader without serious prospects of victory.[33] This change in treatment was seen in both
print and broadcast media. Negative mentions of Harper in the press, which
had fallen dramatically from Weeks 1 through 3 (24 percent, 9 percent, and then
6 percent, respectively), rose back to 15 percent in Week 4.[34] Television's about-
face in its treatment of the Conservatives was demonstrated by CTV in the final
week of the campaign, when it aired almost no positive statements about the
Conservatives.

The Conservative Party's fortunes moved in tandem with the kind of stories
that appeared in the media. It was no coincidence that Conservative momentum peaked in Week 3 when the networks' leading stories were about traditional
Conservative strengths: justice issues at 21 percent, and the economy, tax cuts,
and the deficit at 18 percent of all press statements made that week.[35] Week 5 saw
a rebound in health care mentions (the Liberal trump card) at 20 percent, up

from 7 percent in Conservative-friendly Week 3. Most tellingly, mentions of government leadership and ethics (including morals and accountability) plummeted to their lowest level of 1 percent in newspapers in week five,[36] demonstrating that the Conservatives had lost their battle for the ballot box question in the campaign's crucial final week.

During the two televised all-party debates, the focus of attention was the incumbent prime minister, who was put on the defensive by the three other leaders' relentless attacks and seemed incapable of citing his own achievements, let alone those of the Chrétien government. Post-debate coverage described Martin's performance as a politician fighting for the survival of his party, and made the case that the election had become "one for the Conservatives to lose."[37] Harper emerged calm, a bit dull, but unscathed from Martin's attack about the "black hole" of his budgetary planning or about his having wanted to send Canadian troops to join the US war on Iraq: "Canadians were not wrong," Martin reprimanded his rival on screen, "You were wrong."[38] In stark contrast to the inflated expectations of Martin, the media's low expectations of Harper meant that he had "won" the debate simply by virtue of not having made any mistakes.

On Day 21 (June 12), the senior columnist of the *Globe and Mail* and "dean of the chattering caste," Jeffrey Simpson, signalled the crucial shift. In his column titled "A Conservative Wolf in Sheep's Clothing," Simpson characterized Harper's openness to free votes on issues of abortion and same-sex marriage as a "constitutional fraud, political sham, even a deceit" and cautioned readers that despite the Progressive Conservative and Canadian Alliance merger, the "Alliance dominates among candidates, organizers, and Mr. Harper's advisers (who are very, very right-wing.)" Simpson went on to accuse Harper of "trying to bribe the Canadian electorate" into believing his party's "new" brand of economic conservatism, which made both tax cuts and "huge amounts of spending" possible, despite all evidence of his puritan conservative economic tendencies.[39] Even if he had relatively few readers on the *Globe and Mail's* op-ed page, Simpson was read by his colleagues, who proceeded to take their cue from him, turn tough on Harper, and, doing to him what they had done to Martin, watered the seeds of doubt already sown by the Liberals.

On Day 25 (June 16), articles reporting Harper's prediction that he would win a majority mocked him for presumptuously "measuring the curtains" at 24 Sussex Drive.[40] His consultations on the transition into governance were also reported as premature, even though, as a leader with a strong chance of defeating the current government, it would have been irresponsible for him not to prepare for office. When on Day 26 (June 17), Premier Ralph Klein announced that he was waiting until just after the federal election to bring in changes to Alberta's health care system that might violate the Canada Health Act, Martin was able to get four days' play in the national media for his claim that this proved the Conservatives had "a hidden agenda" after all. With the press hounds baying, the CPC's most extreme candidates' well-known views on social issues were played up, giving Martin a chance to express his horror at the threat they posed to Canadian values.

By Day 25 (June 16), the Conservatives had fallen back to being in a dead heat with the Liberals, 35 percent to 34 percent. On Day 27, the media gave prominent play to a press release from Harper's war room that egregiously suggested Martin favoured child pornography. For the first time, in Week 4, Harper's negative mentions in the media exceeded those for Martin.[41] Stories on social issues exceeded those on economic issues, playing into the Liberals' fear-mongering campaign.

On Day 29 (June 20), it was bilingualism in Air Canada that was under threat. The Liberals alleged on their website that Harper would relax the airline's bilingualism requirements, citing a leaked pre-writ memo from the Conservative Party. On Day 34, then-Conservative Justice critic Randy White was shown saying in an interview conducted months prior to the election that he was personally in favour of using the Charter's notwithstanding clause to override court rulings such as those pertaining to the definition of marriage.[42] By Week 5, when 40 percent of the voters had still to make up their mind, the Liberals, though still in a virtual tie with the Conservatives, returned to promoting their platform, which seemed no longer to be falling on deaf ears.[43] Their final attack ad encapsulated all the fears they were trying to evoke. The buyer should beware. NDP voters should "think twice, vote once." And, to conclude, the slogan: "Choose your Canada." If at the very end of the campaign the public forgot their fury at the Liberals, and former Tory voters in Ontario moved to Martin, it was less for what he stood for than for what he said Harper stood for.

Poll-saturated coverage had a discernible impact not only on the way campaigns conducted themselves but also on voter behaviour.[44] This became especially apparent when polling numbers for the Conservatives began to rise, changing the way the media covered both Stephen Harper and Paul Martin. The former received what ultimately proved to be a fatal sense of momentum; the latter a boost to his scare campaign. Now Martin's "devil you know" plea was given more careful consideration. Stephen Harper's talk of Conservative consultations regarding a possible transition into governance meant that the prime minister could now warn Canadians to be wary of the kind of change they would be voting for. Suddenly faced with the prospect of a Conservative majority, those voters leaning toward the NDP found themselves turning back to the Liberals, who had the greater chance of preventing a Conservative government. Moderate voters in Ontario who were supporting the Conservatives as a protest against perceived Liberal abuses suddenly got cold feet when confronted with the possibility of a majority government harkening back to Harris and Mulroney days, with the likes of Randy White at the helm.

If the Liberals' negative commercials finally worked after their initial failure, it was thanks to the media having switched from enemy to ally, helping convince Canadians that the Harper Conservatives lived up to their scary billing after all. In this way, the Liberals' paid advertisements bought them "earned media," through increased news stories commenting on social conservatism. Because voters typically distrust politicians but trust journalists, the earned media dulled criticism of Liberal attack ads. In Week 4, there was a discernible rise in coverage of the same-sex marriage and abortion issues – about one in every three campaign-related articles dealt with social issues, displacing health, taxes, and accountability.[45]

The Regions: Continuity in the Party System

The struggle for the hearts and minds of the national press gallery was important, but not necessarily more important than what went on locally in each region. Just over ten years after 1993's electoral earthquake seemed to have fragmented the Canadian party system along regional lines, the Martin Liberals revealed that doing politics differently did not preclude such traditional governing-party behaviour as appointing MPs from each region to the cabinet, recruiting local stars, and making promises to fix local problems, all the while maintaining a pan-Canadian thrust to their policy.

The Atlantic Provinces

Back in December 2003, Martin had brought Geoff Regan, whose father was a former premier and federal cabinet minister, into his cabinet as minister of fisheries and had made Newfoundlander John Efford minister of natural resources. With discontent running high among genuine Tories about their party's takeover from the far West's far right, the Liberals were pleased to have induced the MPs John Herron from New Brunswick and Scott Brison from Nova Scotia to cross the floor; the latter was appointed parliamentary secretary to the prime minister responsible for Canadian-American relations. In Nova Scotia, they also recruited local stars Sheila Fougere, a municipal politician, and Mike Savage, son of another former premier. In St. John, New Brunswick, they recruited Paul Zed, president of Summa Strategies and legal counsel at Clark Drummie, a leading Atlantic Canada law firm.

In the pre-writ months, Martin promised $400 million to clean up the environmental disaster of the tar ponds in Sydney, Nova Scotia, and $300 million for improving Prince Edward Island's harbours. One pan-Canadian policy with a distinctly regional tilt toward the Maritimes and Quebec was easing the eligibility criteria to give the seasonally unemployed more access to employment insurance (EI). During the campaign itself, Martin promised a Liberal government would strengthen or withdraw from the North Atlantic Fishing Organization if abuses by Portuguese fishermen continued,[46] and he undertook to give the provinces a greater share of the taxes generated by offshore oil and natural gas royalties.

Quebec

With separatism in apparent decline, *la belle province* initially presented the Martinites with an attractive prospect. From winning fifty-four seats and forming the Official Opposition in 1993, the Bloc Québécois had slipped to forty-four and then thirty-eight seats in the intervening elections. The Parti Québécois' defeat by the provincial Liberals in the 2003 election had put the BQ on the defensive over the sensitive issue of independence, forcing Gilles Duceppe to distance himself from the PQ's leader, Bernard Landry, to keep the volatile former PQ premier, Jacques Parizeau, under wraps, and, in his platform, to put Quebec's role in the world (a euphemism for sovereignty) in last place.

Then came Adscam, whose impact on the Liberals was far more devastating in Quebec than elsewhere. Not only did it show flagrant corruption within the federal government; Quebeckers also felt collectively insulted by Martin's unilingual anglophone handlers for suggesting that the scandal was a function of the province's old-style patronage politics. References to Quebec's "tribal politics" and its "culture of corruption" were widely disseminated in francophone Canada as proof positive of the Liberals' hostility to Quebec. Even if the anger was more deeply felt among the elite than the general francophone public,[47] the Liberals' political support fell ten percentage points (five times more than the rest of Canada). It was not Harper but Gilles Duceppe as BQ leader who picked up this disaffected part of the electorate, with his double-entendre slogan, "Un parti propre au Quebec" subtly rubbing salt in the Liberals' wounds. Not only did the BQ belong to Quebec, its hands were clean.

In contrast, the Liberals' slogan – "Tout droit d'abord" – was that of the Martin family corporation, Canada Steamship Lines, whose use of offshore tax havens had landed the PM in considerable difficulty. His key organizational decision made things much worse. Having focused before the scandal on winning away soft federalist support from the Bloc, he had appointed as his lieutenant in charge of the Quebec campaign Jean Lapierre, a former Liberal who had abandoned the party in 1990 to become a founding member of the Bloc. Host of a talk-radio show for several years, Lapierre was not used to keeping his opinions to himself. He quickly alienated Quebec nationalists by pooh-poohing the importance of Adscam. Declaring Chrétien's anti-separatist Clarity Act "useless," he also managed to outrage the party's federalists who were already smarting from the appointment of someone they had long deemed a traitor.

Within this context, none of the Liberals' traditional pre-writ tricks worked: neither the change in EI for seasonal workers, nor $900,000 for a marine biology centre in Rimouski, nor $1.1 million for *tourisme Outaouais*. Martin had banished Stéphane Dion from his cabinet and promoted backbenchers Irwin Cotler, Hélène Scherrer, and Denis Paradis, but it was in vain that his reshuffled team of Quebec ministers tirelessly brought the message of these and other goodies to local communities. The former prime minister's supporters angrily sat on their hands in the face of the Martin team's intransigence. In a flagrantly gratuitous insult to the former prime minister on his home turf, former Chrétien aide Stephen Hogue, who had been working since September 2003 to succeed his boss in St. Maurice-Champlain, the riding he had held for forty years, was told that the riding was reserved for a woman, Marie Eve Bilodeau, who turned out to be a Martin supporter.[48]

With the Liberals falling 20 percent behind the Bloc in the opening days of the campaign, Jean Lapierre was increasingly sidelined. After three weeks, Dion was brought back from political oblivion to connect the campaign with its alienated federalist core by warning of the danger represented by the Bloc. Together with Pierre Pettigrew, he published an open letter maintaining that a vote for the BQ would help bring to power Harper's Conservatives whose values were inimical to those of Quebeckers. Further shifting the Liberal message by replacing reconciliation for confrontation, the foreign minister, Bill Graham, was brought in from Toronto to affirm that the BQ shared the same values as the Liberals.

The Liberals' Quebec ad campaign, run separately from the campaign in the rest of Canada as always, kept up the message that a vote for the Bloc would produce a Conservative government committed to cancelling women's right to abortions and would leave Ottawa with no minister from Quebec.[49] The menacing style, which reminded Quebeckers of threats made by Paul Martin during the 1995 referendum, was deemed a political disaster. New ads were more positive, suggesting that the Liberals would open the Canadian economy to Quebec business and claiming that they would fight in Ottawa for the social needs of a unique Quebec.

Ontario

The battleground where Harper's reconstituted party could credibly hope for its breakthrough to government was Ontario, which also had the 106 seats that Martin needed if he were to rescue a minority from his self-made debacle. Vast in its geography and varied in its demography, Ontario presented several different political challenges to the Liberals. Most comfortable in the megalopolis of Toronto, the Liberals managed to attract some star candidates, notably the former Montreal Canadiens' goalie, Ken Dryden, who was given the riding of former Chrétien cabinet minister Art Eggleton. Having put themselves on the wrong side of newly elected Mayor David Miller on the Toronto Island airport issue, thanks in part to the antics of maverick MP Dennis Mills, they had difficulty capitalizing on Martin's previously announced commitment to increase federal financing for Canada's cities. On social questions, Foreign Affairs Minister Bill Graham championed the gay rights that the Martin team had finally, if reluctantly, brought itself to support.

In the broad, urbanizing semi-circle around Toronto known for its telephone area code, 905, the Liberals offered $1 billion to support the development of GO transit and nominated a goodly number of visible minority candidates. In the outer "blue belt" made up of smaller cities and agricultural areas, where the Conservatives were making their major gains, the party offered nothing specific, relying on the national campaign to save the situation, and leaving their candidates to fend for themselves.[50] In the north, which had been taken for granted as a solidly red zone, Martin had to make visits later in the campaign to point out Harper's opposition to such regional development initiatives as FedNor and the Community Futures Program.

The McGuinty Liberals' provincial budget, delivered on May 18, only days before Martin announced the date of the election, served to exacerbate the general sense of mistrust of government. In response to the outcry against the provincial "Fiberals," Martin initially defended McGuinty's budget, arguing it was necessary to deal with what he considered the Harris social deficit and Eves fiscal deficit. But it became evident in that first week on the campaign trail that the five-percentage-point drop suffered by the federal Liberals between mid-May and June 1 was caused exclusively by the McGuinty budget.[51] By Day 9, Martin had begun distancing himself from McGuinty: "I believe it is very important for political leaders to keep their promises ... But don't over-promise, and then whatever you say you're going to do, do."[52] A variety of high-profile Liberals, such as Anne McLellan, began to publicly accuse the McGuinty government of hurting federal Liberal support.[53] Ironically, McLellan and Martin were disavowing a provincial budget that the federal Liberals had helped to orchestrate as a symbol of federal co-operation to "save" the health care system. A highly publicized meeting between Ontario Health Minister George Smitherman and federal Health Minister Pierre Pettigrew had occurred less than a month before the budget was delivered, and only weeks after a meeting between McGuinty and Martin in Ottawa had specifically addressed health care.[54] The federal Liberals had put themselves in the paradoxical position of denouncing the outcome of their own pre-campaign tactics.

The West

Like John Turner before him, Paul Martin had come to the country's highest office having raised great expectations about how he would bring the West into a revivified Ottawa. His debut was promising. Even before his elevation, he met the premiers at the Grey Cup football game in Regina. He then brought Reg Alcock into his cabinet from Manitoba to be head of the Treasury Board, promoted Ralph Goodale from Saskatchewan to the government's number-two post of finance minister, and made Anne McLellan from Alberta deputy prime minister and minister in charge of his new Department of Public Safety and Emergency Preparedness, the next highest portfolio in his government.

On the pre-writ policy front, Martin was no less prolific in his regionally focused promises than he had been elsewhere in the country: $1 billion for Alberta's beef industry to help it recover from the American embargo following the discovery of one cow in the province with BSE, the mad cow disease; a commitment to adjust the much-loathed gun registry; an International Centre for Infectious Disease for Winnipeg; and more cash for Saskatoon's Synchrotron Institute. Having spent his ammunition, Martin had little more for the Prairies during the campaign, apart from his pledge to give its cities the same new deal he was peddling in the rest of the country.

Although the Martin team worked hard on the recruitment front, their only major coup was persuading the ex-mayor of Winnipeg, Glen Murray, to run for the Liberals. Strong-arm tactics to get their favourites nominated yielded the same bitterness within the ranks as elsewhere in the country. Also as elsewhere, the plunge in Liberal ratings that followed Adscam drastically dashed their hopes of making any gains and forced them to struggle just to hold on to the few seats they had. British Columbia was the only province where there was a genuine three-way split, with each party hovering around 30 percent in the polls. Here the Liberals had a double message, attacking the Conservatives on the one hand and courting the NDP's supporters on the other. Stumbling as badly in BC as elsewhere by angering minority groups and party loyalists with their heavy-handed interventions in riding nominations, they nevertheless produced a so-called "dream team" by poaching three major figures from the NDP, including former premier Ujjal Dosanjh, along with Keith Martin from the Conservatives, and parachuting a major business figure, David Emerson, into a safe seat.

The Liberals' behaviour in British Columbia provided some evidence to support the Carty thesis about Canada's evolving party system: following the new partisan constellation introduced by 1993's electoral earthquake, federal politics had become increasingly regionalized.[55] Unique in anglophone Canada, *B.C. Agenda* was a separate provincial platform making special promises, including a crackdown on drug use and moving the headquarters for the federal tourism promotion department to Vancouver in anticipation of the winter Olympics of

2010 at Whistler.[56] The BC campaign organization also produced its own com-mercial, featuring its three former NDP candidates and pleading for support from the province's progressives.[57]

Further apparent evidence for political balkanization came on Day 33 (June 24), when a reference to the Kyoto Protocol on climate change was spliced into the Liberals' last national attack ad, "The Harper We Know," for BC eyes only – the Conservatives had said they would withdraw from the treaty if elected. The Grits practised regional differentiation elsewhere as well. For Saskatchewan, the ad attacking Harper for his debt-deepening promises substituted former Con-servative premier Grant Devine for Mike Harris as bogeyman. But these last two actions could be given an alternative interpretation. While the Kyoto and Grant Devine mentions certainly added a regional reference, they were changes to com-mercials whose messages were nevertheless uniform across Canada.

A different regional element in the campaign was the last-minute fight that Martin picked over Alberta Premier Ralph Klein's expected further privatization of health care. Since few votes could be gained in Alberta by this manoeuvre, turning Klein into a scarecrow was an obvious case of mobilizing pro-medicare bias against Conservatives across the country. A parallel nationalization of a regional question could be seen in the Liberals' pitch in Quebec, where voting for the Bloc was castigated as helping bring the Conservatives to power.[58] Be-yond spelling out the national implications of voting for the BQ, the Liberals put a more positive, pan-Canadian spin on Quebec by celebrating its exemplary child care program, undertaking to use it as a model for the rest of Canada.[59]

The Results: A Last-Minute Reprieve

Surprising most observers who, on the strength of the poll results in Week 5, expected a photo finish, the Liberal Party received 822,000 more votes than the Conservatives on June 28. Their 37 percent of the vote won them 44 percent, or 135, of the House of Commons's 308 seats: 22 of the Atlantic provinces' 32 seats; 21 of Quebec's 75; 75 of Ontario's 106; 6 of the Prairies' 56; and 8 of British Columbia's 36. The Bloc's sweep of 54 ridings outside Montréal, and the CPC's 99, left the NDP just 19, not enough to hold the balance of power and extract proportional representation as its price for propping up the Liberals. With the electoral system intact and the Conservatives' party restored as the only political formation on the right, the prospects seemed good for the new two plus two party system – two major parties of the centre and right coexisting with a weak left-wing NDP and a regional Bloc Québécois.

Thirty-four of the sixty-five women elected to the House of Commons were Liberals – a healthy share considering the dismal overall representation of fe-males (21 percent of Parliament). The Liberal Party had the third-largest per-centage of female candidates to run in the election, and the second-highest success rate among the four. Martin awarded senior posts to women (nine in total for his new cabinet), notably Anne McLellan as deputy prime minister and minister of public safety and preparedness, Carolyn Bennett as minister of state (public health), and Judy Sgro as short-lived minister of citizenship and immigration.

In the end, enough voters had second thoughts to turn Paul Martin's succession story from that of a Judas to one of a Lazarus. According to a COMPAS/ Global Television survey of voters having cast their ballots on election day, 40 percent decided who they would vote for in the previous week; and 25 percent only decided within twenty-four hours of the election.[60] At this last minute, mistrust of the Conservatives' putative hidden agenda trumped mistrust of the Liberals' corruption – largely in Ontario.

In virtually all post-campaign analysis, the minority government that the Liberals won at the last moment was credited to the impact of their advertising. Though no explicit correlation between ads and electoral outcomes exists, the coexistence of the appetite for change with the re-election of the incumbent government can be explained only by the voters' overriding concern about the incumbent's rival. Since the Liberals' fear campaign had not initially triumphed, it appeared that the media's autonomous role in constructing the election as a decision about extreme social conservatism ultimately delivered the Liberal minority. As a result, Paul Martin did not follow John Turner all the way down the road to self-destruction. Instead, he was put on a short leash by uncommitted voters relenting in their anger over Adscam and by Tory voters agreeing with Joe Clark's publicly stated preference for the old Liberals over the new Conservatives.[61]

The Liberals' decade of apparently unchallengeable hegemony had been shaken to the core. With the partisan succession resolved, the question became what kind of prime ministerial succession was Paul Martin going to make as leader of a minority government. Like John Turner before him, he had failed to make his promised breakthrough in the West and bled support from both Quebec and the jewel in the Liberal crown, Ontario. Would he take his lead from Lester Pearson (1963-8) and, negotiating support for every issue with the opposition, produce a creative, highly productive government? Would he follow Pierre Trudeau's model (1972-4) and govern just long enough to regain his political balance and then provoke another election on his own terms? Or would he take his cue from Joe Clark (1979) and, running the PMO as if he had a majority, turn the provisional mandate received from the voters into a game of political chicken? Only time would tell how long and how well this revivified Lazarus would stay on his feet.

Conclusion

The Liberal Party As Hegemon: Straddling Canadian History

We generally analyze election campaigns with two basic questions in mind: Why did the winners win? Why did the losers lose? With these two issues in mind, election results are understood as the outcome of various interacting causes that, when combined in different proportions, result in a party's victory or defeat at the polls. For example, a mixture of weak leadership, poor campaign organization, and unfocused policies left the Liberals high and dry in the 1984 and 1988 elections, whereas Jean Chrétien's successful response to public cynicism about politicians' broken promises by issuing his Red Book contributed to his 1993 victory.

When a number of elections are examined together in this fashion, we can see just what factors have been most decisive in determining their outcome over the years. Leadership has mattered, of course, but not in a way in which parties can derive simple lessons from history and apply them to future campaigns. Surely it was improbable in 1968 that a shy millionaire intellectual from Montreal with no political experience to speak of should have transmogrified into a charismatic figure who brought the Liberals their first majority in fifteen years. It was just as unlikely that a handsome, intelligent, engaging corporate lawyer from western Canada with connections across the country should have proven a dud in 1984. Similarly, money has remained the mother's milk of electoral politics, but unless the business community engages in all-out political warfare by intervening directly in an election campaign with its own advocacy advertising, as it did in the 1988 free trade election, it is unlikely to prove the decisive factor.

Far more interesting are the insights that we can gain by putting a number of elections end to end to look at the broader changes that have occurred between election years. Since political parties are the main institutions linking civil society to the executive, legislative, and administrative machinery of a democratic state, changes in the internal structure of parties, in their methods of campaigning, and in the party system they form as they interact with one another should help us understand the evolving nature of the Canadian polity. This concluding chapter will relate the mutating face of Canada's partisan politics and the country's changing place in the world to the electoral record of what, despite its recent troubles, remains Canada's hegemonic political party.

The Fourth Party System

It seemed obvious that Canadian politics had entered a new phase following the double shock of the polarizing free-trade campaign of 1988 and the 1993 electoral earthquake. Gone was the "two-party-plus-one" system in which the Liberals and the Progressive Conservatives competed for the reins of power, while the New Democrats struggled on, always hoping to regain the influence they had exerted in the Liberal minority governments of 1963-5, 1965-8, and 1972-4. The elections of 1997 and 2000 appeared to confirm that the realignment of 1993 had produced a new "one-party-plus-four" configuration, with the LPC, which remained the only national party able to claim representation from every region, continuing to propound a pan-Canadian vision for the country. For their part, the Bloc Québécois, the New Democratic Party, and the country's Conservatives in their Reform/Alliance and Progressive Conservative manifestations divided up the opposition's duties from their regional bases as they responded to their localized bases of support.[1]

What makes the Liberal Party of Canada crucial for this discussion is its centrality in the fourth party system. Having long been the "government party," it was more dominant at the time of Jean Chrétien's retirement than it had ever been. Its policies could be contested by the other parties, but its control of government seemed unchallengeable as late as the fall of 2003, given its surging popularity in such traditionally hostile territory as British Columbia and Alberta upon Paul Martin's succession to the leadership and the narrow regional appeal of the opposition parties.

That the Liberal Party returned from its 2004 electoral outing having lost its parliamentary majority and with less representation than before from regions in which it had been poised to make a breakthrough (notably Quebec and the West) showed that Paul Martin had managed to fritter away the hegemonic position he had inherited. In the language of Machiavelli used for the 1984 campaign chapter, the poor Liberal showing in 2004 demonstrated how sadly the party leader lacked the Virtù – or political judgment – required to deal with a set of political conjunctures that, for all the difficulties they have brought him, still saw Fortuna smiling broadly in his direction.

Not only did Martin mishandle the "Adscam" issue as a short-term matter in the winter of 2004, when he was positioning himself for an early election. By establishing a judicial inquiry to dig further into the funding of federalist propaganda in Quebec, he initiated a long-term self-wounding process that – over a year later – was challenging the Liberals' chances even to be re-elected as a minority government. The daily revelations of corruption broadcast live from the Gomery inquiry heralded the possibility that, with the Bloc Québécois capitalizing on the collapse of the Liberals' credibility in its domain, Stephen Harper's reconstituted Conservative Party could successfully bring the past decade of Liberal dominance to an end. That it was only Belinda Stronach's defection from the Conservative Party on May 17, 2005, that saved Paul Martin's government from defeat in a non-confidence motion underlined just how tenuous the Liberal grip on power had become. In restoring an alternation between the Liberals and the Conservatives, Canadian politics would then have moved still further back toward the two-plus party system, which had been obliterated – at least for a decade – by the electoral cataclysm of 1993.

Adapting to Globalization

At the same time as Canadian party politics was becoming more and more regionalized during the 1990s,[2] the Liberal Party was paradoxically taking the lead in integrating the country into the new global economy. This book's nine elections span thirty years and two distinct periods in Canada's evolution. As the debate over wage and price controls indicated, the 1974 election marked the watershed of the postwar political and economic paradigm. The Keynesian welfare state with its related "Fordist" system of industrial organization based on mass production and unionized labour was entering a period of prolonged crisis throughout the developed world due to the oil price shock precipitated in 1973 by the Organization of Petroleum Exporting Countries and the resultant phenomenon of "stagflation," or simultaneous high inflation and high unemployment.

In the subsequent three decades, the context within which Canadian political parties operated was transformed. The generous and expansive state was replaced by a neoconservative order in which government-provided public services were significantly reduced. The postwar foundations of economic prosperity based on import substitution, resource exports, and branch-plant manufacturing were shattered thanks to the crumbling of international economic barriers under trade liberalization, the globalization of financial markets thanks to new satellite- and computer-based information technology, and the resulting continentalization of corporate production strategies and distribution systems.

When in power during the first, second, and third party systems, political parties focused their energies on national integration. When in opposition, they criticized the government of the day for mismanaging this task. In office or not, their policy horizon was set by the country's territorial boundaries. In times of peace, the very notion of "foreign" policy confirmed the distinction between government, which was practised within the nation-state, and diplomacy, which dealt with issues outside its borders. In the Liberal Party's case, policies aimed at national consolidation had a distinctly continental touch. Under the leadership of C.D. Howe, Canada's American-born "minister of everything" during the Mackenzie King and St. Laurent eras, the Grits openly courted American capital to help develop Canada's industrial base and its vast natural resource endowment by integrating the Canadian with the American economy. Continental integration of Canada's armed forces and military industries under American control was formalized in the 1950s, with the creation of the North American Air (now Aerospace) Defense Command (NORAD) and the signature of the Canada-United States defence production sharing agreements. Lester Pearson took a further step toward North American economic integration in 1965 when he signed the Canada-United States Auto Pact, which gave US-owned Canadian car manufacturers preferential access to the American market.

It was only after 1972 that the Liberals started having second thoughts about their previous embrace of continentalism. This shift began with the establishment of the Foreign Investment Review Agency and Petro-Canada and culminated with the launching of the ill-fated National Energy Program in 1980. Although John Turner ultimately reinforced the nationalist thrust, which the Liberal Party had only half-heartedly adopted under Trudeau, by vigorously opposing the Canada-United States Free Trade Agreement, his successors brought the party back to its continentalist ways. As the leader of the opposition, Jean Chrétien may have mouthed an anti-NAFTA position for electoral reasons, but as prime minister he and his main economic minister, Paul Martin, wholeheartedly endorsed the North American Free Trade Agreement, welcomed the World Trade Organization, which the Mulroney government had helped negotiate, and went on to sign bilateral trade and investment agreements with as many other countries as would agree to talk.

Constructing the "external constitution" that these agreements comprise has meant adopting continental and global norms in areas such as health policy (reducing the market share for cheaper generic drugs because of new trade-related intellectual property rights favouring brand-name drug companies), cultural policy (agreeing to "split-run" American magazines that siphon off the periodical industry's advertising market), agricultural policy (breaking up the supply management system), and environmental policy (accepting the use of the toxic gasoline additive MMT).[3] Despite performing public hand-wringing acts when these examples of economic globalization cast doubt on the federal government's claim to manage the country's own affairs, the Liberal Party in power has steadfastly supported these new continental and global economic regimes.

In the aftermath of the September 11, 2001, terrorist attacks on the United States, the Liberals responded to Washington's strident new obsession with national security by acquiescing to its demands for tighter Canadian border and immigration controls. Only with its refusal to join the American war in Iraq did the Chrétien government overtly resist the George W. Bush administration's rash foreign policy. As prime minister in his turn, Martin proceeded to restructure Canada's national security apparatus along the lines of the US Department of Homeland Security by creating a new super-Ministry of Public Safety and Emergency Preparedness. More surprisingly, having endorsed Canada's continued participation in NORAD, which had become the Pentagon's space-based global command and control system, he refused to support its corollary, the US National Missile Defence system.

When it wears its electoral mask, however, the Liberal Party reverts to a more centrist and nationalistic stance, playing on the themes of sovereignty and national pride. In its ideational role, it collaborates with the other parties in perpetuating a national sovereignty discourse that gives the voters the impression that their government is indeed capable of addressing their social, economic, and cultural concerns. Federal power may have been displaced vertically to continental and global institutions, it may have been transferred horizontally to market forces, it may have been downloaded to the provincial level, but the language of the hustings remains primarily Ottawa-centric. Although globalization is invoked from time to time, and party platforms intone the mantra about making the economy "second to none" and "globally competitive," federal parties implicitly deny in their introverted campaign mode the radical shift that has taken place in Canada's international context.

Over the decades, political parties have been leading actors in our consociational democracy, in which the elites from the country's constituent regional, linguistic, and sectoral groups come together periodically at the summit of the political system to work out some kind of a modus vivendi, allowing their constituencies – however antagonistic they might be toward one another – to get enough of what they need from the system. In a globalized world, however, consociation takes place at the international level as well, when national political elites gather to construct the market-liberation consensus that is expressed in the rules of the WTO or in the practices of the International Monetary Fund.

Just as the Liberals under Chrétien and Martin have proceeded to integrate Canada into the global economy, they have reinforced the legacy left by the Mulroney Conservatives by entrenching neoconservative norms in federal policy. The concerted attack they made on the federal government's deficits and the accompanying erosion of the government's entrepreneurial, regulatory, and redistributive capacities are well known. To the extent that the fourth party system is directly linked to neoconservative globalization, the Liberal Party has become its prime Canadian mover.

Campaign Policy

While recent Liberal governments have played a central role in propelling Canada into a globalized world, the Liberal Party's electoral behaviour was more ambiguous. Its 1993 critique of the Conservatives' preoccupation with zero inflation was modulated by the promise of an economic development strategy with a prominent role for government investment that had clear links to policies practised by the Trudeauites. Brandishing the wand of economic interventionism was accompanied by explicitly left-leaning promises to buttress the health care, cultural, and Aboriginal policies that were seen to have been jeopardized by the Mulroney Conservatives. While vaguer in every respect, the Liberal Party's three subsequent campaign platforms reaffirmed these social priorities. The Liberals still claimed to be the champions of a self-defined national unity, an autonomous foreign policy, and a humane society in which government, in Chrétien's frequently expressed phrase, is "a force for good" having a noble mission to improve conditions for its citizenry.

If its discourse belonged more to the third than the fourth party system, was its method of policy delivery not an indication that the leopard had indeed changed its spots? The carefully written, detailed analyses and prescriptions of the 1993 Liberal platform, *Creating Opportunity*, were heralded as an innovation that would transform the way elections were conducted thereafter. In the words of the party leader, it was the ultimate indicator of democratic politics, since it would allow the voters to hold him accountable for his acts if and when he was elected prime minister.

The claim to trail-blazing innovation had some merit. Not only did the Liberals issue similar policy platforms in their subsequent re-election bids in 1997, 2000, and 2004, but provincial politicians also acknowledged the Red Book's success by taking their cue from Chrétien's campaign prop. The Ontario Progressive Conservatives, for example, issued a platform document, *The Common Sense Revolution*, a whole year in advance of their 1995 electoral victory.

This focus on a platform document can be read in two ways. In one light, it can be identified with the media-hyped populism characteristic of the fourth party system. It signals accountability, even if the actual accounting that takes place is bound to be highly subjective. But those with long memories might see the Red Book as a return to the general practice observed in the first and second party systems, when parties routinely issued a manifesto describing what they would do if entrusted with power. Such documents might reflect the personal ideas of the leader (as was the case with Laurier) or of the party's advertising agency (as was often the case during Mackenzie King's tenure as leader).[4]

The Red Books made the same genuflection toward democratic norms as the Liberal Party's 1962 and 1963 election manifestos, which reflected resolutions passed in a policy convention held in 1961 under the careful control of Lester

Pearson's right-hand man, Walter Gordon. Chrétien's campaign documents may have been glossily produced, but they bore a strong resemblance to those early moments of diffident party democratization in their mix of vaunted party-member input and backroom control by the leader. They marked a definite change from the Trudeau campaigns, when comprehensive documents were eschewed in order to give the leader's tour maximum flexibility for making news with surprise policy announcements from day to day during the campaign proper.

Further evidence that the Red Books do not indicate a shift into a new era for the Liberal Party is their connection with a leader-managed process of intellectual renewal characteristic of the third system. The intellectual origins of the 1962 and 1963 party manifestos lay not in the 1961 policy convention but in a thinkers' conference held in Kingston in 1960. Deriving party policy from consultations with non-partisan intellectuals also inspired the Trudeau Liberals' first efforts at participatory democracy – their assemblage of policy wonks in 1969 at Harrison Hot Springs, BC, was modelled on the 1960 Kingston conference. It is not surprising, then, that when Jean Chrétien launched a process of policy renewal as new leader in 1990, he too started with a thinkers' conference held across the river from Parliament in Aylmer, Québec. As dauphin-in-exile, Paul Martin spent a year presiding over a "virtual" thinkers' conference for which he commissioned dozens of papers on policy priorities.

Beyond the continuity represented by the thinkers'-conference approach to a leader-managed process of policy development, the Liberal Party further fails to conform to the norms of the new fourth party system by resisting the siren calls of direct democracy. It has shunned referenda, recalls, and other nostrums of plebiscitarian politics, clinging instead to the representative principles of the parliamentary system that have served it so well.

Electoral System

The Liberals' success in retaining their status as a truly national party has had much to do with their capacity to profit from the single-member-constituency first-past-the-post electoral system, which tends to give the party with a plurality of votes a commanding majority of seats in Parliament.[5] At the same time, it discriminates against less successful national parties (the old PCs and NDP) and benefits those parties with a regional base and appeal (the Bloc Québécois and the new Conservative Party of Canada's western wing). Since the first-past-the-post system has been a common thread through all mutations of the Canadian party system, it cannot be considered an element either defining or explaining what is novel about the fourth system, even if the Liberals have benefited from it far more than any other party in recent decades (see Figures 3 and 4).

Given how the Liberal Party depends on the plurality system to give it a far greater share of the seats in the Commons than the proportion of votes it

Figure 3

Effects of the first-past-the-post system in Canada, 1972-2004

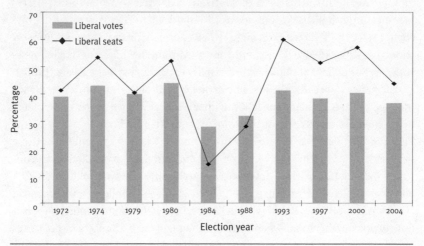

Source: Reports of the Chief Electoral Officer for each election.

Figure 4

Effects of the first-past-the-post system in Quebec, 1972-2004

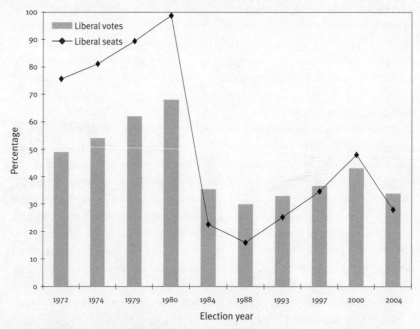

Source: Reports of the Chief Electoral Officer for each election.

receives from the electorate, any move to dilute the first-past-the-post system with elements of proportional representation (PR) would pose an existential threat to the Liberals' dominance. Although the NDP had vowed to champion reforms to the electoral system that would see Canada move toward PR in the 2004 minority Parliament, the danger this poses to the Liberals' prospects is minimal, given how the two other opposition parties also depend on the plurality system to deliver them more seats than the votes they receive would justify under PR.

Leadership Selection

Leadership conventions have come into question due to the need, in the face of the public's declining faith in representative institutions, to rectify their sometimes outrageously unethical campaign procedures.[6] As a result, parties are moving to abandon traditional convention-based methods for choosing leaders in favour of universal ballot mechanisms on the grounds that they empower all party members.[7] Since 1985, most of Canada's major federal and provincial political parties have switched from delegated leadership conventions, a staple of Canadian politics since the 1920s, to various forms of universal membership voting, which have been described as the "latest step in a historical progression from closed and exclusive to open and participatory leadership selection in Canadian parties."[8]

The LPC carefully studied the alternative selection processes but balked at making radical changes.[9] The desire to find a compromise between the idea of greater democratization and the need to remain competitive as a brokerage party led it to adopt a compromise system that combines both the direct vote and the leadership convention. Although it was the first of the national parties to amend its constitution (in 1990) to ensure that future leaders will be elected by a direct vote of all its members, the LPC's new selection format was neither a total acceptance of the one-member-one-vote principle, nor a total rejection of the familiar convention format. Local associations would continue to elect delegates, but with a different ballot and under different rules. Introducing proportional representation in the riding delegate selection contests was a way to deal with traditional delegate selection abuses while at the same time incorporating some of the strengths of the universal suffrage system. Delegates from across the country would still gather at a central convention site to select a leader, and, in theory, the party would retain such positive aspects of the convention as the excitement generated by the horse-race atmosphere, the resulting colourful media coverage, the anticipated boost in the polls, the morale building among the elite of the party, and the strengthening of personal contacts between delegates and leaders.

In practice, however, the leading contender to replace Jean Chrétien so completely captured the party's extra-parliamentary organization that the race turned into a long coronation procession for Paul Martin, reminiscent of the leadership transitions from Mackenzie King to St. Laurent and from St. Laurent to Pearson during the second party system. Reminiscent but not identical, for instead of the retiring prime minister (King) selecting both his successor and his successor's successor, aspiring dauphin Martin wrested the crown from the incumbent and placed it on his own head.

In addition to the modalities of the convention itself, the conditions under which a leadership contest can be launched in the Liberal Party also reflect the restricted degree of internal democracy in the LPC leadership selection process. While the LPC constitution, like those of all other federal parties, mandates a leadership convention to be held following the death or resignation of an incumbent, it requires that a leadership review be held at the party's first convention following every general election, regardless of the election result. Such leadership reviews were expected to be a formality for a Liberal leader who led the party to victory in the previous election, but the threat of a grassroots revolt at the approaching leadership review was sufficient to force Jean Chrétien to announce his intention to retire in the period immediately preceding the party's first convention following the 2000 election.

The Leader

Old leaders, like old soldiers, do not simply die, but are prone to fading away slowly and persisting over a very long time. They may even be called back into battle as was Trudeau in 1979. It may seem perverse to argue that leadership represents another element of continuity in the present phase of the Liberal Party's history given the striking differences between Pierre Trudeau's continuing charisma over his sixteen years as leader, Turner's embarrassing failures during his inglorious interregnum, Jean Chrétien's generally cautious, sometimes belligerent, but unexpectedly successful approach, and Paul Martin's technocratic, dithering, and focus-group-tested style of leadership.[10]

For all the stylistic differences in their leadership, both Jean Chrétien in 1993 and Paul Martin in 2003 displayed greater continuities with Liberal leaders from previous party systems than the discontinuities that the paradigm-shift argument would lead us to expect. In an apparent rejection of the demands in the fourth party system for greater democratic participation in policy making Chrétien and Martin have followed Trudeau in "governing from the centre" – both by vesting greater powers in the Prime Minister's Office and the Privy Council Office, and by instituting policy through orders-in-council rather than by legislation duly passed by Parliament.[11] Employing techniques reminiscent of the second party system, both men have recruited local stars into their cabinets to appease regional discontents. Both happily continued to play the third party system's elitist game of federal-provincial diplomacy to create bold new national programs like the National Child Benefit and the Health Care Accord of 2004. And in their management of internal party affairs, both men have displayed an authoritarian proclivity to discipline those who crossed them. Jean Chrétien sacked Paul Martin from his cabinet once his leadership machinations became Ottawa's worst-kept secret. Later, Martin's team dispatched Sheila Copps in her bid to win the Liberal nomination in the redrawn riding of Hamilton East-Stoney Creek and expelled Carolyn Parrish from caucus for being too overtly anti-American in her behaviour in public.

Internal Party Autocracy

As with its leadership, so with the moves to democratize its inner workings: the bigger transformation took place in the LPC from the second to the third party system. The Liberal Party in the fourth era of party politics is much the same as it was in the third. Although Mackenzie King willed an extra-parliamentary organization into being in the 1930s, he never gave his National Liberal Federation the chance to develop a democratic culture. Only the reforms made possible by the party's double defeat of 1957 and 1958, plus the concomitant decimation of its old guard, brought democratic norms into the Liberals' internal practices. Spearheaded by Cell 13, a group of young and ambitious Toronto-based professionals keen to bring energy, openness, and their own moxie to the Liberal Party, significant reforms were introduced to the party constitution in order to make the leader somewhat accountable to the grassroots.

These efforts at reform were both endorsed and promoted in Pierre Trudeau's first years as leader following his campaigning for power on the strength of such slogans as "participatory democracy" and a "just society," but they soon hit the glass wall of parliamentary sovereignty and centralized government. The cabinet rejected the extra-parliamentary party's newly asserted right to determine the contents of the election platform. When the dust had settled by the early 1970s, the Liberal Party's internal organization remained democratic in its constitutional form but autocratic in its day-to-day practice. Impotent in terms of policy power, the extra-parliamentary party reverted to its culture of latency between elections, an organization available as an entry channel into the gladiatorial stratum of political activists, a training ground for potential candidates, and a site where young hacks could learn the skills of organization and the behavioural norms of discipline, opportunism, and manipulation necessary for a career in the back rooms or front halls of partisan politics.

In some respects, and particularly in the leader's power over the nomination process, the Liberal Party under Jean Chrétien and Paul Martin is more authoritarian than it has been at any time since Cell 13 started pressing for change in the late 1950s. On the whole, however, the extra-parliamentary party remains essentially the same as it has been since the early 1960s. Its membership fluctuates in sync with the electoral cycle, rising steeply during a leadership campaign or in the ridings' nomination battles before an election, and falling off subsequently until the prospect of another election causes hopeful candidates to recruit supporters. In effect, the Liberal Party remains a leader-centred organization both at the riding level and at its headquarters. While the longevity in office of the party's leaders gives an impression of continuity in personnel, its membership rolls are characterized by high levels of instability and discontinuity from campaign to campaign, there being little reason for party members to stay active once an election is over or a leader is selected. The LPC is far from having become the "mass party" envisaged in 1968 by Richard Stanbury in his project to generate active relations between a participatory grassroots and a responsive caucus. Its formal structures remain largely an empty shell.

For all its democratic failings, the Liberal Party outclasses its rivals in attracting citizens into its ranks. Not only does it report the largest number of party members, but these members' participation rates are higher than those of their opponents. Research executed in 2000 by William Cross and Lisa Young shows that Liberals out-participate other parties' members in displaying election signs (at the rate of 91 percent), attending nomination meetings (88 percent), volunteering in election campaigns (86 percent), attending local party meetings (89 percent), and serving on their local riding executive (59 percent).[12] One out of three of these activists dedicate over five hours per month to party work, compared with one out of ten in the other parties. One-quarter of the Liberals surveyed attended more than ten party functions in 1999 compared with one-twentieth of the other parties' members.[13]

Further strengths of the LPC's membership base are indicated by women and men being present in roughly equal numbers and by francophones being especially well represented in its ranks. Still other indicators suggest that, while the LPC may have lost its undisputed hegemony on Paul Martin's watch, its vital signs promise it a bright future. Compared to its rivals, it has the largest proportion of its members under 40 (19 percent). Its relative youthfulness is confirmed by having the smallest proportion of members over 65 (33 percent). Its place as a party of knowledgeable citizens is further suggested by its members boasting the highest university attendance (65 percent).[14]

These data notwithstanding, the LPC's machinery is maintained by a small staff so that it can be activated when an election or leadership campaign appears on the horizon. In the wings behind the political stage, hundreds of former ministers and MPs, pollsters and advertising people, fundraisers and political operatives constitute the informal party, a mostly invisible phalanx of loyalists who wield very considerable clout behind the scenes.

Election Financing

The legal framework for party fundraising is another respect in which the fourth party system represents strong continuity with the vision of the third, in contrast with the norms and the practices of the second. The watershed year was 1974, when tri-partisan agreement produced the Election Expenses Act and a number of other legislative amendments that brought the rule of law to the murky world of political fundraising. The legislation turned those political parties from private clubs into publicly accountable organizations that became legally bound to submit for official inspection professionally audited records of campaign-related financial receipts and expenses. In return for a number of carrots (tax credits to encourage citizens to donate, subsidies to candidates and to party organizations, guaranteed allocations of air time for the now-limited period of campaign advertising), the legislation introduced a corresponding series of sticks (limits on campaign spending, requirements for disclosure, a strict enforcement mechanism complete with severe legal penalties for infractions). The enhanced capacity of ridings to raise funds, the augmented constituency autonomy, the increased levels of citizen participation, and a decreased reliance on corporate financing represented an important, if insufficient, step toward heightened democratic practice. Insufficient, because major loopholes allowing parties to exclude pre-writ expenses and such research costs as opinion polling from their spending limits undermined the legislation's capacity to create a level playing field for all contenders. Exempting from the legislation's reporting requirements both the constituency fundraising between elections and the money raised by aspiring candidates for a riding nomination or the party leadership only perpetuated the unregulated conditions that had prevailed under the brokerage system.

Further holes were punched in the election expense legislation by the Alberta Court of the Queen's Bench, which, in a 1984 ruling, considerably weakened the legislation's potential to make election financing fair by exempting interest-group advocacy advertising from its aegis. The resulting orgy of big business spending in favour of the Conservatives' free trade policy in 1988 made the corporate control exercised in the brokerage system appear positively benign. Pressure to repair this gaping breach in the election financing rules led to the extensive research and substantial report of the Royal Commission on Electoral Reform and Party Financing of 1991, which pointed in the direction of strengthening the third party system's legal regime. When a 1991 federal amendment restricting "third party" advertising to $1,000 per advocacy group per election was also struck down as a result of a legal challenge in Alberta, it appeared that the courts were moving to promote the kind of pluralistic, identity-based politics more in tune with a postmodern party system.

Although the Alberta courts showed themselves ready to sanction a move toward an American model of electoral politics, Jean Chrétien sought to reassert the primacy of political parties in electoral politics by blocking the financial intrusion of other groups onto the hustings. A key element in Chrétien's reform legacy of 2003, Bill C-24, was the most substantial change to the federal election financing system since the watershed legislation of 1974. It adopted Quebec's rigorous and long-standing interdiction of corporate and labour-union political contributions, gave more generous tax incentives to stimulate individual contributions, required riding associations to register with Elections Canada, applied spending limits to candidate nominations and party leadership campaigns, and increased the public subsidy for elections to 90 percent of their costs.[15] The bill received the support of the Bloc Québécois, the Progressive Conservatives, and the NDP in the House.

Not surprisingly, the Canadian Alliance led the parliamentary opposition to the reforms. During an interregnum from politics, Stephen Harper had headed the National Citizens' Coalition (NCC) – the group that had successfully litigated in the courts against the Election Expense Act's restrictions on third-party advertising in 1984 and 1991. At the time C-24 was passed, the NCC had a case before the Supreme Court concerning a 1997 amendment to the Canada Elections Act that restricted third-party advertising. On May 18, 2004, just five days before the writs were issued for the thirty-eighth general election, the Supreme Court of Canada decisively resolved a twenty-year uncertainty about the capacity of wealthy groups from civil society to participate alongside or in competition with the national parties. The majority of the justices upheld the law limiting civil society organizations' spending to $3,000 per candidate for a total of $150,000 per election.[16] The interdictions placed by Bill C-24 on corporate, union, and third-party participation in elections have made the political parties even more dominant as the principal institutions connecting citizens to their lawmakers.[17]

Campaign Organization

The previous chapters have shown how the formal, constitutionalized structures of the Canadian extra-parliamentary party have little to do with its reality during election campaigns, when the lip service paid to rank-and-file control gives way to the reality of military-like, centralized command organizations operating under the conditions of political warfare. These high-spending, short-lived, maximum-stake operations bear little resemblance to the phenomena known by sociological labels such as "oligarchy" or "stratarchy."[18]

The campaign's organization chart may resemble a business school management model, but its various functional substructures – leader's tour, policy development, speech writing, opinion polling, fundraising, advertising – are generally situated in geographically dispersed sites and staffed by personnel who are largely out of touch with one another. They are separately linked to a campaign committee that rarely meets as a body and is largely disconnected from the chief wielders of campaign power, who are generally away from Ottawa for days at a time as they accompany their leader around the country trying to create telegenic tableaux and reportable sound bites for the daily consumption of a hungry pack of reporters and camera operators.

While political campaigns have always been centred on the party leader and have always been concerned about communicating through the media, the most significant changes in this regard occurred in the 1960s when the Liberal Party's managers sat at the knee of John Kennedy's campaign wizards, reading the breathless account of his electoral success in *The Making of the President,* and inviting his pollster Lou Harris secretly to visit Toronto to show them how to link campaign advertising with attitudinal survey research.[19] It was indeed the same young men[20] of Cell 13 (who had argued in the late 1950s for the democratization of the party to whose control they aspired) who imported the new, US-tested techniques of opinion manipulation that enormously enhanced the party leader's capacity to affect voting behaviour directly.

In every decade since then, commentators have been able to point to some new communication technology that has allegedly revolutionized election campaigning. Being able to fax a text to the leader's hotel in a far-off city for his speech that evening; being able to talk by telephone from Ottawa with the leader in her plane; being able to communicate through e-mail to every riding campaign office in the country; being able to intercept news media communications in the party war room to warn the leader of an opponent's gaffe; being able to target individual voters' concerns about issues and use direct mail to explain how the party will address them: technological change has certainly affected the speed, mood, and behaviour of both politicians and news reporters. But these accelerations in the communication of information do not appear to justify the claim that the 1990s *transformed* the parties' electoral behaviour from the patterns established during the previous period.

For the Liberal Party, at least, continuity in organizational technique is more striking than is change. Its campaign structure is still characterized by a leader's tour that has the leader plus a small coterie of trusted intimates accompanying him around the country in six-day circuits, punctuated by a Sunday in Ottawa to take stock and recharge batteries. Fundraisers, advertisers, and pollsters still operate in their own vacuums, loosely connected to a virtual executive centre. On the ground, riding organizations are still left on their own, with basic but not overwhelming communications support from the central office. Candidates still feel largely disconnected from a campaign that they hear about in the media and in the daily morale-boosting banalities they receive from the national office. Their influence over the conduct of that larger campaign is still negligible.

We are left with a paradox. On the one hand, it makes evident sense to talk about a fourth party system for both macro- and micro-political reasons. On the macro side, the ground has definitely moved. Trade liberalization has shaken the forms and functions of the state. Technological, economic, cultural, and de-mographic globalization have made it meaningful to talk of a post-national so-ciety. On the micro level, 1997 and 2000 confirmed that the 1993 federal election had indeed proven critical, with two regionally based parties and two pretend-ers to national party status crowding the opposition benches in the House of Commons.

On the other hand, the reunification of the right in 2004 seemed to restore another third-party-system feature: elections as battles between the Liberals and the Conservatives. Within that pattern, the Liberal Party of Canada stands as a monument to political continuity. To the extent that it has changed, its movement has been as much regress backwards as progress forwards. Its extra-parliamentary organization, its campaign structure, its leadership, and even its revised method for selecting a successor all testify to the persistence of features that characterized the Pearson/Trudeau era and are anchored in the King/St. Laurent period. This evidence of stability is puzzling, given that parties are epiphenomena in the political economy. They are poorly structured, with few organic ties to local communities. They are continually reconstructed by the ambitious, the parvenus, and those power-struck young people who swell their ranks in search of success outside the confines of normal career patterns.

This lack of change raises a major question. Why, when globalization in all its forms has so substantially changed our social, cultural, and economic lives, have the politics practised by the Liberal Party of Canada changed so little? This ques-tion itself contains three others. By what means have the Liberals been able to resist change? Why has this unresponsiveness to a changed global and social context been electorally successful? And what are the implications of having minor micro-change amidst major macro-change?

Standing against the Current

The first question is easily answered. In an age characterized by a "decline of deference" among a vastly better-educated public that is skeptical about politi-cians and markedly more individualistic and autonomous in its values,[21] most Canadian political parties have tried to become more open, more member-driven, more responsive to social pressures, and more reflective of new post-materialist values. It is thanks to its *lack* of democratic practices that the Liberal Party has been able to resist these pressures. The access gate to the parliamentary party is heavily guarded by such figures as the leader's regional chairs. No new social movement, no special interest, no ethnic group came close to taking over the party in the 1990s. No tree-hugging environmentalism, no flag-waving nationalism, no social-equality activism, no right-to-life evangelism was able to rock the cautious, balanced approach upon which Jean Chrétien insisted, in the mode of Mackenzie King. The Liberal Party has remained successful precisely because it had become – or better, because it had remained – undemocratic and autocratic.

The Appeal of the Old and Unimproved

The second question is less easy to answer, other than superficially. It makes a mockery of the sophisticated value research performed by my colleagues to claim that the Liberals' defiance of post-national values has only been successful because the public does not care how it is governed. Citizens may not care how the governing party runs its own internal affairs, as long as it remains free of corruption. But they do apparently care about government. Canadians want a good public education system and an excellent health care system. They want a clean environment and good jobs in a prosperous economy. And, most of all, they still believe that government should play a major role in achieving all these goals.

This leaves us with the possibility that the growing political sophistication of the public – with its heightened skepticism about politicians – and its difficulty in penetrating the parties' organizations, makes it resigned to a politics it dislikes. Within this political standoff, citizens with idealistic motivations turn to non-partisan means of political action, such as social movements, voluntary associations, and non-government organizations, where they can be directly effective and perhaps can indirectly affect the policies of their governments, whether local, national, or transnational. Non-democracy in the party system may lead to greater democracy within civil society as a reaction.

Implications of Stasis

The implications of this paradox are not encouraging. The systematic blockage of public participation in the parliamentary system can only lead to a perpetuation of its legitimacy deficit, a problem that has itself increased in the wake of two simultaneous challenges to its authority. From the inside, Parliament has lost authority ever since the Charter of Rights and Freedoms gave the courts enormous new opportunities to extend their policy-making authority. From the outside, economic liberalization has bled power away from the state system toward the continental and global levels of governance. NAFTA and the WTO establish powerful sets of rules that constrain or even prohibit Parliament from passing laws and regulations that would formerly have been considered the appropriate responsibility of the Canadian government. If the Technology Partnerships Fund, which promotes companies such as Bombardier, is declared "illegal" by the WTO, that program has to be dismantled or reconfigured, sending a clear message to Canadian voters that their government is no longer in charge.

If government is now less important, perhaps it does not matter so much whether it is run by someone who hailed from another era, provided he does his job without scandal, without offending the public's sensibilities, without embarrassing the citizens with the way he represents their country abroad. Jean Chrétien may have been petty-minded in refusing Conrad Black the government's blessing to take up the title offered him in England while retaining his Canadian citizenship. He may have been insensitive in dismissing with a joke the trampling of civil liberties in the pepper spraying of legitimately demonstrating citizens. He may have spoken in incomprehensible sentences and acted more like a bodyguard than a prime minister when he was challenged by protesters.

For all his faults and flaws, though, all Jean Chrétien initially had to do to win was prove he was not the much-reviled Brian Mulroney. Once elected, he merely had to prove he was competent. Even if he went further than his Progressive Conservative predecessor in entrenching the policies of neoconservative self-restraint, he was able to identify himself with the basic tenets of Canadian nationalism, appealing to the country's idealism by endorsing international efforts to ban land mines and create a permanent international criminal court, appealing to its chauvinism by practising gunboat diplomacy to defend the Atlantic fisheries against an apparently marauding Spanish fishing armada, and standing up to the United States even on such an important issue as its second war against Iraq. Indeed, it was only in early 2004, when news of the scandal over the federal government's Quebec sponsorship program tarnished the Liberals' sheen of managerial competence and integrity that their long-standing double-digit lead in the polls shrank, their parliamentary majority evaporating in the subsequent election.

An alternative explanation for what appears to be the cognitive dissonance between the public's actual post-national, democratic values and its acquiescence to government by a pre-modern, authoritarian party may lie in deception. Or self-deception. When a political party promises a modified welfare state but actually delivers a neoconservative set of policies, the most obvious observation to make is that it deceived the public. Doublespeak was not invented by Jean Chrétien or Paul Martin. Talking in the language of social liberalism during campaigns and practising business liberalism in power has been one of the hallmarks of the Liberal Party ever since Mackenzie King turned public ambiguity into a political art form.

A more nuanced explanation would include the public in this hypothesis, making the voters willing accomplices in their self-deception. They participate in the charade of democracy – watching the political news and the partisan commercials, reading the canvassers' brochures, sometimes making a political donation or putting a sign in their window or attending an all-candidates' meeting – and they vote, albeit in ever-decreasing numbers. However much of a mockery this process may be in terms of strict criteria for what would constitute real government by the people, they wearily accept that these elaborate rituals for renewing their elites are labelled democratic.

Given the enormous volatility of the voter due to the decline of long-standing partisan commitments, one might be tempted to conclude that every campaign is up for grabs, that every party has a fighting chance. This would be a mistake, for parties do carry with them their past history, their identity, their organizational culture, their freight of rivalries and infighting among their elites. Some residue of their image in the public mind governs their behaviour as they proceed into each new campaign. The NDP's principles may be up for discussion, but they are variations on the definition of social democracy for a country in an advanced stage of globalization. The Bloc Québécois is caught by its self-definition in its Quebec stronghold, its appeal linked to the referendum prospects of its provincial senior partner. And it remains to be seen whether the product of the same-sex marriage between the Canadian Alliance and the Progressive Conservatives will be able in the long run to secure the Tory supporters of the old PC Party in central and eastern Canada without alienating the old Reform Party's populist base in the West.

It would appear that the Liberal Party has constructed for itself from this new party system a position of centrality unrivalled since Sir John A. Macdonald first put together a government for the newborn Dominion of Canada. While none would be foolhardy enough to predict it will last forever, it would take a disaster far greater than the revelations of the sponsorship scandal – such as a successful secession by Quebec from the federation or a move away from the first-past-the-post electoral system – to cause the Liberal order to collapse utterly.

Less cataclysmic scenarios offer more hope than gloom for the Grits. Time would appear to be on their side, rather than on that of their opponents. The appeal of the Bloc fluctuates with the fall and rise in separatist support in Quebec, despite the upturn in their fortunes owing to anger over the sponsorship scandal. On the left, any winds blowing toward a Third Way have been caught in the sails of the Liberal Party, leaving the NDP becalmed. And it remains a significant challenge for the new Conservative Party to make the inroads it needs in central Canada to win enough seats to cross the aisle in the Commons, without forsaking their western Canadian base and seeing their party split again, as happened under Brian Mulroney. This will be an uphill battle, as only 14 percent of voters outside Quebec rank the Conservatives as their second choice, compared to 25 percent for the Liberals and 24 percent for the NDP.[22]

For his part, if Paul Martin proves not to have the Virtù to navigate the party around the shoals of minority government, it may fall to his successor to play the double game of fraternizing with international elites and selling a watered down, national-unity conservatism as the only sensible position that can realistically be taken under the circumstances of globalized interdependence. But play that game the Liberal Party will, for it remains the only machine able to deliver electoral success in a Canadian polity still deeply fractured on regional and ideological lines.

Wilfrid Laurier was a little off in his prediction that the twentieth century would belong to Canada. Even if the last century did not belong to Canada, Canada turns out to have belonged to the Liberal Party, which has managed to adapt to changing times Laurier's and King's winning formulas in the clientelist and brokerage party systems. Under Pearson, and Trudeau, the party continued to straddle the ideological centre in the pan-Canadian era, leaning to the left to co-opt the ideas and feed off the reformist energy of its social-democratic challengers. The party under Jean Chrétien leaned to the right to co-opt the ideas and borrow the energy from its neoconservative challengers in the fourth party system. Curiously, the threat of separatism strengthened, rather than weakened, the party's appeal throughout the country, giving credence to the hallmark Liberal Party policy of bilingualism and validating the party's claim to be the only credible bridge between the two nations and so the champion of national unity. As seen by those who rejected secession in Quebec, the Liberal Party's strength in much of the rest of Canada made it the only valid federalist party to support. And, as the only viable national party, it had prime claim to the purse strings of the business community.

Adept at patronage, skilled at brokerage, a purveyor of pan-Canadian messages, and an apostle of globalization, the Liberal Party of Canada bears the DNA of each of Canada's party systems. It has fought many electoral battles over the decades to achieve its present mastery. No doubt it will carry into future partisan wars the techniques it has developed and the memories it retains from its past campaigns, striving to make the twenty-first century belong to it as well. Future voters in future election campaigns will, of course, have the final word on how long the Big Red Machine can continue to dominate Canadian politics.

Appendix

Table A.1

Liberal Party revenue and expenses, 1974-2004

	Total revenue	Total year expenditures	Election expenses	Percentage of limit	Revenue less expenditures
1975[a]	2,216,700	1,962,807	–	–	253,893
1976[b]	5,822,908	4,706,545	–	–	1,116,363
1977	4,586,606	4,186,708	–	–	399,898
1978	5,017,511	5,283,026	–	–	(265,515)
1979	7,020,054	6,683,449	3,912,826	86.2	336,605
1980	8,367,078	7,548,028	3,846,223	84.6	819,050
1981	5,592,109	5,116,282	–	–	475,827
1982	6,746,594	6,780,896	–	–	(34,302)
1983	7,736,361	6,277,009	–	–	1,459,352
1984	13,014,211	18,292,289	6,292,983	98.5	(5,278,078)
1985	6,163,001	8,148,592	–	–	(1,985,591)
1986	10,718,738	11,166,265	–	–	(447,527)
1987	8,881,704	9,274,313	–	–	(392,609)
1988	17,897,024	17,015,487	6,839,875	85.7	881,537
1989	6,397,280	7,115,151	–	–	(717,871)
1990	13,777,976	13,326,648	–	–	451,328
1991	7,203,991	7,196,230	–	–	7,761
1992	7,631,350	7,007,779	–	–	623,571
1993	19,795,203	20,584,601	9,913,190	94.1	(789,398)
1994	11,764,405	11,706,926	–	–	57,479
1995	13,229,459	10,687,039	–	–	2,542,420
1996	14,112,746	13,192,805	–	–	919,941
1997	26,817,965	20,022,369	11,247,141	99.0	6,795,596
1998	13,763,008	12,790,570	–	–	972,438
1999	15,411,552	12,605,399	–	–	2,806,153
2000	26,527,162	19,569,874	12,525,174	98.5	6,975,288
2004	–	–	16,604,528	94.4	–

▶

◀ Table A.1

Notes: Financial data for party activities except for electioneering are not included after 2000 due to changes in Elections Canada data collection methods which make it impossible to draw meaningful comparisons with earlier election data or even to know the party's expenditures.

a   Figures for 1975 run from August 1974 to July 1975.

b   Figures for 1976 run from August 1975 to December 1976.

Sources:

1974 to 1990: W.T. Stanbury, *Money in Politics: Financing Federal Parties and Candidates in Canada,* Vol. 1, Royal Commission on Electoral Reform and Party Financing (Toronto: Dundurn Press, 1991), Table 5.1.

1991-5 revenue: Elections Canada, "Table 2: Sources of Revenue of Registered Political Parties," <http://www.elections.ca/ecFiscals/1995/table02_e.html> accessed March 2005.

1991, 1992, 1994, and 1995 expenses: Elections Canada, "Table 4: Nature of Expenses of Registered Political Parties," <http://www.elections.ca/ecFiscals/1995/table04_e.html> accessed March 2005.

1993 expenses: W.T. Stanbury, "Regulating the Financing of Federal Parties and Candidates" in *Canadian Parties in Transition,* 2nd ed., ed. A. Brian Tanguay and Alain-G. Gagnon (Scarborough, ON: International Thomson Publishing, 1996), Table 17.3.

1996-2000 revenue: Elections Canada, "Table 2: Sources of Revenue of Registered Political Parties," <http://www.elections.ca/ecFiscals/2000/table02_e.html> updated May 21, 2003.

1996-2000 expenses: Elections Canada, "Table 1: Summary of Contributions and Expenses, by Registered Political Party," <http://www.elections.ca/ecFiscals/2000/table01_e.html> updated May 21, 2003.

2000 election expenses: Elections Canada, "Election Expenses and Reimbursement, by Registered Political Party," <http://www.elections.ca/content.asp?section=fin&document=table1&lang=e&textonly=false> updated September 3, 2004.

2004 election expenses: Elections Canada, "Total Election Expenses and Reimbursements, by Registered Political Party – 2004 General Election," <http://www.elections.ca/content.asp?section=fin&document=table1_04&lang=e&textonly=false> updated February 17, 2005.

Table A.2

Government funding of the Liberal Party and Liberal candidates, 1979-2004

	Party election expenses	Party reimbursement	Candidate election expenses	Candidate reimbursement
1979	3,913,000	718,000	6,186,000	3,594,000
1980	3,846,000	910,000	6,074,000	3,656,000
1984	6,293,000	1,416,000	8,835,000	4,081,000
1988	6,840,000	1,539,000	9,677,000	4,565,000
1993	9,828,000	2,077,000	12,257,000	5,890,000
1997	11,247,141	2,180,000	13,864,000	6,638,000
2000	12,525,174	2,809,219	14,633,510	7,036,924
2004	16,604,528	9,962,717	–	–

Sources:

1979-93 reimbursement data: W.T. Stanbury, "Regulating the Financing of Federal Parties and Candidates" in *Canadian Parties in Transition,* 2nd ed., ed. A. Brian Tanguay and Alain-G. Gagnon (Scarborough, ON: International Thomson Publishing, 1996), Table 17.6.

1979-88 candidate expenditures: W.T. Stanbury, *Money in Politics: Financing Federal Parties and Candidates in Canada,* Vol. 1, Royal Commission on Electoral Reform and Party Financing (Toronto: Dundurn Press, 1991), Table 12.17.

1993 candidate expenditures: W.T. Stanbury, "Regulating the Financing of Federal Parties and Candidates" in *Canadian Parties in Transition,* 2nd ed., ed. A. Brian Tanguay and Alain-G. Gagnon (Scarborough, ON: International Thomson Publishing, 1996), Table 17.2; *party expenditures,* appendix 1.

1997 party expense and reimbursement data: Elections Canada, "Election Expenses and Reimbursements, by Registered Political Party," <http://www.elections.ca/eccandidates/191/table06.html> updated October 19, 2000.

1997 candidate expense and reimbursement data: Elections Canada, "Summary of Candidates' Expenses, by Political Affiliation," <http://www.elections.ca/eccandidates/191/table12.html> accessed March 2005.

2000 party expenses and reimbursement data: "Election Expenses and Reimbursement, by Registered Political Party," <http://www.elections.ca/content.asp?section=fin&document=table1&lang=e&textonly=false> updated September 3, 2004.

2000 candidate and reimbursement data: "Reimbursement of Candidates' Election Expenses by Political Party," <http://www.elections.ca/content.asp?section=fin&document=table&dir=rem&lang=e&textonly=false> updated September 11, 2003.

2004: "Total Election Expenses and Reimbursements, by Registered Political Party – 2004 General Election," <http://www.elections.ca/content.asp?section=fin&document=table1_04&lang=e&textonly=false> updated February 17, 2005.

Table A.3

Contributions by individuals to the Liberal and Conservative parties, 1974-2000

	Liberal			Conservative		
	No.	Average ($)	Total ($)	No.	Average ($)	Total ($)
1974 (5-month period)	4,117	112	1,104,659	6,243	99	1,280,659
1979	13,025	91	1,184,755	34,952	91	3,182,897
1980	17,670	141	2,277,650	32,720	98	3,043,829
1984	29,056	178	5,181,097	93,199	109	10,142,398
1988	30,642	155	4,748,305	53,893	189	10,181,404
1993	41,058	150	6,228,624	44,728	203	9,060,423
1997	21,906	182	5,701,064	20,353	162	4,545,316
2000	*	*	6,966,801	*	*	2,778,118

* Elections Canada no longer provides this information.

Sources:

1974 to 1988: W.T. Stanbury, "Regulating the Financing of Federal Parties and Candidates," in *Canadian Parties in Transition,* 2nd ed., ed. A. Brian Tanguay and Alain-G. Gagnon (Scarborough, ON: International Thomson Publishing, 1996), Table 17.4; and W.T. Stanbury, *Money in Politics: Financing Federal Parties and Candidates in Canada,* Vol. 1, Royal Commission on Electoral Reform and Party Financing (Toronto: Dundurn Press, 1991), Tables 4.1 and 5.1.

1993: Report of the Chief Electoral Officer Respecting Election Expenses, 1993.

1997 and 2000: Elections Canada, "Contributions to Registered Political Parties, by Donor Category," <http://www.elections.ca/ecFiscals/2000/table03_e.html> updated May 21, 2003.

Table A.4

Contributions by corporations to the Liberal and Conservative parties, 1974-2000

	Liberal			Conservative		
	No.	Average ($)	Total ($)	No.	Average ($)	Total ($)
1974 (5-month period)	2,430	410	993,177	2,046	477	1,447,968
1979	3,737	1,037	3,875,567	7,752	651	5,020,285
1980	4,420	844	3,730,983	5,011	872	4,367,936
1984	6,494	822	5,339,729	21,286	517	11,003,522
1988	7,238	1,167	8,449,440	14,032	1,023	14,358,842
1993	7,557	1,099	8,307,383	8,898	1,484	13,215,683
1997	10,315	464	11,229,938	7,157	353	6,435,732
2000	*	*	11,862,693	*	*	2,777,286

* Elections Canada no longer provides this information.

Sources:

1974 to 1988: W.T. Stanbury, "Regulating the Financing of Federal Parties and Candidates" in *Canadian Parties in Transition,* 2nd ed., ed. A. Brian Tanguay and Alain-G. Gagnon (Scarborough, ON: Nelson Canada, 1996), Table 17.5; W.T. Stanbury, *Money in Politics: Financing Federal Parties and Candidates in Canada,* vol. 1, Royal Commission on Electoral Reform and Party Financing (Toronto: Dundurn Press, 1991), Tables 4.1 and 5.1.

1993: Report of the Chief Electoral Officer Respecting Elections Expenses, 1993.

1997 and 2000: Elections Canada, "Contributions to Registered Political Parties, by Donor Category," <http://www.elections.ca/ecFiscals/2000/table03_e.html> updated May 21, 2003.

Table A.5

Liberal election expenses, 1979-2004

	1979	1980	1984	1988	1993	1997	2000	2004
Advertising	576,168	402,504	763,482	812,365	1,887,313	2,959,048	3,552,138	2,589,017
Broadcasting – radio	563,029	578,597	1,069,248	1,023,465	1,103,984	970,699	662,450	*
Broadcasting – TV	1,295,208	1,612,532	1,695,186	2,024,456	3,128,401	2,838,083	3,508,420	7,578,406 **
Rent, heat, and light	53,996	15,514	41,092	28,378	64,415	78,446	57,227	**
Salaries and benefits	145,942	155,254	202,760	483,623	347,930	573,160	799,542	1,076,300
Professional services	231,146	373,928	128,640	332,321	204,298	143,974	197,021	252,967
Leader's tour	***	***	***	1,066,972	1,538,614	1,697,242	2,283,346	2,836,782
Travel and vehicle rental	691,019	420,914	880,817	151,766	223,147	453,586	429,913	468,934 **
Fundraising	–	–	–	27,353	300,200	284,597	253,466	**
Administration expenses	356,318	184,377	431,321	667,557	827,486	698,278	426,455	641,515[a]
National office expenses	–	–	1,080,437	221,619	287,402	547,897	382,620	313,532
Miscellaneous expenses	0	2,603	0	0	0	2,131	2,576	847,075
Total	3,912,826	3,746,223	6,292,983	6,839,875	9,913,190	11,247,141	12,555,174	16,604,528

* Included with TV

** Data no longer available on this category from Elections Canada. This expense is included under miscellaneous expenses.

*** Included with travel

a Figure given is for the new "elections surveys or other surveys or research" category in the 2004 return

Sources:

1979 and 1980: F. Leslie Seidle and Khayyam Zey Paltiel, "Party Finance, the Election Expenses Act and Campaign Spending in 1979 and 1980," in *Canada at the Polls, 1979 and 1980,* ed. Howard R. Penniman (American Enterprise Institute for Public Policy Research, 1980).

1984: Khayyam Zey Paltiel, "The 1984 Federal General Election and Developments in Canadian Party Finance," in *Canada at the Polls, 1984,* ed. Howard Penniman (American Enterprise Institute for Public Policy Research, 1988).

1988 and 1993: Report of the Chief Electoral Officer Respecting Election Expenses, 1988, 1993.

1997: Elections Canada, "Table 7: Breakdown of Election Expenses of Registered Political Parties," <http://www.elections.ca/eccandidates/19i/table07.html> accessed March 2005.

2000: Elections Canada, "Breakdown of Election Expenses of Registered Political Parties – 2000 General Election," <h:tp://www.elections.ca/content.asp?section=fin&document=table2&lang=e&textonly=false> updated December 10, 2004.

2004: Elections Canada, "Breakdown of Paid Election Expenses by Expense Category and Registered Political Party – 2004 General Election," <http://www.elections.ca/content.asp?section=fin&document=table2_04&lang=e&textonly=false> updated February 1, 2005.

Notes

Preface

1 The initiative to start this series was taken in the early 1970s by Howard Penniman, a fellow at the American Enterprise Institute in Washington, DC, as part of his ambitious project to edit a book on every democratic election in the world. Apart from his books on many other countries' elections, his enterprise caused volumes to be produced on the Canadian federal elections of 1974, 1979, and 1984. Following Penniman's retirement, Jon Pammett and Alan Frizzell repatriated responsibility for what had become a respected series, and they have edited the books on the elections of 1988, 1993, 1997, 2000, and 2004 from their base in Carleton University. I am the only scholar to have written in each of these collections.

   Chapters in this book are greatly reworked from that earlier writing as follows: *1974,* "Pierre Trudeau and the Liberal Party: The Jockey and the Horse," in *Canada at the Polls: The Federal Election of 1974,* ed. Howard Penniman (Washington, DC: American Enterprise Institute, 1976), 57-96; *1979 and 1980,* "The Defeat of the Government, the Decline of the Liberal Party, and the (Temporary) Fall of Pierre Trudeau," in *Canada at the Polls, 1979 and 1980: A Study of the General Elections,* Howard R. Penniman (Washington, DC: American Enterprise Institute, 1981), 152-89; *1984,* "The Dauphin and the Doomed: John Turner and the Liberal Party's Debacle," in *Canada at the Polls, 1984: A Study of the Federal General Elections,* ed. Howard Penniman (Duke University Press, 1988), 97-119; *1988,* "The Liberals: Disoriented in Defeat," in *The Federal Election of 1988,* ed. Alan Frizzell, Jon Pammett, and Tony Westell (Ottawa: Carleton University Press, 1989), 27-41; *1993,* "Yesterday's Man and His Blue Grits: Backward into the Future," in *The Canadian General Election of 1993,* ed. Alan Frizzell, Jon H. Pammett, and Anthony Westell (Ottawa: Carleton University Press, 1994), 27-42; *1997,* "Securing their Future Together: The Liberals in Action," in *The Canadian General Election of 1997,* ed. Alan Frizzell and Jon H. Pammett (Toronto: Dundurn, 1997), 39-70; *2000,* "The Liberal Threepeat: The Multi-System Party in the Multi-Party System," in *The Canadian General Election of 2000,* ed. Jon H. Pammett and Christopher Dornan (Toronto: Dundurn, 2000), 13-59; *2004,* "Disaster and Recovery: Paul Martin As Political Lazarus," in *The Canadian General Election of 2004,* ed. Jon Pammett and Christopher Dornan (Toronto: Dundurn, 2000), 28-65.

2 I analyzed this watershed campaign – which failed in its attempt to introduce party politics into Toronto's municipal arena but succeeded as the first in a progressive, two-round battle to save the city from rampant expressway construction and overdevelopment – in *City Lib: Parties and Reform* (Toronto: Hackert, 1972).

3 Edward Greenspon, "Reading the Tea Leaves Points to a Chrétien Exit," *Globe and Mail,* October 25, 2001, A19.

Introduction

1 Although the Reform Party of Canada was replaced at the so-called "United Alternative" convention in 2000 by the Canadian Reform Conservative Alliance, which subsequently merged with the Progressive Conservatives in 2003 to form a new Conservative Party, the word "Reform" remains identified with right-wing populist politics in Canada.

2 David E. Smith, "Party Government in Canada," in *Canadian Political Party Systems: A Reader,* ed. R. Kenneth Carty (Peterborough, ON: Broadview Press, 1992), 531-62.

3 R. Kenneth Carty, "Three Canadian Party Systems," in *Canadian Political Party Systems,* ed. Carty, 563-86.

4   R. Kenneth Carty, William Cross, and Lisa Young, *Rebuilding Canadian Party Politics* (Vancouver: UBC Press, 2000).

5   James Bickerton, Alain Gagnon, and Patrick J. Smith, *Ties That Bind: Parties and Voters in Canada* (Toronto: Oxford University Press, 1999).

6   "Grits" is a label that has stuck to the Canadian Liberals, just as "Whig" has clung to English Liberals. It derives from "clear grit," which was a special sand used by the stone masons in southwestern Ontario, where the emerging radical movement was based. Similarly, the free-thinking, anticlerical radicals in French Canada were branded "Rouges" to identify them with the revolutionary tradition in Europe.

7   John Willison, *Sir Wilfrid Laurier and the Liberal Party: A Political History* (Toronto: G.N. Morang, 1903), 18.

8   Under the principle of "representation by population," each constituency in a legislature should contain approximately the same number of people. The distribution of seats in the legislature of the Province of Canada was based on the alternative "two nations" principle, with each of the two former colonies receiving the same number of seats, even though Upper Canada's population was only two-thirds of Lower Canada's. The charge for representation by population was led by an Upper Canadian because of the torrid pace of population growth in Upper Canada, whose population greatly exceeded that of Lower Canada by the end of the 1850s.

9   Willison, *Sir Wilfrid Laurier*, 18.

10 The Pacific Scandal broke in 1873 when it became known that Sir Hugh Allan, a promoter who was awarded the contract to build a railway linking British Columbia with the rest of Canada, had donated the then colossal sum of $360,000, raised in the United States, to the Conservative Party's 1872 re-election bid. The Macdonald government resigned and opened the door for Alexander Mackenzie's Liberals to win the election.

11 *House of Commons Debates*, March 2, 1877.

12 Hugh G. Thorburn, "The Development of Political Parties in Canada," in *Party Politics in Canada*, 7th ed., ed. Hugh G. Thorburn (Scarborough, ON: Prentice-Hall Canada, 1996), 7.

13 Joseph Schull, *Laurier: The First Canadian* (Toronto: Macmillan of Canada, 1965), 269-70.

14 David Jay Bercuson, *True Patriot: The Life of Brooke Claxton, 1898-1960* (Toronto: University of Toronto Press, 1993).

15 Thorburn, "Development of Political Parties," 9.

16 Reginald Whitaker, *The Government Party: Organizing and Financing the Liberal Party of Canada, 1930-58* (Toronto: University of Toronto Press, 1977), 32, 37.

17 Ibid., 171.

18 The story of the decline in Liberal fortunes in western Canada is told in David E. Smith, *The Regional Decline of a National Party: Liberals on the Prairies* (Toronto: University of Toronto Press, 1981).

19 This problem began during the Mackenzie King years. In his diary, King wrote, "It is perfectly appalling how little many ministers will exercise themselves and how completely they get into the hands of members of the permanent service." Whitaker, *Government Party*, 89.

20 The one notable exception to this rule is an episode in 1930 involving a $700,000 donation by the Beauharnois Power Corporation of Quebec to the Liberal Party. Although the company was not in line for any major federal contracts, the size of this donation – which was more than double what the party would collect from all other businesses in the next two elections – suggested that the Beauharnois "donation" was more of a bribe than anything else. The taint created by this episode would help the Liberals to their 1930 election defeat. Ibid., 12-13.

21 Under the plurality system, the candidate who receives the most votes in a given constituency wins the seat. When multiple candidates compete for a single seat, it is possible for an individual to be elected with much less than a simple majority of the votes cast. Aggregated across the nation, the plurality system can produce large parliamentary majorities for parties without their receiving a simple majority of the overall vote but winning with slim margins in various ridings.

22 Although Brian Mulroney would win 211 seats in the 1984 general election, compared to Diefenbaker's 208 seats in 1958, the former represented only 75 percent of the seats in a House of Commons that then had representatives from 282 ridings. J. Murray Beck, *Pendulum of Power: Canada's Federal Elections* (Scarborough, ON: Prentice-Hall of Canada, 1968), 326-7.

23 Donald V. Smiley, "The Two Party System and One-Party Dominance in the Liberal Democratic State," *Canadian Journal of Economics and Political Science* 24 (1958): 312-22.

24 Marshall McLuhan, *Understanding Media: The Extensions of Man,* 2nd ed. (New York: New American Library, 1964).

25 Charles Taylor, *Snow Job: Canada, the United States and Vietnam (1954 to 1973)* (Toronto: Anansi, 1974).

26 Christina McCall-Newman, *Grits: An Intimate Portrait of the Liberal Party* (Toronto: Macmillan of Canada, 1982), 90-1.

27 Gad Horowitz, "Conservatism, Liberalism and Socialism in Canada: An Interpretation," in *Party Politics in Canada,* 2nd ed., ed. Hugh G. Thorburn (Scarborough, ON: Prentice-Hall Canada, 1967), 55-73.

28 John Meisel, "Recent Changes in Canadian Parties," in *Party Politics,* 2nd ed., ed. Hugh G. Thorburn, 33-54.

29 John Meisel, *Working Papers on Canadian Politics,* Enl. ed. (Montreal and Kingston: McGill-Queen's University Press, 1973), 13.

30 Ibid., 25.

31 Ibid., 38.

32 For example, in the Toronto riding of Davenport in 1968, the four candidates for the nomination recruited 5,400 people as instant party members (author's observation).

33 Joseph Wearing, "Mutations in a Political Party: The Liberal Party in Canada in the Fifties and Sixties," paper presented at the 47th annual meeting of the Canadian Political Science Association, University of Alberta, Edmonton, June 2-6, 1975, n. 59.

34 Meisel, "Recent Changes," 54.

35 Samuel James Eldersveld, *Political Parties: A Behavioral Analysis* (Chicago: Rand McNally, 1964), chapter 1.

36 W.T. Stanbury, *Money in Politics: Financing Federal Parties and Candidates in Canada,* vol. 1 of the Research Series, Royal Commission on Electoral Reform and Party Financing (Dundurn Press, 1991), 107.

37 Jerry Grafstein and Pierre Lapointe, "Editors' Forward," *Journal of Liberal Thought* 1, 1 (1965): 2-3.

38 Thomas S. Axworthy, "Innovation and the Party System: An Examination of the Career of Walter L. Gordon and the Liberal Party" (MA thesis, Queen's University, 1970), 238.

39 For a description of the reforms attempted by party insiders in the 1960s, see Wearing, "Mutations in a Political Party."

40 Jerry Grafstein and Claude Frenette, "Editorial," *Journal of Liberal Thought* 3, 1 (1967): 7-15.

41 A similar innovation around this time in the constitution of the Progressive Conservative party allowed for the 1966 ouster of John Diefenbaker from his position as party leader.

42 McCall-Newman, *Grits,* 94.

43 For an example of Trudeau's scorn for the Liberals, when Lester Pearson flip-flopped in 1963 on his earlier refusal to allow American nuclear weapons on Canadian soil, despite widespread public opposition, Pierre Trudeau condemned "the anti-democratic reflexes of the spineless Liberal herd" and called Pearson "the defrocked priest of peace" in an article in *Cité libre,* a magazine that Trudeau had helped found in 1950. Cited in Stephen Clarkson and Christina McCall, *Trudeau and Our Times,* vol. 1 (Toronto: McClelland and Stewart, 1990), 90.

44 Beck, *Pendulum of Power,* 399.

45 McCall-Newman, *Grits,* 117.

46 On the movement for increased democracy in Quebec provincial politics, see Clarkson and McCall, *Trudeau and Our Times,* vol. 1, ch. 3.

47   Pierre Elliott Trudeau, "Notes for Remarks by the Prime Minister at the Harrison Liberal Con-
     ference" (Ottawa: Office of the Prime Minister, 1969), 2.
48   Thomas Alexander Hockin, "Pierre Trudeau on the Prime Minister and the Participant Party,"
     in *Apex of Power: The Prime Minister and Political Leadership in Canada,* ed. Thomas Alexander
     Hockin (Scarborough, ON: Prentice-Hall Canada, 1971), 98.
49   Stephen Clarkson, "Democracy in the Liberal Party," in *Party Politics in Canada,* 4th ed.
     (Scarborough, ON: Prentice-Hall Canada, 1979), 154-60.
50   Allen M. Linden, ed., *Living in the Seventies* (Toronto: P. Martin Associates, 1970).
51   Stephen Clarkson, *Feedback from Active Liberals: Study of Attitudes Towards Party Involvement
     of 1,000 Ontario Liberal Activists* (Toronto: Liberal Party of Canada [Ontario], 1973), 29.
52   Ibid., 24.
53   Ibid.
54   McCall-Newman, *Grits,* 130.
55   Ibid., 131.

1974

1   Jerry Grafstein, interview with the author, October 18, 1974.
2   In Quebec, by contrast, the French-language media were so supportive of Trudeau and his
     party that the influential *La Presse* printed its editor's endorsement of the Liberals on the front
     page of its June 29, 1974 issue.
3   Lawrence LeDuc, "The Measurement of Public Opinion," in *Canada at the Polls: The General
     Election of 1974,* ed. Howard Rae Penniman (Washington, DC: American Enterprise Institute,
     1975), 220-3.
4   "National Campaign Headquarters Candidates' Update," Ottawa, Liberal Party of Canada, May
     24, 1974.
5   Blair Williams, "Note to Newspaper Editors," Liberal Party of Canada, Ottawa, June 25, 1974, 4.
6   Ibid., 7.
7   Ibid., 5.
8   Ibid., 5.
9   Frederick J. Fletcher, "The Mass Media and the 1974 Canadian General Election," in *Canada at
     the Polls,* ed. Penniman, 253.
10   *Globe and Mail,* May 24, 1974, A1.
11   Ibid., 285.
12   *Globe and Mail,* June 5, 6, 7, 12, 14, 17, and 18, 1974, A1.
13   *La Presse,* May 25, 27, 29, and 30, June 2, 3, 4, and 5, 1974, A1.
14   *La Presse,* May 24, June 4, 6, and 13, July 1, 1974, A1.
15   Stephen Clarkson and Christina McCall, *Trudeau and Our Times,* vol. 1 (Toronto: McClelland
     and Stewart, 1990), 133.
16   Joseph Wearing, *The L-Shaped Party: The Liberal Party of Canada 1958-1980* (Toronto: McGraw-
     Hill Ryerson, 1980), 201.
17   Christina McCall-Newman, *Grits: An Intimate Portrait of the Liberal Party* (Toronto: Macmillan
     of Canada, 1982), 369. Keith Davey, *The Rainmaker: A Passion for Politics* (Toronto: Stoddart,
     1986), 165.
18   *Toronto Star,* June 29, 1974, B8.
19   *Toronto Star,* July 6, 1974, A1.
20   LeDuc, "Measurement of Public Opinion," 238.
21   Ibid., 224.
22   Keith Davey, interview with the author, October 13, 1974.
23   "Candidates' Update," Nos. 8 to 15, author's files.
24   "Candidates' Update," May 24, 1974, 3.
25   McCall-Newman, *Grits,* 163.
26   For a discussion of the changing face of Quebec politics during the 1960s and 1970s, see Ken-
     neth McRoberts, *Quebec: Social Change and Political Crisis,* 3rd ed. (Toronto: Oxford Univer-
     sity Press, 1999).

27 Author's notes.
28 Boyd Upper, "Speech to Ontario Liberal Candidates' College," May 18, 1974, York University.
29 W.T. Stanbury, *Money in Politics: Financing Federal Parties and Candidates in Canada,* vol. 1 of the Research Series, Royal Commission on Electoral Reform and Party Financing (Toronto: Dundurn Press, 1991), 107.
30 Ibid., 111.
31 All figures appearing in parentheses convert values in the text into 2002 dollars using data obtained from Statistics Canada, Table 326-0002, Consumer price index (CPI), 2001 basket content, annual (Index, 1992 = 100). Khayyam Zey Paltiel, "Campaign Financing in Canada and Its Reform," in *Canada at the Polls,* ed. Penniman, 185.
32 Ibid., 190.
33 Blair Williams, "Note to Newspaper Editors," Ottawa, Liberal Party of Canada, June 25, 1974, 2.
34 LeDuc, "Measurement of Public Opinion," 233.
35 *Globe and Mail,* May 31, June 3 and 12, 1974, A1.
36 Harold D. Clarke et al., "The 1974 Federal Election: A Preliminary Report," presented at the 47th annual meeting of the Canadian Political Science Association, University of Alberta, Edmonton, June 2-6, 1975, 10-12.
37 LeDuc, "Measurement of Public Opinion," 220.
38 Ibid., 238.
39 Ibid., 220, 237.
40 Harold D. Clarke et al., *Absent Mandate: Interpreting Change in Canadian Elections,* 2nd ed. (Toronto: Gage, 1991), 135.
41 Ibid.
42 Ibid.
43 LeDuc, "Measurement of Public Opinion," 220, 241.
44 Clarke et al., *Absent Mandate,* 136.
45 LeDuc, "Measurement of Public Opinion," 220, 230.
46 Ibid., 230.
47 Lisa Young, *Feminists and Party Politics* (Vancouver: UBC Press, 2000), 142.
48 Ibid.
49 Lise Gotell and M. Janine Brodie, "Women and Parties in the 1990s: Less Than Ever an Issue of Numbers," in *Party Politics in Canada,* 7th ed., ed. Hugh G. Thorburn (Scarborough, ON: Prentice-Hall Canada, 1996), 55.
50 John Saywell, "Parliament and Politics," in *The Canadian Annual Review of Politics and Public Affairs 1974,* ed. John Saywell (Toronto: University of Toronto Press, 1975), 70.
51 Christina Newman, "That Big Red Machine Is the Daveymobile," *Globe and Mail,* July 7, 1975.
52 Jerry Grafstein, interview with the author, October 18, 1974.

1979
1 Harold D. Clarke, *Political Choice in Canada* (Toronto: McGraw-Hill Ryerson, 1980), 381, 391.
2 George Radwanski, *Trudeau* (Toronto: Macmillan of Canada, 1978), 291. Margaret Trudeau, *Margaret Trudeau: Beyond Reason* (New York: Paddington Press, 1979), 193.
3 John Saywell, "Parliament and Politics," in *The Canadian Annual Review of Politics and Public Affairs 1975,* ed. John Saywell (Toronto: University of Toronto Press, 1976), 52.
4 Christina McCall and Stephen Clarkson, *Trudeau and Our Times: The Heroic Delusion,* vol. 2 (Toronto: McClelland and Stewart, 1994), 124.
5 In the end, a compromise was reached that allowed for the provision of air traffic control services in both official languages to domestic air traffic in Quebec.
6 Saywell, "Parliament and Politics," 3. R.B Bennett was the Conservative prime minister during the Depression; Mackenzie Bowell was one of the hapless prime-ministerial successors of Sir John A. Macdonald during the 1890s.
7 John Meisel, "The Larger Context: The Period Preceding the 1979 Election," in *Canada at the Polls, 1979 and 1980: A Study of the General Elections* (Washington, DC: American Enterprise Institute, 1981), 36.

8   Saywell, "Parliament and Politics," 27.

9   Meisel, "The Larger Context," 35.

10 Ibid., 36.

11 Saywell, "Parliament and Politics," 27.

12 James Laxer and Robert M. Laxer, *The Liberal Idea of Canada: Pierre Trudeau and the Question of Canada's Survival* (Toronto: J. Lorimer, 1977), 76.

13 Lawrence Martin, *Chrétien: The Will to Win* (Toronto: Lester Publishing, 1995), 262.

14 Ibid.

15 John Saywell, "Parliament and Politics," 11.

16 Proposition 13, passed by California voters on June 13, 1978, is thought by many to mark the beginning of the tide of anti-governmental sentiment in the United States. Its passage led, almost overnight, to a 53 percent reduction in property taxes collected by municipal governments, thus paralyzing them.

17 Roy MacLaren, MP, interview with the author, August 15, 1979.

18 Kathy Robinson, interview with the author, July 9, 1979.

19 Martin Goldfarb, interview with the author, August 22, 1979.

20 Christina Newman, "That Big Red Machine Is the Daveymobile," *Globe and Mail,* July 7, 1975.

21 "Ministerial politics" was Reg Whitaker's phrase to describe the system that developed under St. Laurent's weak leadership.

22 Maurice Duverger famously distinguished between cadre parties run by political elites and mass parties that emerged from major social-reform movements. The notables who animated a cadre party could be displaced by the leader's clique. Duverger, *Political Parties: Their Organization and Activity in the Modern State* (London: Methuen, 1954).

23 Stephen Clarkson, "Democracy in the Liberal Party," in *Party Politics in Canada,* 4th ed., ed. Hugh G. Thorburn (Scarborough: Prentice-Hall Canada, 1979), 154-60.

24 Kenny would also find the reward for his loyal service in a tenured Senate seat.

25 Allan Fotheringham, "Davey and Coutts, Packagers of the New and Increasingly Isolated Pierre Trudeau," *Maclean's,* February 23, 1976, 56. Bob Haldeman was Richard Nixon's chief of staff, and a key figure in the burglary of the Democrats' Watergate headquarters; he served eighteen months in prison for his part in the scandal. During his time at the White House, Haldeman was accused of insulating Nixon from the public and the press.

26 Michael Webb to Christina McCall-Newman, May 24, 1979.

27 Michael Webb, *Report of the Alberta Commissioner* (Calgary: Liberal Party of Canada, 1977), 20.

28 Saywell, "Parliament and Politics," 11-12, 18.

29 Blair Williams, "The Transformation of the Federal Cabinet under P.E. Trudeau," paper presented at the 51st Annual Meeting of the Canadian Political Science Association, University of Saskatchewan, Saskatoon, May 30-June 1, 1979, 30.

30 The following analysis is based on several dozen interviews conducted in person and by telephone with candidates, senior members of the national campaign committee, staff officers in the Prime Minister's Office, provincial campaign committee chairmen, and personnel across the country over the summer following the May 22, election. Requests for confidentiality dictate that precise attributions of information be dispensed with.

31 Data derived from *Ontario Riding Histories* (Ottawa: Office of the Prime Minister, 1979).

32 All figures appearing in parentheses convert values in the text into 2002 dollars using data obtained from Statistics Canada, Table 326-0002, Consumer price index (CPI), 2001 basket content, annual (Index, 1992 = 100).

33 *Canada Elections Act, RSC* 1970, c. 14 (1st Supp.), s. 1.

34 W.T. Stanbury, *Money in Politics: Financing Federal Parties and Candidates in Canada,* vol. 1 of the Research Series, Royal Commission on Electoral Reform and Party Financing (Toronto: Dundurn Press, 1991), 147.

35 Royal Commission on Electoral Reform, "Financing Contemporary Party Problems," in *Canadian Political Party Systems: A Reader,* ed. R. Kenneth Carty (Peterborough, ON: Broadview Press, 1992), tables 2 and 3.

36 Stanbury, *Money in Politics*, 113.
37 Ibid.
38 Royal Commission on Electoral Reform, "Financing Contemporary Party Problems," 463.
39 Lisa Young, *Feminists and Party Politics* (Vancouver: UBC Press, 2000), 152.
40 Ibid. On the "Towards Equality" report, see M. Janine Brodie and Jill Vickers, "The More Things Change ... Women in the 1979 Federal Campaign," in *Canada at the Polls, 1979 and 1980: A Study of the General Elections*, ed. Howard Rae Penniman (Washington, DC: American Enterprise Institute, 1981), 334.
41 Brodie and Vickers, "The More Things Change," 334.
42 Audrey Gill, "Memorandum," May 8, 1979.
43 Keith Davey, "Memorandum to All Liberal Candidates," March 29, 1979.
44 Ibid.
45 "Non response" was the construction used by Pierre Trudeau in an interview with the author, July 21, 1979.
46 Lorna Marsden, "Memorandum," May 12, 1979.
47 "Nobodies," famous tirade by Pierre Trudeau in the House of Commons, July 25, 1969, in John Robert Colombo, *Colombo's New Canadian Quotations* (Edmonton: Hurtig, 1987), 167.
48 Davey, "Memorandum," March 29, 1979.
49 "Political tactician" was the phrase Pierre Trudeau used in describing Jim Coutts to the author in an interview, July 21, 1979.
50 Davey, "Memorandum," March 29, 1979.
51 V.J. Bell, Donald C. Wallace, and R.B. Byers, *Canadian Annual Review of Politics and Public Affairs 1979* (Toronto: University of Toronto Press, 1981), 28.
52 On the danger of media hostility, see Frederick J. Fletcher, "Playing the Game: The Mass Media and the 1979 Campaign," in *Canada at the Polls, 1979 and 1980*, ed. Penniman, 287.
53 Ibid.
54 Clarke, *Political Choice*, 280.
55 Bell, Wallace, and Byers, *Canadian Annual Review, 1979*, 31.
56 Fletcher, "Playing the Game," 287.
57 Bell, Wallace, and Byers, *Canadian Annual Review, 1979*, 32.
58 Ibid., 29.
59 *Maclean's*, April 9, 1979, as cited in Bell, Wallace, and Byers, *Canadian Annual Review, 1979*, 33.
60 Bell, Wallace, and Byers, *Canadian Annual Review, 1979*, 29.
61 Ibid.
62 Ibid., 25.
63 Ibid., 41.
64 Bell, Wallace, and Byers, *Canadian Annual Review, 1979*, 41. The first leaders' debate took place in 1968, featuring Trudeau, Robert Stanfield, and T.C. Douglas.
65 Ibid.
66 Ibid., 42.
67 Lawrence LeDuc, "The Contest for Media Attention: 1979 and 1980 Federal Election Campaigns," in *Politics and the Media: An Examination of the Issues Raised by the Quebec Referendum and the 1979 and 1980 Federal Elections* (Toronto: Reader's Digest Foundation of Canada and Erindale College, University of Toronto, 1981), 125.
68 Fletcher, "Playing the Game," 309.
69 Ibid., 306.
70 Ibid.
71 Michael Valpy, *Sunday Morning*, CBC Radio, May 29, 1979.
72 "Vote for Trudeau, Support the Amending Formula," was the slogan proposed in despairing jest by one member of the Liberals' advertising group.
73 Christopher Lasch, *The Culture of Narcissism: American Life in an Age of Diminishing Expectations* (New York: Norton, 1978), 78.
74 *Maclean's*, June 4, 1979, as cited in Bell, Wallace, and Byers, *Canadian Annual Review, 1979*, 41.

75 May Gallup poll published in the *Toronto Star,* May 13, 1979, A26, as cited in William P. Irvine, "The Canadian Voter," in *Canada at the Polls, 1979 and 1980,* ed. Penniman, 27.

76 *Toronto Star,* April 24, 1979, A6.

77 *Toronto Star,* July 7, 1979, A1.

78 Harold D. Clarke et al., "Voting Behaviour and the Outcome of the 1979 Election: The Impact of Leaders and Issues," in *The Ballot and Its Message: Voting in Canada,* ed. Joseph Wearing (Toronto: Copp Clark Pitman, 1991), 243.

79 Ibid.

80 May Gallup poll published in the *Toronto Star,* May 13, 1979, A26, as cited in Irvine, "The Canadian Voter," 27.

81 Clarke et al., "Voting Behaviour," 258.

82 Lawrence LeDuc and Richard Price, "Great Debates: The Televised Leadership Debates of 1979," in *The Ballot and Its Message,* ed. Wearing, 278.

83 Clarke et al., "Voting Behaviour," 261.

84 Harold D. Clarke et al., *Absent Mandate: Interpreting Change in Canadian Elections,* 2nd ed. (Toronto: Gage, 1991), 138.

85 Ibid.

86 Clarke et al., "Voting Behaviour," 260.

87 Irvine, "The Canadian Voter," 83.

88 Ibid.

89 Ibid., 84.

90 Brodie and Vickers, "The More Things Change," 334.

91 Ibid., 329.

92 The other four seats were evenly split between the Tories and the NDP.

93 John Courtney, "Campaign Strategy and Electoral Victory: The Progressive Conservatives and the 1979 Election," in *Canada at the Polls, 1979 and 1980,* ed. Penniman, 150.

94 Ibid.

95 Clarke et al., "Voting Behaviour," 260.

1980

1 Stephen Clarkson and Christina McCall, *Trudeau and Our Times: The Magnificent Obsession,* vol. 1 (Toronto: McClelland and Stewart, 1990), 147.

2 Richard Gwyn, "Will Trudeau Ever Be the PM Again? I Think Not," *Toronto Star,* July 21, 1979, B5.

3 Author's observations.

4 Joseph Wearing, *The L-Shaped Party: The Liberal Party of Canada 1958-1980* (Toronto: McGraw-Hill Ryerson, 1980), 241.

5 Jimmy Gardiner was the Liberal premier of Saskatchewan from 1926-9 and 1934-5, and then was a member of King's cabinet. He built a fabled patronage machine during his years in power that was unrivalled in its effectiveness.

6 The first page of the letter of invitation to the Grindstone conference titled, "Canada, The Political Process, and the Liberal Party: A Two Day Conference, The Ramada Inn, Winnipeg, 12-14 October, 1979." The quoted remarks were made by Hu Harries, Tony Merchant, John Reid, Michel Rochon, and Gary Wilson (author's notes).

7 Wearing, *The L-Shaped Party,* 241.

8 For the concept of the leader's clique, see Robert Michels, *Political Parties: A Sociological Study of the Oligarchical Tendencies of Modern Democracy* (New York: Dover, 1959), 24, 104: "There arises in the leaders a tendency to isolate themselves, to form a sort of cartel, and to surround themselves, as it were, with a wall, within which they will admit only those who are of their own way of thinking."

9 Information about Trudeau's response to party complaints are from Pierre Trudeau, interview with the author, July 21, 1979; and James Coutts, interview with the author, December 19, 1985.

10 On the contents of the budget, see Frederick J. Fletcher and Donald C. Wallace, "Parliament and Politics," in *Canadian Annual Review of Politics and Public Affairs 1979*, ed. V.J. Bell, Donald C. Wallace, and R.B. Byers (Toronto: University of Toronto Press, 1981).

11 For a description of the thinking in the Department of Finance and the debate within the Clark cabinet over this measure, see Jeffrey Simpson, *Discipline of Power: The Conservative Interlude and the Liberal Restoration* (Toronto: Personal Library, 1980), 227-31.

12 Roy had telephoned René Lévesque for tactical guidance, but the Quebec premier could not return his call, and Claude Morin was in Africa, leaving Roy to take his policy cue from the PQ's finance minister, Jacques Parizeau, who had already denounced Crosbie's gas tax as an incursion into Quebec's jurisdiction. (Daniel Latouche, conversation with the author, March 2, 1990; Latouche was a policy adviser in the premier's office in 1979.)

13 Wearing attributes the masterminding of this decision to Davey, Coutts, MacEachen, Lalonde, and Trudeau. Wearing, *The L-Shaped Party*, 242.

14 The surprising Quebec exception who didn't want Trudeau returned was Marc Lalonde. He felt that Trudeau should be spared the ordeal of yet another election campaign, which he thought the Liberals would lose. Stephen Clarkson and Christina McCall, *Trudeau and Our Times: The Magnificent Obsession*, vol. 1 (Toronto: McClelland and Stewart, 1990), 166.

15 Wearing, *The L-Shaped Party*, 243.

16 Information on the National Executive meeting is from Gordon Dryden and Lorna Marsden, interviews with the author, March 3, 1980.

17 Wearing, *The L-Shaped Party*, 243.

18 Ibid.

19 Ibid.

20 Lorna Marsden, LPC vice-president, interview with Jospeh Wearing, cited in ibid., 244.

21 All figures appearing in parentheses convert values in the text into 2002 dollars using data obtained from Statistics Canada, Table 326-0002, Consumer price index (CPI), 2001 basket content, annual (Index, 1992 = 100).

22 W.T. Stanbury, "Elections, Party Finance, and Political Marketing," in *Canadian Parties in Transition*, ed. Alain Gagnon and Brian Tanguay (Scarborough, ON: Nelson, 1996), table 17.1.

23 Wearing, *The L-Shaped Party*, 244.

24 William P. Irvine, "Epilogue: The 1980 Election," in *Canada at the Polls, 1979 and 1980: A Study of the General Elections*, ed. Howard Rae Penniman (Washington, DC: American Enterprise Institute, 1981), 363.

25 Trudeau was himself leery – as he had been back in the heyday of Trudeaumania – of making campaign promises that he might have difficulty keeping, so he was willingly complicit with Coutts's suppression of most of the policies that had been frenetically negotiated by the platform committee.

26 Irvine, "Epilogue," 362.

27 Keith Davey and Jacques Bouchard, "Backroom Planning: The Anatomy of a Campaign," in *Politics and the Media: An Examination of the Issues Raised by the Quebec Referendum and the 1979 and 1980 Federal Elections* (Toronto: Reader's Digest Foundation of Canada and Erindale College, University of Toronto, 1981), 54.

28 David V.J. Bell and Donald C. Wallace, "Parliament and Politics," *Canadian Annual Review of Politics and Public Affairs*, ed. R.B. Byers, 5-109 (Toronto: University of Toronto Press, 1980), 87.

29 Val Sears, "The Cardboard Campaign: How the Liberals Backed out of the National TV Debate," *Toronto Star*, February 16, 1980, B2.

30 Lisa Young, *Feminists and Party Politics* (Vancouver: UBC Press, 2000), 152.

31 Fletcher and Wallace, "Parliament and Politics," 88.

32 Ibid.

33 Irvine, "Epilogue," 363.

34 Ibid., 364.

35 Ibid., 363.

36 Ibid., 370.
37 *Globe and Mail,* January 9, 1980, as cited in Bell and Wallace, *Canadian Annual Review 1980,* 7.
38 Irvine, "Epilogue," 369.
39 "A better Canada is possible. Vote Conservative; we'll do it." Ibid., 370.
40 Bell and Wallace, *Canadian Annual Review 1980,* 6.
41 *Winnipeg Free Press,* February 13, 1980, A13, as cited in Bell and Wallace, *Canadian Annual Review 1980,* 6.
42 Irvine, "Epilogue," 370.
43 Davey and Bouchard, "Backroom Planning," 54.
44 Frederick J. Fletcher, "Appendix: The Contest for Media Attention: 1979 and 1980 Federal Election Campaigns," in *Politics and the Media: An Examination of the Issues Raised by the Quebec Referendum and the 1979 and 1980 Federal Elections,* 125-41 (Toronto: Reader's Digest Foundation of Canada and Erindale College, University of Toronto, 1981), 130.
45 Ibid., 129.
46 Bell and Wallace, *Canadian Annual Review 1980,* 12.
47 Ibid., 11, 12.
48 Fletcher, "Appendix," 134.
49 Ibid., 138.
50 Wearing, *The L-Shaped Party,* 245.
51 Davey and Bouchard, "Backroom Planning," 54.
52 Hugh G. Thorburn, *Party Politics in Canada,* 7th ed. (Scarborough, ON: Prentice-Hall Canada, 1996), 623.
53 Harold D. Clarke et al., "Voting Behaviour and the Outcome of the 1979 Election: The Impact of Leaders and Issues," in *The Ballot and Its Message: Voting in Canada,* ed. Joseph Wearing (Toronto: Copp Clark Pitman, 1991), 262.
54 Harold D. Clarke et al., *Absent Mandate: Interpreting Change in Canadian Elections,* 2nd ed. (Toronto: Gage, 1991), 140.
55 Irvine, "Epilogue," 384.
56 Ibid., 371.
57 Clarke et al., *Absent Mandate,* 141.
58 Ibid., 142.
59 Ibid.
60 Ibid.
61 Ibid.
62 Wearing, *The L-Shaped Party,* 235.

1984

1 Carol Goar, "Canada after Trudeau," *Maclean's,* March 12, 1984, 20.
2 I am indebted to Johanna Superina for suggesting Machiavelli's relevance to John Turner's political performance.
3 Niccolò Machiavelli, *The Prince,* in *The Portable Machiavelli,* ed. Peter Bondarella and Mark Musa (New York: Penguin Books, 1981), 159ff.
4 Mary Janigan, "Turner's Race for the Crown," *Maclean's,* March 26, 1984, 11.
5 Mary Janigan, "The Political Shape of 1984," *Maclean's,* January 16, 1984, 11.
6 Walter Stewart, "The Natural," *Toronto Life,* June 1983, 30.
7 Léon Dion, "The Concept of Political Leadership: An Analysis," *Canadian Journal of Political Science* 1, 1 (1968): 4-6.
8 "Liberal Leadership Convention Questionnaire," unpublished survey of 1,019 cases carried out for the Canadian Broadcasting Corporation, conducted by Professor George Perlin, Queen's University, June 6, 1984, 11, author's files.
9 John Courtney, "Reinventing the Brokerage Wheel," in *Canada at the Polls, 1984: A Study of the Federal General Elections,* ed. Howard Rae Penniman (Durham, NC: Duke University Press, 1988), 186.

10   Robert J. Drummond, "Parliament and Politics," in *Canadian Annual Review of Politics and Public Affairs 1984,* ed. R.B. Byers (Toronto: University of Toronto Press, 1987), 17.

11   Ibid., 17-18.

12   Ibid., 18.

13   Ibid.

14   This analysis draws heavily on some of the excellent post-mortem analyses written by senior writers in the main national newspapers: Jeffrey Simpson, "Liberal Ruins Offer Clues to Party's Collapse," *Globe and Mail,* September 6, 1984, A1, A8; Val Sears, "A Month Ago John Turner Admitted: 'I've Screwed Up,'" *Toronto Star,* September 6, 1984, A1, A8; Greg Weston, "Anatomy of Defeat," *Ottawa Citizen,* September 5, 1984, A9; Linda Diebel, "Why the Liberals Bombed," *Montreal Gazette,* September 8, 1984, B1, B4; plus Jeffrey Simpson, "The Vincible Liberals," in *The Canadian General Election of 1984,* ed. Alan Stewart Frizzell, Jon H. Pammett, and Anthony Westell (Ottawa: Carleton University Press, 1985).

15   W.T. Stanbury, *Money in Politics: Financing Federal Parties and Candidates in Canada,* vol. 1 of the Research Series, Royal Commission on Electoral Reform and Party Financing (Toronto: Dundurn Press, 1991), 130. All figures appearing in parentheses convert values in the text into 2002 dollars using data obtained from Statistics Canada, Table 326-0002, Consumer price index (CPI), 2001 basket content, annual (Index, 1992 = 100).

16   For the amounts spent, see Stanbury, *Money in Politics,* table 13.1.

17   Ibid., table 3.7.

18   Ibid., table 3.1.

19   Simpson, "The Vincible Liberals," 26.

20   Drummond, "Parliament and Politics," 23.

21   Frederick J. Fletcher, "The Media and the 1984 Landslide," in *Canada at the Polls, 1984,* ed. Penniman, 182.

22   Ibid., 181.

23   R.H. Wagenberg et al., "Campaigns, Images and Polls: Mass Media Coverage of the 1984 Canadian Election," *Canadian Journal of Political Science* 21, 1 (1988): 117-29.

24   Courtney, "Reinventing the Brokerage Wheel," 195.

25   Ibid., 180.

26   Fletcher, "The Media and the 1984 Landslide," 181.

27   Barry Kay et al., "The Character of Electoral Change: A Preliminary Report from the 1984 Election Study," in *The Ballot and Its Message: Voting in Canada,* ed. Joseph Wearing, (Mississauga: Copp Clark Pitman, 1991), 296.

28   Fletcher, "The Media and the 1984 Landslide," 183.

29   Ibid.

30   Keith Davey, "Mr Davey Protests," *Globe and Mail,* September 3, 1984, A6. The Davey letter was itself reported with editorial reaction in the same paper: *Globe and Mail,* "Davey Says That Globe Was Biased in Campaign," September 3, 1984, A5.

31   "Turner Contradicts Policy Adviser, Says All Must Pay Minimum Tax," *Globe and Mail,* August 27, 1984, A4.

32   Michael Tenszen, "Axworthy Rues Liberal Strategy," *Globe and Mail,* August 31, 1984, A1, A2.

33   Bob Hepburn, quoted in Alan Stewart Frizzell and Anthony Westell, "Analysis of the Vote," in *Canadian General Election of 1984,* ed. Frizzell, Pammett, and Westell, 55-6.

34   Fletcher, "The Media and the 1984 Landslide," 168.

35   Ibid., 168-9.

36   Ibid., 168.

37   Ibid., 171.

38   Fletcher, "The Media and the 1984 Landslide," 170. For the statistics on polls being used in news stories, see Wagenberg et al., as cited in ibid.

39   Keith Davey, *The Rainmaker: A Passion for Politics* (Toronto: Stoddart, 1986), 353.

40   Fletcher, "The Media and the 1984 Landslide," 170.

41   Kay et al., "Character of Electoral Change," 32.

42 For the statistics on Turner's negative press coverage, see Wagenberg et al., "Campaigns, Images and Polls," 129.
43 Drummond, "Parliament and Politics," 27.
44 Michael Adams, *The Focus Canada Quarterly Report* (Toronto: Focus Canada, 1984), 13.
45 Ibid., 17-18.
46 Fletcher, "The Media and the 1984 Landslide," 166.
47 Ibid., 165.
48 Ibid.
49 Richard Gwyn, cited in Drummond, "Parliament and Politics," 250.
50 "Mulroney Appeals to Referendum Yes Votes," *Montreal Gazette,* August 7, 1984, A1.
51 Fletcher, "The Media and the 1984 Landslide," 165.
52 Ibid., 166.
53 Ibid., 167.
54 Frizzell and Westell, "Analysis of the Vote," 71.
55 Fletcher, "The Media and the 1984 Landslide," 183.
56 Ibid., 185.
57 *Halifax Chronicle-Herald,* August 2, 1984, as cited in Drummond, "Parliament and Politics," 28.
58 Fletcher, "The Media and the 1984 Landslide," 166.
59 Jeffrey Simpson, "Last Hurrah," *Globe and Mail,* September 3, 1984, A6.
60 Jeffrey Simpson, "The Last Resort," *Globe and Mail,* August 28, 1984, A6.
61 Drummond, "Parliament and Politics," 25.
62 Fletcher, "The Media and the 1984 Landslide," 161.
63 Frizzell and Westell, "Analysis of the Vote," 89.
64 James Bickerton, Alain Gagnon, and Patrick J. Smith, *Ties That Bind: Parties and Voters in Canada* (Toronto: Oxford University Press, 1999), 39.
65 Lawrence LeDuc, "The Flexible Canadian Electorate," in *Canada at the Polls, 1984: A Study of the Federal General Elections,* ed. Howard Rae Penniman (Durham, NC: Duke University Press, 1988), 48.
66 Harold D. Clarke et al., *Absent Mandate: Interpreting Change in Canadian Elections,* 2nd ed. (Toronto: Gage, 1991), 145.
67 Wagenberg et al., "Campaigns, Images and Polls," 119.
68 LeDuc, "The Flexible Canadian Electorate," 48.
69 Barry Kay et al., "The Character of Electoral Change," 310.

1988

1 For a thoughtful analysis of the distinction between the "accommodative" and "pan-Canadian" models of party organization, see David E Smith, "Party Government, Representation, and National Integration in Canada," in *Party Government and Regional Representation in Canada,* ed. Peter Aucoin (Ottawa: Royal Commission on the Economic Union and Prospects for Canada, 1986).
2 Joseph Wearing, *The L-Shaped Party: The Liberal Party of Canada 1958-1980* (Toronto: McGraw-Hill Ryerson, 1980).
3 Bob Bragg, "Turner Pledges Western Base," *Calgary Herald,* January 19, 1985, A1.
4 Rt. Hon. John Napier Turner, "Speech to the Liberal Party of Canada (Ontario) Annual Meeting" (Toronto, 1985).
5 Anthony Westell, "Setting the Stage," in *The Canadian General Election of 1988,* ed. Alan Stewart Frizzell, Jon H. Pammett, and Anthony Westell (Ottawa: Carleton University Press, 1989), 11-12.
6 Robert Everett, "Parliament and Politics," in *Canadian Annual Review of Politics and Public Affairs 1988,* ed. David Layton-Brown (Toronto: University of Toronto Press, 1995), 19.
7 Ibid., 18.

8   Joseph Wearing, "Can an Old Dog Teach Itself New Tricks? The Liberal Party Attempts Reform," in *Canadian Parties in Transition,* ed. Alain Gagnon and Brian Tanguay (Scarborough, ON: Nelson Canada, 1988).

9   Greg Weston, *Reign of Error: The Inside Story of John Turner's Troubled Leadership* (Toronto: McGraw-Hill Ryerson, 1988).

10   Westell, "Setting the Stage," 12.

11   Everett, "Parliament and Politics," 19.

12   Ibid., 18.

13   Ibid.

14   Ibid.

15   Ibid., 15.

16   Patrick Johnston, a social-policy expert and co-chair of the Liberals' platform committee, worked for ten months recruiting members to support his candidacy for the nomination in Scarborough West. He lost to an anti-abortion candidate sponsored by Campaign Life, a militant organization that mobilized all the Catholic churches in the riding and pumped in large amounts of money to finance a virulent campaign in this one of the four constituencies it had targeted.

17   All figures appearing in parentheses convert values in the text into 2002 dollars using data obtained from Statistics Canada, Table 326-0002, Consumer price index (CPI), 2001 basket content, annual (Index, 1992 = 100).

18   Everett, "Parliament and Politics," 20.

19   Martin Goldfarb and Tom Axworthy, *Marching to a Different Drummer: An Essay on the Liberals and Conservatives in Convention* (Toronto: Stoddart, 1988).

20   Everett, "Parliament and Politics," 20; Westell, "Setting the Stage," 12.

21   *Globe and Mail,* September 29, 1988, as cited in Everett, "Parliament and Politics," 21.

22   Duncan Cameron, interviews with the author, August 3 and 30, 1988; assessment confirmed by Marjorie Griffin Cohen.

23   For the assessment of Turner as the nervous achiever, see Christina McCall-Newman, *Grits: An Intimate Portrait of the Liberal Party* (Toronto: Macmillan of Canada, 1982), Part V.

24   Westell, "Setting the Stage," 12.

25   The $90,000 Angus Reid poll was paid for by the Department of Finance. *Globe and Mail,* "PCs Tipped on Pollution by Survey; Public Paid," December 30, 1988, A1.

26   F. Leslie Seidle and Khayyam Zey Paltiel, "Party Finance, the Election Expenses Act, and Campaign Spending in 1979 and 1980," in *Canada at the Polls, 1979 and 1980: A Study of the General Elections,* ed. Howard Rae Penniman (Washington, DC: American Enterprise Institute, 1981), 239.

27   Constitution of the Liberal Party of Canada, subsection 12(2), available from Liberal Party of Canada, http://liberal.ca/documents_e.aspx.

28   Ibid., subsection 12(4).

29   Ibid., subsection 12(4).

30   W.T. Stanbury, *Money in Politics: Financing Federal Parties and Candidates in Canada,* vol. 1 of the Research Series, Royal Commission on Electoral Reform and Party Financing (Toronto: Dundurn Press, 1991), 133.

31   Ibid.

32   Ibid., tables 10.3 and 10.4.

33   Ibid., table 10.2.

34   Ibid., 133.

35   Ibid., table 3.4.

36   John Duffy, *Fights of Our Lives: Elections, Leadership and the Making of Canada* (Toronto: HarperCollins Publishers, 2002), 339.

37   Gerald L. Caplan, Michael J.L. Kirby, and Hugh Segal, *Election: The Issues, the Strategies, the Aftermath* (Scarborough, ON: Prentice-Hall Canada, 1989), 131-43.

38 Everett, "Parliament and Politics," 24.

39 R.A. Young, "The End of the Political Centre, 1988" (University of Western Ontario Working Paper, London, Ontario), 6.

40 Alan Stewart Frizzell and Anthony Westell, "The Media and the Campaign," in *Canadian General Election of 1988*, ed. Frizzell, Pammett, and Westell, 79.

41 Michael Adams, Donna Dasko, and James Matsui, "Liberals Move Ahead of PCs in Wake of Leaders' Debates," *Globe and Mail*, November 1, 1998, A1.

42 Turner volunteered to pay air-time costs for a third debate devoted solely to free trade, but Mulroney refused. Everett, "Parliament and Politics," 23.

43 Ibid., 26.

44 Diane Francis, "A New Attack on Freedom of Speech," *Maclean's*, May 31, 1993, 9.

45 Brian Mulawka, "Elections Are for Political Parties, Not Citizens," *Alberta Report*, November 3, 1997, 8.

46 David Laycock, "Organized Interests in Canada and the Free Trade Election of 1988" (paper presented at the Centre for International Affairs, Harvard University, Cambridge, MA, n.d.), 10.

47 Donald C. MacDonald, "1988 Election Expenditures: A Canadian-American Comparison," in *Canadian Legislatures, 1992: Issues, Structures and Costs*, ed. Robert J. Fleming (Agincourt, ON: Global Press, 1992), 22.

48 Ibid., 21.

49 Ibid., 20-1.

50 Everett, "Parliament and Politics," 26.

51 Ibid., 22.

52 There were a total of 295 seats. Hugh G. Thorburn, ed., *Party Politics in Canada*, 7th ed. (Scarborough, ON: Prentice-Hall Canada, 1996), 623.

53 Based on the 1988 Federal Election Studies, as cited in Jon H. Pammett, "The 1988 Vote," in *Canadian General Election of 1988*, ed. Frizzell, Pammett, and Westell, 118.

54 Ibid., 123.

55 Harold D. Clarke et al., *Absent Mandate: Interpreting Change in Canadian Elections*, 2nd ed. (Toronto: Gage, 1991), 138.

56 H.D. Forbes, "Absent Mandate '88?" in *Party Politics*, ed. Thorburn, 265.

57 Clarke et al., *Absent Mandate*, 145.

58 Pammett, "The 1988 Vote," 122.

59 Ibid., 121.

60 Ibid., 122.

61 Cathy Widdis Barr, "The Importance and Potential of Leaders' Debates," in *Media and Voters in Canadian Election Campaigns*, ed. Frederick J. Fletcher (Ottawa: Royal Commission on Electoral Reform and Party Financing, 1991), 121.

62 Richard Johnston, *Letting the People Decide: Dynamics of a Canadian Election* (Montreal: McGill-Queen's University Press, 1992), 160.

63 Ibid.

64 Ibid.

65 Pammett, "The 1988 Vote," 115.

66 Ibid., 128.

67 Ibid., 129.

68 Ibid.

69 Ibid.

70 Ibid.

71 Shelagh M. Dunn, "The Free Trade Initiative and Regional Strategies," in *Canada: The State of the Federation 1987-1988*, ed. Peter M. Leslie and Ronald Watts (Kingston, ON: Institute of Intergovernmental Relations, Queen's University, 1988).

72 Alan Stewart Frizzell, Jon H. Pammett, and Anthony Westell, "Conclusion," in *Canadian General Election of 1988*, ed. Frizzell, Pammett, and Westell, 132.

1993

1 I am grateful to Jeffrey Johnstone for assistance in researching this chapter.

2 Stephen Clarkson and Christina McCall, *Trudeau and Our Times: The Magnificent Obsession,* vol. 1 (Toronto: McClelland and Stewart, 1990), 47.

3 On the idea of the losing-party syndrome, see George C. Perlin, *The Tory Syndrome: Leadership Politics in the Progressive Conservative Party* (Montreal: McGill-Queen's University Press, 1980), 10.

4 John Fraser, "Jean Chrétien: The Sequel," *Saturday Night,* February 1994, 12.

5 W.T. Stanbury, *Money in Politics: Financing Federal Parties and Candidates in Canada,* vol. 1 of the Research Series, Royal Commission on Electoral Reform and Party Financing (Toronto: Dundurn Press, 1991), 141.

6 Ibid., 140. All figures appearing in parentheses convert values in the text into 2002 dollars using data obtained from Statistics Canada, Table 326-0002, Consumer price index (CPI), 2001 basket content, annual (Index, 1992 = 100).

7 Stanbury, *Money in Politics,* 145.

8 Ibid., 378.

9 W.T. Stanbury, "Regulating the Financing of Federal Parties and Candidates," in *Canadian Parties in Transition,* ed. Alain Gagnon and Brian Tanguay (Scarborough, ON: Nelson Canada, 1996), 372.

10 Jeffrey Simpson, quoted in John C. Courtney, *Do Conventions Matter? Choosing National Party Leaders in Canada* (Montreal: McGill-Queen's University Press, 1995), 67.

11 The Conservatives fell drastically from 14,032 corporate contributions in 1988 to 8,898 in 1993, while the Liberals had a small increase from 7,238 to 7,557 (see Table A.4, p. 289). Geoffrey York, "Liberal Coffers Grow As Business Smells a Winner," *Globe and Mail,* July 2, 1993, A3.

12 Mitchell Sharp, *Which Reminds Me: A Memoir* (Toronto: University of Toronto Press, 1994), 88-93.

13 All of these perspectives are represented in Jean Chrétien, ed., *Finding Common Ground* (Hull, QC: Voyageur Publishing, 1992). On the right of centre, see Peter Nicholson, "Globalization: The Economic Impact," 24-37; on the left activist perspective, see Mary Eberts, "Politics and the Community in an Information Age," 209-13; on active government, see Lester Thurow, "The Need for Strategic Approaches," 72-83; on social programs, see Ken Battle, "The Economy, Social Policy and the Environment," 145-68; and on cultural institutions, see Rosemary Kaptana, "Developing Institutions for the 21st Century," 221-7.

14 Chrétien, *Finding Common Ground,* 245; and Hugh Winsor, "Liberal Conference Tests Icy Economic Waters," *Globe and Mail,* November 26, 1991, A1, A8.

15 Rosemary Speirs, "Where Is Chrétien Taking the Liberals?" *Toronto Star,* February 16, 1992, B1, B5.

16 "Adopted Resolutions, Biennial Convention," Liberal Party of Canada, 1992. On Martin's view, see Carol Goar, "Martin Sets Chrétien Agenda," *Toronto Star,* February 25, 1992, A21.

17 Chaviva Hošek, interview with the author, February 7, 1994.

18 R. Kenneth Carty, William Cross, and Lisa Young, *Rebuilding Canadian Party Politics* (Vancouver: UBC Press, 2000), 91.

19 Constitution of the Liberal Party of Canada, subsection 14(6), as amended at the 1992 Biennial Convention in Hull, Quebec, available from Liberal Party of Canada, http://liberal.ca/documents_e.aspx.

20 Carol Goar, "Liberal Candidates Give Substance to Leader's Bravado," *Toronto Star,* May 13, 1993, A1.

21 Lise Gotell and M. Janine Brodie, "Women and Parties in the 1990s: Less Than Ever an Issue of Numbers," in *Party Politics in Canada,* 7th ed., ed. Hugh G. Thorburn (Scarborough, ON: Prentice-Hall Canada, 1996), 62.

22 Lisa Young, *Feminists and Party Politics* (Vancouver: UBC Press, 2000), 69.

23 Ibid.

24 Alan Whitehorn, "The NDP's Quest for Survival," in *The Canadian General Election of 1993*, ed. Alan Stewart Frizzell, Jon H. Pammett, and Anthony Westell (Ottawa: Carleton University Press, 1994), 43.

25 Gotell and Brodie, "Women and Parties," 61.

26 Opinion data courtesy of Michael Adams, President, Environics Ltd.

27 Jeff Sallot, "Jobless Rate Won't Drop Soon, Campbell Warns," *Globe and Mail*, September 9, 1993, A6.

28 Susan Delacourt, "Election Crossfire Begins Quickly," *Globe and Mail*, September 9, 1993, A6.

29 William Walker, "Hidden High Tech Toys Help Big Parties Battle for Voters," *Toronto Star*, September 21, 1993, A11.

30 Rosemary Speirs, "Election Not Time to Debate Cuts: PM," *Toronto Star*, September 24, 1993, A1.

31 CBC Prime Time News, September 23, 1993.

32 CBC Prime Time News, September 26, 1993.

33 Frizzell, Pammett, and Westell, *Canadian General Election of 1993*, 12.

34 Hugh Winsor, "The Two Faces of Jean Chrétien," *Globe and Mail*, September 20, 1993, A4.

35 Richard Gwyn, "Momentum Shifting to Chrétien As Tired PM Falters," *Toronto Star*, September 26, 1993, B3.

36 Edison Stewart, "Jobs: Battle Lines Drawn," *Toronto Star*, September 9, 1993, A26.

37 R. Kenneth Carty et al. report that political cynicism in Canada "appeared to have peaked in 1993, the year of the electoral earthquake." Carty, Cross, and Young, *Rebuilding Canadian Party Politics*, 28.

38 Frizzell, Pammett, and Westell, eds., *Canadian General Election of 1993*, 115.

39 Liberal Party of Canada, *Creating Opportunity: The Liberal Plan for Canada* (Ottawa: Liberal Party of Canada, 1993), 11.

40 Ibid., 82.

41 Ibid., 88.

42 Gwyn, "Momentum Shifting to Chrétien," B3.

43 Frizzell, Pammett, and Westell, eds., *Canadian General Election of 1993*, 134.

44 Ibid.

45 Rosemary Speirs, "Chrétien Gained Most in Debates, Pundits Say," *Toronto Star*, October 6, 1993, A14.

46 Frizzell, Pammett, and Westell, eds., *Canadian General Election of 1993*, 135.

47 Ibid., 137.

48 Ibid.

49 Marlene Hore, interview with the author, January 31, 1994.

50 Frizzell, Pammett, and Westell, eds., *Canadian General Election of 1993*, 115.

51 Marlene Hore, interview with the author, January 31, 1994.

52 Winsor, "Two Faces of Jean Chrétien," A1, A4.

53 Robert Sheppard, interview with the author, November 1, 1993.

54 Frizzell, Pammett, and Westell, eds., *Canadian General Election of 1993*, 93.

55 Jim Bridges, "Media and the 1993 Canadian Election" (unpublished manuscript), 8.

56 Frizzell, Pammett, and Westell, eds., *Canadian General Election of 1993*, 122.

57 "Funny looking face? Perhaps. But what vision!" CBC *Prime Time News*, political advertisement, October 11, 1993.

58 CBC *Prime Time News*, October 15, 1993. The overreaction to the Conservative ad is analyzed in Kenneth Whyte, "The Face That Sank a Thousand Tories," *Saturday Night* 109, 1 (February 1994): 14-21.

59 CBC *Prime Time News*, October 19, 1993.

60 Cited in Carty, Cross, and Young, *Rebuilding Canadian Party Politics*, 32.

61 Jon H. Pammett, "Analyzing Voting Behaviour in Canada: The Case of the 1993 Election," in *Party Politics*, 7th ed., ed. Thorburn, 581.

62 Ibid., 581-2.
63 Harold D. Clarke et al., *Absent Mandate: Canadian Electoral Politics in an Era of Restructuring,* 3rd ed. (Toronto: Gage, 1996), 142.
64 Pammett, "Analyzing Voting Behaviour," 583; and Clarke et al., *Absent Mandate,* 142.
65 Pammett, "Analyzing Voting Behaviour," 586.
66 Ibid., 584; and Clarke et al., *Absent Mandate,* 142.
67 Pammett, "Analyzing Voting Behaviour," 586.
68 Clarke et al., *Absent Mandate,* 141.
69 Ibid.
70 Pammett, "Analyzing Voting Behaviour," 591-2.
71 Ibid., 593.
72 In offering his support for Pierre Trudeau's constitutional hatchet man, Ryan was magnanimous: "you cannot live perpetually with bad memories." Susan Delacourt, "Liberal Campaign Gets a Huge Shot in the Arm," *Globe and Mail,* October 16, 1993, A7.
73 Carty, Cross, and Young, *Rebuilding Canadian Party Politics,* 12.
74 Ibid., 6.
75 Ibid.
76 Ibid., 7.
77 Ibid., 178.
78 Ibid., 224.

1997

1   This chapter was written with the research assistance of Franca Fargione, Isher Kaila, Sharoni Sibony, and Priya Suagh.
2   Edward Greenspon, "Liberals Practice Practicality," *Globe and Mail,* January 15, 1994, A1, A4.
3   Susan Delacourt, "Liberals Brandish Vow Keeping Record on Modest Goals," *Globe and Mail,* October 25, 1996, A13. In their report, the Liberals claimed that 80 percent of their 1993 promises were kept.
4   Ibid.
5   Gordon Gibson, "Jean Chrétien Loses a Crucial Bit of Teflon," *Globe and Mail,* December 16, 1996, A19.
6   Peter Donolo's comment on *The Unofficial Story,* CBC Television, June 1997.
7   Edward Greenspon, "Wanted: A National Agenda," *Globe and Mail,* July 5, 1997, A2.
8   R. Kenneth Carty, William Cross, and Lisa Young, *Rebuilding Canadian Party Politics* (Vancouver: UBC Press, 2000), 81.
9   *The National,* CBC Television, May 9 and 30, 1997.
10 Lawrence LeDuc, "The Leaders' Debates (... and the Winner Is ...)," in *The Canadian General Election of 1997,* ed. Alan Stewart Frizzell and Jon H. Pammett (Toronto: Dundurn Press, 1997), 215.
11 Ibid.
12 Ibid.
13 James Travers and David Vienneau, "National Unity Sets Off Sparks in Leaders' Debates," *Toronto Star,* May 13, 1997, A1, A11.
14 LeDuc, "The Leaders' Debates," 215.
15 Ibid., 217.
16 Ibid., 213.
17 Ibid., 218.
18 Ibid., 219.
19 Ibid.
20 Ibid., 221.
21 Susan Delacourt, "Campaign Lacking Female Touch," *Globe and Mail,* May 20, 1997, A10.
22 Cited in Lisa Young, *Feminists and Party Politics* (Vancouver: UBC Press, 2000), 182.

23 Ibid, 79.
24 David Vienneau, "PM Denounces Charest's Unacceptable Comment," *Toronto Star,* May 20, 1997, A8.
25 Tu Thnah Ha and Anne McIlroy, "Chrétien Counterpunches Charest Jab," *Globe and Mail,* May 16, 1997, A8.
26 Tim Harper, "Chrétien Accuses Charest of Hiding from His Conservative Heritage," *Toronto Star,* May 7, 1997, A16.
27 "Chrétien Calls Reform Policies Divisive," *Globe and Mail,* May 7, 1997, A9.
28 David Vienneau, "Deep in Reform Country, PM Slams Manning," *Toronto Star,* May 27, 1997, A1, A11.
29 David Vienneau, "Chrétien Pleads for Tolerance and Unity," *Toronto Star,* May 30, 1997, A11. On the risk of coming back as a minority government, see Michael Marzolini, "The Regionalization of Canadian Electoral Politics," in *Canadian General Election of 1997,* ed. Frizzell and Pammett, 193-205.
30 "A man among the girls and boys" is Mark Kingwell's phrase, on *Studio Two,* TVOntario, May 30, 1997.
31 Anthony Wilson-Smith, "The Unity Bomber," *Maclean's,* May 19, 1997, 14.
32 LeDuc, "The Leaders' Debates," 217.
33 Le Réseau de l'information, May 25, 1997.
34 David Vienneau, "PM Rips Reform for 'Politics of Intolerance,'" *Toronto Star,* May 27, 1997, A1.
35 Peter Donolo, interview with Sharoni Sibony, August 19, 1997.
36 Sharoni Sibony, "Television and the Liberal Party in the 1997 Canadian Federal Election Campaign" (unpublished essay, University of Toronto), table 2.6.
37 Ibid., table 4.2.
38 Ibid., tables A1 and C1.
39 *The National,* CBC Television, May 9, 1997.
40 Ibid., May 22, 1997.
41 Ibid., May 20, 1997.
42 Carty, Cross, and Young, *Rebuilding Canadian Party Politics,* 191.
43 Scott Feschuk, "Voters' Cynicism Greets Campaign Ads," *Globe and Mail,* May 12, 1997, A8.
44 Sibony, "Television and the Liberal Party," table 4.2.
45 Le Téléjournal, Radio-Canada, May 3, 1997.
46 Daniel Leblanc, "Liberals Dominate Fundraising," *Globe and Mail,* July 6, 1999, A1, A7. All figures appearing in parentheses convert values in the text into 2002 dollars using data obtained from Statistics Canada, Table 326-0002, Consumer price index (CPI), 2001 basket content, annual (Index, 1992 = 100).
47 Tu Thanh Ha, "Liberal Says He Gave Candidates Secret Cash," *Globe and Mail,* May 11, 2005, A8.
48 Ibid.
49 Ibid.
50 Tu Thanh Ha, "Liberals Took Illicit Cash in 2000 Campaign, Probe Told," *Globe and Mail,* May 10, 2005, A7.
51 Liberal Party of Canada, "The 1997 Liberal Platform: Fiscal Responsibility," Talking Point, May 1, 1997.
52 Edison Stewart, "Liberal Fax Calls Charest Separatist," *Toronto Star,* May 17, 1997, A12.
53 Letter to the author, July 31, 1997.
54 Jon H. Pammett, "The Voters Decide," in *Canadian General Election of 1997,* ed. Frizzell and Pammett, 228.
55 Ibid., 227.
56 Ibid., 228.
57 Ibid., 233.
58 Ibid., 236.

59 Ibid., 235.

60 Ibid.

61 Elisabeth Gidengil et al., "Making Sense of Regional Voting in the 1997 Canadian Federal Election," *Canadian Journal of Political Science* 32, 2 (1997): 271.

62 Marzolini, "Regionalization of Canadian Electoral Politics," 203.

63 Brian Underhill and Cameron McKeen, "Unemployed Offended by PM's Parallel," *Halifax Chronicle-Herald,* May 31, 1997, A1.

64 Gidengil et al., "Making Sense of Regional Voting," 262.

65 Carty, Cross, and Young, *Rebuilding Canadian Party Politics,* 223.

66 Karen Unland, "Liberals Give Montrealers Pointed Reminder," *Globe and Mail,* May 21, 1997, A8.

67 Formally the Liberals received 101 of 103 seats, but one of the missing ridings was lost to John Nunziata, a renegade Liberal who, claiming to be an independent, ran a campaign that was Liberal in all but name. Even the Liberals' loss of York South had less to do with support for the Conservatives than with voter revulsion at the scandal over the credentials of their 1993 MP, Jag Bhaduria.

68 Gidengil et al., "Making Sense of Regional Voting," 262, 267.

69 Pammett, "The Voters Decide," 231.

70 Dalton Camp, "Reform's Reckless Rhetoric Didn't Sell East of Manitoba," *Toronto Star,* June 4, 1997, A21.

71 Gidengil et al., "Making Sense of Regional Voting," 262.

72 While opinion research did not focus on this kind of strategic voting, evidence gathered from NDP candidates suggests this was a factor, at least in Toronto.

73 The University of Saskatchewan political scientist is quoted in Mark Wyatt, "Saskatchewan Maintains Tradition," Regina *Leader-Post,* June 3, 1997, B2.

74 Murray Mandruk, "Saskatchewan Won't Decide the Election," Regina *Leader-Post,* May 13, 1997, A4.

75 Gidengil et al., "Making Sense of Regional Voting," 266.

76 *Vancouver Sun,* "No Time to Switch: Canada Needs a Party That Represents All Regions and Can Steer a Middle Course," May 30, 1997.

77 Carty, Cross, and Young, *Rebuilding Canadian Party Politics,* 82.

78 Marzolini, "Regionalization of Canadian Electoral Politics," 194.

79 Ibid.

80 Ibid.

81 Carty, Cross, and Young, *Rebuilding Canadian Party Politics,* 85.

82 Ibid., 52.

83 Lisa Young, "Comment on Johnson, 'Canadian Elections at the Millennium,'" *Choices: Strengthening Canadian Democracy* 6, 6 (2000): 37.

2000

1 This chapter was prepared with the assistance of Jane Abrahim, Cheryl Auger, Josh Koziebrocki, Vivek Krishnamurthy, and Graeme Norton. I am also grateful to Gordon Ashworth, national campaign director of the Liberal Party of Canada, and to Ken Carty for their criticisms and comments on its earlier drafts.

2 R. Kenneth Carty, William Cross, and Lisa Young, *Rebuilding Canadian Party Politics* (Vancouver: UBC Press, 2000).

3 Ibid., 7, 34.

4 Ibid., 9, 28-30.

5 Ibid., 8, 178, 224.

6 Ibid., 224.

7 Ibid.

8 Jeffrey Simpson, "The Masters and the Slaves," *Globe and Mail,* August 19, 1998, A16.

9   The term "selective activism" comes from Geoffrey E. Hale, "Managing the Fiscal Dividend: The Politics of Selective Activism," in *How Ottawa Spends 2000-2001: Past Imperfect, Future Tense,* ed. Leslie A. Pal (Toronto: Oxford University Press, 2000), 60.

10 Carty, Cross, and Young, *Rebuilding Canadian Party Politics,* 224.

11 Shawn McCarthy, "Liberals on the Knife Edge," *Globe and Mail,* November 26, 2000, A1.

12 Don Macdonald, "Beware of Grits – Indeed All Parties – Bearing Gifts," *Halifax Herald,* November 3, 2000, 12.

13 One hundred of Chrétien's most infamous malapropisms were collected by Pascal Beausoleil and published as a bestselling booklet: Pascal Beausoleil, *Les Chrétienneries* (Montréal: Les intouchables, 2000).

14 David Gamble, "Help Us to Block Alliance: Pettigrew," *Montreal Gazette,* November 3, 2000, A10.

15 Valérie Dufour, "Deux ponts et des kilomètres de route pour battre Daniel," *Le Devoir,* November 15, 2000, A4.

16 Tu Thanh Ha, "Liberal Says He Gave Candidates Secret Cash," *Globe and Mail,* May 11, 2005, A8.

17 Ibid.

18 Tu Thanh Ha, "Liberals Took Illicit Cash in 2000 Campaign, Probe Told," *Globe and Mail,* May 10, 2005, A7.

19 Daniel Leblanc, "Insider Backs Brault Story," *Globe and Mail,* April 21, 2005, A8.

20 Ipsos Reid, "Federal Political Scene September 2000" (October 1, 2000), http://www.ipsos-na.com/news/pressrelease.cfm?id=1084

21 Hugh Winsor, "Martin One-Ups Day in Budget Battle," *Globe and Mail,* October 19, 2000, A9.

22 William Walker, "Romanow Looks Set to Jump to Liberals," *Toronto Star,* September 20, 2000, A6.

23 Larry Johnsrude, "Mar Accuses Chrétien of Politicking with Bill 11," *Edmonton Journal,* November 2, 2000, A10.

24 John Cotter, "West May Be Liberal Write-Off," *Edmonton Journal,* October 23, 2000, A3.

25 Vaughn Palmer, "Loyalty Runs Shallow with BC Liberals," *National Post,* October 14, 2000, A17.

26 Ibid.

27 Peter O'Neil and Scott Simpson, "Liberals Offer Transit Money, but Levy Will Remain," *Vancouver Sun,* November 1, 2000, A4.

28 Paul Willcocks, "Be Aware of Liberals Bearing Gifts for Votes," *Vancouver Sun,* November 3, 2000, A18.

29 Carty, Cross, and Young, *Rebuilding Canadian Party Politics,* 181.

30 Ibid., 198.

31 Ibid.

32 Ibid.

33 Liberal Party of Canada, "Health Care," Campaign 2000 television advertisement.

34 Liberal Party of Canada, "Health Care BC," Campaign 2000 television advertisement.

35 Liberal Party of Canada, "Quality Health Care," Campaign 2000 television advertisement.

36 CFRB Radio, November 27, 2000.

37 Robert Matas, "'Scurrilous' Ads Enrage Alliance: Liberals Using Chinese-Language Media to Paint Portrait of Rival as 'Scary' and 'Racist,'" *Globe and Mail,* November 24, 2000, A7.

38 Carty, Cross, and Young, *Rebuilding Canadian Party Politics,* 197.

39 Ibid., 178.

40 Ibid., 199.

41 Ibid., 51.

42 André Siegfried, *The Race Question in Canada* (Toronto: Macmillan of Canada with the Institute of Canadian Studies, Carleton University, 1978), 136.

43 Donald J. Savoie, *Governing from the Centre: The Concentration of Power in Canadian Politics* (Toronto: University of Toronto Press, 1999).

44 Anne McIlroy, "Youth Wing Cheers PM's Populist Theme," *Globe and Mail*, March 17, 2000, A9.

45 Jeffrey Simpson, "Two Scorpions in a Bottle," *Globe and Mail*, April 23, 2000, A19.

46 Shawn McCarthy and Paul Adams, "Chrétien Defends Early Vote," *Globe and Mail*, October 23, 2000, A1.

47 Shawn McCarthy, "Alliance Supports Two-Tier Health Care: Government Should Give Provinces Leeway in Promoting Private Clinics, Co-Chair Says," *Globe and Mail*, October 31, 2000, A1.

48 John Ibbitson, "Day's Plan Found in Secret Paper," *Globe and Mail*, November 7, 2000, A1.

49 Shawn McCarthy and Brian Laghi, "Chrétien Pounded again As Day Puts on Show," *Globe and Mail*, November 11, 2000, A1.

50 Edward Greenspon, "Straight for the Jugular," *Globe and Mail*, November 11, 2000, A15.

51 Brian Laghi, "Chrétien Evokes Image of Team Spirit," *Globe and Mail*, November 14, 2000, A7.

52 Brian Laghi, "Chrétien Says He'll Consider Quitting," *Globe and Mail*, November 17, 2000, A1.

53 *The National*, CBC Television, November 24, 2000. Author's italics.

54 Carty, Cross, and Young, *Rebuilding Canadian Party Politics*, 21.

55 Ibid., 81.

56 Ibid., 118.

57 Ibid., 224.

58 Ibid., 9.

59 Ibid., 200.

60 *Sunday Report*, CBC Television, October 22, 2000.

61 Fifty-two percent of the election coverage on CBC's *The National* was general. Of the coverage devoted to specific parties, 15 percent was on the Liberals and 16 percent was on the Alliance, whereas the PCs received 7 percent, the NDP 7 percent, and the Bloc 3 percent. (In 1997 the equivalent figures were 59 percent general, 9.5 percent Liberal, 9.4 percent Reform, 7 percent PC, 7 percent NDP, and 9 percent Bloc.)

62 Paul Attallah and Angela Burton, "Television, the Internet, and the Canadian Federal Election of 2000," in *The Canadian General Election of 2000*, ed. Jon H. Pammett and Christopher Dornan (Toronto: Dundurn Press, 2001), 217.

63 Carty, Cross, and Young, *Rebuilding Canadian Party Politics*, 180.

64 Ibid., 224.

65 Lisa Young, "Comment on Johnson, 'Canadian Elections at the Millennium,'" *Choices: Strengthening Canadian Democracy* 6, 6 (2000): 37.

66 Carty, Cross, and Young, *Rebuilding Canadian Party Politics*, 8, 181.

67 Ibid., 210.

68 Ibid., 200-1, 210.

69 Ibid., 200, 208.

70 Ibid., 208.

71 Joanne Pratt, campaign manager for the Jim Peterson campaign in Willowdale, interview with Vivek Krishnamurthy, November 28, 2000.

72 Susan Bourette, "Campaigning in the Age of the Internet a Cyber-Letdown," *Globe and Mail*, October 30, 2000, A9.

73 Those candidates whose sites had visible hit counters reported 400-600 hits total by the final weekend of the campaign. Only 67 of 141 Liberal candidate websites achieved a "top 20" ranking on the Google search engine, and 59 sites achieved a similar score on the Altavista.ca search engine.

74 Warren Kinsella, interview with Vivek Krishnamurthy, November 9, 2000.

75 Carty, Cross, and Young, *Rebuilding Canadian Party Politics*, 200.

76 Ibid., 203-4.

77   Paul Mang, manager of information technology for the Jim Peterson campaign in Willowdale, interview with Vivek Krishnamurthy, November 28, 2000.
78   Joanne Pratt, interview with Vivek Krishnamurthy, November 28, 2000.
79   Paul Mang, interview with Vivek Krishnamurthy, November 28, 2000.
80   Carty, Cross, and Young, *Rebuilding Canadian Party Politics,* 208.
81   Ibid., 210.
82   Gary W. Selnow, *Electronic Whistle-Stops: The Impact of the Internet on American Politics,* Praeger Series in Political Communication (Westport, CT: Praeger, 1998), 98.
83   Joanne Pratt, interview with Vivek Krishnamurthy, November 28, 2000.
84   Ibid.
85   Sasa Petricic, reporter for CBC news, interview with Graeme Norton, December 5, 2000.
86   Ibid.
87   Roy MacGregor, "Wired Media Have Changed the Message: A Leader Barks on the West Coast, and One Yelps Back from the East," *National Post,* November 25, 2000, A6.
88   Warren Kinsella reported that more and more journalists were contacting the Liberal Party's national office for information to use in their reports. Warren Kinsella, interview with Vivek Krishnamurthy, November 9, 2000.
89   Richard Nadeau et al., "Pourquoi les libéraux ont-ils gagné?" *La Presse,* December 2, 2000, A21.
90   Pierre Drouilly, "Le vote nationaliste toujours solide," Cyberpresse, http://www.cyberpresse.ca (accessed December 1, 2000).
91   This compares with forty-two seats won by the Liberals from vote-splitting in Ontario in 1993 and twenty-six seats won this way in 1997. André Turcotte, Roundtable on the Federal Election, University of Toronto, November 29, 2000.
92   Carty, Cross, and Young, *Rebuilding Canadian Party Politics,* 82.

2004

1   This chapter is based on research executed by Erik Bruveris, Dennis Laberge, John Mackay, Chris Piggott, and Annette Yuen. Invaluable information and commentary was also contributed by Peter Donolo, Akaash Maharaj, and Priya Suagh.
2   John Gray, *Paul Martin: The Power of Ambition* (Toronto: Key Porter, 2003), 89.
3   Susan Delacourt, *Juggernaut: Paul Martin's Campaign for Chrétien's Crown* (Toronto: McClelland and Stewart, 2003), 118.
4   Ibid., 138-9.
5   Campbell Clark, "Membership Rules Have Martin Rivals Grumbling," *Globe and Mail,* January 25, 2003, A4.
6   Gray, *Paul Martin,* 189.
7   Lawrence Martin, *Iron Man: The Defiant Reign of Jean Chrétien* (Toronto: Viking, 2003), 387.
8   Delacourt, *Juggernaut,* 24.
9   James Travers, "PM Names Players for Key Roles," *Toronto Star,* July 20, 2004, A17.
10 "I am mad as hell that some people did this ... This isn't a question of the Liberals' election. Liberals are mad ... I am very mad that some people may have enriched themselves, and I am very determined to get to the bottom of this and punish those who were involved." Jim Brown, "Martin 'Mad As Hell,'" *Globe and Mail,* February 15, 2004, A21.
11 Paul Martin himself suggested that there "had to be political direction" on February 12 (at an impromptu press conference following the release of Auditor General Sheila Fraser's report), but later backpedalled that statement in an interview on CPAC's "Primetime Politics" with Peter Van Dusen on June 7, 2004.
12 Jane Taber, "Liberals Tell PM to Ease Up," *Globe and Mail,* February 19, 2004, A1.
13 Jane Taber, "Liberals Move to Ease Nomination Challenges," *Globe and Mail,* January 15, 2004, A4.
14 Graeme Smith, "How Winnipeg's Mayor Cleared Commons Path," *Globe and Mail,* May 8, 2004, A5.
15 John Ibbitson, "Liberals Take No Prisoners," *Globe and Mail,* May 5, 2004, A4.

16 *Hill Times,* "Incumbent MPs Not Running in Next Election: 57," May 24-30, 2004, 16.

17 Anne Dawson, "PM's Adviser Admits to Making 'Rookie' Mistakes: Alienating Chrétien Loyalists an Error, Says Martin Campaign Manager," *Ottawa Citizen,* May 21, 2004, A4.

18 Warren Kinsella, Latest Musings, http://www.warrenkinsella.com/musings.htm (accessed June 4, 2004).

19 Daniel Leblanc and Rhéal Séguin, "Attacks Haven't Allowed Martin to 'Be Himself,' Liberals Feel," *Globe and Mail,* June 3, 2004, A4.

20 Brian Tobin, interviewed on CTV's "Question Period," May 30, 2004.

21 CBC News Online, "Liberal MP Calls Her Party's Campaign 'Comedy of Errors,'" June 9, 2004, http://www.cbc.ca/story/canada/national/2004/06/09/parrish_lib040609.html (accessed February 21, 2005).

22 Jane Taber, "Liberals 'Are in a Spiral,' Top Martin Adviser Says," *Globe and Mail,* June 10, 2004, A1.

23 By Day 2 of the campaign, Paul Martin drew a sharp distinction between Canada and the United States at a rally in Charlottetown, PEI: "you can't have a healthcare system like Canada's, you can't have social programs like Canada's with taxation levels like those in the United States."

24 Though Martin's $9 billion commitment to health care led the CBC's election coverage on May 25, 2004, it was followed immediately by a "Reality Check" that characterized his previous treatment of health care when he was finance minister as "scourging health care, not nurturing it."

25 McGill University Observatory for Media and Public Policy, "2004 Federal Election Newspaper Content Analysis: Cumulative Results, from 17 May to 25 June 2004," http://www.ompp.mcgill.ca/pages/reports/CumulativeReport(June25).pdf (accessed February 21, 2005).

26 Ibid.

27 Heather Scofield and Campbell Clark, "Martin's Big Pledge: $9 Billion for Health," *Globe and Mail,* May 26, 2004, A6.

28 Drew Fagan, "Poll Puts Martin's Stumbling Liberals ahead by 4 Points," *Globe and Mail,* June 1, 2004, A1.

29 These ads appeared nationwide with the caption "It's not which Canadian you choose. It's which Canada." For instance, *Globe and Mail,* May 22, 2004, A6.

30 Jane Taber and Campbell Clark, "Liberals Plan Early Attack Ad on Harper," *Globe and Mail,* May 13, 2004, A1.

31 Drew Fagan, "Liberals Target Klein, Mulroney," *Globe and Mail,* June 18, 2004, A1.

32 Minority government coverage began two days before the writ even dropped and, fuelled by daily polls, began in earnest by Day 7 of the campaign.

33 McGill University Observatory for Media and Public Policy, "2004 Federal Election Newspaper Content Analysis: Weekly Results from 17 May to 16 June 2004," http://www.ompp.mcgill.ca/pages/reports/WeeklyReport(June16).pdf (accessed February 21, 2005).

34 Erin Research Inc., "Balance in Coverage of the 2004 Federal Election Campaign: 2004 Content Analysis Conducted for CBC (Report 6)," 21. Report graciously supplied to the author by the CBC.

35 Ibid., 31.

36 McGill University Observatory for Media and Public Policy, "2004 Federal Election Newspaper Content Analysis: Weekly Results from 17 May to 16 June 2004."

37 Don Martin, "Martin Failed to Land Crucial Knockout Blow," *Calgary Herald,* June 16, 2004, A5.

38 English-language leaders' debate, June 15, 2004.

39 Jeffrey Simpson, "A Conservative Wolf in Sheep's Clothing," *Globe and Mail,* June 12, 2004, A27.

40 The first day after the English debate, headlines across the country reflected either Harper's comments on a transition to power, or poll numbers that put him firmly in minority territory.

41 McGill University Observatory for Media and Public Policy, "2004 Federal Election Newspaper Content Analysis: Weekly Results from 17 May to 16 June 2004."

42 Mark Hume, "For Whistle Blower, It Got Personal," *Globe and Mail,* June 12, 2004, A4.

43   Allan Woods, "Undecided Voters Handed Victory to Grits," *National Post,* June 29, 2004, A4.
44   "Horserace" stories led "issues" stories by 67 percent to 32 percent by the end of the campaign. McGill University Observatory for Media and Public Policy, "2004 Federal Election Newspaper Content Analysis: Weekly Results from 17 May to 16 June 2004."
45   Stuart Soroka et al., "What Will the Important Issues Be?" *Globe and Mail,* June 15, 2004, <www.theglobeandmail.com>.
46   John Ibbitson, "Politicos Forcefully Wag the Cod," *Globe and Mail,* May 28, 2004, A4.
47   Patrick Fournier et al., "How the Liberals Lost Quebec," *Globe and Mail,* July 21, 2004, A15.
48   *Globe and Mail,* "Mr. Martin's Cavalcade of Instant Nominations," May 13, 2004, A20.
49   This astonishing attack ad began airing June 10, 2004, or Week 3 of the campaign, which would turn out to be the strongest week of the campaign for the Conservative Party.
50   Gloria Galloway, "Ontario Blue-Belt May Be Grits' Noose," *Globe and Mail,* April 17, 2004, A7.
51   Drew Fagan, "Poll Puts Paul Martin's Stumbling Liberals Ahead by Four Points," *Globe and Mail,* June 1, 2004, A1.
52   Paul Martin, statement made in Sault Ste. Marie, Ontario, May 31, 2004.
53   Richard Mackie, "Not Our Fault Federal Party Lags, Ontario Liberals Say," *Globe and Mail,* June 3, 2004, A4.
54   Murray Campbell, "Ontario Quarterbacking Medicare Change," *Globe and Mail,* May 6, 2004, A7.
55   R. Kenneth Carty, William Cross, and Lisa Young, *Rebuilding Canadian Party Politics* (Vancouver: UBC Press, 2000).
56   Peter O'Neil, "B.C. Grits to Set out a Distinct Agenda," *Vancouver Sun,* June 7, 2004, A1.
57   Liberal Party of Canada, "British Columbia and the NDP" (television commercial, June 2004).
58   On June 7 (only two weeks into the campaign), the Liberals launched their Quebec-targeted negative print ad that likened a vote for the Conservatives to one for separatism amidst talk that a Conservative minority would necessarily be propped up by the Bloc Québécois.
59   Les Whittington and Graham Fraser, "New Spending, No Deficit Pledged," *Toronto Star,* June 4, 2004, A6.
60   Woods, "Undecided Voters Handed Victory to Grits."
61   Jane Taber, "Report of Tory's Political Death Premature," *Globe and Mail,* June 30, 2004, A11.

Conclusion

1   Thomas J. Scotto, Laura B. Stephenson, and Allan Kornberg, "From a Two-party-plus to a One-party-plus? Ideology, Vote Choice, and Prospects for a Competitive Party System in Canada," *Electoral Studies* 23 (2004): 475.
2   William Cross, *Political Parties,* Canadian Democratic Audit (Vancouver: UBC Press, 2004), 128.
3   On the topic of the external constitution, see Stephen Clarkson, "Locked In? Canada's External Constitution under Global Trade Governance," *American Review of Canadian Studies* 33, 2 (2003): 145-72.
4   Reginald Whitaker, *The Government Party: Organizing and Financing the Liberal Party of Canada, 1930-58* (Toronto: University of Toronto Press, 1977).
5   Alan C. Cairns, "The Electoral System and the Party System in Canada," *Canadian Journal of Political Science* 1, 1 (1968): 55-80; and J.A.A. Lovink, "The Impact of the Electoral System on the Party System in Canada," *Canadian Journal of Political Science* 3, 1 (1970): 497-516. Also John C. Courtney, *Elections,* Canadian Democratic Audit (Vancouver: UBC Press, 2004), 139-42, and Lawrence LeDuc, "Making Votes Count: How Well Did Our Election System Perform?" *Electoral Insight* 4, 1 (2005): 37-41.
6   Heather MacIvor, "From Emergence to Electronics: Explaining the Changes in Canadian Party Leadership Selection," *National History* 1, 2 (1997): 173-85.
7   John C. Courtney, *Do Conventions Matter? Choosing National Party Leaders in Canada* (Montreal and Kingston: McGill-Queen's University Press, 1995).
8   MacIvor, "From Emergence to Electronics," 173.

9 Courtney, *Do Conventions Matter?*, 254.

10 Lawrence Martin, *Iron Man: The Defiant Reign of Jean Chrétien* (Toronto: Viking, 2003).

11 Donald J. Savoie, *Governing from the Centre: The Concentration of Power in Canadian Politics* (Toronto: University of Toronto Press, 1999). The one "she," Kim Campbell, did not hang on to prime ministerial power long enough to prove that she could practise a more inclusive style of governance. If it is the office that makes the politician rather than the reverse, it is likely that the vast powers concentrated in the PMO would have forced Campbell into the same mould adopted by her male predecessors and successors.

12 Cross, *Political Parties*, 27.

13 Ibid., 26.

14 Ibid., 20-3.

15 William Cross, seminar presentation, University of Toronto, March 30, 2004.

16 Kirk Makin and Brian Laghi, "Top court upholds spending limits," *Globe and Mail*, May 19, 2004, A8.

17 Ian Stewart, "Bill-C-24: Replacing the Market with the State?" *Electoral Insight* 7, 1 (2005): 32-6.

18 On oligarchy, see Robert Michels, *Political Parties: A Sociological Study of the Oligarchical Tendencies of Modern Democracy* (New York: Dover Publications, 1959). On stratarchy, see Samuel James Eldersveld, *Political Parties: A Behavioral Analysis* (Chicago: Rand McNally, 1964).

19 Theodore Harold White, *The Making of the President* (New York: Atheneum, 1973).

20 Judy LaMarsh is sometimes credited with membership in this group.

21 Neil Nevitte, *The Decline of Deference: Canadian Value Change in Cross-National Perspective* (Peterborough, ON: Broadview Press, 1996).

22 Elisabeth Gidengil, André Blais, Joanna Everitt, Patrick Fournier, and Neil Nevitte, "Back to the Future? Making Sense of the 2004 Canadian Election outside Quebec," paper presented at the annual meeting of the Canadian Political Science Association, London, Ontario, June 2005, Figure 8.

Bibliography

Adams, Michael. *The Focus Canada Quarterly Report.* Toronto: Focus Canada, 1984.

Adams, Michael, Donna Dasko, and James Matsui. "Liberals Move Ahead of PCs in Wake of Leaders' Debates." *Globe and Mail,* November 1, 1988, A1.

Attallah, Paul, and Angela Burton. "Television, the Internet, and the Canadian Federal Election of 2000." In *The Canadian General Election of 2000,* ed. Jon H. Pammett and Christopher Dornan, 215-41. Toronto: Dundurn Press, 2001.

Beausoleil, Pascal. *Les Chrétienneries.* Montréal: Les intouchables, 2000.

Bell, V.J., Donald C. Wallace, and R.B. Byers. *Canadian Annual Review of Politics and Public Affairs 1979.* Toronto: University of Toronto Press, 1981.

Bickerton, James, Alain Gagnon, and Patrick J. Smith. *Ties That Bind: Parties and Voters in Canada.* Toronto: Oxford University Press, 1999.

Bourette, Susan. "Campaigning in the Age of the Internet a Cyber-Letdown." *Globe and Mail,* October 30, 2000, A9.

Bragg, Bob. "Turner Pledges Western Base." *Calgary Herald,* January 19, 1985, A1.

Bridges, Jim. "Media and the 1993 Canadian Election." Unpublished ms.

Brodie, M. Janine, and Jill Vickers. "The More Things Change ... Women in the 1979 Federal Campaign." In *Canada at the Polls, 1979 and 1980: A Study of the General Elections,* ed. Howard Rae Penniman, 322-6. Washington, DC: American Enterprise Institute, 1981.

Brown, Jim. "Martin 'Mad As Hell.'" *Globe and Mail,* February 15, 2004, A21.

Cairns, Alan C. "The Electoral System and the Party System in Canada." *Canadian Journal of Political Science* 1, 1 (1968): 55-80.

Camp, Dalton. "Reform's Reckless Rhetoric Didn't Sell East of Manitoba." *Toronto Star,* June 4, 1997, A21.

Campbell, Murray. "Ontario Quarterbacking Medicare Change." *Globe and Mail,* May 6, 2004, A7.

Caplan, Gerald L., Michael J.L. Kirby, and Hugh Segal. *Election: The Issues, the Strategies, the Aftermath.* Scarborough, ON: Prentice-Hall Canada, 1989.

Carty, R. Kenneth, ed. *Canadian Political Party Systems: A Reader.* Peterborough, ON: Broadview Press, 1992.

Carty, R. Kenneth, William Cross, and Lisa Young. *Rebuilding Canadian Party Politics.* Vancouver: UBC Press, 2000.

CBC News Online, "Liberal MP Calls Her Party's Campaign 'Comedy of Errors,'" June 9, 2004. <www.cbc.ca>.

Chrétien, Jean, ed. *Finding Common Ground.* Hull, QC: Voyageur Publishing, 1992.

Clark, Campbell. "Membership Rules Have Martin Rivals Grumbling." *Globe and Mail,* January 25, 2003, A4.

Clarke, Harold D. *Political Choice in Canada.* Toronto: McGraw-Hill Ryerson, 1980.

Clarke, Harold D., Jane Jenson, Lawrence LeDuc, and Jon H. Pammett. *Absent Mandate: Interpreting Change in Canadian Elections.* 2nd ed. Toronto: Gage, 1991.

–. "Voting Behaviour and the Outcome of the 1979 Election: The Impact of Leaders and Issues." In *The Ballot and Its Message: Voting in Canada,* ed. Joseph Wearing, 237-65. Toronto: Copp Clark Pitman, 1991.

–. *Absent Mandate: Canadian Electoral Politics in an Era of Restructuring.* 3rd ed. Toronto: Gage, 1996.

Clarke, Harold D., Lawrence LeDuc, Jane Jenson, and Jon H. Pammett. "The 1974 Federal Election: A Preliminary Report." Paper presented at the 47th annual meeting of the Canadian Political Science Association, University of Alberta, Edmonton, 2-6 June 1975, v. 4, 1-71.

Clarkson, Stephen. "Locked In? Canada's External Constitution under Global Trade Governance." *American Review of Canadian Studies* 33, 2 (2003): 145-72.

Clarkson, Stephen, and Christina McCall. *Trudeau and Our Times.* Vol. 1, *The Magnificent Obsession.* Toronto: McClelland and Stewart, 1990.

Colombo, John Robert. *Colombo's New Canadian Quotations.* Edmonton: Hurtig, 1987.

Cotter, John. "West May Be Liberal Write-Off." *Edmonton Journal,* October 23, 2000, A3.

Courtney, John. "Campaign Strategy and Electoral Victory: The Progressive Conservatives and the 1979 Election." In *Canada at the Polls, 1979 and 1980: A Study of the General Elections,* ed. Howard Rae Penniman, 121-51. Washington, DC: American Enterprise Institute, 1981.

–. "Reinventing the Brokerage Wheel." In *Canada at the Polls, 1984: A Study of the Federal General Elections,* ed. Howard Rae Penniman, 190-208. Durham, NC: Duke University Press, 1988.

–. *Do Conventions Matter? Choosing National Party Leaders in Canada.* Montreal: McGill-Queen's University Press, 1995.

–. *Elections.* Canadian Democratic Audit. Vancouver: UBC Press, 2004.

Cross, William. *Political Parties.* Canadian Democratic Audit. Vancouver: UBC Press, 2004.

Davey, Keith. "Mr Davey Protests." *Globe and Mail,* September 3, 1984, A6.

–. *The Rainmaker: A Passion for Politics.* Toronto: Stoddart, 1986.

Davey, Keith, et al. "Backroom Planning: The Anatomy of a Campaign." In *Politics and the Media: An Examination of the Issues Raised by the Quebec Referendum and the 1979 and 1980 Federal Elections,* 53-76. Toronto: Reader's Digest Foundation of Canada and Erindale College, University of Toronto, 1981.

Dawson, Anne. "PM's Adviser Admits to Making 'Rookie' Mistakes: Alienating Chrétien Loyalists an Error, Says Martin Campaign Manager." *Ottawa Citizen,* May 21, 2004, A4.

Delacourt, Susan. "Campaign Lacking Female Touch." *Globe and Mail,* May 20, 1997, A10.

–. "Election Crossfire Begins Quickly." *Globe and Mail,* September 9, 1993, A6.

–. *Juggernaut: Paul Martin's Campaign for Chrétien's Crown.* Toronto: McClelland and Stewart, 2003.

–. "Liberals Brandish Vow Keeping Record on Modest Goals." *Globe and Mail,* October 25, 1996, A13.

–. "Liberal Campaign Gets a Huge Shot in the Arm." *Globe and Mail,* October 16, 1993, A7.

Diebel, Linda. "Why the Liberals Bombed." *Montreal Gazette,* September 8, 1984, B1, B4.

Dion, Léon. "The Concept of Political Leadership: An Analysis." *Canadian Journal of Political Science* 1, 1 (1968): 2-17.

Drouilly, Pierre. Le vote nationaliste toujours solide. Cyberpresse. http://www.cyberpresse.ca (accessed December 1, 2000).

Drummond, Robert J. "Parliament and Politics." In *Canadian Annual Review of Politics and Public Affairs 1984,* ed. R.B. Byers, 5-35. Toronto: University of Toronto Press, 1987.

Duffy, John. *Fights of Our Lives: Elections, Leadership and the Making of Canada.* Toronto: HarperCollins Publishers, 2002.

Dufour, Valérie. "Deux ponts et des kilomètres de route pour battre Daniel." *Le Devoir,* November 15, 2000, A4.

Dunn, Sheilagh M. "The Free Trade Initiative and Regional Strategies." In *Canada: The State of the Federation 1987-1988,* ed. Peter M. Leslie and Ronald Watts, 57-76. Kingston, ON: Institute of Intergovernmental Relations, Queen's University, 1988.

Duverger, Maurice. *Political Parties: Their Organization and Activity in the Modern State.* London: Methuen, 1954.

Eldersveld, Samuel James. *Political Parties: A Behavioral Analysis.* Chicago: Rand McNally, 1964.

Erin Research Inc. *Balance in Coverage of the 2004 Federal Election Campaign: 2004 Content Analysis Conducted for CBC (Report 6).* Provided to the author courtesy of CBC.

Everett, Robert. "Parliament and Politics." In *Canadian Annual Review of Politics and Public Affairs 1988*, ed. David Layton-Brown. Toronto: University of Toronto Press, 1995.

Fagan, Drew. "Liberals Target Klein, Mulroney." *Globe and Mail*, June 18, 2004, A1.

–. "Poll Puts Paul Martin's Stumbling Liberals Ahead by Four Points." *Globe and Mail*, June 1, 2004, A1.

Feschuk, Scott. "Voters' Cynicism Greets Campaign Ads." *Globe and Mail*, May 12, 1997, A8.

Fletcher, Frederick J. "Appendix: The Contest for Media Attention: 1979 and 1980 Federal Election Campaigns." In *Politics and the Media: An Examination of the Issues Raised by the Quebec Referendum and the 1979 and 1980 Federal Elections*, 125-41. Toronto: Reader's Digest Foundation of Canada and Erindale College, University of Toronto, 1981.

–. "The Mass Media and the 1974 Canadian General Election." In *Canada at the Polls: The General Election of 1974*, ed. Howard Rae Penniman, 243-89. Washington, DC: American Enterprise Institute, 1975.

–. "The Media and the 1984 Landslide." In *Canada at the Polls, 1984: A Study of the Federal General Elections*, ed. Howard Rae Penniman, 161-89. Durham, NC: Duke University Press, 1988.

–. "Playing the Game: The Mass Media and the 1979 Campaign." In *Canada at the Polls, 1979 and 1980: A Study of the General Elections*, ed. Howard Rae Penniman, 280-321. Washington, DC: American Enterprise Institute, 1981.

Fletcher, Frederick J., and Donald C. Wallace. "Parliament and Politics." In *Canadian Annual Review of Politics and Public Affairs 1979*, ed. V.J. Bell, Donald C. Wallace, and R.B. Byers, 5-125. Toronto: University of Toronto Press, 1981.

Fotheringham, Allan. "Davey and Coutts, Packagers of the New and Increasingly Isolated Pierre Trudeau." *Maclean's*, February 23, 1976, 56.

Fournier, Patrick, André Blais, Joanna Everitt, Elisabeth Gidengil, and Neil Nevitte. "How the Liberals Lost Quebec." *Globe and Mail*, July 21, 2004, A15.

Francis, Diane. "A New Attack on Freedom of Speech." *Maclean's*, May 31, 1993, 9.

Fraser, John. "Jean Chrétien: The Sequel." *Saturday Night*, February 1994, 11.

Frizzell, Alan Stewart, Jon H. Pammett, and Anthony Westell. *The Canadian General Election of 1993*. Ottawa: Carleton University Press, 1994.

–. "Conclusion." In *The Canadian General Election of 1988*, ed. Alan Stewart Frizzell, Jon H. Pammett, and Anthony Westell, 131-2. Ottawa: Carleton University Press, 1989.

Frizzell, Alan Stewart, and Anthony Westell. "Analysis of the Vote." In *The Canadian General Election of 1984: Politicians, Parties, Press and Polls*, ed. Alan Stewart Frizzell, Jon H. Pammett, and Anthony Westell. Ottawa: Carleton University Press, 1985.

–. "The Media and the Campaign." In *The Canadian General Election of 1988*, ed. Alan Stewart Frizzell, Jon H. Pammett, and Anthony Westell, 75-90. Ottawa: Carleton University Press, 1989.

Galloway, Gloria. "Ontario Blue-Belt May Be Grits' Noose." *Globe and Mail*, April 17, 2004, A7.

Gamble, David. "Help Us to Block Alliance: Pettigrew." *Montreal Gazette*, November 3, 2000, A1.

Gibson, Gordon. "Jean Chrétien Loses a Crucial Bit of Teflon." *Globe and Mail*, December 16, 1996, A19.

Gidengil, Elisabeth, André Blais, Richard Nadeau, and Neil Nevitte. "Making Sense of Regional Voting in the 1997 Canadian Federal Election." *Canadian Journal of Political Science* 32, 2 (1997): 247-72.

Globe and Mail, "Chrétien Calls Reform Policies Divisive," May 7, 1997, A9.

–. "Davey Says That Globe Was Biased in Campaign," September 3, 1984, A5.

–. "Mr. Martin's Cavalcade of Instant Nominations," May 13, 2004, A20.

–. "Turner Contradicts Policy Adviser, Says All Must Pay Minimum Tax," August 27, 1984, A4.

Goar, Carol. "Canada after Trudeau." *Maclean's*, March 12, 1984, 20.

–. "Liberal Candidates Give Substance to Leader's Bravado." *Toronto Star*, May 13, 1993, A23.

–. "Martin Sets Chrétien Agenda." *Toronto Star,* February 25, 1992, A21.

Goldfarb, Martin, and Tom Axworthy. *Marching to a Different Drummer: An Essay on the Liberals and Conservatives in Convention.* Toronto: Stoddart, 1988.

Gray, John. *Paul Martin: The Power of Ambition.* Toronto: Key Porter, 2003.

Greenspon, Edward. "Liberals Practice Practicality." *Globe and Mail,* January 25, 1994, A1, A4.

–. "Reading the Tea Leaves Points to a Chrétien Exit." *Globe and Mail,* October 25, 2001, A19.

–. "Straight for the Jugular." *Globe and Mail,* November 11, 2000, A15.

–. "Wanted: A National Agenda." *Globe and Mail,* July 5, 1997, A2.

Gwyn, Richard. "Momentum Shifting to Chrétien As Tired PM Falters." *Toronto Star,* September 26, 1993, B3.

–. "Will Trudeau Ever Be the PM Again? I Think Not." *Toronto Star,* July 21, 1979, B5.

Ha, Tu Thnah, and Anne McIlroy. "Chrétien Counterpunches Charest Jab." *Globe and Mail,* May 16, 1997, A8.

Hale, Geoffrey E. "Managing the Fiscal Dividend: The Politics of Selective Activism." In *How Ottawa Spends 2000-2001: Past Imperfect, Future Tense,* ed. Leslie A. Pal, 59-129. Toronto: Oxford University Press, 2000.

Harper, Tim. "Chrétien Accuses Charest of Hiding from His Conservative Heritage." *Toronto Star,* May 7, 1997, A16.

Hill Times, "Incumbent MPs Not Running in Next Election: 57," May 24-30, 2004, 16.

Hume, Mark. "For Whistle Blower, It Got Personal." *Globe and Mail,* June 12, 2004, A4.

Ibbitson, John. "Day's Plan Found in Secret Paper." *Globe and Mail,* November 7, 2000, A1.

–. "Liberals Take No Prisoners." *Globe and Mail,* May 5, 2004, A4.

–. "Politicos Forcefully Wag the Cod." *Globe and Mail,* May 28, 2004, A4.

Irvine, William P. "The Canadian Voter." In *Canada at the Polls, 1979 and 1980: A Study of the General Elections,* ed. Howard Rae Penniman, 55-85. Washington, DC: American Enterprise Institute, 1981.

–. "Epilogue: The 1980 Election." In *Canada at the Polls, 1979 and 1980: A Study of the General Elections,* ed. Howard Rae Penniman, 337-98. Washington, DC: American Enterprise Institute, 1981.

Janigan, Mary. "The Political Shape of 1984." *Maclean's,* January 16, 1984, 11.

–. "Turner's Race for the Crown." *Maclean's,* March 26, 1984, 11.

Johnsrude, Larry. "Mar Accuses Chrétien of Politicking with Bill 11." *Edmonton Journal,* November 2, 2000.

Johnston, Richard. *Letting the People Decide: Dynamics of a Canadian Election.* Montreal and Kingston: McGill-Queen's University Press, 1992.

Kay, Barry, Stephen D. Brown, James Curtis, Ronald Lambert, and John M. Wilson. "The Character of Electoral Change: A Preliminary Report from the 1984 National Election Study." Paper presented at the 57th annual meeting of the Canadian Political Science Association, Université de Montréal, Montreal. May 31, June 1, 2, 1985.

–. "The Character of Electoral Change: A Preliminary Report from the 1984 Election Study." In *The Ballot and Its Message: Voting in Canada,* ed. Joseph Wearing. Mississauga, ON: Copp Clark Pitman, 1991.

Laghi, Brian. "Chrétien Evokes Image of Team Spirit." *Globe and Mail,* November 14, 2000, A7.

–. "Chrétien Says He'll Consider Quitting." *Globe and Mail,* November 17, 2000, A1.

Laghi, Brian, and Kirk Makin. "Top Court Upholds Spending Limits." *Globe and Mail,* May 19, 2004, A8.

Lasch, Christopher. *The Culture of Narcissism: American Life in an Age of Diminishing Expectations.* New York: Norton, 1978.

Laxer, James, and Robert M. Laxer. *The Liberal Idea of Canada: Pierre Trudeau and the Question of Canada's Survival.* Toronto: J. Lorimer, 1977.

Laycock, David. "Organized Interests in Canada and the Free Trade Election of 1988." Paper presented at the Centre for International Affairs, Harvard University, Cambridge, MA, n.d.

Leblanc, Daniel. "Liberals Dominate Fundraising." *Globe and Mail*, July 6, 1999, A1, A7.

Leblanc, Daniel, and Rhéal Séguin. "Attacks Haven't Allowed Martin to 'Be Himself,' Liberals Feel." *Globe and Mail*, June 3, 2004, A4.

LeDuc, Lawrence. "The Flexible Canadian Electorate." In *Canada at the Polls, 1984: A Study of the Federal General Elections*, ed. Howard Rae Penniman. Durham, NC: Duke University Press, 1988.

–. "The Leaders' Debates (... And the Winner Is ...)." In *The Canadian General Election of 1997*, ed. Alan Stewart Frizzell and Jon H. Pammett, 207-24. Toronto: Dundurn Press, 1997.

–. "Making Votes Count: How Well Did Our Electoral System Perform?" *Electoral Insight* 4, 1 (2005): 37-41.

–. "The Measurement of Public Opinion." In *Canada at the Polls: The General Election of 1974*, ed. Howard Rae Penniman, 209-41. Washington, DC: American Enterprise Institute, 1975.

LeDuc, Lawrence, and Richard Price. "Great Debates: The Televised Leadership Debates of 1979." In *The Ballot and Its Message: Voting in Canada*, ed. Joseph Wearing, 266-82. Toronto: Copp Clark Pitman, 1991.

Liberal Party of Canada. *Creating Opportunity: The Liberal Plan for Canada*. Ottawa: Liberal Party of Canada, 1993.

Lovink, J.A.A. "The Impact of the Electoral System on the Party System in Canada." *Canadian Journal of Political Science* 3, 1 (1970): 497-516.

McCall-Newman, Christina. *Grits: An Intimate Portrait of the Liberal Party*. Toronto: Macmillan of Canada, 1982.

McCall, Christina, and Stephen Clarkson, *Trudeau and Our Times*. Vol. 2, *The Heroic Delusion*. Toronto: McClelland and Stewart, 1994.

McCarthy, Shawn. "Alliance Supports Two-Tier Health Care: Government Should Give Provinces Leeway in Promoting Private Clinics, Co-Chair Says." *Globe and Mail*, October 31, 2000, A1.

–. "Liberals on the Knife Edge." *Globe and Mail*, November 26, 2000.

McCarthy, Shawn, and Paul Adams. "Chrétien Defends Early Vote." *Globe and Mail*, October 23, 2000, A1.

McCarthy, Shawn, and Brian Laghi. "Chrétien Pounded again As Day Puts on Show." *Globe and Mail*, November 11, 2000, A1.

Macdonald, Don. "Beware of Grits – Indeed All Parties – Bearing Gifts." *Halifax Herald*, November 3, 2000.

MacDonald, Donald C. "1988 Election Expenditures: A Canadian-American Comparison." In *Canadian Legislatures, 1992: Issues, Structures and Costs*, ed. Robert J. Fleming, 16-26. Agincourt, ON: Global Press, 1992.

McGill University Observatory for Media and Public Policy. *2004 Federal Election Newspaper Content Analysis: Weekly Results from 17 May to 16 June 2004*. June 16, 2004. http://www.ompp.mcgill.ca/pages/reports/WeeklyReport(June16).pdf (accessed June 18, 2004).

–. *2004 Federal Election Newspaper Content Analysis: Cumulative Results from 17 May to 25 June 2004*. June 25, 2004. http://www.ompp.mcgill.ca/pages/reports/cumulativereport(june25).pdf (accessed June 27, 2004).

MacGregor, Roy. "Wired Media Have Changed the Message: A Leader Barks on the West Coast, and One Yelps Back from the East." *National Post*, November 25, 2000, A6.

Machiavelli, Niccolò. "The Prince." In *The Portable Machiavelli*, ed. Peter Bondarella and Mark Musa. New York: Penguin Books, 1981.

McIlroy, Anne. "Youth Wing Cheers PM's Populist Theme." *Globe and Mail*, March 17, 2000, A9.

MacIvor, Heather. "From Emergence to Electronics: Explaining the Changes in Canadian Party Leadership Selection." *National History* 1, 2 (1997), 173-85.

Mackie, Richard. "Not Our Fault Federal Party Lags, Ontario Liberals Say." *Globe and Mail*, June 3, 2004, A4.

McRoberts, Kenneth. *Quebec: Social Change and Political Crisis,* 3rd ed. Toronto: Oxford University Press, 1999.

Mandruk, Murray. "Saskatchewan Won't Decide the Election." *Regina Leader-Post,* May 13, 1997, A4.

Martin, Don. "Martin Failed to Land Crucial Knockout Blow." *Calgary Herald,* June 16, 2004.

Martin, Lawrence. *Chrétien.* Toronto: Lester Publishing, 1995.

–. *Iron Man: The Defiant Reign of Jean Chrétien.* Toronto: Viking, 2003.

Marzolini, Michael. "The Regionalization of Canadian Electoral Politics." In *The Canadian General Election of 1997,* ed. Alan Stewart Frizzell and Jon H. Pammett, 193-205. Toronto: Dundurn Press, 1997.

Matas, Robert. "'Scurrilous' Ads Enrage Alliance: Liberals Using Chinese-Language Media to Paint Portrait of Rival as 'Scary' and 'Racist.'" *Globe and Mail,* November 24, 2000, A7.

Meisel, John. "The Larger Context: The Period Preceding the 1979 Election." In *Canada at the Polls, 1979 and 1980: A Study of the General Elections,* ed. Howard Rae Penniman, 24-52. Washington, DC: American Enterprise Institute, 1981.

Michels, Robert. *Political Parties: A Sociological Study of the Oligarchical Tendencies of Modern Democracy.* New York: Dover Publications, 1959.

Mulawka, Brian. "Elections Are for Political Parties, Not Citizens." *Alberta Report,* November 3, 1997.

Nadeau, Richard, Neil Nevitte, Elisabeth Gidengil, and André Blais. "Pourquoi les libéraux ont-ils gagné?" *La Presse,* December 2, 2000, A21.

Nevitte, Neil. *The Decline of Deference: Canadian Value Change in Cross-National Perspective.* Peterborough, ON: Broadview Press, 1996.

Newman, Christina. "That Big Red Machine Is the Daveymobile." *Globe and Mail,* July 7, 1975, 2.

O'Neil, Peter. "B.C. Grits to Set out a Distinct Agenda." *Vancouver Sun,* June 7, 2004, A1.

O'Neil, Peter, and Scott Simpson. "Liberals Offer Transit Money, but Levy Will Remain." *Vancouver Sun,* November 1, 2000, A4.

Ontario Riding Histories. Ottawa: Office of the Prime Minister, 1979.

Palmer, Vaughn. "Loyalty Runs Shallow with BC Liberals." *National Post,* October 14, 2000, A17.

Paltiel, Khayyam Zev. "Campaign Financing in Canada and Its Reform." In *Canada at the Polls: The General Election of 1974,* ed. Howard Rae Penniman, 181-208. Washington, DC: American Enterprise Institute, 1975.

Pammett, Jon H. "The 1988 Vote." In *The Canadian General Election of 1988,* ed. Alan Stewart Frizzell, Jon H. Pammett, and Anthony Westell, 115-30. Ottawa: Carleton University Press, 1989.

–. "The Voters Decide." In *The Canadian General Election of 1997,* ed. Alan Stewart Frizzell and Jon H. Pammett, 225-48. Toronto: Dundurn Press, 1997.

Perlin, George C. *The Tory Syndrome: Leadership Politics in the Progressive Conservative Party.* Montreal and Kingston: McGill-Queen's University Press, 1980.

Radwanski, George. *Trudeau.* Toronto: Macmillan of Canada, 1978.

Royal Commission on Electoral Reform. "Financing Contemporary Party Problems." In *Canadian Political Party Systems: A Reader,* ed. R. Kenneth Carty, 445-63. Peterborough, ON: Broadview Press, 1992.

Sallot, Jeff. "Jobless Rate Won't Drop Soon, Campbell Warns." *Globe and Mail,* September 9, 1993, A6.

Savoie, Donald J. *Governing from the Centre: The Concentration of Power in Canadian Politics.* Toronto: University of Toronto Press, 1999.

Saywell, John. "Parliament and Politics." In *The Canadian Annual Review of Politics and Public Affairs 1974,* ed. John Saywell, 3-153. Toronto: University of Toronto Press, 1975.

–. "Parliament and Politics." In *The Canadian Annual Review of Politics and Public Affairs 1975,* ed. John Saywell, 3-114. Toronto: University of Toronto Press, 1976.

–. "Parliament and Politics." In *The Canadian Annual Review of Politics and Public Affairs 1976*, ed. John Saywell, 3-164. Toronto: University of Toronto Press, 1977.

Scofield, Heather, and Campbell Clark. "Martin's Big Pledge: $9 Billion for Health." *Globe and Mail*, May 26, 2004, A6.

Scotto, Thomas J., Laura B. Stephenson, and Allan Kornberg. "From a Two-Party-Plus to a One-Party-Plus? Ideology, Vote Choice, and Prospects for a Competitive Party System in Canada," *Electoral Studies* 23 (2004): 463-83.

Sears, Val. "The Cardboard Campaign: How the Liberals Backed out of the National TV Debate." *Toronto Star*, February 16, 1980, B2.

–. "A Month ago John Turner Admitted: 'I've Screwed Up.'" *Toronto Star*, September 6, 1984, A1, A8.

Seidle, F. Leslie, and Khayyam Zey Paltiel. "Party Finance, the Election Expenses Act, and Campaign Spending in 1979 and 1980." In *Canada at the Polls, 1979 and 1980: A Study of the General Elections*, ed. Howard Rae Penniman, 226-79. Washington, DC: American Enterprise Institute, 1981.

Selnow, Gary W. *Electronic Whistle-Stops: The Impact of the Internet on American Politics*. Westport, CT: Praeger, 1998.

Sharp, Mitchell. *Which Reminds Me: A Memoir*. Toronto: University of Toronto Press, 1994.

Siegfried, André. *The Race Question in Canada*. Toronto: Macmillan of Canada with the Institute of Canadian Studies, Carleton University, 1978.

Simpson, Jeffrey. "A Conservative Wolf in Sheep's Clothing," *Globe and Mail*, June 12, 2004, A27.

–. *Discipline of Power: The Conservative Interlude and the Liberal Restoration*. Toronto: Personal Library, distributed by J. Wiley, 1980.

–. "Last Hurrah." *Globe and Mail*, September 3, 1984, A6.

–. "The Last Resort." *Globe and Mail*, August 28, 1984, A6.

–. "Liberal Ruins Offer Clues to Party's Collapse." *Globe and Mail*, September 6, 1984, A1, A8.

–. "The Masters and the Slaves." *Globe and Mail*, August 19, 1998, A16.

–. "Two Scorpions in a Bottle." *Globe and Mail*, April 23, 2000, A19.

–. "The Vincible Liberals." In *The Canadian General Election of 1984*, ed. Alan Stewart Frizzell, Jon H. Pammett, and Anthony Westell, 15-28. Ottawa: Carleton University Press, 1985.

Smith, David E. "Party Government, Representation, and National Integration in Canada." In *Party Government and Regional Representation in Canada*, ed. Peter Aucoin, 1-68. Ottawa: Royal Commission on the Economic Union and Prospects for Canada, 1985.

Smith, Graeme. "How Winnipeg's Mayor Cleared Commons Path." *Globe and Mail*, May 8, 2004, A5.

Soroka, Stuart, Antonia Maioni, Kenneth Whyte, and Elizabeth Goodyear-Grant. "What Will the Important Issues Be?" *Globe and Mail*, June 15, 2004, <www.theglobeandmail.com>.

Speirs, Rosemary. "Chrétien Gained Most in Debates, Pundits Say." *Toronto Star*, October 6, 1993, A14.

–. "Election Not Time to Debate Cuts: PM." *Toronto Star*, September 24, 1993, A1.

–. "Where Is Chrétien Taking the Liberals?" *Toronto Star*, February 16, 1992, B1, B5.

Stanbury, W.T. "Elections, Party Finance, and Political Marketing." In *Canadian Parties in Transition*, ed. Brian Tanguay and Alain-G. Gagnon. Scarborough, ON: Nelson Canada, 1996.

–. *Money in Politics: Financing Federal Parties and Candidates in Canada*. Volume 1 in the Research Series, Royal Commission on Electoral Reform and Party Financing. Toronto: Dundurn Press, 1991.

–. "Regulating the Financing of Federal Parties and Candidates." In *Canadian Parties in Transition*, ed. Brian Tanguay and Alain-G. Gagnon, 372-402. Scarborough, ON: Nelson Canada, 1996.

Stewart, Edison. "Jobs: Battle Lines Drawn." *Toronto Star*, September 9, 1993, A26.

–. "Liberal Fax Calls Charest Separatist." *Toronto Star*, May 17, 1997, A12.

Stewart, Ian. "Bill C-24: Replacing the Market with the State," *Electoral Insight* 7, 1 (2005): 32-6.

Stewart, Walter. "The Natural." *Toronto Life,* June 1983, 30.

Taber, Jane. "Liberals 'Are in a Spiral,' Top Martin Adviser Says." *Globe and Mail,* June 10, 2004, A1.

–. "Liberals Move to Ease Nomination Challenges." *Globe and Mail,* January 15, 2004, A4.

–. "Liberals Tell PM to Ease Up." *Globe and Mail,* February 19, 2004, A1.

–. "Report of Tory's Political Death Premature." *Globe and Mail,* June 30, 2004, A11.

Taber, Jane, and Campbell Clark. "Liberals Plan Early Attack Ad on Harper." *Globe and Mail,* May 13, 2004, A1.

Tenszen, Michael. "Axworthy Rues Liberal Strategy." *Globe and Mail,* August 31, 1984, A1, A2.

Thorburn, Hugh G., ed. *Party Politics in Canada,* 2nd ed. Scarborough, ON: Prentice-Hall Canada, 1967.

–. *Party Politics in Canada,* 4th ed. Scarborough, ON: Prentice-Hall Canada, 1979.

–. *Party Politics in Canada,* 6th ed. Scarborough, ON: Prentice-Hall Canada, 1991.

–. *Party Politics in Canada.* 7th ed. Scarborough, ON: Prentice-Hall Canada, 1996.

Travers, James. "PM Names Players for Key Roles." *Toronto Star,* July 20, 2004, A17.

Travers, James, and David Vienneau. "National Unity Sets Off Sparks in Leaders' Debates." *Toronto Star,* May 13, 1997, A1, A11.

Trudeau, Margaret. *Margaret Trudeau: Beyond Reason.* New York: Paddington Press, 1979.

Turner, Rt. Hon. John Napier. "Speech to the Liberal Party of Canada (Ontario) Annual Meeting." Toronto, 1985.

Underhill, Brian, and Cameron McKeen. "Unemployed Offended by PM's Parallel." *Halifax Chronicle-Herald,* May 31, 1997, A1.

Unland, Karen. "Liberals Give Montrealers Pointed Reminder." *Globe and Mail,* May 21, 1997, A8.

Vancouver Sun. "No Time to Switch: Canada Needs a Party That Represents All Regions and Can Steer a Middle Course," May 30, 1997, A22.

Vienneau, David. "Chrétien Pleads for Tolerance and Unity." *Toronto Star,* May 30, 1997, A11.

–. "Deep in Reform Country, PM Slams Manning." *Toronto Star,* May 27, 1997, A1, A11.

–. "PM Denounces Charest's Unacceptable Comment." *Toronto Star,* May 20, 1997, A8.

–. "PM Rips Reform for 'Politics of Intolerance.'" *Toronto Star,* May 27, 1997, A1.

Wagenberg, R.H., W.C. Soderlund, W.I. Romanow, and E.D. Briggs. "Campaigns, Images and Polls: Mass Media Coverage of the 1984 Canadian Election." *Canadian Journal of Political Science* 21, 1 (1988): 117-29.

Walker, William. "Hidden High Tech Toys Help Big Parties Battle for Voters." *Toronto Star,* September 21, 1993, A11.

–. "Romanow Looks Set to Jump to Liberals." *Toronto Star,* September 20, 2000, A6.

Wearing, Joseph. "Can an Old Dog Teach Itself New Tricks? The Liberal Party Attempts Reform." In *Canadian Parties in Transition,* ed. Alain-G. Gagnon and Brian Tanguay, 272-86. Scarborough, ON: Nelson Canada, 1988.

–. *The L-Shaped Party: The Liberal Party of Canada 1958-1980.* Toronto: McGraw-Hill Ryerson, 1980.

Webb, Michael. *Report of the Alberta Commissioner.* Calgary: Liberal Party of Canada, 1977.

Westell, Anthony. "Setting the Stage." In *The Canadian General Election of 1988,* ed. Alan Stewart Frizzell, Jon H. Pammett, and Anthony Westell, 1-14. Ottawa: Carleton University Press, 1989.

Weston, Greg. "Anatomy of Defeat." *Ottawa Citizen,* September 5, 1984, A9.

–. *Reign of Error: The Inside Story of John Turner's Troubled Leadership.* Toronto: McGraw-Hill Ryerson, 1988.

Whitaker, Reginald. *The Government Party: Organizing and Financing the Liberal Party of Canada, 1930-58.* Toronto: University of Toronto Press, 1977.

White, Theodore Harold. *The Making of the President.* New York: Atheneum, 1973.

Whitehorn, Alan. "The NDP's Quest for Survival." In *The Canadian General Election of 1993,* ed. Alan Stewart Frizzell, Jon H. Pammett, and Anthony Westell, 43-58. Ottawa: Carleton University Press, 1994.

Whittington, Les, and Graham Fraser. "New Spending, No Deficit Pledged." *Toronto Star,* June 4, 2004, A6.

Whyte, Kenneth. "The Face That Sunk a Thousand Tories." *Saturday Night,* February 1994, 14-18, 58-60.

Widdis Barr, Cathy. "The Importance and Potential of Leaders' Debates." In *Media and Voters in Canadian Election Campaigns,* ed. Frederick J. Fletcher, 107-56. Ottawa: Royal Commission on Electoral Reform and Party Financing, 1991.

Willcocks, Paul. "Beware of Liberals Bearing Gifts for Votes." *Vancouver Sun,* November 3, 2000.

Williams, Blair. "The Transformation of the Federal Cabinet under P.E. Trudeau." Paper presented at the 51st Annual Meeting of the Canadian Political Science Association, University of Saskatchewan, Saskatoon, May 30, 31, June 1, 1979, 1-34.

Wilson-Smith, Anthony. "The Unity Bomber." *Maclean's,* May 19, 1997, 14.

Winsor, Hugh. "Liberal Conference Tests Icy Economic Waters." *Globe and Mail,* November 26, 1991, A1, A8.

–. "Martin One-Ups Day in Budget Battle." *Globe and Mail,* October 19, 2000, A9.

–. "The Two Faces of Jean Chrétien." *Globe and Mail,* September 20, 1993, A4.

Woods, Allan. "Undecided Voters Handed Victory to Grits." *National Post,* June 29, 2004, A4.

Wyatt, Mark. "Saskatchewan Maintains Tradition." *Regina Leader-Post,* June 3, 1997, B2.

York, Geoffrey. "Liberal Coffers Grow As Business Smells a Winner." *Globe and Mail,* July 2, 1993, A3.

Young, Lisa. "Comment on Johnson, 'Canadian Elections at the Millennium.'" *Choices: Strengthening Canadian Democracy* 6, 6 (2000): 37.

–. *Feminists and Party Politics.* Vancouver: UBC Press, 2000.

Young, R.A. "The End of the Political Centre, 1988." University of Western Ontario Working Paper, London, Ontario, n.d.

Index

Printed and bound in Canada by Friesens

Set in Minion and MetaPlus by Artegraphica Design Co. Ltd.

Copyeditor: Andy Carroll

Proofreader: Gail Copeland

Indexer: Margaret Menton Manery